CW01650142

THE FILM BOOK

THE FILM BOOK

A COMPLETE GUIDE TO THE WORLD OF CINEMA

Ronald Bergan

DK

LONDON ▪ NEW YORK
MUNICH ▪ MELBOURNE ▪ DELHI

Senior Editor Gareth Jones
Art Editor Katie Eke
Designer Joanne Clark
Editor Natasha Kahn
Senior Production Editor Jennifer Murray
Production Controller Sophie Argyris
Jacket Designer Mark Cavanagh
Managing Editor Stephanie Farrow
Managing Art Editor Lee Griffiths

Dorling Kindersley (India)

Managing Art Editor Ashita Murgai
Managing Editor Saloni Talwar
Senior Art Editor Ivy Roy
Project Editor Samira Sood
Designers Akanksha Gupta, Neetika Vilash
Editor Shatarupa Chaudhuri
Assistant Editor Bincy Mathew
Production Manager Pankaj Sharma
DTP Manager Balwant Singh
Senior DTP Designer Harish Aggarwal
DTP Designers Shanker Prasad, Mohammad Usman, Rajesh Singh Adhikari
Managing Director Aparna Sharma

This edition published in 2013
First published in Great Britain in 2011
by Dorling Kindersley Limited
80 Strand, London WC2R 0RL
Penguin Group (UK)

001 – 179525 – Nov/13

Copyright © 2011 Dorling Kindersley Limited
All rights reserved.

No part of this publication may be reproduced, stored in a retrieval system, or transmitted in any form or by any means, electronic, mechanical, photocopying, recording, or otherwise without the prior written permission of the copyright owners.

A CIP catalogue record for this book is available from the British Library

ISBN 978-1-4093-5000-2

Based on content previously published in *Eyewitness Companions: Film*

Printed and bound in China by
Leo Paper Products Ltd.

Discover more at **www.dk.com**

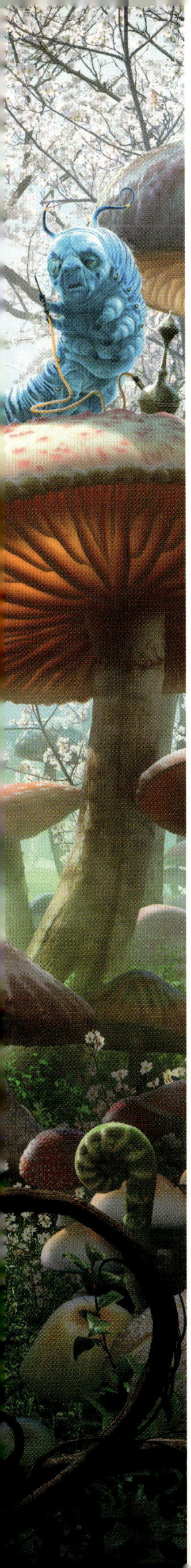

Contents

In the US, movies began in the penny-arcade kinetoscopes of the 1890s. You dropped a penny in a slot and peered through a viewfinder at a grainy image. In time, this new medium became the largest entertainment industry the world has ever known, developing into the 20th century's new art form.

From its very beginnings, cinema provided romance and escapism for millions of people all over the globe. It was the magic carpet that took them away from the harsh realities of life. The movies offered a panacea in the years of the Great Depression in the US; were the opium of the people through World War II; and continued to transport the public away from reality throughout the following decades. It was Hollywood, California, known as "the Dream Factory", which eventually supplied most of "the stuff that dreams are made of".

However, although Hollywood has dominated the worldwide film industry since the 1920s, it is not the only "player" in a truly global market. What makes film the most international of the arts is the vast range of movies that come from more than 50 countries – films that are as multifarious as the cultures that produce them. More and more countries, long ignored as film-making nations, have produced films that have entered the international consciousness.

Certainly in the last few decades, creative cinema has spread from the US and Europe to Central and Eastern Asia, and to the developing world – the most amazing example of which is Iran. African nations have given birth to directors of unique imagination, such as Ousmane Sembene and Souleymane Cissé. China, Hong Kong, Taiwan, and Korea have produced films of spectacular visual quality as well as absorbing content. There has also been a huge revival of cinema in Spain and the Latin American countries. Denmark, neglected as a film-making nation since the days of the great director Carl Dreyer, started to experience a renaissance in the late 1980s.

The barriers between English-language films and those of the rest of the world are disappearing every day, as witnessed by the cultural cross-fertilization of stars and directors. A child in the US is just as likely to watch Japanese "anime" movies as Walt Disney cartoons, and young people in the West are as familiar with Asian martial arts films or mainstream Hindi ones, as audiences in the East are with US movies.

However, not only does cinema provide pure entertainment to audiences across the world, it is also known as "the seventh art". Writing about film as early as 1916, German psychiatrist Hugo Münsterberg discussed the unique properties of cinema, and its capacity to reformulate time and space.

« **An exuberant Gene Kelly** is seen here in a publicity still from ***Singin' in the Rain*** (1952), a musical which affectionately satirizes the early days of sound.

Another Fine Mess (1930) starred the hapless comic duo Stan Laurel and Oliver Hardy in a characteristically perilous situation.

Riccioto Canudo, an Italian-born French critic, argued in 1926 that cinema must go beyond realism and express the film-makers' emotions as well as the characters' psychology, and even their unconscious. These possibilities of cinema were expressed by French "impressionist" film-makers and theorists – Louis Delluc and Jean Epstein – and were underlined by the montage theory that was expounded by the great Russian film-makers of the 1920s. They disturbed the accepted continuity of chronological development and attempted new ways of tracing the flow of characters' thoughts, replacing straightforward storytelling with fragmentary images and multiple points of view.

Cinema began to equal other arts in seriousness and depth, not only with so-called "art cinema", but also in mainstream filming, in which directors such as D.W. Griffith, Fritz Lang, Charlie Chaplin, Busby Berkeley, Walt Disney, Jean Renoir, Orson Welles, John Ford, and Alfred Hitchcock can be counted as pioneers. Technical developments, such as fast film, sound, Technicolor, CinemaScope, and lightweight camera equipment, were used to look into new ways of expression on the big screen.

Maggie Cheung plays Flying Snow in Zhang Yimou's spectacular ***Hero*** (2002), an example of an Asian martial arts film entering the mainstream in Western cinema.

In the last decade of the 20th century, computer-generated imagery (CGI) continued this exploration, while digital cameras enabled more people to make features than ever before. With the emergence of videos and DVDs, and the downloading of movies from the internet, films can be viewed in a variety of ways. As British director Peter Greenaway said, "More films go to people nowadays than people go to films." Directors are learning to come to grips with these new methods of film-watching. Yet, whatever technical advances have been made, no matter where and how we watch films, whether seen on a cell phone or on a giant screen, whether it is an intimate drama in black-and-white or a spectacular epic in Technicolor, it is the intrinsic quality of the film – the direction, the screenplay, the cinematography, and the acting – that continues to astonish, provoke, and delight audiences.

We have attempted to make this guide to cinema as objective as possible, and to include films and directors that have made a difference to cinema, although some subjective selectivity is unavoidable.

A note about foreign-language titles: in many cases, both the English title and the original title of the movie are given. However, when the title of the film has never been translated or the movie is best known under its original title (for example, *La Dolce Vita* rather than *The Sweet Life*), the original title is used. If the film is better known by its English title (such as *In the Mood For Love* rather than *Fa yeung nin wa*), we have given the English version only.

Edmund (Skandar Keynes) is confronted by the CGI-created lion Aslan, in ***The Chronicles of Narnia: The Lion, the Witch and the Wardrobe*** (2005).

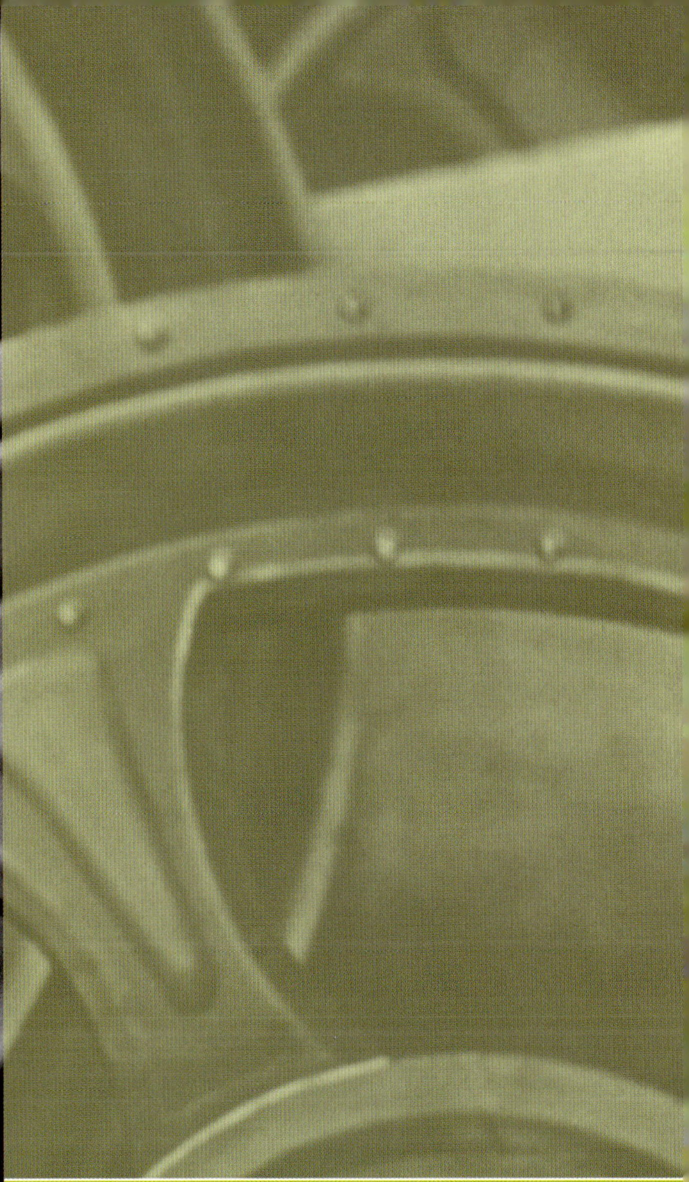

The Story **of Cinema**

1895–1919 The Birth of Cinema

In 1995, the world celebrated the centenary of cinema, marking the date the Lumière brothers had patented a device that displayed moving images. From the late 19th century into the first decades of the 20th century, the love affair with cinema grew.

The Arrival of a Train at a Station (*L'Arivée d'un Train en Gare de la Ciotat*, 1895) was a single-shot sequence lasting 50 seconds, filmed by Louis Lumière. The audience ducked under their seats, convinced that the train was real.

The Lumières' first showing of the Cinématographe Lumière attracted little attention, but the crowds swelled, and soon, more than 2,000 people were queuing up daily.

Why did the world celebrate the centenary of cinema in 1995? Thomas Alva Edison patented his invention of the Kinetoscope in 1891. This was first shown publicly in 1893. It was a peep-show device in which a 1.5m (50ft) loop of film gave continuous viewing. The first pictures were of dancing girls, performing animals, and men at work. However, one could go even further back than this. Film – photographic images printed on a flexible, semi-transparent celluloid base and cut into strips – was devised by Henry M. Reichenbach for George Eastman's Kodak company in 1889. It was based on inventions variously attributed to the brothers J.W. and I.S. Hyatt (1865), to Hannibal Goodwin (1888), and to Reichenbach himself.

However, this would be dating the cinema from its conception rather than its birth, and is only one step along the road to film as we know it.

1895–1919

1895
The Lumière brothers patent and demonstrate the Cinématographe.

1897
Méliès builds a studio at Montreuil-sous-Bois, near Paris, where he eventually produces more than 500 films.

1899
Humphrey Bogart, Fred Astaire, James Cagney, Noel Coward, and Alfred Hitchcock are born.

1900
At the World Fair in Paris, 1.5 million gaze at a giant Cinématographe.

1903
The Great Train Robbery is released, launching the Western as a movie genre.

1905
The first Nickelodeon opens in Pittsburgh, USA, seating 100.

The American entertainment trade journal *Variety* begins publication.

The Lumière brothers

In France, brothers Auguste and Louis Lumière were working in their father Antoine's photographic studio in Lyon. Thomas Edison's Kinetoscope was shown in Paris in 1894; in the same city, Louis Lumière began work on a machine to compete with Edison's device. The Cinématographe – initially a camera and projector in one – was patented in the brothers' names on 13 February 1895.

The first public performance of the Cinématographe took place on 28 December 1895 at the Salon Indien in the Grand Café on the Boulevard des Capucines in Paris. It was a 20-minute programme of 10 films recorded with an immobile camera, with occasional panning. The first film seems to have been ***Workers Leaving the Lumière Factory*** (1895), in which a few hundred people pour out of the gates, including a man on a bicycle, a dog, and a horse. Some have argued that the film was staged, because none of the workers look at the camera or walk towards it.

Other Lumière films shown at this first cinema show included ***The Demolition of a Wall*** (1896), in which reverse motion was used to "rebuild" a wall, making it the first film with special effects. Louis Lumière's ***Watering the Gardener*** (1895) is considered the first comedy. It shows a gardener receiving a jet of water in the face when a naughty boy steps on a hose and then releases it.

Among the audience at this Cinématographe presentation was Georges Méliès. He was a conjurer, cartoonist, inventor, and mechanic, and was greatly excited by what he saw. On 4 April 1896, Méliès opened his Théatre Robert Houdin as a cinema. In 1898, the shutter of his camera jammed while he was filming a street scene. This incident made him realize the potential of trick photography to create magical effects. He went on to develop many cinematic devices, such as superimposition and stop motion. For example, in ***The Melomaniac*** (1903), Méliès plays a music master who removes his head, only for it to be replaced by another and another. As the music master throws each head onto a telegraph wire, they form a series of musical notes.

NICKELODEONS

The first cinemas were called nickelodeons. The price of a ticket was just a nickel, or five cents, and "odeon" is the Greek word for theatre. They seated about 100 and showed films continuously, ensuring a steady flow of spectators. The first was built in the US in 1905, and by 1907, around two million Americans were going to nickelodeons every day. However, the boom was short-lived. By 1910, theatres with larger seating capacity, capable of showing longer films, were starting to replace them.

In 1908, there were around 8,000 nickelodeons throughout the US. The Comet Theatre in New York City was one of them.

A Trip to the Moon *(Le Voyage dans la Lune*, 1902) was one of Georges Méliès' fantastical films.

1906
The Story of the Kelly Gang premieres in Melbourne, Australia. At 70 minutes, it is the longest feature film till then.

1908
The first movie star, Florence Lawrence, appears in 38 films.

1911
Credits begin to appear at the beginning of films.

1913
The "Hollywood" name is formally adopted, and becomes the centre of the film industry.

1914
The first "picture palace", The Strand, opens in New York. It seats 3,300.

Charlie Chaplin appears as the "Little Tramp" in *Kid Auto Races at Venice*.

1915
D.W. Griffith's 3-hour epic, ***The Birth of a Nation*** premieres.

The Squaw Man (1914), a Western adapted from the stage and directed by Cecil B. DeMille, was the first feature-length film to be produced in Hollywood.

THE FIRST BOX OFFICE HITS

1	*Workers Leaving the Lumière Factory* (Lumière brothers, France,1895)
2	*Watering the Gardener* (Louis Lumière, France, 1895)
3	*The Demolition of a Wall* (Louis Lumière, France, 1896)
4	*A Trip to the Moon* (Georges Méliès, France, 1902)
5	*The Great Train Robbery* (Edwin S. Porter, US, 1903)
6	*The Melomaniac* (Georges Méliès, France, 1903)
7	*20,000 Leagues Under the Sea* (Georges Méliès, France, 1907)
8	*The Tunnel Under the English Channel* (Georges Méliès, France, 1907)
9	*The Squaw Man* (Cecil B. DeMille, US, 1914)
10	*The Birth of a Nation* (D.W. Griffith, US, 1915)

Fantasy and reality

Film scholars have pointed out that the films of the Lumière brothers and of Méliès reveal the distinction between documentary and fiction films. The Lumières employed cameramen to travel the world, while Méliès remained in his studio making his fantastic films. Among the hundred or so Méliès films still in existence are two adaptations of novels by Jules Verne: ***A Trip to the Moon*** (1902) and ***20,000 Leagues Under the Sea*** (1907).

The birth of Hollywood cinema

In the early 20th century, American movie production companies were situated in New York. Biograph Studios (est. 1896) was an early home of the creative forces behind many major silent films. Slapstick pioneer Mack Sennett worked there and at another New York studio, Keystone (est. 1912). There Charlie Chaplin also made movies, until, already famous, he was lured away to Essanay (est. 1907) in 1915. However, the man with the greatest influence on

the movies as an art form was David Wark (D.W.) Griffith. From his first film, ***The Adventures of Dollie*** (1908), he transformed the medium. Originally an actor, he learned about film-making from his employer, Edwin S. Porter, whose movie ***The Great Train Robbery*** (1903) was the first to convey a defined story and use long-shot and a final close-up (of a bullet fired at the audience). Between 1908 and 1913, he directed 450 titles, in which he developed film grammar and camera placement, and learned to elicit naturalistic acting from his players. The Biblical spectacle ***Judith of Bethulia*** (1914) was America's first four-reeler and ***The Birth of a Nation*** (1915) was its first masterpiece.

Just before the start of World War I, a number of independent producers moved to a small suburb to the west of Los Angeles; Hollywood, as we know it today, began to take shape. More and more films were shot there because of the space and freedom the area provided. In 1913, Cecil B. DeMille directed ***The Squaw Man*** there, and in March 1915, Carl Laemmle opened Universal Studios at a cost of US$165,000. A pioneering role can be ascribed to Thomas Ince, who devised the standard studio system, which concentrated production into vast, factory-like studios.

At the same time, the star system was developed and refined. The first performer to lay claim to the title of film star was Florence Lawrence, "The Biograph Girl". Theda Bara was the subject of the first full publicity campaign to create a star image. Her background was tailored to fit the role of the exotic "vamp". At the same time, other stars were gaining influence. Three of the most famous, worldwide, were Mary Pickford, Douglas Fairbanks, and Charlie Chaplin. Pickford, who made her name as "Little Mary", made enormous amounts of money with films such as ***Little Rich Girl*** and ***Rebecca of Sunnybrook Farm*** (both 1917). In 1920, she married Fairbanks, who gained a following after several satires on American life. On 15 January 1919, unhappy with the lack of independence in working under contract to others, Chaplin, Pickford, Fairbanks, and D.W. Griffith founded the United Artists Corporation. Unlike the other big companies, United Artists owned no studio of its own and rented the space required for each production. Moreover, it had no cinema holdings and had to arrange the distribution of its products with cinemas or circuits. Despite these drawbacks, however, United Artists was able to sustain itself, and survived.

Cleopatra (1917) starred Theda Bara, aka Theodosia Goodman from Cincinnati, USA. Her pseudonym was an anagram of "Arab Death".

This silent movie camera stands on top of a sturdy tripod, and was cranked by hand.

1920–1929 Silence is Golden

The Silent Film Era saw the consolidation of the studio system that continued into the 1950s. The 1920s was also a decade in which the first great stars lit up the screen, including Garbo and Dietrich. By 1929, however, a technological innovation had changed the course of cinema.

Rudolph Valentino (1895–1926), supreme Latin lover, is seen here in a scene from one of his greatest hits, *Blood and Sand* (1922), in which he played a hot-blooded matador.

In the economic boom that followed World War I, cinema moguls Carl Laemmle, Adolph Zukor, William Fox, Louis B. Mayer, Samuel Goldwyn, and Jack Warner with his brothers Harry, Albert, and Samuel (all European Jewish emigrants), tightened their grip on the film industry.

Genres and stars

The studios began to turn out stories that repeated themes and structures, forming what would later be dubbed "genres". Westerns became a staple of the studios in the 1920s. These films made good use of Californian locations. Cowboy stars, who seldom deviated from their established screen roles, included W.S. Hart, Tom Mix, and Hoot Gibson. Both James Cruze's

BOX OFFICE HITS OF THE 1920s

1. *The Big Parade* (King Vidor, US, 1925)
2. *The Four Horsemen of the Apocalypse* (Rex Ingram, US, 1921)
3. *Ben-Hur* (Fred Niblo, US, 1925)
4. *The Ten Commandments* (Cecil B. DeMille, US, 1923)
5. *What Price Glory* (Raoul Walsh, US, 1926)
6. *The Covered Wagon* (James Cruze, US, 1923)
7. *Way Down East* (D.W. Griffith, US, 1920)
8. *The Singing Fool* (Lloyd Bacon, US, 1928)
9. *Wings* (William A. Wellman, US, 1927)
10. *The Gold Rush* (Charlie Chaplin, US, 1925)

1920–1929

1920

The "marriage of the century", between stars Douglas Fairbanks and Mary Pickford, takes place. He buys her a lodge – and names it Pickfair.

1921

Fatty Arbuckle is acquitted of the rape and manslaughter of Virginia Rappe.

1922

Robert J. Flaherty releases *Nanook of the North*, about the life of an Eskimo family, the first film to be called a documentary.

Rin Tin Tin becomes cinema's first canine star, helping to save Warner Bros. from bankruptcy.

1924

Metro-Goldwyn-Mayer (MGM) is founded by the merging of three production companies.

> **Collective madness,** incarnating the tragic comedy of a **new fetishism.**

The Vatican, 1926, on the orgy of mourning following the death of Valentino

The Covered Wagon (1923) and John Ford's *The Iron Horse* (1924) showed the epic and artistic possibilities of the genre.

However, it was American comedy that reached the widest audiences worldwide during the Silent Film Era. This was due mainly to the comic genius of Charlie Chaplin, Buster Keaton, Harold Lloyd, Harry Langdon, and Stan Laurel and Oliver Hardy – all of whom reached their apogee in the 1920s.

The studios recognized the value of typecasting, so that the audience quickly identified the persona of the stars by the roles they played. One of the biggest of these stars was Rudolph Valentino. Valentino came to the US from Italy in 1913 as a teenager. After becoming a professional dancer in the cafés of New York, he ventured out to California in 1917. In 1921, he appeared as the playboy hero in Rex Ingram's *The Four Horsemen of the Apocalypse*, and became the unrivalled Latin lover of the screen – the male equivalent of the vamp. *The Sheik* (also 1921) sealed his seductive image forever.

In the optimism and materialism of the 1920s, Hollywood began to represent glamour, as well as a defiance of conventional morality. Because of concerns over the immorality of the film business both off and on screen, in 1921, the Motion Picture Producers and Distributors of America (MPPDA) was founded as a self-regulating body. Will H. Hays, former Post-Master General, was its first president. Serving until his retirement in 1945, Hays tried to mould the Hollywood product into a wholesome and totally inoffensive form of family entertainment. His singular power led to the MPPDA being known as the Hays Office; the Production Code on matters of morality was called the Hays Code (est. 1934).

Film poster, 1926

STAR SCANDALS

During the 1920s, a rash of scandals broke out in the Hollywood community. There was the unsolved murder of director William Desmond Taylor, involving film star Mabel Normand (Mack Sennett's lover); Thomas Ince's mysterious death on newspaper tycoon William Randolph Hearst's yacht; and the trial of comedian Roscoe "Fatty" Arbuckle, for rape and murder.

Fatty Arbuckle (1887–1933) was cleared of the charges brought against him, but his career was finished.

1925

The Phantom of the Opera is released, starring Lon Chaney in his most notable role.

Charlie Chaplin's *The Gold Rush* is released.

1926

Don Juan is released by Warner Bros., with sound effects and music but no dialogue.

Rudolph Valentino dies. Some 100,000 fans attend his funeral; a few even attempt suicide.

1927

Fox's *Movietone* newsreel, the first sound news film, is released.

1928

Mickey Mouse appears for the first time, in *Steamboat Willie*.

1929

George Eastman demonstrates his first film in Technicolor.

The first Academy Awards ceremony is held in Hollywood.

Pola Negri (1894–1987) started her career in Germany before coming to Hollywood with Ernst Lubitsch in the 1920s.

Sin and sophistication

Nevertheless, "It Girl" Clara Bow and "Flapper" Joan Crawford were seen as freewheeling symbols of the jazz age, replacing the post-Victorian ideals of womanhood as exemplified by Mary Pickford, Lillian and Dorothy Gish, and Bessie Love. D.W. Griffith's melodramas, ***Broken Blossoms*** (1919) and ***Way Down East*** (1920) marked the end of an era, while Cecil B. DeMille made a series of risqué domestic comedies that tested limits. Six of these moral tales, such as ***Male and Female*** (1919), starred Gloria Swanson as an extravagantly dressed sophisticate, more sinned against than sinning. European sophistication was offered by Erich von Stroheim, who built almost the whole of Monte Carlo on the Universal backlot for ***Foolish Wives*** (1922). Among the marital comedies of manners that Ernst Lubitsch directed at Warner Bros. were ***The Marriage Circle*** (1924) and ***Lady Windermere's Fan*** (1925). At the time, Lubitsch admitted that he had been inspired by Charlie Chaplin's ***Woman of Paris*** (1923), in which Edna Purviance, Chaplin's leading lady in almost 30 comedies, played a high-class prostitute.

The studios, now strongly established in Hollywood, started to buy up talented directors from Europe. These included Ernst Lubitsch and F.W. Murnau from Germany, Michael Curtiz from Hungary, and Mauritz Stiller and Victor Sjöström from Sweden. There were also leading players to enrich the star system, such as Polish-born Pola Negri. She was the first European actress to be given the full Hollywood star treatment. Another European-born star was the imposing Swiss-born Emil Jannings, who arrived in Hollywood from Germany in 1927. He was the first to win the Best Actor Oscar twice, for ***The Way of All Flesh*** (1927) and ***The Last Command*** (1928).

Garbo and Gilbert

Swedish-born Greta Gustafsson (1905–1990) was brought to Hollywood by Louis B. Mayer in 1925 with her mentor, Mauritz Stiller, who had renamed her Garbo, made her lose 10kg (22lb), and created her mystique. However, Stiller was

PICTURE PALACES

The heyday of the picture palaces was roughly the period spanning the two world wars. During these years, hundreds of movie houses were built all over the world, and with splendid foyers, imposing staircases, and mighty Wurlitzer organs, many were masterpieces of Art Deco architecture. On average, they were capable of seating about 2,000 people, and ran three or four movie shows every day. These opulent pleasure palaces insulated the public from the harsh outside world and were as much a part of the experience of movie-going as the film itself. However, by the end of the 1930s, box office returns were failing to keep pace with the vast investment required by the studios to maintain the lavish picture palaces.

The illustration shows London's Art Deco Regal Cinema, which was opened in 1932.

Flesh and the Devil (1926) was the first and most memorable of the three silent films in which Greta Garbo and her lover, John Gilbert, were paired. Garbo, at her most seductive, plays a *femme fatale*.

not chosen to direct her first American film, ***The Torrent*** (1925), and was replaced by Clarence Brown (1890–1987) after only ten days on her second film, ***Flesh and the Devil*** (1926).

The urgency of Garbo's love scenes with John Gilbert, with whom she was involved offscreen, conveyed a mature sexuality and vulnerability never before seen in American films. The cinematographer William Daniels, who shot nearly all her Hollywood movies, devised a subtle romantic lighting for her that did much to enhance her screen image.

Garbo and Gilbert were paired for the last time in ***Queen Christina*** (1933). While the film launched Garbo into a series of tragic roles on which her reputation as an actress rests, Gilbert starred in just one further picture before dying of a heart attack brought on by excessive drinking.

Action and horror

Home-grown talent was also in evidence in Hollywood. Lon Chaney was justly famed for his make-up skills and was known as "The Man With a Thousand Faces". However, his portrayal of a series of grotesques in such films as ***The Hunchback of Notre Dame*** (1923) and ***The Phantom of the Opera*** (1925) was based not only on external distortion but sensitive acting, bringing a quality of humanity even to these most warped and terrifying characters.

Also hugely popular was the derring-do of Douglas Fairbanks, who went from strength to strength in ***The Mark of Zorro*** (1920), ***Robin Hood*** (1922), ***The Thief of Bagdad*** (1924), and ***The Black Pirate*** (1926), all of which were built around the star's muscular athleticism. Fairbanks had a hand in every aspect of film-making and was particularly interested in set design.

The final shot of Raoul Walsh's spectacular ***The Thief of Bagdad*** (1924) shows Douglas Fairbanks (in the title role) and Julanne Johnston (as his princess), sailing over the rooftops on a magic carpet.

The German poster for *Pandora's Box* (1929) shows the unique allure of Louise Brooks.

Europe and Russia

After World War I, the prosperity of the film industry in France and Italy was eclipsed by increased imports of American films. Nevertheless, despite the flood of Hollywood movies, Europe continued to produce works of great artistic quality. Among the masterpieces were Abel Gance's *Napoléon* (1927) and Carl Dreyer's *The Passion of Joan of Arc* (1928) from France; and G.W. Pabst's *Pandora's Box* (1929) and Fritz Lang's *Metropolis* (1927) from Germany. In the Soviet Union, the release of Sergei Eisenstein's *Strike* (1924) paved the way for one of the most exciting periods of experimentation and creative freedom in the history of Soviet cinema.

The coming of sound

In contrast, barring notable exceptions such as F.W. Murnau's *Sunrise* (1927), Frank Borzage's *Seventh Heaven* (1927) – which won three of the very first Oscars – and King Vidor's *The Crowd* (1928), Hollywood production was unremarkable in the late 1920s. Conditions were ripe for radical innovation. In August 1926, Warner Bros., ailing financially, presented the first synchronized programme using a sound-on-disc system called Vitaphone. Their main intention was to offer cinema owners a substitute for the live performers in their programmes – in particular the cinema orchestra and the stage show. Because of this,

An unemployed man in a soulless big city appeals for help in King Vidor's silent, poignant masterpiece, *The Crowd* (1928).

New Yorkers queue to see *The Jazz Singer* (1927), eager to experience the novelty of synchronized sound – the "talkies" – for the first time.

their first feature film with sound (*Don Juan*, 1926, starring John Barrymore) was not a talking picture at all. It used only a musical score recorded on discs to accompany the silent images, thus saving on the extra cost of hiring an orchestra.

The breakthrough came in October 1927, when Warner Bros. launched the first commercially successful feature film with sound – *The Jazz Singer* – this time featuring lip-synch recordings of songs as well as some dialogue. The success of this movie gave impetus to the installation of sound recording and projection equipment in studios and cinemas.

In May 1928, after a thorough examination of the different sound techniques, almost all the studios decided to adopt Western Electric's more flexible sound-on-film recording process, which meant the end of Warner's Vitaphone. By 1929, thousands of cinemas were equipped with sound and dozens of silent films had added dialogue sequences.

During the filming of Stroheim's *Queen Kelly* (1928), starring Gloria Swanson, the producers (including Swanson herself and Joseph P. Kennedy, father of the future US president) called a halt. They claimed that, with a third of the film already shot without sound, it was impossible to reshoot it with sound, and therefore the film was redundant. In reality, however, it was because Swanson and

Kennedy came to consider the film's sado-masochistic subject matter too shocking. ***Queen Kelly*** was hastily edited, given an arbitrary ending, and a music track was added. While Swanson's luminous career survived the arrival of sound, ***Queen Kelly***, although released in Europe, never secured a commercial release in the US. Twenty-two years later, Swanson and Stroheim would come together again in Billy Wilder's ***Sunset Boulevard*** (1950), about a forgotten star of silent films. In this movie, the sequences screened by Norma Desmond (Swanson) at her home are taken from ***Queen Kelly***, and there are other allusions to Stroheim's unfinished and largely unseen masterpiece.

MGM interfered with the editing and added a soundtrack to one of Victor Sjöström's finest achievements in the US, ***The Wind*** (1928). The film featured Lillian Gish – one of the greatest silent screen stars – giving the performance of her life.

Some Hollywood directors were able to use the new technology creatively. Rouben Mamoulian, on his first film, ***Applause*** (1929), used two microphones on certain scenes, later mixing the sound.

The birth of RKO

Sound led to the creation of a new major studio, Radio-Keith-Orpheum or RKO, in 1928, whose trademark was a pylon on a globe transmitting radio signals. Sound also led to a new genre – the musical. MGM's *The Broadway Melody* (1929), which won the Academy Award for Best Film, opened the floodgates for other musicals, dozens of which appeared before the decade was out.

The coming of sound was as seismic in other countries as in the US. In Great Britain, the success of American "talkies" resulted in a wild scramble for the new techniques. Other countries began to demand dialogue in their own languages, which led to the disintegration of the international film market – dominated by Hollywood for more than a decade. It split into as many markets as there were languages.

Directors experimented with multi-lingual films. For example, E.A. Dupont's ***Atlantic*** (1929) was shot in English, French, and German, with three different casts – a very expensive solution.

Sound affected not only film content and style, but the structure of the industry. Artistically, it immobilized the camera and froze the action in the studio.

Most of the early talkies were commercially successful, but many were of poor quality – dialogue-dominated play adaptations, with stilted acting by inexperienced performers, and an unmoving camera or microphone. (Hollywood's shift to the talkies was wittily recreated in ***Singin' in the Rain***, 1952, see p.292.) Screenwriters had to place more emphasis on characters in their scripts, and title-card writers became redundant. Most entries were literal transcriptions of Broadway shows put on the screen. However, directors and studio technicians gradually learned how to mask camera noise, free the camera, and mobilize microphones and sound recording equipment. Technology became subservient to direction and not vice versa. Now there was no looking back: the talkies were here to stay.

The Broadway Melody (1929), was the first "100% All-Talking, All-Singing, All-Dancing Motion Picture".

Garbo talks! The Swedish star made a smooth transition to sound in *Anna Christie* (1930).

1930–1939 **The Cinema Comes of Age**

Besides changing the shape of the entire film industry, the coming of sound also affected the careers of many directors and actors. During the 1930s, many genres went from strength to strength, and a new generation of stars, including Fred Astaire and Ginger Rogers, Joan Crawford, Spencer Tracy, and Clark Gable, transfixed viewers.

Three of the four founders of United Artists – Douglas Fairbanks, D.W. Griffith, and Mary Pickford – made unsuccessful attempts at the talkies. Griffith, one of the film world's most important figures, suddenly became one of its most old-fashioned. Fairbanks and Pickford, teaming up just once, in *The Taming of the Shrew* (1929), revealed their vocal deficiencies, and the film flopped. Only Chaplin survived into the sound era, ignoring spoken dialogue until *The Great Dictator* (1940). He sensed, rightly, that words would weaken the international appeal and effectiveness of much of his comedy. Thus in *City Lights* (1931), perhaps the peak of his career, he used only music and realistic sound effects.

In the mid and late 1920s, Hungarian-born Vilma Banky had been one of Hollywood's most bankable stars, but now her Hungarian accent was deemed too thick. Norma Talmadge retired after *Du Barry, Woman of Passion* (1930), when critics reviled her Brooklyn accent – rather out of keeping with the 18th-century costumes. John Gilbert is chiefly remembered as a casualty of sound. When dialogue was added to *His Glorious Night* (1929), his high-pitched voice was ridiculed. Gilbert's attempts at a comeback failed, despite his efforts as Greta Garbo's leading man in Mamoulian's *Queen Christina* (1933) – the sexual electricity was no longer there. Garbo's deep, accented voice was, however, instantly acceptable from the moment she spoke her first line in *Anna Christie* (1930). Similarly, Marlene Dietrich's celebrated husky contralto was heard in six baroque Hollywood dramas directed by Josef von Sternberg, who made her a star overnight in Germany's first film with dialogue, *The Blue Angel* (1930).

Some directors really came into their own with the talkies: Frank Capra and Howard Hawks with their machine-gun dialogue; George Cukor with his glossy, literate films at MGM; and Ernst Lubitsch, who demonstrated his sophistication and cynical wit in films such as *Trouble in Paradise* (1932) as well as in musicals starring Maurice Chevalier.

The supreme dancing duo of Fred Astaire and Ginger Rogers performs in *Top Hat* (1935). This film is perhaps the most popular of their nine black-and-white musicals.

1930–1939

1930

The daily trade paper *The Hollywood Reporter* debuts, later becoming an institution.

The movie industry begins to dub in the dialogue of films exported to foreign markets.

1931

Fritz Lang's influential *M* appears, the first psychodrama about a serial killer.

1932

Four-year-old Shirley Temple is signed to Twentieth Century Fox.

1933

King Kong is released, featuring stop-motion special effects.

The first drive-in movie theatre opens in New Jersey, US.

1934

The Hays Code is established.

Warner Bros. shuts down its German distribution office in protest against Nazism.

European films in the 1930s

In France, René Clair and Jean Renoir made good use of sound. Clair's first film with sound, ***Sous les Toits de Paris*** (***Under the Roofs of Paris***, 1930) used songs and street noises, and minimum dialogue. Renoir's ***La Chienne*** (***The Bitch***, 1931) made brilliant use of direct sound. The director also made two of the most important films of this rich period in French cinema – ***La Grande Illusion*** (1937) and ***La Règle du Jeu*** (1939). In 1936, Henri Langlois, Georges Franju, and Jean Mitry founded Cinémathèque Française. Its first task was to save old films from destruction.

In 1935, supported by Mussolini, the famous studio Cinecittá was built on Rome's outskirts. However, the quality of the films – grandiose propaganda epics and "white telephone" films (unreal, glamorous tales) – was low. Until the Nazis came to power in Germany, films there showed an awareness of social and political trends, notably G.W. Pabst's ***Westfront 1918*** (1930) and ***Kameradschaft*** (1931), and Fritz Lang's ***M*** (1931). In the Soviet Union, socialist realism, an ideological interpretation of history told in a straightforward style, was becoming entrenched, and all artists had to toe the party line.

In Great Britain, the outstanding figure in the industry at the time was Hungarian emigré Alexander Korda, who settled in England in 1931 and formed his own production company, London Films. His Denham Studios was built in an attempt to rival Hollywood.

Boom and bust

Meanwhile Hollywood, having recovered from the Wall Street Crash of 1929, was reaching its apogee. First there was a "talkie boom" in the late 1920s, and the industry enjoyed its best year ever in 1930, when theatre admissions and studio profits reached record levels. Then, in 1931, the Great Depression caught up with the movie industry and profits fell drastically.

Jean Gabin gives a spellbinding performance of tragic stature in *Daybreak* (*Le Jour Se Lève*, 1939), Marcel Carné's masterpiece of "poetic realism".

The rapid rise of the double feature, with a cheaply made second or "B-movie", was a direct result of the Great Depression. To attract patrons in those troubled times, most of the theatres offered two features in each programme, changing the programmes two or three times a week. As a result, "Poverty Row" studios, such as Monogram and Republic, could specialize in B-movies, usually Westerns or action adventures.

Major Hollywood studios

In the 1930s, the greatest asset of Columbia Pictures, which grew from a Poverty Row company into a major contender under the dictatorial Harry Cohn (1891–1958), was Frank Capra. The director made a succession of films that earned critical acclaim and secured Capra an unusual degree of independence. These included ***It Happened One Night*** (1934), ***Mr. Deeds Goes to Town*** (1936), and ***Mr. Smith Goes to Washington*** (1939).

James Whale's *Frankenstein* (1931) marked the beginning of Universal Pictures' horror movie output.

1935
It Happened One Night (1934) becomes the first film to sweep the Oscars, winning five major awards – a feat unrepeated until 1975.

1936
Chaplin's *Modern Times*, a comment on the Great Depression, is released.

1937
The first US full-length animated feature, Disney's *Snow White and the Seven Dwarfs*, is released.

1938
African-American leaders challenge the Hays Office to make roles other than those of servants and menials available to blacks.

1939
Gone With the Wind premieres.

Leo the lion poses for MGM's studio logo, which is still in use today; on the circle framing Leo was the MGM motto: *"Ars Gratia Artis"* – art for art's sake.

Universal Pictures, which started the decade with Lewis Milestone's celebrated anti-war film ***All Quiet on the Western Front*** (1930), established itself as the horror movie studio by producing all the early classics of the genre. These included ***Frankenstein*** (1931) and ***The Bride of Frankenstein*** (1935) – both directed by James Whale – with Boris Karloff as the monster. The studio also produced Tod Browning's ***Dracula*** (1931), starring Hungarian-born Bela Lugosi in the role that typecast him for the rest of his career. In the mid-1930s, wholesome teenage soprano Deanna Durbin almost single-handedly rescued the studio from bankruptcy with ten light-hearted, economical musicals, all produced by Hungarian-born Joe Pasternak, the most successful purveyor of popular classics in movies.

RKO produced nine chic Fred Astaire-Ginger Rogers musicals, from ***Flying Down to Rio*** (1933) to ***The Story of Vernon and Irene Castle*** (1939), and Katharine Hepburn's earlier films, including Howard Hawks' ***Bringing Up Baby*** (1938). The groundbreaking ***King Kong*** (1933) was also a monster hit for RKO.

Twentieth Century Fox was a latecomer among the major Hollywood studios. It was formed in 1935 by a merger of Twentieth Century Pictures and Fox Film Corporation. The company's impressive logo – searchlights on sky-scraping letters spelling out its name – became synonymous with big-feature entertainment, but the company only really started to make its mark at the beginning of the 1940s.

Warner Bros. became associated with gangster pictures that often starred James Cagney, Edward G. Robinson, and George Raft. Also on their roster were Bette Davis, Humphrey Bogart, and Errol Flynn, who was at his swashbuckling best in ***Captain Blood*** (1935), ***The Charge of the Light Brigade*** (1936), and ***The Adventures of Robin Hood*** (1938), all directed by Hungarian-born Michael Curtiz. Another European emigré at Warner was German-born William Dieterle, who directed two successful "biopics" (see p.86), on Louis Pasteur and Emile Zola – both starring Paul Muni.

Warner Bros. musicals were grittier than those of other studios, but they also contained the most fantastic cinematic numbers ever committed to film. The studio's dance director, Busby Berkeley, became known for his use of kaleidoscopic camera tricks between 1933 and 1937, while working at Warner.

If Warner Bros. was considered working-class, then MGM could be deemed middle-class. Driven by Louis B. Mayer and, until his premature death, "Boy Wonder" Irving Thalberg, MGM operated on a lavish budget making "beautiful pictures for beautiful people". The studio had Garbo, Jean Harlow, Norma Shearer (Thalberg's wife), Joan Crawford, Clark Gable, Spencer Tracy, William Powell, and Myrna Loy. Powell and Loy were very popular as the husband-wife detective team in the "Thin Man" series. Olympic swimmer Johnny Weissmuller made his debut for MGM as the vine-swinging hero in ***Tarzan the Ape Man*** (1932), which led to a string of sequels.

MGM devised the formula of providing idealistic folksy films of Americana, and glamorous and prestigious romantic screen classics, such as George Cukor's ***David Copperfield*** (1935). Other hits for the studio included ***The Great Ziegfeld*** (1936), the longest Hollywood talkie released up to that time – at 2 hours, 59 minutes – and ***Boys Town*** (1938), which won Spencer Tracy consecutive Best Actor Oscars.

Tarzan the Ape Man (1932) introduced Johnny Weissmuller, the most successful Tarzan of them all. Jane was played by Maureen O'Sullivan.

BOX OFFICE HITS OF THE 1930s

1	*Gone With the Wind* (Victor Fleming, US, 1939)
2	*Snow White and the Seven Dwarfs* (David Hand, US, 1937)
3	*The Wizard of Oz* (Victor Fleming, US, 1939)
4	*Frankenstein* (James Whale, US, 1931)
5	*King Kong* (Merian Cooper and Ernest Schoedsack, US, 1933)
6	*San Francisco* (Woody Van Dyke, US, 1936)
7=	*Hell's Angels* (Howard Hughes, US, 1930)
=	*Lost Horizon* (Frank Capra, US, 1937)
=	*Mr. Smith Goes to Washington* (Frank Capra, US, 1939)
8	*Maytime* (Robert Z. Leonard, US, 1937)

Clark Gable and Claudette Colbert share a motel room in *It Happened One Night* (1934). The screwball comedy was a surprise hit, winning five Oscars.

Paramount, in sharp contrast to MGM's middle-class values, had aristocratic pretensions. Run by Adolph Zukor, it had Lubitsch's elegance, Sternberg's exoticism, and DeMille's extravagance. Players under contract to Paramount included Dietrich, Gary Cooper, Claudette Colbert, the Marx Brothers (until 1933), W.C. Fields, and Mae West, whose saucy humour was partly responsible for the creation of the Legion of Decency in 1934.

Seal of approval

In September 1931, the Production Code was tightened and the submission of scripts to the Hays Office was made compulsory. By 1934, with the cooperation of the largely Catholic Legion of Decency, members pledged to condemn "all motion pictures except those that did not offend decency and Christian morality". The Production Code Administration (PCA) was set up to give a Seal of Approval on every film; most studios agreed not to release a film without this certificate. As a result, a number of films were withheld from release, and drastic reconstruction undertaken. The conversion of Mae West's *It Ain't No Sin* into the innocuous *Belle of the Nineties* (1934) was the most prominent. The Production Code even found the cartoon character Betty Boop immoral and demanded that her sexiness be hidden. Among the proscriptions were: profanity, nudity, sexual perversion, miscegenation, and scenes of childbirth. The Code also suggested that respect must be given to the flag; no sympathy for criminals must be shown; and a man and woman, even if married, could not be seen in bed together. The Code thus amounted to a form of censorship, but although it inhibited some film-makers, it did help to ensure a steady flow of high-quality family entertainment.

The films of 1939 – a golden year for Hollywood – included *Mr. Smith Goes to Washington*, *The Wizard of Oz*, John Ford's mould-breaking Western *Stagecoach*, *Dark Victory*, with Bette Davis, *Goodbye Mr. Chips*, starring Robert Donat (who won the Best Actor Oscar for this film), Lewis Milestone's *Of Mice and Men*, Lubitsch's *Ninotchka*, and *Gone With the Wind*. We will not see its like again.

GLORIOUS TECHNICOLOR

By the 1930s, Technicolor had become such a successful cinematography process that it was often used as the generic name for any colour film. Walt Disney (1901–66) enjoyed the exclusive rights to make animated films in colour from 1932–35, producing Oscar-winning shorts, such as *Flowers and Trees* (1932) and *The Three Little Pigs* (1933). By the mid-1930s, colour was no longer a novelty, but was being used for about 20 per cent of Hollywood's output. Technicolor reached its zenith at the end of the decade with two MGM movies – *The Wizard of Oz* and *Gone With the Wind* – both credited to Victor Fleming.

Technicolor cameras, seen here with film rolls on top, were mainly used in studios.

1940–1949 The Cinema Goes to War

The outbreak of World War II in Europe finally brought the economic problems of the 1930s to an end in the US. There was a return to full employment, which led to a boom in film attendance. During the post-war years, however, the studios were troubled by union problems and strikes, followed by the notorious anti-Communist "Hollywood witch-hunt".

In October 1940, the *New York Herald Tribune* wrote, "The incomparable Charles Chaplin is back on the screen in an extraordinary film. ***The Great Dictator*** is a savage comic commentary on a world gone mad. It has a solid fabric of irresistible humour and also blazes with indignation". Chaplin's first talkie, a thinly disguised satire on Nazi Germany, earned more money than any of his other pictures. However, he, and the world, had much to be indignant about.

Film fights Fascism

Although the US remained neutral in the war until the bombing of Pearl Harbor by Japan on 7 December 1941, Hollywood seemed to be on pre-war alert, with several related films made before the attack. Howard Hawks' ***Sergeant York***, starring Gary Cooper, although set in the First World War, was an assault on isolationism. Other calls for America to take up arms, which also extolled the virtues of democracy over the brutality of Fascist regimes, were William Wyler's ***Mrs. Miniver***, Michael Curtiz's ***Casablanca***, set in 1941 war-time Morocco, and Ernst Lubitsch's ***To Be or Not To Be*** (all 1942). Tragically, Carole Lombard, the star of the latter, did not live to see its release. In early 1942, while on a War Bond tour, she was killed in a plane crash. She was just 34 years old.

William Wyler's *Mrs. Miniver* (1942) shows how an upper middle-class English family bore up bravely during World War II.

The outbreak of war in Europe threatened to devastate Hollywood's vital overseas trade. The studios' exports to the Axis nations – principally Germany, Italy, and Japan – had declined to almost nil in 1937–38, but Hollywood still derived about one-third of its total revenue from overseas markets, the United Kingdom in particular. By late 1940, Britain stood alone as Hollywood's significant remaining overseas market.

In Britain, more than half the studio space was taken up by the making of propaganda films for the government. Many were of real merit, like ***London Can Take It!*** (1940), ***The Foreman Went to France*** (1942), and ***The First of the Few*** (1942). The movement also produced Humphrey Jennings, a poet of the documentary, whose best work, ***Listen to Britain*** (1942) and ***Fires Were Started*** (1943), summed up the spirit of Britain at war. Laurence Olivier's ***Henry V*** (1944), the making and release of which coincided with Britain's invasion of occupied France, used the patriotic fervour of the Shakespeare play to good effect. Weekly attendance by wartime British audiences trebled between 1939 and 1945.

The film industry in France fell under Nazi control in 1940 and all English-language films were banned. René Clair and Jean Renoir left for Hollywood. To avoid censorship, directors chose non-political subjects, although Marcel Carné's ***Les Visiteurs du Soir*** (***The Devil's Envoys***, 1942) was regarded by the French as an allegory of their situation, with the Devil (played with relish

1940–1949

1940

Alfred Hitchcock's first American film, *Rebecca*, is released. It goes on to win the Best Picture Oscar.

1941

Bette Davis becomes the first female president of the Motion Picture Academy of Arts and Sciences.

John Huston's *The Maltese Falcon* is the first of the classic film noir.

1942

Paul Robeson leaves the industry because of the lack of quality roles for black actors.

1944

The first TV ad for a film is broadcast by Paramount.

BOX OFFICE HITS OF THE 1940s

1 *Bambi* (David Hand, US, 1942)
2 *Pinocchio* (Hamilton Luske and Ben Sharpsteen, US, 1940)
3 *Fantasia* (11 directors, US, 1940)
4 *Song of the South* (Harve Foster and Wilfred Jackson, US, 1946)
5 *Mom and Dad* (William Beaudine, US, 1945)
6 *Samson and Delilah* (Cecil B. DeMille, US, 1949)
7 *The Best Years of Our Lives* (William Wyler, US, 1946)
8 *The Bells of St. Mary's* (Leo MacCarey, US, 1945)
9 *Duel in the Sun* (King Vidor, US, 1946)
10 *This is the Army* (Michael Curtiz, US, 1943)

by Jules Berry) seen as Hitler. Henri-Georges Clouzot's ***Le Corbeau*** (*The Raven*, 1943), made by a German-run company, was temporarily banned after Liberation.

Other films were more overtly pro-Axis. Jean Delannoy's ***L'Eternel Retour*** (*Love Eternal*, 1943), with a screenplay by Jean Cocteau, was an update of the Tristan and Isolde legend featuring Aryan lovers, which was pleasing to the Occupiers. In all, Germany made 1,100 feature films under the Nazi regime, many of them harmless entertainment, with anti-Semitic propaganda films among the dross. Emil Jannings, who had returned to Germany from Hollywood to co-star with Marlene Dietrich in ***The Blue Angel*** (1930), and remained there, was appointed head of the country's biggest studio, UFA, in 1940. In the following year, he played the title role of ***Ohm Krüger***, an anti-British film set in the time of the Boer War. However, because of his cooperation with the Nazi Ministry of Propaganda, he was blacklisted by the Allies, and spent his last years in retirement in Austria.

Humphrey Jennings showed the National Fire Service at work during the London Blitz in his beautifully photographed documentary ***Fires Were Started*** (1943).

Studio fare

Back in Hollywood, to meet the increased demand for top features, studios either turned to independent producers, whose ranks grew rapidly in the 1940s, or granted their own contract talent greater freedom over their productions. At Paramount, Cecil B. DeMille was given the status of "in-house independent" producer, which got him a profit participation deal on his pictures.

The growing power of independent film-makers and top contract talent in the early 1940s was reinforced by the rise of the talent guilds. The Screen Writers Guild, the Screen Directors Guild, and the Screen Actors Guild provided a serious challenge to studio control, particularly in terms of the artists' authority over their work. Moreover, top contract talent was going freelance, further undermining the established contract system, which was a crucial factor in studio hegemony.

1945

Open City, Roberto Rossellini's Italian realist masterpiece, is released.

Restrictions on the allocation of raw film stock are lifted with the end of World War II.

1946

The Cannes Film Festival debuts on the French Riviera.

The Jolson Story, a popular biopic of Al Jolson, is released.

1947

As a result of HUAC investigations, the "Hollywood Ten" are jailed for refusing to cooperate.

1949

The US Supreme Court rules that Hollywood-based studios must end monopolization of US movie-making, heralding the end of the studio system.

In Jacques Tourneur's *Cat People* (1942), Simone Simon plays a feline heroine afraid that an ancient curse would turn her into a panther when sexually aroused.

Despite the success of Walt Disney's ***Fantasia*** and Alfred Hitchcock's first American film, ***Rebecca*** (both 1940), RKO was in serious financial difficulties. Its distribution was adversely affected when Walt Disney, David O. Selznick (who had brought Hitchcock to Hollywood), and Samuel Goldwyn set up their own releasing companies. Looking for a quick return, RKO took a chance on the 26-year-old Orson Welles with ***Citizen Kane*** (1941), but though it brought them prestige, it didn't bring in funds. They had more success with Val Lewton, who produced a series of subtle, low-budget psychological thrillers, such as Jacques Tourneur's ***Cat People*** (1942).

The Saturday morning matinee was a staple of children's film-going from the 1940s to the 1960s. The programme was mostly cartoons, serials, and B-westerns.

Hollywood's war effort

Ironically, the war years were a comparatively good time for Hollywood. With America suddenly engaged in a global war, Hollywood's social, economic, and industrial fortunes changed virtually overnight. The government now saw "the national cinema" as an ideal source of diversion, information, morale boosting, and propaganda for citizens and soldiers alike. Within a year of Pearl Harbor, nearly one-third of Hollywood's feature films were war-related. The studios reasserted their hold over the industry and enjoyed record revenues, while playing a vital role in the war effort.

The American film industry was extremely prolific, affluent, powerful, and productive during the 1940s. While European film production suffered because of the impact of hostilities, Hollywood film production reached its peak during the years 1943 to 1946, with cinema attendance at pre-Depression levels. The Big Five studios – RKO, Warner Bros., Fox, Paramount, and MGM – radically reduced their output from an average of 50 films a year to 30, concentrating on bigger movies that played longer runs.

Motion pictures offered the masses an easy, inexpensive, and accessible means of escape from long working hours, austerity, and the horrifying news from abroad. Westerns, Technicolor musicals, and sophisticated comedies were the perfect tranquilizers. To make films more topical, established genres, such as the gangster movie and the thriller, often substituted a Nazi or a Fifth Columnist for the traditional underworld baddie. But wartime audiences also wanted to be uplifted by the movies, and dramas, such as ***Casablanca*** (1942) and ***Mrs. Miniver*** (1942), were very popular.

A woman's place

America's entry into the war in 1942 meant big changes in the position of women in society. Traditional models to represent male-female relationships came into increasing conflict with the realities of the world, where women were doing men's jobs and looking after the home alone, while the men were away fighting. Many of the films of the time reflected this, with forceful female stars, such as Barbara Stanwyck, Bette Davis, and Joan Crawford, in powerful melodramas, including ***Now, Voyager*** (1942) and ***Mildred Pierce*** (1945).

ENTERTAINING THE TROOPS

Big-name stars who enlisted in the US Army included James Stewart and Clark Gable. Others performed for the forces at military bases, or contributed to the war effort in other ways. Some of Hollywood's best directors – John Ford, Frank Capra, John Huston, and William Wyler – made war-related documentaries or training films. The US Government's Office of War Information (OWI), formed in 1942, served as an important propaganda agency during World War II, and coordinated its efforts with those of the film industry.

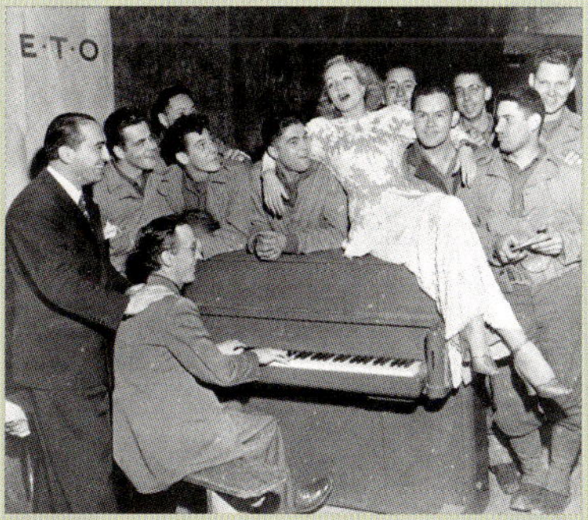

» **Marlene Dietrich** became less mysterious when she helped the Allied cause by entertaining US troops.

Shooting stars

Despite losing Gable and others to the armed services, and 36-year-old Garbo to permanent retirement from the screen in 1941, MGM could still boast of "more stars than there are in the heavens". Throughout the 1940s, songwriter Arthur Freed (1894–1973) headed MGM's top musical production unit, making the studio synonymous with the best screen musicals. Among the talents Freed gathered were artists Gene Kelly, Fred Astaire, Frank Sinatra, Judy Garland, and June Allyson; directors Vincente Minnelli, Stanley Donen, George Sidney, and Charles Walters; and lyricists Betty Comden, Adolph Green, and Alan Jay Lerner. Freed also signed Lena Horne, the first African-American woman to have a long-term contract with a major studio. Horne negotiated a clause that prevented her from playing domestics, jungle natives, or other racial stereotypes. However, she was used as a speciality performer so that her numbers could be edited out for theatres in the Southern states.

Columbia was fortunate in having flame-haired screen goddess Rita Hayworth under contract. Charles Vidor, the Hungarian-born director, brought out the best in her in ***Cover Girl*** (1944) and ***Gilda*** (1946). In the latter, she "sang" (dubbed by Anita Ellis) *Put the Blame on Mame*, peeling off her long gloves, as Glenn Ford – and millions of hot-blooded men – lusted after her.

The biggest wartime star at Twentieth Century Fox was leggy blonde Betty Grable, a favourite forces pin-up, who appeared in several highly Technicolored musicals. However, when studio head Darryl F. Zanuck returned after his war service, he made Fox's output more serious-minded.

« **Rita Hayworth** in Charles Vidor's ***Gilda*** (1946), the role with which she was most identified, epitomized 1940s Hollywood glamour.

Post-war boom

In 1940s Great Britain, the average annual cinema attendance reached 1,462 million. In 1947, the new Labour Government imposed a 75 per cent tax on foreign film imports; the US responded by placing an embargo on the export of films to Britain. The sudden shortage of American films was a challenge to the British film industry. When an agreement was signed with the Motion Picture Association of America (MPAA) in 1948, a flood of Hollywood films hit the market and, at the same time, Americans were obliged to spend 75 per cent of their British earnings to make American films in British studios. In the late 1940s, the Rank Organization owned the two largest studios in Britain – Denham and Pinewood – and several smaller ones.

The end of World War II brought rapid changes in the industry, particularly with the application of the anti-trust legislation that signalled the end of the old Hollywood. Forced by law to divest themselves of financial control of the theatres, the major studios lost guaranteed outlets for their products just as audiences started to decline in numbers. France reinforced the quota system on American films. It also initiated co-productions between itself and Italy, which helped to finance independent production.

The most important aesthetic change that took place in films at the time was Italian neorealism. This term was first applied to Luchino Visconti's ***Ossessione*** (1943), shown only clandestinely at the time, but which had a profound influence on other young directors in Italy, such as Roberto Rossellini and Vittorio De Sica, and even directors in other countries.

Split into two countries, East and West Germany had two separate film industries. A certain number of directors who worked during the Nazi era, such as Leni Riefenstahl, were blacklisted. In East Germany, Russian films dominated the cinemas, while in the West, mostly American films were shown, with the aim, it was stated, of aiding de-Nazification. Similarly, Japan was flooded with American films that were supposed to show the people a modern democratic society.

Challenging authority

The release of the Billy the Kid Western, ***The Outlaw***, by the maverick millionaire Howard Hughes, caused a huge censorship uproar. The film was completed in 1941, but not given a general release until 1946, having been withdrawn after a limited release in 1943. The delay came about when producer Hughes

John Mills (right) plays Pip and Alec Guinness plays Herbert Pocket in David Lean's ***Great Expectations*** (1946), perhaps the finest of all Dickens screen adaptations, and part of the Denham Studios stable.

"Are you now or have you ever been a member of the **Communist Party**?"

HUAC, 1947

"How Would You Like To Tussle With Russell" was the slogan for *The Outlaw* (1943), dreamt up by the producer-director Howard Hughes, who discovered Jane Russell.

challenged the legal authority of the Production Code when the film was refused a Seal of Approval for "glamorizing crime and immorality". However, it could have had more to do with Jane Russell's cantilevered bra, specially designed by Hughes.

More realistic representations of sexual and psychological problems and psychopathic behaviour could be found in the film noir genre, as well as movies such as Elia Kazan's ***Gentleman's Agreement*** and Edward Dmytryk's ***Crossfire*** (both 1947), about anti-Semitism in the US. Kazan's ***Pinky*** and Clarence Brown's ***Intruder in the Dust*** (both 1949) dealt with racial prejudice, while Billy Wilder's ***The Lost Weekend*** (1945) explored alcoholism.

This willingness to engage in serious confrontations with social problems and religious and racial bigotry emerged just as the House of Un-American Activities Committee (HUAC), spurred on by Senator Joseph McCarthy, began its investigations into alleged Communist infiltration of the motion picture industry. After declaring that Hollywood film-makers "employed subtle techniques in pictures glorifying the Communist system", the HUAC held public hearings in October 1947 to question "friendly" witnesses (friendly to the purposes of the committee), who included Adolphe Menjou, Ronald Reagan, Robert Taylor, and Gary Cooper. Ten so-called "unfriendly" witnesses were subpoenaed. The Hollywood Ten, as they became known, were imprisoned after they claimed that the Fifth Amendment of the US Constitution gave them the right to refuse to answer the question of whether or not they had been Communists. One of them, director Edward Dmytryk, later recanted. Eventually, more than 300 film artists and technicians were blacklisted, their contracts terminated and careers finished. Some worked under assumed names or went abroad. Others, including Larry Parks (who had risen to fame in ***The Jolson Story***, 1946, a popular biopic), Lee J. Cobb, Budd Schulberg, and Elia Kazan, were so afraid of going to prison that they named people who had been members of left-wing groups. It was one of the shabbiest periods in the history of Hollywood, and sapped its creative spark into the 1950s.

The mid-1940s also saw the emergence of Ealing Studios in Britain, formed by a team of directors, writers, and technicians who believed that the way to an international market was to capture and exploit the British spirit with all its oddities and humour. It could be described as a genuine indigenous school of film-making.

Humphrey Bogart and his wife Lauren Bacall, leading a line of Hollywood artists, scriptwriters, and directors, march in protest against the McCarthy witch-hunts.

1950–1959 The Cinema Fights Back

The 1950s gave cinema a rival – television. Throughout the decade, cinema attendance dropped as people tuned in to the small black-and-white screens in their living rooms. The big Hollywood studios responded by developing a series of devices and new tricks to tempt audiences back in front of the silver screen.

In *From Here To Eternity* (1953), the fact that the hitherto ladylike Deborah Kerr played the adulterous army wife caught up in an affair with Burt Lancaster added to the frisson felt by audiences – especially evident during the celebrated erotic beach scene.

In the early 1950s, the House of Un-American Activities Committee (HUAC) was at its peak, interrogating Americans about their Communist connections and distributing millions of pamphlets to the American public, with titles such as "One Hundred Things You Should Know About Communism". The second wave of HUAC hearings began in 1951, with Republican Senator Joseph McCarthy leading the charge. Over the next three years, McCarthy subpoenaed some of the most prominent entertainers of the era. However, in 1954, with the help of Edward Murrow's unedited footage of the hearings (the subject of George Clooney's *Good Night and Good Luck*, 2005), the public was able to see McCarthyism for what it really was – a witch-hunt.

While Senator McCarthy was seeing villainous Reds under every bed, film moguls saw the box in people's living rooms as the real enemy. Although cinema audience figures had already started to decline in 1947, the main cause for the drastic reduction in cinema admissions was blamed on the television sets that were proliferating in homes across the US. In the first years of the 1950s, 50 per cent of US homes had at least one TV set, a number that was set to grow dramatically. As Samuel Goldwyn commented, "Why should people go out and pay money to see bad films when they can stay at home and see bad television for nothing?"

Jack Warner stipulated that no TV set was to be seen in a Warner Bros. movie. Television, which was added to the list of taboos, was seldom

1950–1959

1950

Gloria Swanson and other actors from the silent screen play aspects of themselves in *Sunset Boulevard*.

1951

HUAC opens a second round of hearings in Hollywood, and blacklists 212 people.

1952

MGM releases *Singin' in the Rain*.

A Streetcar Named Desire is the first film to win three acting Oscars, for Vivien Leigh, Karl Malden, and Kim Hunter.

1953

The Academy Awards are televised for the first time.

Single- or multi-film contracts replace seven-year contracts for actors.

1954

The Seven Samurai, Akira Kurosawa's influential epic, is released.

mentioned in films except in a satirical context, as in the MGM musical *It's Always Fair Weather* (1955) and Elia Kazan's *A Face in the Crowd* (1957) – a biting attack on the manipulation of the masses by TV.

Ironically, the arch-enemy provided Hollywood with some of the best screenplays of the era, as well as the first generation of directors to come to the movies via the TV studio. These included John Frankenheimer, who made *The Manchurian Candidate* (1962), Sidney Lumet, Robert Mulligan (best known for *To Kill A Mockingbird*, 1962), and Delbert Mann. Mann's *Marty* (1955), based on a Paddy Chayefsky teleplay about a lonely butcher from the Bronx (movie heavy Ernest Borgnine, cast against type, winning the Best Actor Oscar), was the "sleeper" of the decade. As a result, other intimate, realistic TV dramas, such as Lumet's *12 Angry Men* (1957), were successfully adapted for the big screen.

AT THE DRIVE-IN

Outdoor drive-in theatres, first introduced in the US in 1933, flourished in the 1950s. Patrons watched a film from their own cars, parked in a semi-circle around a giant screen. The sound was supplied by small speakers attached inside each car. Drive-in theatres attracted families with small children, avoiding the need for a babysitter, and young couples. With the latter in mind, many of the drive-ins showed "B" horror movies, dubbed "drive-in fodder".

Some 4,000 drive-ins were constructed across America but their popularity started to decline in the 1960s. Only a few still exist today, frequented by nostalgic audiences.

A lion in your lap

The existence of a financial competitor to Hollywood stimulated all sorts of movie innovations. One novelty that had mixed results was 3-D movie-making. The first colour feature-length Hollywood film made in Natural Vision (soon to be dubbed 3-D) was *Bwana Devil* (1952); the film's publicity slogan was "A Lion in your lap". Arch Oboler, who produced, directed, and wrote it, made a huge profit on his comparatively small investment due to the novelty value of the film's pioneering technique. However, these films, which could only be seen through cheap cardboard Polaroid spectacles, were still fairly crude, with images changing in quality and causing "ghosts" on the screen. Nevertheless, Hollywood began

The 3-D experience was uncomfortable for those who already wore glasses; headaches were common; and the novelty soon wore thin.

1955

James Dean is killed in a car accident.

On the Waterfront wins eight Oscars.

RKO sells its film library to television.

1956

Cecil B. DeMille remakes his own silent epic, *The Ten Commandments*. It is nominated for seven Oscars.

1957

The first kiss between a black man and a white woman (Harry Belafonte and Joan Fontaine) is featured in ***Island in the Sun***.

1958

The horror film *The Fly* appears.

1959

Hitchcock's film *North by Northwest* is released.

making about 30 3-D films a year, with audiences being subjected to all sorts of missiles hurtling towards them. Gradually, the glasses became an increasing annoyance and many good films produced in 3-D, such as MGM's *Kiss Me Kate* (1953) and Alfred Hitchcock's *Dial M For Murder* (1954), were released as ordinary "flat" films.

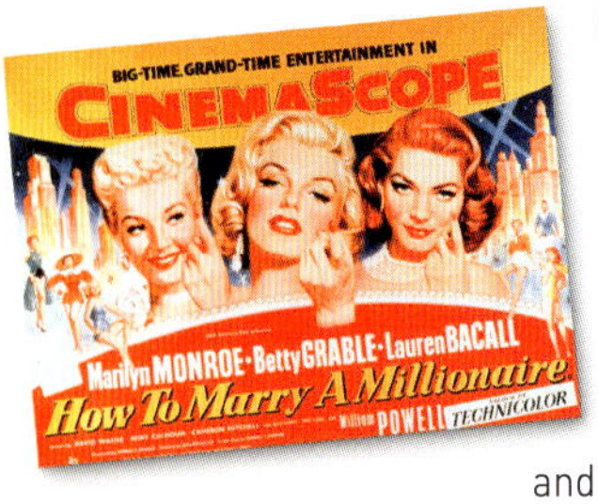

Film poster, 1953

Stretching the screen

In 1952, a film was released showing how a technology called Cinerama could make films more realistic by involving viewers' peripheral vision. *This is Cinerama* informed its audiences that "you will be gazing at a movie screen – you'll find yourself swept right into the picture, surrounded by sight and sound". A series of short subjects followed, including scenes of a roller coaster, a bullfight, and Niagara Falls.

The process had three 35mm projectors, three screens curved to cover 140 degrees, and stereophonic sound. However, theatres that showed films in this new way were required to employ three full-time projectionists and invest thousands of dollars in new equipment, and Cinerama's popularity was short-lived.

Todd-AO was developed in the early 1950s to produce a widescreen image by photographing on 65mm and printing on a 70mm positive. The remaining space at the side of the print allowed room for six stereophonic soundtracks. The process was developed by the American Optical Company (hence AO) for showman Mike Todd. Todd-AO was successfully used for *Oklahoma!* (1955) and the star-studded *Around the World in Eighty Days* (1956). Todd married Elizabeth Taylor in 1956, but their stormy marriage was cut short when he was killed in a plane crash.

In 1953, Twentieth Century Fox unveiled CinemaScope, a process that used an anamorphic (distortable) lens to expand the size of the image. *The Robe*, a Biblical epic starring British actor Richard Burton, was the first CinemaScope feature. By the end of 1953, every major studio except Paramount – whose rival VistaVision process had a 35mm film running horizontally instead of vertically – was making films in CinemaScope.

The size of the screen dictated the content of the movies to a large extent, so that *Knights of the Round Table* (1953), *Land of the Pharoahs* (1955), and *Helen of Troy* (1955) filled the screens, if not the theatres. The need to cram every inch of the screen with spectacle was an expensive operation, and CinemaScope films seldom recouped their costs. Exceptions included Elia Kazan's *East of Eden* (1955), Nicholas Ray's *Rebel without a Cause* (1955), Vincente Minnelli's *Lust for Life* (1956), and Otto Preminger's *River of No Return* (1954).

Carroll Baker plays the virgin bride in Elia Kazan's *Baby Doll* (1956), a film that scandalized puritan America because of provocative poses such as this.

The movies mature

There was a more interesting device for getting people to leave their TV sets for a movie theatre: controversial and adult subjects deemed unsuitable by TV's sponsors for family viewing at home. So if someone wanted to hear the words "virgin" and "seduce", they would have to go out to the movies to see Preminger's *The Moon is Blue* (1954), which was released without the Production Code's Seal of Approval. This film helped to create a permissiveness that wrested Hollywood from the puritan values that had gripped it for so long.

Independent producers were also breaking the hold of the major studios and tackled more daring subjects, delving into areas that Hollywood had previously avoided. Movies such as Kazan's *Baby Doll* (1956) led to revisions of the Production Code, after which "mature" subjects such as prostitution, drug addiction, and miscegenation could be shown if "treated within the limits of good taste".

Hollywood themes

Despite the Communist witch-hunts against the background of the Cold War, Hollywood continued to explore liberal themes. Native Americans were, for the first time, sympathetically treated in films like Delmer Daves' ***Broken Arrow*** (1950) and Robert Aldrich's ***Apache*** (1954). Racial intolerance was examined in Joseph Mankiewicz's ***No Way Out*** (1950) and Stanley Kramer's ***The Defiant Ones*** (1958). Juvenile delinquency was explored in Richard Brooks' ***The Blackboard Jungle*** (1955), the first major Hollywood film to use rock'n'roll on its soundtrack. Preminger's ***The Man with the Golden Arm*** (1955) and Fred Zinnemann's ***A Hatful of Rain*** (1957) tackled the subject of drug addiction with a frankness hitherto unknown. With the Korean War over and wounds beginning to heal, Stanley Kubrick was able to make ***Paths of Glory*** (1957), one of the screen's most powerful anti-militarist statements.

Saul Bass created this classic poster for Otto Preminger's ***The Man With The Golden Arm*** (1955), in which Frank Sinatra played a professional gambler hooked on narcotics.

The steep decline in weekly theatre attendance forced studios to find creative ways to make money from the new medium. Converted studios were beginning to produce more hours of film for TV than for feature films. Although their vast structure was weakened, the studios still had a certain identity and continued to turn out good films under their banners. At MGM, the artistic status of the musical was raised by Vincente Minnelli's ***An American in Paris*** (1951) and Gene Kelly and Stanley Donen's ***Singin' in the Rain*** (1952). Although Republic Pictures produced some of their best films in the 1950s – Nicholas Ray's ***Johnny Guitar*** (1954) and John Ford's ***Rio Grande*** (1950) and ***The Quiet Man*** (1952) – it abandoned making films in 1958. RKO, which businessman Howard Hughes had bought in 1948 for US$9 million, later paying a further US$23 million for ownership of the subsidiaries, ceased production in 1953. In 1957, it was sold to Desilu Productions, a TV company owned by Lucille Ball.

Columbia recovered in the early 1950s, with the support of independent producers – David Lean (***The Bridge on the River Kwai***, 1957), Elia Kazan (***On the Waterfront***, 1954), and Fred Zinnemann (***From Here To Eternity***, 1953). The latter was notable

Alec Guinness (left) is the stubborn English POW colonel in the seven Oscar-winning ***The Bridge on the River Kwai*** (1957). The bridge is in the background.

for showing the usually ladylike Deborah Kerr in an adulterous affair with Burt Lancaster and reviving Frank Sinatra's flagging career. Lancaster and Kirk Douglas emerged as the most versatile stars of the 1950s, gaining greater independence by going freelance and becoming producers. Other stars, such as Bette Davis, successfully reinvented themselves.

Hip new stars

With youth culture beginning to infiltrate the movies in the 1950s, it was now possible for young people to identify with certain stars. Joan Crawford, a remnant of past glamour, was scathing about the "ordinary" characters in films that were becoming popular with young people. However, it was precisely because of their youth that audiences could imagine the new stars living next door, and that made them attractive.

Marlon Brando projected an anti-conformist image, especially in *The Wild One* (1954), the film noted for a dialogue that typified his attitude. "What are you rebelling against?" Brando is asked. "Whaddaya got?" he replies.

James Dean (1931–55), who starred in only three films – *Rebel without a Cause* (1955), *East of Eden* (1955), and *Giant* (1956) – was the personification of adolescent rebellion and despair. Dean died on 20 September 1955 when the silver Porsche Spyder he was driving had a head-on collision with another vehicle. His death resulted in a level of hysteria among fans not seen since the untimely demise of Rudolph Valentino in 1926.

> "I don't believe you want to go to the theatre to see **somebody you can see next door**."

Joan Crawford, 1950

BOX OFFICE HITS OF THE 1950s

1. *Lady and the Tramp* (Clyde Geronimi, Wilfred Jackson, and Hamilton Luske, US, 1955)
2. *Peter Pan* (Clyde Geronimi, Wilfred Jackson, and Hamilton Luske, US, 1953)
3. *Cinderella* (Clyde Geronimi, Wilfred Jackson, and Hamilton Luske, US, 1950)
4. *The Ten Commandments* (Cecil B. DeMille, US, 1956)
5. *Ben-Hur* (William Wyler, US, 1959)
6. *Sleeping Beauty* (Clyde Geronimi, US, 1959)
7. *Around the World in Eighty Days* (Michael Anderson, US, 1956)
8. *This is Cinerama* (Merian C. Cooper, US, 1952)
9. *South Pacific* (Joshua Logan, US, 1958)
10. *The Robe* (Henry Koster, US, 1953)

In Laslo Benedek's *The Wild One* (1954), Marlon Brando's inarticulate biker character made him the idol of the erotic and anarchic motorcycle cult, and spawned a series of biker movies.

Brando and Dean were able to attract a new type of youngster to the cinema – those who preferred their heroes more non-conformist than the clean-cut, studio-bred idols of the 1930s and 1940s.

The legacy of the 1950s

Away from the new wave of anarchic performers, there were still a number of stars in the glamorous Hollywood tradition, such as Ava Gardner, Susan Hayward, Elizabeth Taylor, Grace Kelly, Rock Hudson, and Audrey Hepburn. Three names from an earlier era made sensational comebacks: Bette Davis played a fading actress in *All About Eve* (1950), Judy Garland played her greatest role in *A Star is Born* (1954), and Ingrid Bergman returned to Hollywood to win an Oscar for *Anastasia* (1956). However, the iconic images of Brando in leather, astride a motorcycle in *The Wild One*, the boyish blond features of rebellious James Dean, and the wide eyes of pin-up idol Marilyn Monroe, who did not live much beyond the end of the decade, remain the predominant US movie symbols of the 1950s. The ghosts of the decade are still there to haunt us.

Film poster, 1954

"THE METHOD"

"The Method" was advanced by a group of actors and directors at the Actors Studio in New York in 1948. It was influenced by the teachings of the Russian stage director Konstantin Stanislavsky, who stressed a more instinctive approach to acting than had been popular until that time. Marlon Brando (1924–2004) typified this style. Many thought there was madness in "The Method" and it became the most caricatured of all acting styles with its mumbled delivery, shrugging of shoulders, fidgeting, and scratching. Humphrey Bogart commented, "I came out here with one shirt and everyone said I looked like a bum. Twenty years later Marlon Brando comes out with only a sweatshirt and the town drools over him. That shows how much Hollywood has progressed".

A "Method" session takes place at the Actors Studio; founded by Elia Kazan and Cheryl Crawford, its most famous teacher was Lee Strasberg.

1960–1969 The New Wave

Much was changing as the new decade dawned. America had a dynamic new leader, John F. Kennedy, and in Europe, more liberated attitudes to sex, fashion, and politics filtered into books, art, and movies. In the film world, the first rumblings of change came about in France with the New Wave, whose influence reached as far as Hollywood.

Shirley MacLaine and Jack Lemmon star in Billy Wilder's comedy *The Apartment* (1960), the last black-and-white film to win the Best Picture Oscar, until Steven Spielberg's *Schindler's List* (1993).

At the start of 1960, the Writers Guild of America went on strike for more equitable contracts and a share of the profits of films sold to TV. The Screen Actors Guild of America demanded a raise in minimum salaries and a share in TV residuals. Both the writers and the actors won their cases – victories that helped to push Hollywood to the brink of economic disaster.

Due to various insecurities and financial difficulties, the studios were quickly taken over by multinational companies. Paramount was rescued by Gulf + Western Industries; Warner Bros. merged with Seven Arts Ltd, a TV company, to become Warner Bros.-Seven Arts; MGM shifted its interests to real estate; and MCA (the Music Corporation of America) acquired Universal-International Studios. The Bank of America absorbed United Artists through its Transamerica Corporation subsidiary. Even without huge overheads and star salaries, this studio continued to attract many leading independent producers and directors, such as Stanley Kramer. He had his greatest ever success with *It's a Mad, Mad, Mad, Mad World* (1963) – a US$10-million earner. United Artists also had directors Billy Wilder (*The Apartment*, 1960), Norman Jewison (*In the Heat of the Night*, 1967), John Sturges (*The Great Escape*, 1963), and Blake Edwards. The latter, with *The Pink Panther* (1963), initiated a slapstick comedy series starring Peter Sellers as the incompetent Inspector Clouseau.

BOX OFFICE HITS OF THE 1960s

1. *One Hundred and One Dalmatians* (Clyde Geronimi, Hamilton Luske, Wolfgang Reitherman, US, 1961)
2. *The Jungle Book* (Wolfgang Reitherman, US, 1967)
3. *The Sound of Music* (Robert Wise, US, 1965)
4. *Thunderball* (Terence Young, UK, 1965)
5. *Goldfinger* (Guy Hamilton, US, 1964)
6. *Doctor Zhivago* (David Lean, US, 1965)
7. *You Only Live Twice* (Lewis Gilbert, UK, 1967)
8. *The Graduate* (Mike Nichols, US, 1967)
9. *Butch Cassidy and the Sundance Kid* (George Roy Hill, US, 1969)
10. *Mary Poppins* (Robert Stevenson, US, 1964)

1960–1969

1960

Alfred Hitchcock's *Psycho* terrifies audiences for the first time.

1961

West Side Story receives 11 Oscar nominations, eventually winning all but one.

1962

Marilyn Monroe is found dead of a drug overdose at her home in Los Angeles.

The first James Bond film, *Dr. No*, is released.

1963

Sidney Poitier becomes the first black actor to win a Best Actor Oscar, for *Lilies of the Field*.

The first video recorder is sold for US$30,000.

Steve McQueen, here commandeering a Nazi soldier's motorbike, contributed as much as anyone to the vast appeal of ***The Great Escape*** (1963).

On the whole, while the studios became administrative centres organizing finance and distribution, they were losing their individual stamp. To fill the gap, independent producers became a more common feature of the movie-making process. They would come to the studio with a package consisting of director, script, writers, and marketable stars.

Although the structure of the industry had changed drastically, most of the pictures still followed the genre pattern initiated by the studios in their heyday. There were musicals: Robert Wise and Jerome Robbins' ***West Side Story*** (1961), George Cukor's ***My Fair Lady*** (1964), and William Wyler's ***Funny Girl*** (1968), all derived from Broadway shows; Westerns, notably from veterans John Ford and Howard Hawks with ***The Man Who Shot Liberty Valance*** (1962) and ***El Dorado*** (1966), respectively, and newcomer Sam Peckinpah with ***Ride the High Country*** (1962), all of them valedictions to the Old West; and romantic comedies like the popular Doris Day–Rock Hudson cycle.

The 1961 screen version of the landmark Broadway musical ***West Side Story*** features finger-snapping, high-kicking street gangs.

1965

The Sound of Music surpasses ***Gone with the Wind*** as the number one box office hit of all time.

1966

Paramount is bought by multinational conglomerate Gulf + Western Industries.

Revisions to the Hays Code allow some films to be recommended for "mature" audiences.

1967

Mike Nichols becomes the first director to be paid US$1,000,000, for one film, ***The Graduate***.

Arthur Penn's *Bonnie and Clyde* is released, with the tagline: "They're young. They're in love. They kill people."

1968

Stanley Kubrick's innovative *2001: A Space Odyssey* is released.

MULTIPLEX CINEMAS

From the mid-1960s, the traditional picture palace with one auditorium was largely replaced by multiplex cinemas. These comprised a single utilitarian building divided into a number of cinemas and about six to eight screens (most of them smaller than the old auditoria). Ostensibly, this gave distributors a wider choice of outlets, and audiences a wider choice of films and times. In the 1990s, many multiplexes grew into megaplexes with 20 or more screens, some showing the same presentations.

One of the Virgin Megaplex cinemas in the UK boasts 20 screens and has the seating capacity for up to 5,000 people.

The movie-going habit

As movie-going was not as popular as it had once been, each film had to attract its own audience, and extravagant advertising campaigns accompanied the many million-dollar spectacles that pushed their way onto the screens, among them Anthony Mann's *El Cid* (1961) and *The Fall of the Roman Empire* (1964); Nicholas Ray's *King of Kings* (1961) and *55 Days at Peking* (1963); and George Stevens' *The Greatest Story Ever Told* (1965). All of them were shot in Spain or Italy, further diminishing Hollywood as a production centre. Movies shot on location in Europe in the 1950s, such as *Roman Holiday* (1953), were considered novel and were, as a result, successful; these later features were not.

Cleopatra (1962), shot on location in Rome, nearly bankrupted Twentieth Century Fox. Starring Elizabeth Taylor (already the highest-paid performer in the history of Hollywood at US$1 million) as the Queen of Egypt, and her future husband Richard Burton as Marc Antony, it cost a record US$44 million. Fox subsequently regained a fortune with Robert Wise's *The Sound of Music* (1965) but lost it all again with Richard Fleischer's *Doctor Dolittle* (1967) and Wise's *Star!* (1968).

The concurrence of Fox's failure and the success of more youth-oriented movies proved to be a major turning point in Hollywood history. In the mid-1960s, Hollywood found itself with a new audience drawn mainly from the 16–24 age group. With different tastes to their elders, this younger generation expressed a growing aversion to traditional values. Hollywood needed to tap into this new audience and its adult tastes. Instead of paying huge amounts to respected and experienced directors like Robert Wise and Richard Fleischer, it suddenly seemed reasonable to take a risk on younger, more experimental directors.

Richard Burton and Elizabeth Taylor caused a scandal with their highly publicized offscreen love affair during the making of *Cleopatra* (1962), since both were married to other people at that time.

Sex and violence

With the demise of the Production Code in the US, the limits of language, topics, and behaviour were considerably widened, almost enough to satisfy young audiences' craving for sex and violence. Films started to depict violence in a more brutal and graphic manner, notably Robert Aldrich's *The Dirty Dozen* (1966), Arthur Penn's *Bonnie and Clyde* (1967), and Peckinpah's *The Wild Bunch* (1969).

Although it made no reference to civil rights or Vietnam, Mike Nichols' *The Graduate* (1967) was taken as a symbol of the counterculture of the time. The title character of Benjamin Braddock (played by Dustin Hoffman) had a great appeal among middle-class college students, and the use of Simon & Garfunkel songs, such as *Mrs. Robinson*, instead of an orchestral music score, added to the film's attraction for young people. It also initiated the trend for pop-song soundtracks in the movies.

It was only after Hoffman came along that the names and faces of movie stars reflected more accurately the diversity of ethnic groups in America, opening up the floodgates for Barbra Streisand, Al Pacino, Elliott Gould, Robert De Niro, and Richard Dreyfuss.

Roger Corman – who, since 1953, had been making "Z movies" (films on a tiny budget and in rented studios) – joined American International. The studio produced ***The Wild Angels*** (1966), a low-budget biker picture, and ***The Trip*** (1967), the title referring to a psychedelic LSD "trip". Both films starred Peter Fonda (son of Henry, brother of Jane, and father of Bridget), who produced, co-wrote, as well as featured in ***Easy Rider*** (1969). This inexpensive biker movie directed by Dennis Hopper went on to earn around US$35 million.

Angry young men

In the late 1950s and early 1960s, there emerged in England a movement of playwrights, novelists, and film-makers who were labelled "Angry Young Men". Much of their work dealt honestly and vigorously with working-class life, and as such, contained an overt criticism of the "never had it so good" philosophy of the Conservative government of the day. Karel Reisz's ***Saturday Night and Sunday***

Playing the title role of ***The Graduate*** (1967), Dustin Hoffman is on the verge of being seduced by his parents' friend, Mrs. Robinson (Anne Bancroft). The film's frank treatment of sex appealed to young audiences.

Thunderball (1965) was the fourth film in the James Bond series, starring Sean Connery as Bond.

Morning (1960), Tony Richardson's ***A Taste of Honey*** (1961) and ***The Loneliness of the Long Distance Runner*** (1962), and Lindsay Anderson's ***This Sporting Life*** (1963) contributed to the movement.

In contrast to these grimy "kitchen sink" dramas, the "sparkle" of Swinging London was depicted in a series of films that showed trendy young people living it up in affluent surroundings. In fact, the phrase "Swinging London" was first used by New York TV columnist John Crosby, who had grown disenchanted with America and come to the city in 1964 looking for a job. In an article for the colour supplement of *The Daily Telegraph*, he described London as being more "swinging" than New York. Curiously, it was a 1963 adaptation of a classic 18th-century novel, Henry Fielding's *Tom Jones*, directed by Tony Richardson and written by *Look Back in Anger* playwright John Osborne, that triggered the vogue for "Swinging London" films. These films reached their apotheosis with Italian Michelangelo Antonioni's ***Blow-Up*** (1966), in which the "Swinging London" society is seen through foreign eyes.

Bond and Spaghetti

The high cost of making films in Hollywood and the shrinking studio size forced many studios to reduce their internal production and increase movie-making elsewhere, mostly in Britain, where they could produce big-budget films on an economically advantageous production base. For example, there was the creation of the most durable series in the history of cinema – the string of 007 James Bond movies. The first, ***Dr. No*** (1962), was made for less than US$1 million. The Bond films got progressively more expensive as they took more at the box office. ***Thunderball*** (1965) became the sixth-highest earning movie of the decade from any source, pulling in nearly US$26 million. The Bond producers with the gold fingers were US agronomist Albert R. "Cubby" Broccoli and Canadian-born Harry Saltzman. They set up Eon productions in England, from where all the Bond features have since originated.

Sean Connery and Ursula Andress starred in *Dr. No* (1962), a successful Bond recipe of sex, violence, and camp humour.

It was three years before Sergio Leone's ***A Fistful of Dollars*** (1964), an Italian-made Western, was picked up for distribution in the US in 1967, although it had been a hit in Italy. It began a whole spate of Spaghetti Westerns, and made Clint Eastwood, after small parts in ten movies and seven years in TV's ***Rawhide*** series, an international superstar at 37. The plot was taken from ***Yojimbo*** (1961), directed by Akira Kurosawa.

French New Wave

Perhaps the main impetus for the change in the way films were made came with the New Wave in France. *La Nouvelle Vague* managed to revitalize French cinema when it was in danger of being totally ossified. Several young critics on the influential magazine *Cahiers du Cinéma* decided to take practical action in their battle against the staid content of French productions by making films themselves. The leading figures of the group were François Truffaut, Jean-Luc Godard, Alain Resnais, Claude Chabrol, Jacques Rivette, Eric Rohmer, and Louis Malle.

These directors shunned conventional filming methods. They took to shooting in the streets with hand-held cameras and a very small team, using jump cuts, improvisation, deconstructed narratives, and quotes from literature and other films. The young directors, producers, and actors captured the life of early 1960s France – especially Paris – as it was lived by young people.

Although these films were radically different from traditional cinema, and were aimed at a young, intellectual audience, many achieved critical and financial success, gaining a wide audience both in France and abroad. Their methods and subject matter were taken up by young directors abroad – especially in the UK and former Czechoslovakia – and eventually paved the way for the American indie movement.

Sami Frey, Anna Karina, and Claude Brasseur, three petty crooks in Jean-Luc Godard's ***Bande à Part*** (1964), do a spontaneous synchronized dance in a café – a scene to which Quentin Tarantino paid homage in ***Pulp Fiction*** (1994).

In 1960 alone, some 18 directors made their first features in France. At the same time, Italian cinema had its own new wave with Federico Fellini, Luchino Visconti, Pier Paolo Pasolini, Michelangelo Antonioni, and Bernardo Bertolucci. Winners at Cannes in 1960 included Fellini's ***La Dolce Vita*** (1960), Kon Ichikawa's ***Kagi*** (1959), Antonioni's ***L'Avventura*** (1960), Ingmar Bergman's ***The Virgin Spring*** (1959), and Luis Buñuel's ***The Young One*** (1960) – all films that were not afraid to enter uncharted territory.

However, towards the end of the decade the mood began to change. At the Cannes Film Festival in May 1968, as French workers went on strike and students in Paris were setting cars alight, digging up paving stones on the Left Bank, and confronting the riot police, French cinema's ruling body adopted a motion demanding that the festival be cancelled as a sign of solidarity with the workers and students. "We refuse to be of service to a brutal capitalist society which we put in question", it stated. Protestors, led by Malle, Truffaut, and Godard, prevented the showing of Carlos Saura's ***Peppermint Frappé*** (1967). The jury resigned and the festival was aborted. Neither France nor its cinema would be the same again. After 1968, the experimental elements of the French New Wave were already starting to get assimilated into mainstream cinema. Many of its technical and conceptual advances were transformed into the clichés of film-making. Truffaut incorporated more traditional elements in his films, while Godard's films became increasingly political and radical. Chabrol continued to make genre thrillers of varying quality and Rohmer pursued his own obsession with the behaviour of young people.

Censorship

In the same year, 1968, the Russian invasion of Prague interrupted one of the most creative periods of film-making that part of the world had ever known. Rigid censorship returned to Eastern Europe. In Poland, the purges that followed the student demonstrations in March 1968 hit the cinema harder than any other art or industry. Every aspect of cinema came under official attack.

In Latin America, political repression intensified and the most famous of Brazil's Cinema Novo directors, Glauber Rocha, went into exile in protest. Meanwhile, in the US, the anti-Vietnam war movement was growing, but this was not addressed by Hollywood till almost ten years later.

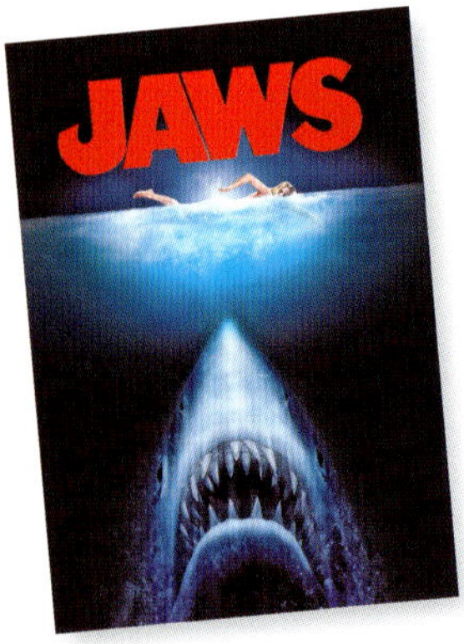

Film poster, 1975

1970–1979 Independence Days

An estimated 43.5 million Americans visited cinemas each week in 1960, compared with only 15 million a decade later. However, when there were pictures that the public really wanted to see – blockbusters like ***Star Wars*** and ***Jaws*** – cinema attendance shot up, and profits soared once again.

The result of this pattern was that certain films grossed a fortune, while many others barely recouped their costs. Escalating production expenses thus made film-making a risky business.

But Hollywood, as ever, recovered well, managing to pour out a stream of pictures that, in terms of richness, variety, and intelligence, compared with the very best of the past. Francis Ford Coppola's success with *The Godfather* (1972) was seminal. Following in his footsteps were Martin Scorsese, Steven Spielberg, George Lucas, Michael Cimino, Brian De Palma, Peter Bogdanovich, Paul Schrader, John Milius, John Carpenter, and many others. These directors ushered in the New Hollywood.

The movie brats

Many of these "movie brats", as they were dubbed, were graduates from film schools, a new phenomenon. Born in the 1940s, they had grown up with cinema and had a passion for the films of classical Hollywood. They had also studied, and were influenced by, the masters of foreign cinema. For example, Lucas' *Star Wars* (1977) was influenced by Akira Kurosawa's *The Hidden Fortress* (1958). The resemblance between the two buffoon farmers in *The Hidden Fortress* and the two talkative droids C-3PO and R2-D2 in *Star Wars* is apparent. Even the name Ben "Obi-Wan" Kenobi (played by Alec Guinness) is Japanese-sounding. Of course, such cinephilia had no effect on the film's immense popularity, and *Star Wars* succeeded in grossing more than US$164 million in only two years in the US. The merchandising of this film was also hugely lucrative. Both Spielberg's *Jaws* (1975) and Lucas' *Star Wars* were the first films to earn more than US$100 million in video rentals.

It was Lucas' *American Graffiti* (1973) that spawned many "rites of passage" films. This dreamy, rock'n'roll-driven vision of adolescent life in a small Californian town in 1962, before the Vietnam War and the drug scene, cost US$750,000 and made US$55 million at the box office. It helped boost the careers of Harrison Ford, Richard Dreyfuss, and Ron (cast as Ronny) Howard. The film's success convinced producer Garry Marshall to reconsider a failed pilot for a TV series eventually called *Happy Days*, featuring 20-year-old Howard. Harrison Ford went on to establish himself as Han Solo in the *Star Wars* cycle. Dreyfuss' fame grew with two Spielberg blockbusters: as an ichthyologist somewhat out-acted by "Bruce", the shark machine in *Jaws*, and as the representative of ordinary

Spectral pirates on a ghost ship get ready to terrorize a coastal town in John Carpenter's chiller, *The Fog* (1980).

1970–1979

1970

CBS hold a demonstration of colour video-recording in New York.

The IMAX wide-screen format premieres in Japan.

1971

Melvin Van Peebles' *Sweet Sweetback's Baadasssss Song* kicks off the blaxploitation genre.

The Beatles' last film *Let It Be* is released.

1972

Two years after *Airport*, the disaster movie trend continues with *The Poseidon Adventure*.

1973

Universal turns down George Lucas' idea for *Star Wars* – and Fox picks it up.

The Exorcist, inspired by a true story about a girl possessed by a demon, shocks audiences.

1974

Roman Polanski's thriller *Chinatown*, starring Jack Nicholson, is a big hit.

mid-western manhood chosen by little green men to take off with them in their flying saucer in *Close Encounters of the Third Kind* (1977).

Most of Spielberg's films were aimed primarily at teenagers, whereas the films of Woody Allen were directed at more mature audiences. *Annie Hall* (1977) won Allen both the Best Picture and Best Director Academy Awards. The film proved to be a breakthrough, capitalizing on the vogue of sexual anxiety and the tendency for self-examination.

Angst and machismo

If Allen represented New York Jewish angst, Scorsese explored the close-knit Italian-American community with its underlying rigid and sentimental codes of masculinity also evident in Coppola's *The Godfather*. As a result of these two Italian-American directors, Al Pacino and Robert De Niro became two of the key stars of the decade. Their acting style was derived from their "Method" predecessors like Marlon Brando, the younger version of whose character Don Corleone was played by De Niro in *The Godfather II* (1974). However, Brando proved he was still a force to be reckoned with in the 1970s, in Bertolucci's *Last Tango in Paris* (1972), and Coppola's *The Godfather* and *Apocalypse Now* (1979). The latter was one of a number of films on the Vietnam War.

The vexing issue of Vietnam

Hollywood had initially been reluctant to come to grips with the war, which had ended in 1975, probably because it was an issue that divided the nation. Commercially, therefore, the subject was bound to offend and alienate a large part of the potential audience. The film-making community split itself between hawks like John Wayne, whose *The Green Berets* (1968) had been contrary to the zeitgeist, and doves such as Jane Fonda, who made her documentary *Vietnam Journey* (1974) on behalf of the anti-war movement. Hollywood could no longer turn a blind eye to the war in Vietnam as a major subject. In 1978, both Michael Cimino's *The Deer Hunter* and Hal Ashby's *Coming Home* appeared. Each reveals the scars, both physical and mental, left behind by the war and the extent to which US soldiers' experiences there had entered the national consciousness. *Coming Home* was

Close Encounters of the Third Kind (1977) was Steven Spielberg's first science fiction movie, a favourite genre of the director.

1975

Jaws is released and becomes a worldwide phenomenon.

Robert Altman's *Nashville*, a complex, epic study of US culture, appears.

1976

Dolby stereo is used in films.

1977

Close Encounters of the Third Kind is released.

Star Wars grosses almost US$200 million on its first release, and receives 10 Oscar nominations.

1978

Woody Allen's 1977 film *Annie Hall* wins the Best Picture Oscar.

Marlon Brando is paid more than US$3 million, plus royalties, for a four-minute appearance in *Superman*.

1979

Miramax Films is set up by brothers Bob and Harvey Weinstein.

Dustin Hoffman and Robert Redford play *Washington Post* investigative reporters in Alan J. Pakula's ***All the President's Men*** (1976).

instigated by its anti-Vietnam War star, Jane Fonda. The film tells of the love affair between a volunteer (Fonda) at a Vietnam veteran's hospital and an ex-soldier confined to a wheelchair by war injuries (Jon Voight). At the Oscar ceremony of that year, Coppola presented Cimino with the award for Best Director. ***The Deer Hunter*** also won Best Picture, while Jon Voight and Jane Fonda won Academy Awards for Best Actor and Best Actress, respectively, for ***Coming Home***.

At the same ceremony, there was a poignant moment when the Old Hollywood made way for the New. John Wayne, who was fighting his last battle with cancer, presented Cimino with the Best Film award. Wayne got the biggest cheer of the evening as, gaunt with illness, he tottered up the Academy staircase and said, "Oscar first came to the Hollywood scene in 1928. So did I. We're both a little weather-beaten but we're still here, and plan to be around a whole lot longer". Sadly, Wayne died a few months later.

The Vietnam War and the Watergate Scandal of 1974 fuelled an American malaise, which was reflected in a spate of so-called "conspiracy" movies that explored the nation's dark underside. The best of these were Alan J. Pakula's ***The Parallax View*** (1974) and ***All the President's Men*** (1976); and Sydney Pollack's ***Three Days of the Condor*** (1975). All three films exposed government cover-ups. Coppola's ***The Conversation*** (1974) was a post-Watergate thriller about a professional eavesdropper (Gene Hackman) who finds himself being bugged.

Warner Bros. withdrew *A Clockwork Orange* (1971), from UK distribution at Kubrick's request.

Violence on screen

Vietnam was the first war to be consistently reported on television. It was one of the many reasons why violence in the movies would increase (race riots and campus unrest were two others). The moral ambiguity of Don Siegel's ***Dirty Harry*** (Clint Eastwood's first incarnation of the cold-blooded rogue cop Harry Callahan, 1971), John Boorman's ***Deliverance*** (1972), Scorsese's ***Taxi Driver*** (1976), and Tobe Hooper's ***The Texas Chainsaw Massacre*** (1974) worried many. Stanley Kubrick's ***A Clockwork Orange*** (1971), about "the adventures of a young man whose principal interests are rape, ultra-violence, and Beethoven", did nothing to set aside these concerns.

The British Board of Film Classification passed the film with an X certificate, claiming that it was "an important social document of outstanding brilliance and quality". However, a group calling itself The Festival of Light found it "sickening and disgusting" and tried to stop it being shown. Eventually, however, a spate of copycat violence and threats against Kubrick's own family persuaded the director himself to request a UK ban. ***A Clockwork Orange*** was not seen again by British film-goers for another 27 years, until Kubrick's sudden death in 1999.

In 1968, the Motion Picture Producers and Distributors of America superseded the Production Code and incorporated a series of ratings for films. These included G for general audiences, M for mature audiences, R for ages 17 and over, and X for over-18s only. The rating system then received

BOX OFFICE HITS OF THE 1970s

1. ***Star Wars*** (George Lucas, US, 1977)
2. ***Jaws*** (Steven Spielberg, US, 1975)
3. ***Grease*** (Randal Kleiser, US, 1978)
4. ***Close Encounters of the Third Kind*** (Steven Spielberg, US, 1977)
5. ***The Exorcist*** (William Friedkin, US, 1973)
6. ***Superman*** (Richard Donner, US, 1978)
7. ***Saturday Night Fever*** (John Badham, US, 1977)
8. ***Jaws 2*** (Jeannot Szwarc, US, 1978)
9. ***Moonraker*** (Lewis Gilbert, UK, 1979)
10. ***The Spy Who Loved Me*** (Lewis Gilbert, UK, 1977)

minor revisions in 1970, 1972, 1984, and 1990. Although the dispute over *A Clockwork Orange* never reached the same pitch in the United States, in 1973, for its American release, Kubrick cut about 30 seconds of footage to win an R rating.

Sex on screen

The market for mainstream films showing sex scenes expanded in the 1970s. There was also a more outspoken approach to sex in films which came to the US from abroad: *Last Tango in Paris* (1972), with its explicit sex scenes; Just Jaeckin's *Emmanuelle* (1974), in which bored bourgeois wife Sylvia Kristel explores all the possibilities of sex; Pier Paolo Pasolini's *Salo* (1975), an update of a Marquis de Sade novel; and Nagisa Ôshima's *Ai No Corrida* (1976), featuring a gangster and a geisha acting out their sexual fantasies. *Pretty Baby* (1978), Louis Malle's first US film, featured a 12-year-old girl (Brooke Shields) being brought up in a turn-of-the-century New Orleans brothel. Public disquiet became vocal and there was again agitation for federal legislation on censorship. In Europe – Spain, Portugal, and the Communist countries – there was some relaxation on censorship. Many of the technical and conceptual advances of the French, Italian, Czech, British, and other New Waves soon got assimilated into mainstream cinema. Rainer Werner Fassbinder, Werner Herzog, and Wim Wenders brought a brief New Wave to German cinema in the 1970s. There were a few other individuals who made an impact, such as Andrei Tarkovsky and Sergei Parajanov in the former USSR and Andrzej Wajda and Krzysztof Kieslowski in Poland, but Eastern European cinema gradually lost its way. Milos Forman had fled the former Czechoslovakia in 1968, but his US career really took off with *One Flew Over the Cuckoo's Nest* (1975). Based on a cult novel of the 1960s, it became the first film in 41 years (since *It Happened One Night*) to fly off with all five major Oscars, and raked in US$56.5 million.

Stallone and Travolta

That sum was almost equalled by *Rocky* (1976), the archetypal rags-to-riches story of the decade. Producer Irwin Winkler recalled: "In comes this big lug who weighed 220lb, didn't talk well, and acted slightly punch drunk. He said he had an idea for a boxing script and wanted to star in it". The "lug" was Sylvester Stallone. It is by now Hollywood folklore how Stallone, with only US$106 in his bank account and three bad movies to his debit, turned down a one-off payment of US$265,000 and instead secured US$70,000, a percentage of the profits, and the lead role. *Rocky* became a box-office hit and won Oscars for Best Picture (the first sports film to do so), and Best Director (John G. Avildsen).

Another of the crop of Italian-Americans who made it big in the 1970s was John Travolta, who gave male dancing the onscreen kiss of life in *Saturday Night Fever* (1977) at the height of the disco craze.

One of the most significant developments of the decade was when Sony brought out the home video-cassette recorder in 1975; it cost around US$2,000 and had a recording time of up to one hour. Its future impact on viewing habits could hardly be imagined at the time.

In *Saturday Night Fever* (1977), Travolta showed the acrobatic exuberance of Gene Kelly, and a strut reminiscent of Fred Astaire – but his riveting dancing was all his own.

1980–1989 The International Years

In the 1980s, the Hollywood machine reasserted itself. The movie brats lost their way as the studios consolidated everything they had learned from the ***Star Wars*** phenomenon, marshalling the power of TV advertising to sell high-concept movie packages, pushing up the cost of marketing, and raising the stakes across the board.

In *Raging Bull* (1980), Robert De Niro gained 27kg (60lb) to play boxer Jake LaMotta in middle age; his reward was one of the film's disappointing haul of just two Oscars.

Martin Scorsese began the 1980s with ***Raging Bull*** (1980) and the 1990s with ***GoodFellas*** (1990). However, his high-calibre output was the exception – and even he talked about giving up the fight in the 1980s. The "Hollywood Renaissance" of the 1970s proved to be a flash in the pan. The power enjoyed by the movie brats reached its apogee with the epic Western ***Heaven's Gate*** (1980), directed by Michael Cimino with such perfectionism that the budget rocketed 500 per cent, to about US$44 million. Although modest by today's standards, these figures were enough to bring United Artists to the brink of bankruptcy. Slow and anti-heroic, this was perhaps the most radical of all the revisionist Westerns but, when the film was previewed at a running time of 219 minutes, the American critics were merciless. The studio panicked, and ***Heaven's Gate*** was cut to 149 minutes – a desecration comparable to the treatment RKO had meted out to Orson Welles' ***The Magnificent Ambersons*** (1942) four decades earlier. The shorter cut did nothing to salvage the film's commercial prospects. It grossed only US$1.5 million and United Artists' illustrious name became history. The studio was sold in 1981 and merged with another fallen giant, MGM.

Heaven's Gate effectively finished off the Western for at least a decade. (The next significant contributions to the genre would be TV's ***Lonesome Dove*** in 1989 and Kevin Costner's ***Dances with Wolves*** in 1990.) More than that, it became a watchword for unchecked directorial megalomania – a widespread condition in the late 1970s and early 1980s (the subject of Peter Biskind's well-sourced history of the period, *Easy Riders, Raging Bulls*).

Francis Ford Coppola had got away with his vastly over-budget ***Apocalypse Now*** (1979), but his bold dreams of a film-makers' studio, Zoetrope, foundered on ***One from the Heart*** (1982), an

1980–1989

1980

Alfred Hitchcock, master of suspense, dies at the age of 80.

Sherry Lansing becomes the first female president of a major studio (Twentieth Century Fox).

1981

Ronald Reagan becomes the first movie-star president.

Katharine Hepburn wins her fourth Best Actress Oscar.

Raiders of the Lost Ark marks Steven Spielberg's first collaboration with George Lucas.

1982

Ridley Scott's *Blade Runner* opens.

Princess Grace of Monaco, formerly actress Grace Kelly (*High Noon, Rear Window*) dies in a car crash.

1984

The US Supreme Court rules that home videotaping does not violate copyright laws.

innovative but expensive exercise in digital cinema that didn't connect with critics or audiences. Its failure plunged him into debt and pulled the plug on a studio that, at one point, housed such eclectic talents as Jean-Luc Godard, Wim Wenders, Gene Kelly, Michael Powell, and Tom Waits.

Such spectacular failures curtailed artistic ambition in American cinema. When a film of real daring did come along, Hollywood seemed bent on suppressing it. Sergio Leone's magnificent gangster opus, ***Once Upon a Time in America*** (1984), was hacked from 229 minutes to 139 for its US release, despite the fact that the film performed well in Europe. Universal sat on Terry Gilliam's ***Brazil*** (1985) for a year, preparing their own edit, before the film-maker shamed them into releasing his cut. The motto that RKO had adopted after ridding themselves of Orson Welles in the 1940s applied across the board in the 1980s: "Showmanship, not genius."

If the balance of power shifted definitively away from the directors (and the big directors' vanity and self-indulgence didn't help their cause), the studios themselves were in a state of flux. Increasing competition from independent production companies like Cannon, DEG, Orion, and Tri-Star had, by 1986, knocked the major studios' share of the US box office to a low of 64 per cent.

Increasingly, the real power fell to the talent agencies. The largest of these was Creative Artists Agency (CAA), which represented numerous A-list stars, writers, and directors. They began to pitch pre-packaged deals to the studios: scripts with their clients already attached. CAA president

Sergio Leone's gangster epic, *Once Upon a Time in America* (1984), was a violent requiem for the immigrant's dream. It was Leone's last film.

1985

The first Blockbuster video store opens in Dallas, Texas.

1986

Media mogul Ted Turner buys MGM's film library and begins "colourizing" its black-and-white films.

Actor Rock Hudson dies of AIDS; the epidemic begins to be acknowledged.

1987

Disney does its first tie-in with McDonalds: a Happy Meals toy based on *Duck Tales*.

1988

Video sales of *E.T.: The Extra-Terrestrial* exceed 15 million.

Martin Scorsese's *The Last Temptation of Christ* is released in spite of protests by some Christians.

1989

Warner Communications merges with Time, Inc. to become the biggest media company in the world.

Michael Ovitz became the most feared and courted man in Hollywood, and star salaries rose steeply, pushing up the average cost of a movie even as admissions continued to flatline. For the agents, the deal was the be-all and end-all.

It's not that there weren't box-office hits. Steven Spielberg's *Raiders of the Lost Ark* (1981) and *E.T.: The Extra-Terrestrial* (1982) consolidated his reputation as the man with the Midas touch. As the decade progressed, Hollywood channelled more and more of its resources into supporting blockbuster "event" movies, generally released on public holiday weekends, with saturation marketing campaigns. These, in turn, aggravated inflationary pressures across the business.

The rewards were phenomenal, both in box office terms and ancillary merchandising deals. However, this model gave less room to the adult dramas that had always been Hollywood's mainstay. Teenagers became the prime audience – the 12–20 age group constituted 48 per cent of audiences in 1980.

Slasher horror movies and risqué adolescent comedies were the new staples: ***Friday the 13th*** (1980) would spawn more than a dozen sequels stretching into the new millennium; ***Porky's*** (1982) would beget innumerable imitations. While established stars like Robert Redford

In the 1980s, popcorn entertainment came back into style. Steven Spielberg's *Indiana Jones* films epitomized the return to mainstream blockbusters.

BOX OFFICE HITS OF THE 1980s

1. *E.T.: The Extra-Terrestrial* (Steven Spielberg, US, 1982)
2. *Return of the Jedi* (Richard Marquand, US, 1983)
3. *The Empire Strikes Back* (Irvin Kershner, US, 1980)
4. *Indiana Jones and the Last Crusade* (Steven Spielberg, US, 1989)
5. *Rain Man* (Barry Levinson, US, 1988)
6. *Raiders of the Lost Ark* (Steven Spielberg, US, 1981)
7. *Batman* (Tim Burton, US, 1989)
8. *Back to the Future* (Robert Zemeckis, US, 1985)
9. *Who Framed Roger Rabbit* (Robert Zemeckis, US, 1988)
10. *Top Gun* (Tony Scott, US, 1986)

Sylvestor Stallone's John Rambo went from underdog in ***First Blood*** (1982) to killing machine in the eponymous ***Rambo*** sequels.

and Clint Eastwood continued to write their own ticket, the teen audience fostered its own stars. The "Brat Pack" included Molly Ringwald, Rob Lowe, Emilio Estevez, Charlie Sheen, and Andrew McCarthy. Although some actors of the 1980s, such as Tom Cruise, Demi Moore, Matt Dillon, and John Cusack, have since enjoyed long film careers, others have not been so fortunate.

Birth of the action hero

Reports of video-savvy audiences ("tape-heads") shouting "Fast forward" at the screen may have been apocryphal, but it's arguably true that the 1980s refined the movie with action sequences into a new genre: the action film. In 1982, it was still possible for Sylvester Stallone to star in a passably serious, if formulaic, thriller about a Vietnam war veteran failing to adapt to life back home (*First Blood*); but three years later, by the time of ***Rambo: First Blood, Part II*** (1985), the character had been transformed into an invulnerable one-man army, and any vestiges of realism had been obliterated. By ***Rambo III*** (1988), Stallone was battling the Soviets in Afghanistan – and earning US$20 million for the picture. The same trajectory is obvious in Stallone's ***Rocky*** films. A credible underdog in the first movie, he became a pumped-up American champ in the later sequels, a warrior wrapped up in the patriotism of Ronald Reagan's presidency.

Even then, another action star was poised to outgun Stallone. Former bodybuilder Arnold Schwarzenegger, probably the most iconic star of the era, had been hanging around Hollywood since the early 1970s. With his strong Austrian accent, negligible acting ability, and physique described by journalist Clive James as "like a walnut wearing a condom", he was an unlikely superstar. John Milius cast him as ***Conan the Barbarian*** (1982), and he then played a taciturn robot assassin in James Cameron's *The Terminator* (1984). Although the character was the villain – literally a killing machine – audiences adored the film, and Schwarzenegger was made.

With the exception of Sigourney Weaver in ***Alien*** (1979) and ***Aliens*** (1986), women in action films of this era are usually relegated to supporting bit roles. These films are characterized by bombast and machismo – explosions, fusillades of bullets, fireballs, and car chases, all as destructive as demolition derbies. The genre was aimed mainly

> "You have **twenty seconds** to comply."
>
> *Robocop*, 1987

at young men, and did well in the increasingly important overseas markets – not least because the films had very little meaningful dialogue. The best action films have an exhilarating cinematic dynamic: Paul Verhoeven's ***Robocop*** (1987), John McTiernan's ***Die Hard*** (1988), and James Cameron's ***Terminator*** films (1984 and 1991) are as accomplished as the 1920s' slapstick comedies or the 1950s' musicals.

Directors had always shot action sequences from multiple angles, and as action sequences became longer and more elaborate, this aesthetic infected Hollywood's visual language. Shot durations shrank and visual continuity was handled by design and back-lighting. The aesthetic was often attributed to the influence of MTV. Music television's non-stop diet of pop promos, with their rapid-fire backbeat montage, became popular with the spread of cable television in the early 1980s, and music promo directors sometimes graduated to feature films. More came from advertising, with their visual skills honed in 30-second segments. Britons Ridley and Tony Scott, Adrian Lyne, Hugh Hudson, and Alan Parker all came up through advertising. Between them, Tony Scott and Adrian Lyne directed ***Top Gun*** (1986), ***Beverly Hills Cop 2*** (1987), ***Flashdance*** (1983), ***9½ Weeks*** (1986), and ***Fatal Attraction*** (1987) – some of the biggest hits of the decade. These were quintessential "high concept" movies – films that could be pitched and sold in 30 words or less.

Tom Cruise attracts Kelly McGillis in ***Top Gun*** (1986), a typical high-velocity movie from US über-producers Jerry Bruckheimer and Don Simpson.

THE VIDEO REVOLUTION

In 1982, MPAA industry spokesman Jack Valenti said, "the VCR is to the American film producer and the American public as the Boston strangler is to the woman home alone". However, his concerns about copyright infringement devastating Hollywood were misplaced. VHS defeated Betamax in the videotape wars, largely because it courted Hollywood. And the video rental market proved to be manna for film producers. Video stores flourished, granting audiences control over what they watched and how: rewind, replay, and fast forward buttons were the first step towards viewer interactivity. A by-product of this success was that cinemas shrank, as single-screen venues were halved and quartered to allow for more flexible programming. Across the US, drive-in theatres were replaced with multiplexes.

After the introduction of VCR, a whole sector of films found their audience at home, on video, instead of on the big screen.

Outside Hollywood

There was a related fashion in France, where Jean-Jacques Beineix pioneered what critic Serge Daney dubbed "le cinéma du look", with the flamboyant ***Diva*** (1981) and ***Betty Blue*** (1986). Luc Besson (***Subway***, 1985) and former critic Leos Carax (***Boy Meets Girl***, 1984) represented the extremes of the style, the first a resolute populist, the second a confrontational intellectual. Ageing practitioners of the *nouvelle vague* continued to work: Jean-Luc Godard returned to cinema after a flirtation with video, as did Maurice Pialat, whose intense emotional authenticity inspired a generation of 1990s film-makers. In 1981, however, French cinema was rocked by the suicide of director Jean Eustache.

Likewise, the New German Cinema was knocked off course in 1982 by the death of its most prolific talent, Rainer Werner Fassbinder, aged just 36. Wim Wenders had a tough Hollywood initiation with ***Hammett*** (1982), but recovered with ***Paris, Texas*** (1984). He returned to Berlin for ***Wings of Desire*** (1987), but then lost his way in a number of ambitious, muddled projects.

Some of the best international cinema of this time came from further east: from China's Fifth Generation film-makers (Chen Kaige and his erstwhile cameraman, Zhang Yimou); from Hong Kong (where Tsui Hark, John Woo, and Stanley Kwan were making their mark); and especially from Taiwan. Two Taiwanese directors – Hou Hsiao-hsien and Edward Yang – were busy constructing a cinematic identity reflecting Taiwan's complex self-image. Hou's films were the antithesis of Hollywood's faster, faster approach. Languorous meditations on the recent past, they were often composed of scenes filmed in a single, unobtrusive master shot.

Designer cinema even prevailed in France, where films like Jean-Jacques Beineix's ***Betty Blue*** (1986) privileged style over content.

1990– Celluloid to Digital

After a century of celluloid, a radical technological shift began to take effect in the 1990s with the advent of digital film-making. While the studios increasingly concentrated their resources on blockbusters like ***Titanic*** (1997), the independents made intelligent, adult drama and reached wider audiences than ever before with movies like ***Pulp Fiction*** (1994).

One hundred years after Louis and Auguste Lumière screened their first one-reelers in Paris, 40 of the world's leading film-makers took up the challenge of making a film using the original Cinématographe camera to create a silent, monochrome movie with no cuts, in natural light, and lasting no more than 52 seconds.

Tom Hanks' *Forrest Gump* (1994) crosses paths with JFK, President Nixon, and Elvis Presley through the magic of CGI.

Lumière and Company (1995) showed both how much and how little cinema had changed over the course of its short history. For all the innovations of sound and colour, the various refinements of film stock and size, in essence, the technology remained the same: strips of celluloid pulled through a shutter to be exposed to light for a fraction of a second.

By the dawn of the 21st century, that technology was superseded with the transition from analogue to digital systems. The cutters were the first to switch, moving from moviolas to computers. This shift was partly necessitated by the increasingly frenetic montage techniques popularized by film-makers such as Martin Scorsese in films like ***GoodFellas*** (1990), and his one-time pupil Oliver Stone in ***JFK*** (1991) and ***Natural Born Killers*** (1994). The first 35mm feature with a digital soundtrack was ***Dick Tracy*** (1990).

The groundbreaking animation ***Toy Story*** (1995) was the first feature film made entirely on computer, but ***Jurassic Park*** (1993) and ***Forrest Gump*** (1994) had already integrated computer-generated imagery (CGI) into live-action films. This technique opened up new avenues for the later spectacular historical epics – ***Titanic*** (1997) and ***Gladiator*** (2000) – and fantasy films, such as the ***Lord of the Rings*** trilogy (2001–03) and the ***Harry Potter*** series (2001–11). These movies dominated the box office, ringing up billion-dollar receipts worldwide.

1990–2010

1990

Cyrano de Bergerac, with Gérard Depardieu, wins a record ten César Awards.

Macaulay Culkin becomes a child star in *Home Alone*.

1993

Disney buys Miramax Films for US$80 million.

Actor Brandon Lee (son of Bruce) is killed by a faulty prop gun during the filming of *The Crow* (1994).

1994

Dreamworks SKG is announced by Steven Spielberg, Jeffrey Katzenberg, and David Geffen.

Spielberg's 1993 film *Schindler's List* wins seven Oscars.

1997

The most expensive film to date, James Cameron's *Titanic*, also becomes the highest grossing.

1999

The first of three prequels, ***Star Wars: Episode I – The Phantom Menace***, makes US$100 million in a record five days.

Going against the grain of the CGI spectacular, ***The Shawshank Redemption*** (1994) was a slow-paced, old-fashioned prison drama that could have been made any time in the last 30 years. Significantly, it was only a minor hit on theatrical release, but became an all-time favourite when audiences saw it on video and DVD.

The more gradual transition to digital cameras was anticipated by a new generation of improved, lightweight video cameras. Although they could not match the aesthetic quality of film, video cameras had one key advantage: they were much cheaper to use.

Digital film-making

Shrewd low-budget film-makers in the early 1990s capitalized on the digital camera's limitations. They employed the extreme handheld *cinema verité* style camerawork, set by Woody Allen's ***Husbands and Wives*** (1992), Mathieu Kassovitz's ***La Haine*** (1995), and Lars von Trier's ***Breaking the Waves*** (1996), and TV shows such as ***NYPD Blue*** (1993–2005). In this idiom, poor image quality translated as gritty realism. No film exemplified this better than ***The Blair Witch Project*** (1999). It purported to be discovered footage shot on camcorder and 16mm film, by a student research team who get lost in the woods and disappear while investigating a local legend. This simple scenario was augmented by an elaborate internet campaign fostering the notion that the film was, in fact, a documentary. ***The Blair Witch Project*** cost about US$35,000 and made a staggering US$248 million worldwide. A sequel followed two years later, but it was a flop.

By shooting in black and white, the talented young French director Mathieu Kassovitz gave his angry youth movie, ***La Haine*** (1995), a patina of realism. The film graphically illustrates the racial divisions that would erupt across France ten years later.

2000
Crouching Tiger, Hidden Dragon is the first Asian action film to find US commercial and critical success.

2001
The final episode of Peter Jackson's critically acclaimed ***Lord of the Rings*** trilogy is released.

2002
Halle Berry is the first black actress to win a Best Actress Oscar. African-American actor Denzel Washington also wins Best Actor.

2009
James Cameron breaks his own record, with ***Avatar*** beating ***Titanic*** to become the highest grossing film worldwide.

2010
Kathryn Bigelow creates history by becoming the first woman to win a Best Director Oscar, for ***The Hurt Locker***.

Dogme 95

With developments encouraging more elaborate fantasies and facilitating back-to-basics realism, four Danish directors seized the moment to announce the *Dogme 95* Manifesto: "Today, a technological storm is raging, the result of which will be the ultimate democratization of the cinema. For the first time, anyone can make movies...". They went on to stress the importance of the avant-garde and denounce the superficial, cosmetic aspects of the Hollywood mainstream.

Signed by the controversial director Lars von Trier, the document concluded with ten "Vows of Chastity" designed to return cinema to its roots in realism: film-makers pledged to shoot on actual locations, using only the props that belonged there; to avoid period and genre films; to dispense with optical effects and "superficial action"; to use a handheld camera; and have no post-recorded music.

Contentious and at least partly tongue in cheek, the *Dogme 95* movement nevertheless struck a chord. Thomas Vinterberg's ***Festen*** (***The Celebration***) was the first film to be released under the banner in 1998 and it won the Jury Prize at Cannes. Lars von Trier's ***The Idiots*** was released the same year, and contrary to the vows' diktats, it was shot on video.

The independents

By 2005, there would be over 50 official *Dogme* films, but that was just a drop in the ocean compared to the booming American independent film scene.

As soon as the technology became available, Digital Video (DV) cameras made an immediate impact – in the year 2000, twice as many independent features were made as in the preceding year.

Among the first major film-makers to go digital was Mike Figgis, who ran four cameras concurrently and quartered the screen in the real-time drama ***Timecode*** (2000). Spike Lee used digital technology for his near-the-knuckle race satire ***Bamboozled*** (2000), while Eric Rohmer recreated Revolutionary France by using digital paintings as backdrops in ***The Lady and the Duke*** (2001). Zacharias Kunuk's digital ***Atanarjuat: The Fast Runner*** (2001) was the first native Inuit feature, and in ***Ali*** (2001), Michael Mann mixed digital and celluloid. Mann went on to exploit digital's superior night vision for ***Collateral*** (2004). Meanwhile, artist David Fincher, who had started out in a special effects production company, showed how seamlessly CGI could be integrated into traditional film drama in ***Fight Club*** (1999).

The indie boom had started in the 1980s, partly due to the proliferation of film festivals such as Sundance, and perhaps because Hollywood films

Octogenarian Eric Rohmer embraced the latest technology to fashion ***The Lady and the Duke*** (2001), a portrait of Revolutionary France that resembled a painting brought to life.

had become conservative and formulaic and thus removed from the realities of American life. A piecemeal movement sprang up around role models John Sayles (social conscience liberalism), who made ***Silver City*** (2004), ***Casa de los Babys*** (2003), and ***Sunshine State*** (2002), and Jim Jarmusch (minimalist cool), director of films including ***Coffee and Cigarettes*** (2003), ***Ghost Dog: The Way of the Samurai*** (1999), and ***Mystery Train*** (1989).

Primarily centred on the US east coast, the 1980s independents produced breakthrough films about African-Americans (Spike Lee's ***She's Gotta Have It***, 1986), gays and lesbians (Sayles' ***Lianna***, 1983, and Gus Van Sant's ***Mala Noche***, 1988), and about women (Susan Seidelman's ***Desperately Seeking Susan,*** 1985). These films found critical support and developed their own arthouse audience. Steven Soderbergh's ***sex, lies, and videotape*** (1989) was a landmark, making US$24.7 million in the US, and another US$30 million internationally. It was the biggest hit to date for New York "speciality" distribution company, Miramax, and the first American indie to break out of the arthouse circuit and into the multiplexes.

Soderbergh immediately landed a studio contract and would become one of the most successful directors of the era, nabbing two Oscar nominations in the same year for ***Erin Brockovich*** and ***Traffic*** in 2000. He was not alone in embracing the mainstream; for most, "independence" was a transitional station on the way to a Hollywood career. Jim Jarmusch was an exception, finding funding from Japan that allowed him to retain copyright to his cool bohemian doodles. Hal Hartley was another who preferred to work cheaply without watering down his deadpan neo-Godardian comedies, such as ***Flirt*** (1995) and ***Henry Fool*** (1997). Soderbergh himself stepped out of the Hollywood mainstream on occasion to recharge his creative batteries with avant-garde experiments like ***Schizopolis*** (1996). And Gus Van Sant went from the arthouse (***My Own Private Idaho***, 1991) to the multiplex (***Good Will Hunting***, 1997) and back again (***Elephant***, 2003). However, most found they could co-exist with the studios – in general, this was not an era of confrontational political film-making or challenging formal innovation.

James Cameron's *Titanic* (1997) cost US$200 million to make, and, despite rocky reviews, became the first film to make over US$1 billion. It ensured mainstream stardom for Leonardo DiCaprio and Kate Winslet.

HOME ENTERTAINMENT

Cinema audiences have declined almost everywhere as widescreen High Definition TV sets, TiVo recorders, and DVD players make home viewing a more attractive proposition. DVDs (Digital Versatile Discs) were introduced in 1997, and their superior reproduction of picture and sound, durability, and slimline packaging proved a runaway success with consumers. By 2005, the DVD market became the film industry's greatest revenue source. DVDs have also given the studios' back catalogues a new lease of life. For Hollywood, this revenue helps to offset high production and marketing costs (about US$30 million apiece) and lower cinema attendance.

Blu-ray Discs, introduced in 2006, took a step further. Developed by the Blu-ray Disc Association (BDA), the discs got their name from the blue–violet laser used to read them, which allows a greater density of information to be stored than is possible with the red laser used on DVDs. A Blu-ray Disc (BD) can store up to ten times more data than a DVD, at a distinctly better viewing and audio quality, and is more scratch-resistant. James Cameron's ***Avatar*** (2009) sold 6 million BDs in three weeks, leading to an 86 per cent surge in Blu-ray sales. However, the home entertainment experience is still undergoing transformation as DVDs and Blu-ray discs have given way to web-enabled set-top boxes and the iPad.

Bill Murray plays a depressed movie actor, Bob Harris, in Tokyo in *Lost in Translation* (2003).

The new indies

Quite a few of the talented young film-makers who emerged from the indie sector contented themselves with working clever, ironic variations on classical Hollywood genres. Joel and Ethan Coen, for example, made a series of stylish pastiches on the works of James M. Cain, Dashiell Hammett, Raymond Chandler, Clifford Odets, and Preston Sturges.

Quentin Tarantino

Cult heroes the Coens were rudely trumped when Quentin Tarantino unleashed his more visceral brand of souped-up cinephilia with ***Reservoir Dogs*** in 1992. Born in 1963, Tarantino had grown up in the video age. In fact, he worked as a clerk in a video store before Harvey Keitel showed interest in his script about an undercover cop infiltrating a gang of jewel thieves. A magpie talent, Tarantino's influences were legion: Hong Kong thrillers (*Reservoir Dogs* borrowed from a Ringo Lam thriller, *City on Fire*, 1987); Jean-Luc Godard; Jean-Pierre Melville; Stanley Kubrick; and Sam Fuller.

In synthesizing these influences, Tarantino also forged something new and arresting: a pop post-modernism that spoke for the young people whom novelist Douglas Coupland referred to as "Generation X" and film-maker Richard Linklater dubbed "Slackers". Non-conformists but avid consumers, this generation was media-savvy, ironic about relationships, cynical about politics, but inclined toward liberal multi-culturalism.

Tarantino's second film, ***Pulp Fiction*** (1994), rocked Hollywood with its audacious approach to narrative structure, outrageously casual violence, and flip, funny dialogue. Produced by Miramax, it became the first "indie" movie to break US$100 million at the US box office. To the dismay of the old guard, it even walked away with the *Palme d'Or* at Cannes, depriving Polish auteur Krzysztof Kieslowski of a third straight festival triumph for his ***Three Colours*** trilogy (1993–94).

Tarantino's success – and the disproportionate influence it bestowed on Miramax – has been criticized for "mainstreaming" arthouse and independent film. Conversely, he could be credited for pushing the borders of the commercial film, breaking ground for the wider acceptance of independent-minded artists such as Richard Linklater, Paul Thomas Anderson, David O. Russell, Spike Jonze, and Sofia Coppola, who became the first American woman to earn an Oscar nomination for Best Director with ***Lost in Translation*** (2003). Tarantino was the most important American film-maker of the 1990s.

BOX OFFICE HITS OF THE 1990s–2000s

1	*Avatar* (James Cameron, US, 2009)
2	*Titanic* (James Cameron, US, 1997)
3	*The Lord of the Rings: The Return of the King* (Peter Jackson, US/New Zealand, 2003)
4	*Pirates of the Caribbean: Dead Man's Chest* (Gore Verbinski, US, 2006)
5	*Toy Story 3* (Lee Unkrich, US, 2010)
6	*Alice in Wonderland* (Tim Burton, US, 2010)
7	*The Dark Knight* (Christopher Nolan, US, 2008)
8	*Harry Potter and the Philosopher's Stone* (Chris Columbus, US/UK, 2001)
9	*Pirates of the Caribbean: At World's End* (Gore Verbinski, US, 2007)
10	*Harry Potter and the Order of the Phoenix* (David Yates, US/UK, 2007)

World cinema

Beyond US borders, Hollywood continued to exert a strong grip on film markets in Europe (with the partial exception of France), Asia, and the southern hemisphere, although India, China, Hong Kong, and South Korea all maintained strong local industries. Initially, it was Hong Kong that made the maximum international impact, with a series of prestigious arthouse films from Wong Kar Wai, such as ***Chungking Express*** (1994), and a cycle of

The popularity of J.K. Rowling's *Harry Potter* books translated into mega box office hits for Warner Bros. The recipe was fidelity to the source, expert British character acting, and – the magic ingredient – dazzling CGI trickery.

Working stylish variations on the classic cops and robbers formula, Hong Kong thriller *Infernal Affairs* (2002) was a smash hit at home and abroad. Two equally inventive sequels followed soon after.

stylish, souped-up urban crime thrillers such as John Woo's *A Better Tomorrow* (1986), Ringo Lam's *Full Contact* (1993), and Wai-keung Lau and Siu Fai Mak's *Infernal Affairs* (2002). Woo and Lam both went on to Hollywood careers, while Martin Scorsese directed Leonardo DiCaprio in *The Departed* (2006), a remake of *Infernal Affairs*.

Hollywood continues to draw fresh blood from the thriving Asian horror market, remaking Japanese hits, such as *Ringu* (1998) and *The Grudge* (2003), and enticing their directors – Hideo Nakata and Takashi Shimizu respectively – to America.

Elsewhere, Mexico produced the thrilling *Amores Perros* (2000) and *Y Tu Mamá También* (2001), and Brazil came up with the incendiary *favela* story *City of God* (2002, see p.342). Isolated from American culture, Iran produced a refracted, poetic take on neorealism through film-makers like Mohsen Makmalbaf, Jafar Panahi, and the minimalist master Abbas Kiarostami (*A Taste of Cherry*, 1997).

Lacking a strong home market for genre films, and failing to compete with the production values of Hollywood, European cinema seems largely irrelevant to most audiences most of the time. Aside from a few arthouse stalwarts like Pedro Almodóvar (*All About My Mother*, 1999), Michael Haneke (*Caché*, 2005), and Lars von Trier (*Dogville*, 2003), there is no guarantee of widespread international distribution beyond the film-festival circuit and DVD.

Digital downloads

Today the industry is facing its next great challenge: the internet. Digital downloads of feature films and streamed video-on-demand have become a reality, raising the spectres of widespread piracy and the collapse of theatrical exhibition. However, cinema has survived such scares before, adapting to new technologies and ultimately profiting from them.

The world wide web holds out promises too: a video jukebox with an infinite range of choice, virtually no delivery costs, and an audience that would have been unimaginable at any time before in the art form's history.

After two Hollywood flops, Alfonso Cuarón put his career back on track by returning to his native Mexico to make the earthy sex comedy *Y Tu Mamá También* (2001).

Crash (2005) was a surprise winner over Ang Lee's *Brokeback Mountain* (2005) at the 2006 Academy Awards, scooping the prize for Best Film. Set in Los Angeles, it highlights racial tensions and the assumptions strangers make about each other.

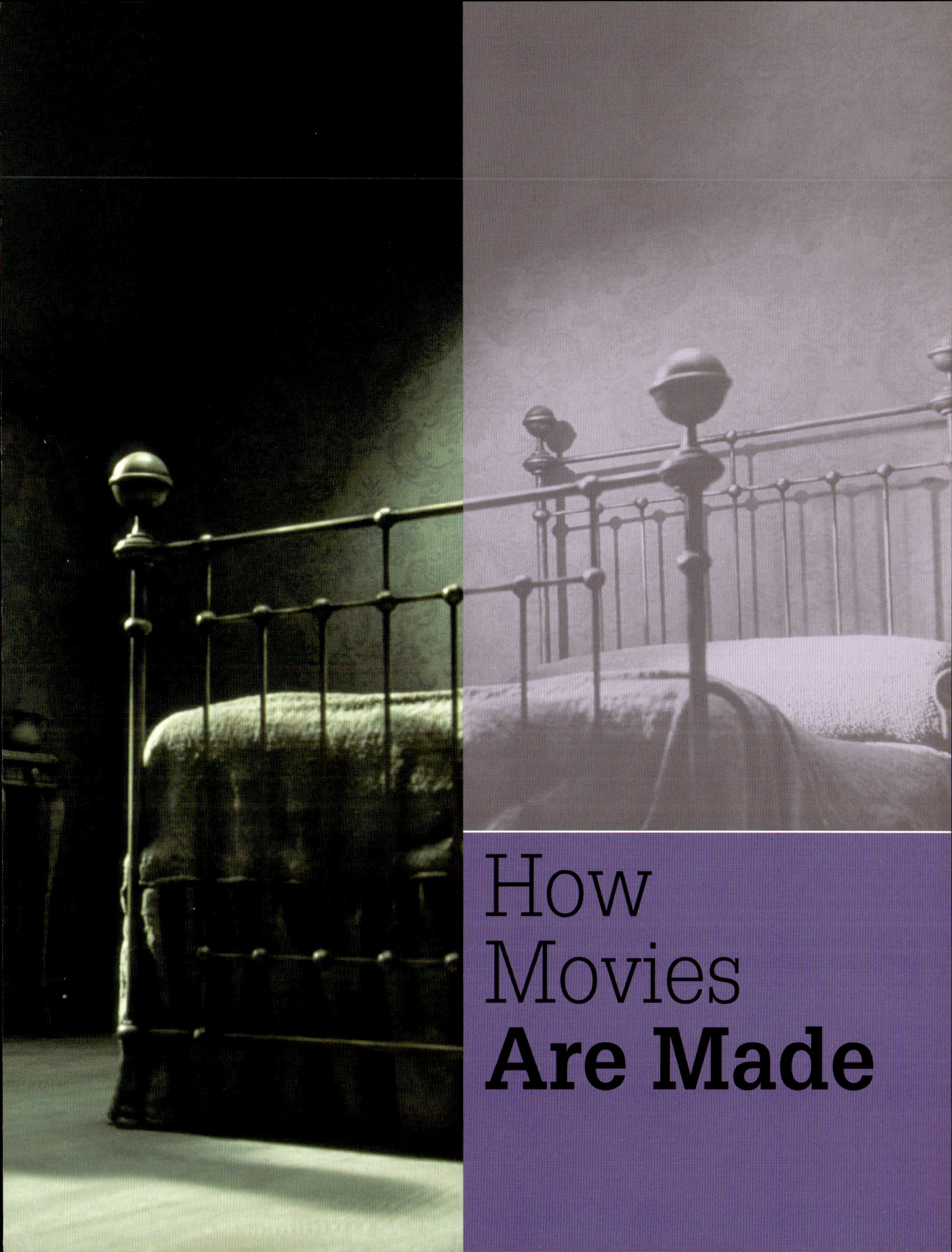

How Movies Are Made

End-of-movie credits run for minutes, and rightly so. It takes many creative, technical, publicity, and distribution talents to take a movie from an idea to the screen. ***The Godfather*** (1972) had crews across several continents, while ***Gone With the Wind*** (1939) had multiple crews in the studio.

The basic stages of making a movie remain the same whatever the size of the budget or the cast. The process begins with pre-production, then moves through production, and post-production. The players in pre-production and production include the producers, directors, screenwriters, and actors – the "above-the-line" people who usually have higher status and wildly varying payment. Below-the-line players generally include the production department, cinematographers, composers, editors, costume designers, production designers, stuntpeople, and sound crew. Their costs are generally lower and more predictable.

After the filming of a movie, post-production begins. This stage involves the editor, sound editor, composer, and special effects crew. The final part of post-production involves getting the movie to its audience, which includes distribution and exhibition. After post-production, the final version of the film goes to distributors and exhibitors. Distributors decide when the movie will be released and get it to the cinemas, and exhibitors show the finished product.

« ***The Perils of Pauline*** (1914) made farmer's daughter Pearl White a star and honed the elements of action films – danger, stunts, and suspense.

Anecdotes about how actors, directors, producers, and screenwriters collaborate are legion. The inception of a film may be straightforward – as with the concept for ***It's a Wonderful Life*** (1946), which was transmitted from Frank Capra to James Stewart – or it may be long and involved, as in the search for a new James Bond, such as Daniel Craig. Equally intricate is the work of technical staff, such as the costume designers who, for example, might have to design authentic Roman Empire-era clothes, as for ***Gladiator*** (2000). Dazzling special effects combine computer-generated images and old-fashioned physical trickery to enliven a story of a giant gorilla or a galaxy far, far away.

After a movie is made, it has to reach the viewer. Distributors set up showing periods with cinemas, then alter the time frame if a film is a surprise hit or underperforms. Movies are also released in international markets, where established stars might save a film that has floundered in its home country. Finally, there is the video market, where all movies end up, often (as with children's classics) resulting in a healthy profit.

The complexity of film-making disproves silent star Norma Desmond's (Gloria Swanson) claim in ***Sunset Boulevard*** (1950) when she says, "I am big. It's the pictures that got small".

Pre-production

The pre-production stage of making a movie usually begins with a conversation. Held anywhere, this discussion will mark the first time producers, screenwriters, and studio executives discuss the concept and potential actors for their movie.

Director Nicholas Ray (left) discusses a project with screenwriter Philip Yordan. They worked together on *Johnny Guitar* in 1954.

The "pitch" and the producer

As captured in movie lore and skewered in Robert Altman's *The Player* (1992), a movie pitch is a short encapsulation of a movie idea which, if it succeeds, pleases a studio executive or other powerful individuals. Some ideas get the go-ahead but fail in execution, such as the remake of *Sabrina* (1995). Others, such as James Cameron's conception of *Titanic* (1997) as primarily a love story, can result in a film classic.

From the beginning, the producer is central to the making of the movie. He may be a forceful, creative type or he may be part of a group of investors who has a more distant relationship with the industry but knows the star. Since the early days of the Hollywood studio system, the definition of a producer has become increasingly fluid and many are now seeking to have the tasks of producers defined more clearly. Traditionally, however, a producer is responsible for securing the money to make the movie.

In most cases, the money for a movie comes from the studio executives. Like producers, the studio executives vary in the scope of their power. Wherever they fit, they will provide money and be highly involved with the screenwriter and producer through the next stage of the movie – the development stage.

The development stage

This part of the process encompasses the activities necessary to get a movie ready for production, that is, filming. These include discussing the concept and script, historical research, story-boarding, and casting.

In restaurants and offices, producers and movie executives cook up a deal and talk it through. At this stage, a screenwriter also produces a draft of the script. The screenwriter is usually known to the producers or executives, having worked with them in the past, or through experience on similar types of projects. Whatever the screenwriter's stature, the script is very often rewritten again and again to please the producers and studios, in a process known as development, which can be so tortuous that it earns the name "development hell". When the script is finished and believed to represent a potentially profitable venture, studio executives "green light" the picture and pre-production begins.

Actors may also be involved at the development stage. This is even more likely to be the case if the script is being written as a vehicle for a particular actor, or is attached to a well-known actor-director/producer team (such as James Cameron/Arnold Schwarzenegger in the 1980s and 1990s). Another situation in which this may be the case is if the actor is the director himself (such as Clint Eastwood or Mel Gibson). Often, stars who are big at the box office are involved during development to secure the necessary funding for a big film. A top US star can command US$30 million per movie – and may also receive a percentage of the gross profit. Less well-known actors are usually signed up during this stage.

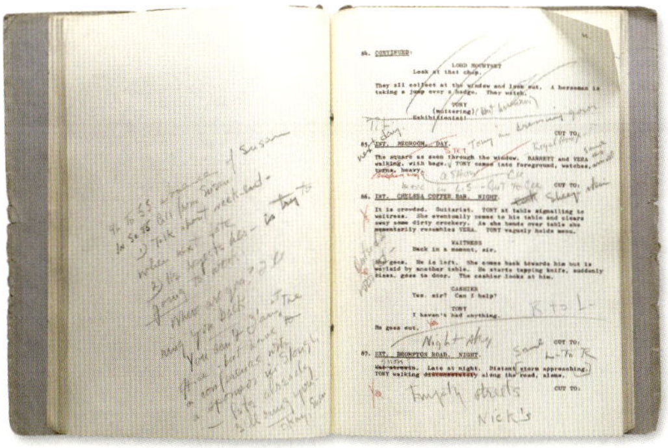

Film scripts are often revised, both before and during filming. This is a marked-up script by Harold Pinter for *The Servant* (1963).

Storyboards help the director visualize each scene – these are from *The Wizard of Oz* (1939).

The Living Daylights (1987), in which Timothy Dalton made his debut as James Bond, was shot in Europe, the US, and in the studio. Here, the crane allows for a panoramic view of the set.

Producer and production crew

At the pre-production stage, the practical members of the production department calculate the cost of the preparation for, and the shooting of, the film. Depending on his level of involvement, the producer may also be responsible for hiring the crew, which includes a director of photography, a production designer, a costume designer, a composer, and an editor. He may also be involved in setting up a shooting schedule and budget, and choosing locations. Generally, the location scout searches for the best locations for the movie. These may be real, for example, New York for ***On the Town*** (1949); or a convincing substitute, such as using Italy for 19th-century New York streets in ***Gangs of New York*** (2002). To film the 16th-century feudal Japan of Akira Kurosawa's ***Throne of Blood*** (1957), the director commissioned a castle to be built. The 19th-century story of love and obsession on the British coast, Karel Reisz's ***The French Lieutenant's Woman*** (1981) was filmed in part on location, in a British town largely untouched by time (Lyme Regis).

Creative crew

To sign up actors, casting directors first break down a script to see what roles have to be cast. They may use a private company like Breakdown Services in the US, which distributes daily lists, or "breakdowns", of available roles to the Screen Actors Guild (SAG, the major association for actors),

WHO'S WHO ON SET

Best boy	Assistant to the gaffer
Boom operator	Positions and operates the microphone
Chief/key/head grip	Moves the camera
Continuity person (script supervisor)	Ensures that make-up, costumes, etc. don't change between scenes
Director of photography (cinematographer/first cameraman/lighting cameraman)	Responsible for the choice of lighting, composition, camera, lens, and film – in fact, the "look" of the film
First assistant cameraman (focus puller)	Maintains the camera, changes lenses and magazines, and operates the focus control
Gaffer	Chief electrician
Grip	Moves equipment on set
Location manager	Finds suitable locations and clears their use with the owner
Mixer (sound recordist)	In overall charge of the sound recording
Production manager (line producer)	In charge of the day-to-day budget
Second assistant cameraman (clapper loader)	Loads magazines, operates the clapperboard, and performs other camera tasks
Set decorator	Finds props and decorates the set
Set designer	Designs the set using sketches and models
Stills person	Takes still photographs of the production
Wardrobe	Responsible for the care and repair of costumes throughout production

franchised agents, and personal managers. The agents and managers then submit the names of clients who might be right for the part. Following auditions and hiring, the casting director then negotiates the contract with the actor.

Meanwhile, the cinematography, production design, and editing components of the movie will be set up. The director and director of photography, or DP, may discuss the intended look for the film and how to achieve it. The DP may also confer with the production designer and crew to make sure that the cameras can be accommodated in the set design. When planning the shoot, the scenes are not shot in order: for example all the action in one location will be filmed together, even though it might be viewed at different times in the final version. During post-production, the editor will put it all together according to the storyline.

Italian producer Giovannella Zannoni and Italian director Franco Zeffirelli look over some footage together on the set of Zeffirelli's film *Tea With Mussolini* (1999).

Production

As immortalized in movies about the movies, such as ***Singin' in the Rain*** (1952), production is the actual process of shooting a movie. It occurs after pre-production is completed and includes the crafts of acting, cinematography, costume design, directing, lighting, and design.

Cinematography

Lighting and photographing a film is known as cinematography, and is the responsibility of the director of photography (DP), also known as the cinematographer. Although the DP is responsible for how the film is lit and photographed, he or she does not run the camera or set up the lights. Instead, under the DP's supervision, these activities are carried out by the cinematographic crew. The camera operator runs the camera; the electrical crew is under the guidance of the gaffer or chief electrician.

In all phases of movie production, the DP is a craftsperson and an artist. He or she has a knowledge of many kinds of technology, such as film stocks and printing processes, cameras, lenses, and filters; and applies artistic sensibilities to place the camera and compose the picture in the frame. Nearly every day, the DP reviews the "rushes" or daily footage and discusses it with the director to make sure the movie has the director's desired approach.

In the US, members of the professional society called the American Society of Cinematographers appear in film credits with "ASC" after their name.

A member of the art department paints a background for an imaginary, historical, or inaccessible location. This department works under the production designer.

Production design

The physical world to be photographed in a movie is created by the production designer. He or she acts as an architect, decorator, and visionary to create everything from elaborate sets to small props that may become totemic items, like the light sabres of *Star Wars* (1977). Among the production designer's duties are designing and overseeing the construction of sets and scenery; designing props and overseeing their purchase or rental; and

Girl with a Pearl Earring (2003) required cinematographer Eduardo Serra to recreate artist Johannes Vermeer's aesthetic sensibility.

working with the costume designer to make sure the actors' wardrobe matches with the rest of the film's look. The production designer usually has knowledge of architecture, engineering, painting, drawing, and theatre and film arts. He or she applies this background to research the historical period of the movie and the material world of its inhabitants, or to realize an imaginary culture, which can range from the look of an Elizabethan theatre in ***Shakespeare in Love*** (1998) to the futuristic world of ***Gattaca*** (1997).

Active in both the pre-production and production stages, the production designer works with the director and producer to create sketches of sets. Implementing these ideas requires adherance to budgets, time constraints, and the vision of the director. It also requires a team, known as the art department, including the art director, set designer, set decorator, scenic artist, property master, construction coordinator, and landscaper.

Acting

Once signed, actors prepare for their roles. They develop appropriate characteristics for their character, such as gaining weight, as Robert De Niro did to play an olderJake LaMotta in ***Raging Bull*** (1980), or finding a walk, as Alec Guinness is said to have done for each of his roles. Some immerse themselves in the period of the film. But nearly all serious actors have prepared beforehand through acting training. One of the best known schools for actors is the Actors Studio in New York City. Founded in 1947 and led by Lee Strasberg, the Actors Studio has encouraged actors to develop a deep understanding of their characters' motivations. Well-known actors who have used the Actors Studio "Method" style (see box, p.37) include Marlon Brando, Robert De Niro, Dustin Hoffman, and Marilyn Monroe. Notable university acting programmes include the Yale School of Drama in the US, while drama schools such as The Royal Academy of Dramatic Arts (RADA) in London have trained many well-known faces. Internationally, drama schools abound. In Paris, there is the national drama and theatre school, Conservatoire National Supérieur d'Art Dramatique. Germany has the Berlin University of the Arts, Spain has the Septima Ars School of Cinema and TV. Finland has its Theatre Academy, and in India, there is the National School of Drama.

While audiences are no longer shocked by actors varying the type of persona they portray, as they were with aspects of James Stewart's performance in ***Anatomy of a Murder*** (1959), most actors still manage their careers effectively by remaining consistent to the sensibilities they have established in their films. So, Tom Hanks will doubtless continue to represent the decent everyman, while Julia Roberts is likely to remain the accessible, practical everywoman.

Film actor in action

Film is a medium that picks up small nuances in expression; the stage represents the character through movement and gesture. On the set, actors endure challenges and advantages unique to the form. Unlike the stage, the set offers no live audience for reaction and support; but it does allow the actor to redo a line or scene he or she is not happy with. The film actor is also in constant collaboration with the various film technicians who handle cinematography, music, and editing. They all come together to highlight the actor's performance. Charlton Heston's Moses in ***The Ten Commandments*** (1956) is accorded stature by the forceful colour on screen and Cecil B. DeMille's direction, which defines Heston's powerful character via a series of sweeping gestures.

In the US, actors are members of the Screen Actors Guild, which has established a minimum payment for its actors. More established or in-demand actors get salaries far beyond scale, but for many actors, the rate is scale plus ten (ten per cent for the agent).

Stunt performers

The players who substitute for the main actors and perform acts involving risk are the stunt performers. These trained men and women are largely unknown to the movie-going audience, but their presence in fires, explosions, or chase scenes is essential. They are chosen for their general resemblance to the star and are dressed to match him or her.

Although some actors do at least some of their own stunts, stunt doubles replace actors when the stunt is considered too dangerous for

Jackie Chan is renowned for doing his own stunts, as seen here in ***Rush Hour*** (1998). Other examples of his stuntwork include ***Rumble in the Bronx*** (1995) and the early masterpiece, ***Drunken Master*** (1978).

anyone but a trained person. In part, a stunt performer is used for economic reasons: to keep the actor in sufficiently good health to complete the movie and make good on the investment. If a stunt is considered too dangerous for a human being, the effects are done by digital imagery and long-established camera tricks. In using stunt performers, the aim is to avoid mishaps, such as the injury sustained by silent comic actor Harold Lloyd, who lost a thumb and forefinger while filming ***Haunted Spooks*** (1920).

In the US, stunt performers are members of the Stuntmen's Association of Motion Pictures and the Screen Actors Guild. Some of them are so accomplished that they receive industry accolades. Perhaps the most honoured was Western and action movie stuntman Yakima Canutt (1895–1986), who appeared in ***Stagecoach*** (1939), and who received a special Academy Award for his extraordinary stuntwork in 1966.

Animals and children

While digital effects and animatronics can be used to create an animal, or at least place it where the director wants it to be, real animals are still effective additions to many movies, particularly family-oriented ones. To circumvent some of the troubles of dealing with animals, multiple look-alike animals are sometimes used, each featuring in a different set of scenes. An animal may also be made to perform by a trainer dangling food before its eyes. In some films, the animals themselves are the stars. Notable examples include Lassie, whose first big-screen feature, ***Lassie Come Home*** (1943), was actually Oscar-nominated; and the killer whale Willy, who makes friends with a young boy in the heart-warming ***Free Willy*** (1993).

Children are also big draws for the movie-goer seeking familiarity. On the set, child actors pose many of the same challenges as animals. Hence, multiple child actors are chosen for a role (such as twins or triplets in a movie calling for a baby), and they perform for only limited periods. In most countries, child labour laws regulate how long child actors may remain on the set. Furthermore, school-age children are usually tutored when they are not filming.

Sound

Sound is a crucial element in films, because it helps to create the required atmosphere as, for example, in *Jaws* (1975).

Sound in film comprises three components – dialogue, sound effects, and music – and is created and implemented by three people – the mixer, sound editor, and composer. These components appear on separate tracks, recorded separately, but run together in the movie. The sound crew works on the film during both the production and post-production stages of making a film.

Racing Stripes (2005) brings the animal/animatronics film into the 21st century but relies on a classic story of wishes coming true; a zebra (voice of Frankie Muniz) believes he is a racehorse and comes to race with thoroughbreds.

The first of two phases of creating a movie's sound occurs during the production stage. This is when most of the dialogue and some sound effects are recorded on the set. The person in charge at this point is the floor mixer, who ensures that the recording is clear and in balance. The dialogue takes priority over background sounds, since the latter can always be dubbed in later. A guide track is used to dub dialogue and background sounds if necessary.

The many tasks involved in creating the sound mix are carried out by the sound crew. This includes the sound mixer (or floor mixer or recordist), who is responsible for the sound recording on the set and directs the rest of the crew. Other members of the sound crew include the sound recorder, boom operator, cablemen, and playback operators.

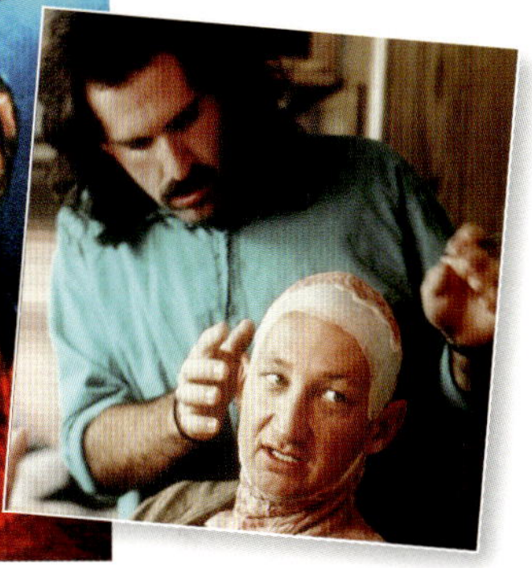

Robert Englund is transformed into Freddy Krueger, the horribly scarred dream monster of ***A Nightmare on Elm Street*** (1984) and its sequels. Creature make-up typically requires several hours daily for application and removal of latex appliances.

Costumes, make-up, and hair

Just as the production designer creates a world on the set or location of a film, the costume designer, make-up artist, and hairstylist change the actors' clothes and their overall appearance so that they fit into the world that is being created onscreen.

The costume designer works closely with the director, cinematographer, and production designer to create a wardrobe. Part of the job is to research the period covered in the film for clothing style, colour, fabric composition, and fit on the body. The different professions that may be included within this area are those of costume supervisor, costumer/stylist, set costumer, tailor/seamstress, wig master or mistress, and wardrobe attendant. Wardrobe pieces that can be purchased off-the-peg (from a shop) may be obtained by the stylist.

Many top costume designers have become known for the looks they create, the actors they have dressed, or the stories they generate. The broad-shouldered look that Adrian created for Joan Crawford was embraced (in modified form) for ladies' wear during the 1940s; Givenchy was the man who dressed Audrey Hepburn; and Travis Banton dressed Marlene Dietrich. Consummate studio designer Edith Head dressed just about everyone – stories and anecdotes abounded about her famous clients' attributes and habits, such as Barbara Stanwyck's tiny waist or Paul Newman and Robert Redford's unfussy ways.

Even more than the costume designer, the make-up artist develops a close relationship with the actor. The make-up artist is responsible for conveying the actor's sensibility for the film by preparing the actor's face, neck, forearms, and hands. The work is redone at least once a day and must remain consistent throughout shooting. Members of the make-up team include the make-up artist and his or her assistant. If relevant to the film, there may also be a body make-up artist, who will often create extraordinary effects with make-up.

There has been a separate category for make-up in the Academy Awards since 1981. Awards have been given to such diverse films as ***Frida*** (2002) and ***The Chronicles of Narnia: The Lion, the Witch and the Wardrobe*** (2005).

Special effects

Beyond the ability of the stuntperson or costume designer lies special effects. In a huge range of movie genres, including drama, epic, and horror, special effects are manufactured illusions that can be imagined, but are impossible to film without trickery. Examples include the sinking of the *Titanic* in James Cameron's 1997 film of the same name, and the transformation of mad scientist Seth Brundle (Jeff Goldblum) into a horrific giant man/fly hybrid in ***The Fly*** (1986). In many cases, special effects are used to reduce costs. Filming in front of a matte painting is less costly than filming on a huge national monument (such as Mount Rushmore in *North by Northwest*, 1959). It can also be used to create the illusion of filming taking place at an off-limits location. Special effects (abbreviated as FX, SFX, SPFX, or EFX) are of two kinds. They are visual or photographic effects, achieved by manipulating the film image, and mechanical or physical effects, achieved using mechanical devices on the set. While a physical effect may be simple, such as using an unseen rope to move or knock over a prop, special effects today are usually much more complicated.

Visual effect techniques include computer-generated imagery (CGI), digital compositing, digital matte paintings, green screen technology, miniatures, morphing, motion-capture, rotoscopes, and travelling mattes.

Mechanical effects include animatronic puppets, explosions, full-scale mock-ups, rain and snow machines, squibs that replicate bloody bullet hits, and wires attached to actors. A complicated FX sequence may include a variety of visual and mechanical effects.

Technological advances

The technology for special effects is changing so rapidly that many long-standing practices, such as brush-and-canvas matte paintings, and rear projection have now fallen out of use. Even animatronics, used (with difficulty) for the shark in *Jaws* (1975) and refined in the films of the 1980s and 1990s, is less widely used today. Yet some established technologies that are still used include rain and snow machines, which permit filming even when the weather is uncooperative. Some digital effects, such as morphing (a computer-generated effect in which one image is transformed into another), have been around so long that they are almost considered old-fashioned nowadays.

Current technologies include motion-capture, in which an actor's movements are translated to a computer-graphics model. Motion-capture can be blended with digital animation to create realistic virtual creatures, such as the giant gorilla in *King Kong* (2005). James Cameron revolutionized film-making in his *Avatar* (2009), in which real footage is mixed with motion-captured CGI in an immersive 3-D technology.

Green screens are green fabric backgrounds positioned behind actors that allow CGI to be integrated into the scene. Blue screens were originally used, but have been largely superseded by green ones because green delivers finer outlines.

King Kong (2005) uses green screen technology (inset) to allow Naomi Watts to interact with Kong.

Post-production

A crucial part of the movie-making process begins once filming is finished. Thousands of frames of film must be assembled in an order that conveys a story, and the scenes may be shortened or reordered so that the finished product reflects the director's vision.

Editing

Most films are shot out of sequence. During filming, it is the editor's job to begin assembling the pieces of film into the order in which they will be seen in the final movie. The editor talks with the director about the previous day's filming, known as "rushes". The film shot may be transferred to a videotape or digital format for ease of rearranging or selection. The film construction made at this point is called the assembly. The bulk of the editing is done during post-production.

Film editors carry out various different stages of editing to shape the final arrangement of shots that makes a finished film. First, they work with the director to refine the assembly of all the different sections of the film into a rough cut, the first fully edited work print, which includes the film's soundtrack. However, the individual shots are not completely determined at this stage. This version of the film is dominated by the director's vision and is known as the director's cut. During post-production, the DP and the director also work together to oversee the timing of the first print. Among the tasks at this stage is the correction of density and colour balance. Following repeated consultations with the director, the editor assembles the shots with visual effects into the fine cut. This runs to the length that the director, editor, and producer have agreed on.

Charlie Chaplin is seen editing a film. He also wrote, directed, and acted in his films in a 50-year career.

The sound mixing desk is where the various tracks of human dialogue, sound effects, and music are combined to create an original to transfer to the film negative.

For the first hundred years of film-making, film-editing meant physically cutting and reassembling the edited film reel itself. Today, however, much film-editing is done electronically, using video and digital technology. Films are transferred to videotape and digital format, and are computer-coded; this allows scenes to be edited on screen. The original negative is cut using the fine cut as a guide.

Post-production sound

There are four post-production stages that go into creating the movie's sound. These include dialogue and sound effects, composed music, the sound mix, and the transfer of the original sound mix on to the film negative. First, the sound editor, or sound effects editor, works with the director and editor to create the soundtracks. Additional sounds are either created by a foley artist – a technician who adds sound effects during the dubbing process – or taken from film library stock.

Composer John Williams has won Academy Awards for Best Score for ***Jaws*** (1975), ***Star Wars*** (1977), ***E.T.: The Extra Terrestrial*** (1982), and ***Schindler's List*** (1993).

A composer (such as John Williams or Danny Elfman) is used if the film requires an original score. A music editor edits the music to fit the film. For existing music under copyright, rights managers agree on fees for its use in the film. A recording or re-recording mixer works with the director to blend together the many tracks of different sound, and the finished mix is transferred on to the original negative. The film sound is recorded with a digital system and reproduced as an optical soundtrack. It is then read as synchronized sound when it is sent through the loudspeakers during an audience showing.

Release prints

Colour testing follows the making of the original negative. Once all phases of the movie are completed, the movie is previewed with audiences; depending on their reaction, final cuts are made.

Film stars often do publicity to promote their recent releases, such as Tom Cruise here on Jay Leno's late-night talk show.

Master prints are made from the original negative when it is finalized, and duplicate negatives are then made from that to produce release prints.

Distribution and exhibition

Once a movie is completed, the distributor gets it to cinemas and exhibitors make sure that it is shown. The distributor is usually the movie studio that financed the film. The distributor plans the release date, licenses the movie to cinemas, arranges to have prints of the film sent to exhibitors, and creates a marketing and advertising programme for it. The exhibitor negotiates a financial deal with the distributor for the financial take at the cinema on the film, including paying advance money to secure an expected hit.

The studio is also responsible for advertising and publicizing the film. This includes market research, advertisements (television, radio, newspaper, and online), "coming attractions" trailers in cinemas, posters, lobby cards, and stills. Other aspects of publicity include press kits and press releases to the media, and booking stars for media interviews and general visibility.

Theatrical release

Once the film is in the cinema, it has only a short time to earn its money as a theatrical release. After a few weeks or (if the movie is a blockbuster or an Academy Award winner) months, attendance will diminish. The days of one film (such as *The Sound of Music*, 1965) playing at the same cinema for a year are gone, and unlikely to return. Therefore, distributors have to judge box office receipts carefully and recalibrate the number of cinemas that are showing a film. A movie with good word-of-mouth and sustained interest (such as *March of the Penguins*, 2005) will be shown on more screens, while an underperforming film may need a different advertising campaign (as with *Munich*, 2005) or might be withdrawn altogether.

After the domestic theatrical release, a film's earning potential is extended by its release in overseas cinemas. There is also revenue to come from DVD and Blu-ray disc sales, internet downloads, and the licensing to a variety of TV rights, including pay-per-view, premium cable channels, basic cable channels, and terrestrial television. The distributor can also extend a film's life by licensing merchandising rights to makers of toys, mugs, T-shirts, recordings, and video games. Since the release of *Star Wars* in 1977, and the highly successful accompanying figurines and book tie-ins, merchandising has taken on a new importance. Many products relating to a movie are now sold even before the release of the film.

The role of the film critic

Good planning and deal-making does not ensure a hit. Neither does advance audience interest. Often, the success of a movie begins (or ends) with film critics.

Film critics are the first to slot a movie into its place in the film canon. They pre-screen the movie and tell the audience whether they believe it is worth the price of admission. Despite the critics, however, the strongest force for the popularity of a movie is the audience. Based on the film's stars, subject matter, director, time of year, and the cultural atmosphere of the time, the public decides whether to go and see a film or not. Audiences are affected by timing: *Jaws*, for example, worked well as a summer blockbuster. They also want an element of familiarity: *Shakespeare in Love* works, but *Marlowe in Love* probably wouldn't. Finally, the time has to be right culturally: the Western *Brokeback Mountain*, about gay ranch hands, was very successful when released in 2005, but 20 years ago, it may have been only an arthouse picture.

A general view of the 81st Academy Awards held at the Kodak Theatre. In recent years, award ceremonies have set fashion trends, as well as invigorating box office takings.

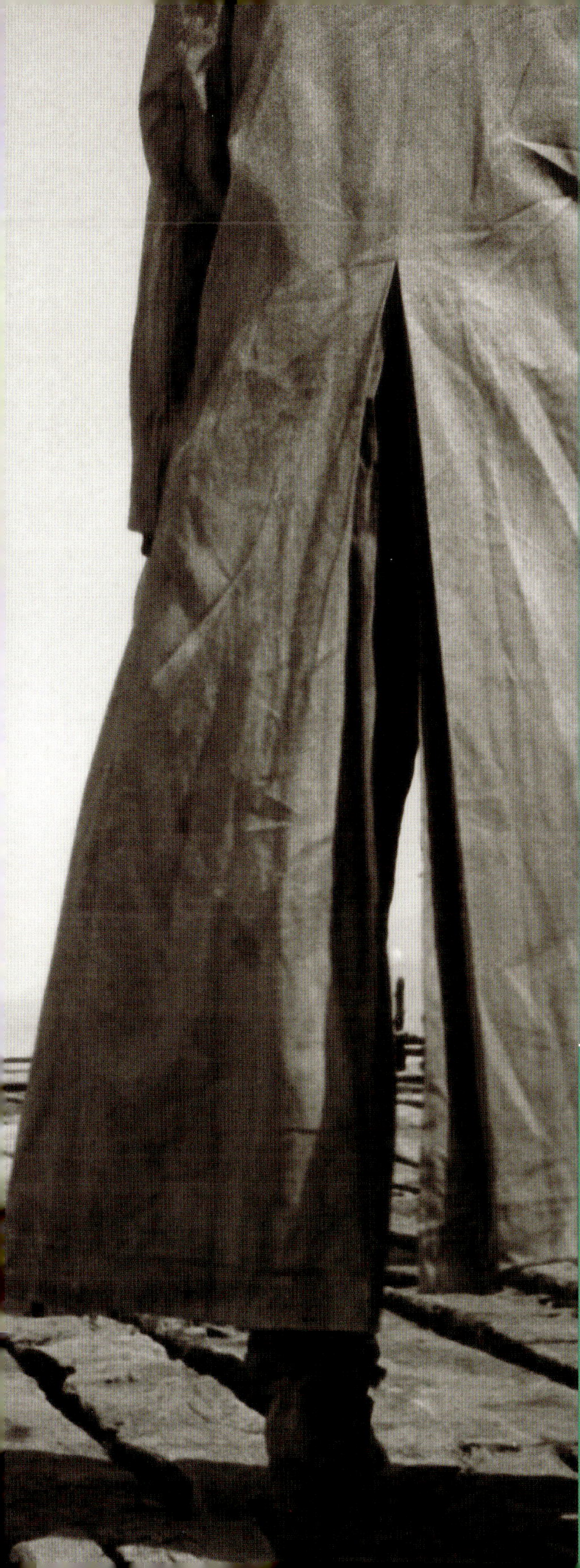

Movie **Genres**

When a film is labelled a Western, a musical, or a comedy, audiences already have certain expectations about it. Within each genre, films may differ in many respects, but they will share comparable, recognizable patterns in theme, period, setting, plot, use of symbols, and characterization.

The concept of genre really began during the Hollywood studio period. It helped production decisions and made a film easier to market. Also, during Hollywood's golden era, when the studios were turning out hundreds of films at a rapid rate, a generic concept provided scriptwriters with a template with which to work.

Each studio specialized in a particular genre: Universal (horror), Warner Bros. (gangster), MGM (musicals), and Paramount (comedy). Some directors became connected with a specific genre: John Ford (Westerns), Cecil B. DeMille (epics), Alfred Hitchcock (thrillers), Vincent Minnelli (musicals), and Douglas Sirk (melodramas). However, it was with the stars that the public most associated certain types of picture: James Cagney, Edward G. Robinson (gangster films); Joan Crawford, Barbara Stanwyck (melodramas); Fred Astaire, Betty Grable (musicals); John Wayne, Randolph Scott (Westerns); and Boris Karloff, Bela Lugosi (horror films). Performers were so closely linked with certain genres that it became an event when they departed from the norm. "Garbo Laughs!" was the publicity line for Ernst Lubitsch's ***Ninotchka*** (1939), which prepared audiences to accept Greta Garbo, who had previously been seen only in melodramas, in a comedy.

Today, genres and actors have become more flexible, although stars such as Bruce Willis and Sylvester Stallone remain linked in the public's mind with action movies; likewise, Jim Carrey and Adam Sandler with comedies. There are still directors who specialize in certain genres: John Hughes in teen movies; Woody Allen in comedy; John Woo in action; and Wes Craven in horror.

Over the years, well-loved conventions have become clichés, such as the good cowboy and the villain having a showdown on a dusty street, and so traditional genres have been reinterpreted, challenged, or satirized. Sam Peckinpah and Sergio Leone's Westerns can be termed revisionist, as can the film noirs of the Coen brothers. Audiences are familiar enough with genres to enjoy lampoons, such as Mel Brooks' ***Blazing Saddles*** (1974) and Jay Roach's ***Austin Powers*** movies of the late 1990s. Despite auteur cinema (the personal expression of a director) being the antithesis of genre cinema, directors such as Jean-Luc Godard, Jean-Pierre Melville, and Wong Kar Wai have used established genres for their own purposes.

Janet Leigh is about to be stabbed in the shower in Alfred Hitchcock's ***Psycho*** (1960), one of the most famous and shocking scenes in cinema history.

Film poster, 1981

Action-adventure

"Lights, camera, action" is the command given by the director at the beginning of each shot. Action films – often linked to adventure – tend to be real crowd-pleasers, with their combination of exciting storylines, physical action, and special effects.

This type of film encompasses several genres – Westerns, war films, crime pictures, and even comedies. The style is associated with non-stop action – dramatic chases, shoot-outs, and explosions – often centred around a male hero struggling against terrible odds. Action films offer pure escapism and entertainment to the audience, and are regularly big box-office hits.

It was in the 1980s that the action-adventure genre became established. The style inherited the law-and-order ideology from the "rogue cop" films of Clint Eastwood – such as the *Dirty Harry* movies – and the vigilante pictures of Charles Bronson in the late 1960s and 1970s. Hollywood's big action films became increasingly gung-ho, with *Top Gun* (1986) as the apotheosis of renewed American power and confidence in the Reagan era. Among the action men who dominated the genre in the 1980s were Harrison Ford (*Raiders of the Lost Ark*, 1981), Bruce Willis (*Die Hard*, 1988), and Mel Gibson (*Lethal Weapon*, 1987).

Errol Flynn (right), as Robin Hood, faces Basil Rathbone, as Sir Guy of Gisbourne, in the exciting climax of Michael Curtiz's classic swashbuckler, *The Adventures of Robin Hood* (1938). The film was a huge hit for Warner Bros.

Action heroes

No hero came larger or more testosterone-filled than former Mr. Universe, Arnold Schwarzenegger. Schwarzenegger made an impact in sword-and-sorcery fantasies (*Conan the Barbarian*, 1982), science-fiction action (*The Terminator*, 1984), and military movies (*Commando*, 1985). An equally macho fantasy figure was Sylvester Stallone as a Vietnam vet in the jingoistic *Rambo* cycle. These films glorified the power of the individual to solve political and social problems through an entertaining combination of excessive musculature and firearms.

Pre-1960s action heroes were far more moral, and their code was to kill only in self-defence. Costume epics featured flamboyant characters played by actors such as Douglas Fairbanks, who swashbuckled his way through *The Mark of Zorro* (1920), *The Three Musketeers* (1921), and *Robin Hood* (1922). Fairbanks' worthy successors were Errol Flynn, Tyrone Power, and Stewart Granger in the US; while in France, Jean Marais, Gérard Philipe, and Jean-Paul Belmondo carried on the tradition. In Japan, Toshiro Mifune starred in numerous samurai films or *jidai-geki*, filled with furious swordplay.

Gender roles

Traditionally, action-adventure movies were aimed mostly at male audiences in their teens to mid-30s. The female characters in these films were generally shown as either having a restraining influence or fuelling men's violence. In the 1990s, however, a new style of action-adventure film began to appear, in which women played roles traditionally taken by men. In Ridley Scott's *Thelma and Louise* (1991), two women (played by Geena Davis and Susan Sarandon) go on a crime spree, while *Lethal Weapon 3* (1992) added a tough female martial-arts expert to the buddy-buddy formula. The genre, however, is still male-dominated, and although the heroes are more clean-cut and cocky, such as Tom Cruise (*Mission: Impossible*, 1996) and Keanu Reeves (*The Matrix*, 1999), they are still as lethal as in earlier films.

Bruce Willis, as one-man army John McClane, survives various hair-raising stunts in the explosive action thriller *Die Hard* (1988).

Uma Thurman plays a ruthless warrior and former assassin, in Quentin Tarantino's *Kill Bill: Volume 1* (2003).

WHAT TO WATCH

- *The Mark of Zorro* (Fred Niblo, US, 1920)
- *The Adventures of Robin Hood* (Michael Curtiz and William Keighley, US, 1938)
- *The Seven Samurai* (Akira Kurosawa, Japan, 1954)
- *Top Gun* (Tony Scott, US, 1986)
- *Lethal Weapon* (Richard Donner, US, 1987)
- *Thelma and Louise* (Ridley Scott, US, 1991)
- *Mission: Impossible* (Brian De Palma, US, 1996)
- *Kill Bill: Volume 1* (Quentin Tarantino, US, 2003)

Animation

Film animation encompasses a multitude of styles, themes, and techniques. From the simplest drawing by hand to images created using the most up-to-date digital technology, the genre has always aimed to appeal to the widest possible age range.

Gene Kelly dances with Tom and Jerry in ***Anchors Aweigh*** (1945), a film that combines animation with live action.

In the mid-19th century, long before the invention of cinema, devices to give drawings an illusion of movement were already in use. In 1832, a Belgian, Joseph Plateau, invented a piece of equipment that produced a moving picture from a series of drawings. The action was viewed through slits on a revolving disc. In 1882, Emile Reynaud introduced his Praxinoscope to the audience at the Musée Grevin in Paris, using perforated film, which projected images on a screen. However, when live action cinema was invented, animation was neglected until 1908, when it was almost reinvented by America's J. Stuart Blackton. He pioneered stop-motion photography, a technique taken up by Émile Cohl in France. Cohl made more than 100 brief animated films between 1908 and 1918, and created the first regular cartoon character.

In 1909, Winsor McCay, an American cartoonist, created Gertie the Dinosaur using simple line drawing. It was the first animated cartoon to be shown as part of a theatrical programme in the US. In 1918, he made probably the first animated feature, ***The Sinking of the Lusitania***.

The years 1919–20 saw the emergence of the first cartoon production units. These turned out one-reel films about ten minutes long, which supported cinema programmes. This was possible due to the labour-saving method of "cel" animation, which allowed the tracing of moving parts of characters on celluloid sheets without having to redraw the entire character and background for every frame of film. In the 1920s, Pat Sullivan's Felix the Cat reigned supreme – his witty thoughts given in bubbles – until the coming of sound transformed animated films.

Mickey Mouse is the sorcerer's apprentice in one of the most memorable musical sequences in Walt Disney's ***Fantasia*** (1940).

WHAT TO WATCH

Steamboat Willie (Ub Iwerks, US, 1928)

Snow White and the Seven Dwarfs (David Hand and William Cottrell, US, 1937)

Pinocchio (Ben Sharpsteen and Hamilton Luske, US, 1940)

Yellow Submarine (George Dunning, UK, 1968)

Akira (Katsuhiro Otomo, Japan, 1988)

Toy Story (John Lasseter, US, 1995)

Spirited Away (Hayao Miyazaki, Japan, 2001)

Belleville Rendez-vous (Sylvain Chomet, France, 2003)

Wallace and Gromit: The Curse of the Were-Rabbit (Steve Box and Nick Park, UK, 2005)

Wall-E (Andrew Stanton, US, 2008)

Up (Pete Docter and Bob Peterson, US, 2009)

How to Train Your Dragon (Chris Sanders and Dean DeBlois, US, 2010)

Walt Disney's ***Steamboat Willie*** (1928) was the first cartoon with sound. It demonstrated the force of music, not as background accompaniment, but as an element intrinsic to the film's structure and visual rhythm. From 1928, cartoon characters such as Max Fleischer's Betty Boop and Disney's Mickey Mouse, Donald Duck, and Goofy became as well-known as film stars. Disney's studio streamlined cartoon production and dominated Hollywood animation in the 1930s, consolidating its position with the hugely successful animation features ***Snow White and the Seven Dwarfs*** (1937), ***Pinocchio*** (1940), ***Fantasia*** (1940 – the first film to use stereo sound commercially), ***Dumbo*** (1941), and ***Bambi*** (1942).

Dave Fleischer, whose Popeye shorts proved very popular from 1933 to 1947, tried to rival Disney's full-length cartoons with ***Gulliver's Travels*** (1939) and *Hoppity Goes To Town* (1941), but they were perhaps too sophisticated for children, and were not commercially successful. In the 1940s, MGM made headway with William Hanna and Joe Barbera's cartoon shorts featuring Tom and Jerry, which had jazzy sound effects, little dialogue, and zany violence as frustrated cat Tom eternally pursued resourceful mouse Jerry. Also at MGM, Tex Avery's anarchism was given free rein in a series of crazy cartoons that exploded the boundaries of the genre. Among the best of these cartoons were *Screwball Squirrel* (1944) and *King-Size Canary* (1947).

At Warner Bros., Chuck Jones helped create Bugs Bunny, Porky Pig, and Daffy Duck. Jones was also responsible for the *Roadrunner/Coyote* series in the 1950s, noted for its speed and devastating use of the desert landscape. Another major force was UPA (United Productions of America), set up in 1948 by a breakaway group of Disney animators. In reaction to the naturalistic graphic style and sentimentality of Disney, UPA developed freer, more economical, contemporary art styles. Among their most famous creations was Mr. Magoo. All this inventive cartoon work was halted with the proliferation of television, when studios began to devote their output almost entirely to low-budget, mass-produced cartoons.

Sylvain Chomet's *Belleville Rendez-vous* (2003) proved a huge success for French animation. Here, the aged song-and-dance team make a comeback.

Animation abroad

While America was developing animation, other countries were also experimenting with the genre. In Canada, Norman McLaren used many techniques, such as drawing directly on film, mixing live action and drawings, and pixillation (the use of a stop-frame camera to speed up and distort movement). In Great Britain, Len Lye painted directly onto film stock, while John Halas and Joy Batchelor made *Animal Farm* (1955), the first British animated feature film. However, it was in the 1990s that British animation was really put on the map by Aardman Animations with their plasticine characters Wallace and Gromit.

Plasticine buddies – cheese-loving Wallace and his faithful dog Gromit – were the Oscar-winning creations of Nick Park and Aardman Animations.

Waltz with Bashir (2008), an animated documentary film from Israel, depicts director Ari Folman's attempts to reconstruct his memories of the 1982 Lebanon War.

After Aardman Animations' Nick Park and team won the Oscar for best short animation with ***The Wrong Trousers*** (1993), they were able to raise the finances to make ***Chicken Run*** (2000) and ***Wallace and Gromit: The Curse of the Were-Rabbit*** (2005). Meanwhile, France came up with a winner in Sylvain Chomet's exhilarating ***Belleville Rendez-vous*** (2003).

In the former Czechoslovakia, puppet animator Jiri Trnka made his feature-length ***A Midsummer Night's Dream*** (1959) without dialogue, and Karel Zeman made ten features, some combining live actors with animated models and drawings. Jan Svankmajer, a graphic artist and puppeteer, made ***Alice*** (***Neco z Alenky***, 1988), which follows Lewis Carroll's heroine (played by an actress) through an animated land of wonders. The Zagreb animation studio in Croatia, formed in 1950, turned out a string of witty and inventive satires, while Polish animator Walerian Borowczyk made bitterly ironic films such as ***Mr. and Mrs. Kabal's Theatre*** (1967).

New talent

In the US, after a decline in the quality of Disney animated features, there was a revival by a new crew of younger talents, who produced a string of hits unequalled since the 1940s, including ***Beauty and the Beast*** (1991) and ***The Lion King*** (1994). A new golden age of animation dawned at the beginning of the 21st century, leading to the creation of an Oscar for the Best Animated Feature. In 2003, it was awarded to Hayao Miyazaki's inventive ***Spirited Away***. In 2004, Pixar Animation Studios won the award for ***The Incredibles***.

The green ogre and the talkative donkey were voiced by Mike Myers and Eddie Murphy, respectively, in the computer-animated ***Shrek*** (2001), which won the first Oscar for Best Animated Feature.

Avant-Garde

Avant-garde is a term applied to any experimental movement in the arts that is in opposition to conventional forms. In cinema, it specifically refers to a group of influential and radical film-makers who were active across Europe from the end of World War I.

WHAT TO WATCH

L'Inhumaine (Marcel L'Herbier, France, 1924)
Un Chien Andalou (Luis Buñuel, France, 1929)
L'Age d'Or (Luis Buñuel, France, 1930)

In 1918, French poet Louis Aragon wrote that "cinema must have a place in the avant-garde's preoccupations...if one wants to bring some purity to the art of movement and light". Critic Riccioto Canudo argued in 1926 that cinema should express the film-maker's emotions as well as a character's psychology and even their unconscious. The formalist possibilities of cinema were expounded by French film-makers and theorists Louis Delluc and Jean Epstein, and underlined by the montage theory of the great Russian film-makers of the 1920s.

Avant-garde cinema disturbed the accepted continuity of chronological development and attempted new ways of tracing the flow of the characters' thoughts. Collages of fragmentary images, complex allusions, and multiple points of view replaced logical explanation of meaning. Avant-garde artists such as Man Ray, Hans Richter, Fernand Léger, Oskar Fischinger, and Walter Ruttmann, made films influenced by such movements as German expressionism, Russian constructuralism, surrealism, and Dadaism. Salvador Dali's contribution to Luis Buñuel's ***Un Chien Andalou*** (1929) and ***L'Age d'Or*** (1930) was invaluable. Marcel L'Herbier, with ***L'Inhumaine*** (1924) and ***L'Argent*** (1928), hoped to create "visual music" by using sets created by modernist artists.

By the 1930s, Hollywood film-makers were experimenting too. Director and editor Slavko Vorkapich called his montage sequences "symphonies of visual movement", and dance director Busby Berkeley used overhead shots, *trompe l'oeil*, superimposition, trick photography, and surreal settings in his musicals.

Each set for Marcel L'Herbier's ***L'Inhumaine*** (1924) was created by a different designer, including Frenchman Fernand Léger.

The spirit of the avant-garde movement lived on in the American Underground and in the films of Jean-Luc Godard, Chris Marker, and Jean-Marie Straub and his wife Danièle Huillet. The latter couple, in particular, have never swerved from making films that break away from accepted notions of realism, disengage from bourgeois values, and question the primacy of narration.

Biopic

By its very nature, the biopic (biographical picture) exists across many genres. It could be a war film (***Patton***, 1970), an epic (***Lawrence of Arabia***, 1962), or a melodrama (***Mommie Dearest***, 1981). Yet there are characteristics that mark the biopic out as a genre of its own.

Joaquin Phoenix plays the role of country music legend Johnny Cash, and Reese Witherspoon plays singer June Carter in *Walk the Line* (2005).

A biopic is essentially a dramatized portrayal of the life of a famous figure. In a conventional biopic, the protagonist falls from the height of fame and then goes on to make a triumphant comeback.

It was German-born William Dieterle who set the pattern with numerous biopics. His most successful ones – *The Story of Louis Pasteur* (1936), *The Life of Emile Zola* (1937), and *Juarez* (1939) – starred a heavily made-up Paul Muni. The most archetypal biopics to follow were *The Story of Alexander Graham Bell* (1939) with Don Ameche; *Young Tom Edison* and *Edison, the Man* (both 1940); *Yankee Doodle Dandy* (1942) with James Cagney as composer-entertainer George M. Cohan; *The Jolson Story* (1946); and *A Song to Remember* (1945), with Cornel Wilde as Chopin.

A close resemblance between the actor and the real-life figure was achieved by Henry Fonda in *Young Mr. Lincoln* (1939), Kirk Douglas as Van Gogh in *Lust for Life* (1956), Ben Kingsley in *Gandhi* (1982), and Anthony Hopkins in *Nixon* (1995). Joaquin Phoenix hit the right notes as Johnny Cash in *Walk the Line* (2005) and Jesse Eisenberg's wardrobe in *The Social Network* (2010) perfectly matched Mark Zuckerberg's. Some biopics focus on a single event that made a person famous, such as *127 Hours* (2010), based on a dramatic incident in mountaineer Aron Ralston's life.

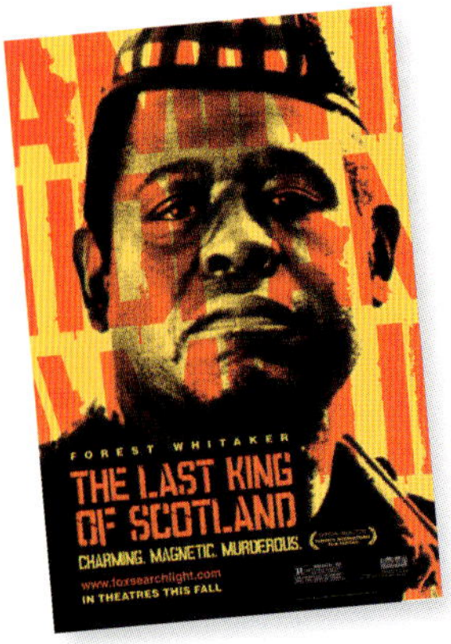

Film poster, 2006

WHAT TO WATCH

Young Mr. Lincoln (John Ford, US, 1939)
Gandhi (Richard Attenborough, UK, 1982)
A Beautiful Mind (Ron Howard, US, 2001)
The Aviator (Martin Scorsese, US, 2004)
Ray (Taylor Hackford, US, 2004)
The Last King of Scotland (Kevin Macdonald, UK, 2006)
Milk (Gus Van Sant, US, 2008)

Comedy

In its various forms, from visual slapstick to verbal repartee, comedy has been part of cinema ever since a naughty boy stepped on a hose in the Lumière brothers' ***Watering the Gardener***, in 1895. Since then, actors have employed many different ways to make us laugh.

Comedy is one of the oldest theatrical genres. Originally derived from the *commedia dell'arte* (improvised comedy from 16th-century Italy) and the burlesque, circus, and vaudeville traditions, it was better suited to silent cinema than tragedy. Slapstick, which derives its name from the wooden sticks that circus clowns slapped together to generate audience applause, was predominant in the earliest silent films, since it didn't need sound to be effective.

The first film comics

Most of the earliest comedies were made by the French and, in 1907, the Pathé Company launched a series of films featuring the character Boireau, played by comedian André Deed – cinema's first true comic star. Other comedians followed, both in France and Italy, each with their own specific character. The most gifted and influential of all the comic artists was Max Linder from France. Charlie Chaplin called him "the Professor to whom I owe everything".

While the other comic stars were manic and grotesque, Linder adopted the character of a handsome young boulevardier, a bemused dandy with sleek hair, a trimmed moustache, and a silk hat that survived all catastrophes. By 1910, Linder was making one film a week, playing the character of a wealthy bachelor in hopeless pursuit of well-bred, pretty ladies. Just a year later, he was the highest-paid entertainer of the time, writing and directing his own films and enjoying fame across Europe.

Early US comics

It was not until 1912 that US comedy emerged, with Mack Sennett's films for the Keystone company and, famously, the Keystone Kops. In five years, Sennett established the type of rapid, irreverent comedy forever associated with his name. Using fast motion, reverse action, and other camera and editing tricks, he usually ended his films with a death-defying chase, with many stunts executed by the comics themselves. Sennett filmed Mabel Normand and Fatty Arbuckle in the first custard pie-throwing scene known in cinema, in ***A Noise from the Deep*** (1913). He also made the first feature-length comedy, ***Tillie's Punctured Romance*** (1914), starring Marie Dressler and Charlie Chaplin.

The four giants of American silent film comedy – Chaplin, Buster Keaton, Harold Lloyd, and Harry Langdon – all emerged from one- or two-reelers to make features in the 1920s. Whereas Chaplin was cocky, Keaton stoical, and Lloyd foolhardy, Langdon cultivated the character of what writer and film critic James Agee called "an elderly baby". With his white moon face and innocent, morose demeanour, he seldom instigated any of the chaos around him. Lloyd's stunt in ***Safety Last!*** (1923), in which he hung precariously on the side of a skyscraper, introduced a comedy of cheap thrills. Although he is now best known for his daredevil feats, only five of the 300 films Lloyd made contain such scenes.

Charlie, The Little Tramp, struggles to survive, in one of Chaplin's best-loved shorts, ***A Dog's Life*** (1918).

The Keystone Kops, a famous slapstick troupe, pose for the camera in 1912. Many famous faces started their careers in the Kops, including Fatty Arbuckle (far right).

Film poster, 1978

Visual gags

Although the coming of sound diminished slapstick comedy, the tradition of visual gags was continued by the teams of Stan Laurel and Oliver Hardy in the 1930s, Bud Abbott and Lou Costello in the 1940s, and Dean Martin and Jerry Lewis in the 1950s. Peter Sellers fell about as the maladroit Inspector Clouseau in Blake Edwards' *Pink Panther* series, first made in the 1960s. In France, the pratfall tradition was carried on by Jacques Tati, Pierre Etaix, and Louis De Funes; and in Italy by Toto. More recent examples include the ***Police Academy*** films of the 1980s, Jim Carrey in ***Ace Ventura Pet Detective*** and ***The Mask*** (both 1994), and the "gross out" comedies of the Farrelly Brothers, such as *There's Something About Mary* (1998).

The birth of the wisecrack

The leading exponent of the wisecracking comedies that inevitably came with the talkies was the bibulous irascible, raspy-voiced W.C. Fields, two of his best films being ***The Bank Dick*** (1940) and ***Never Give a Sucker an Even Break*** (1941). Fields co-starred with Mae West in ***My Little Chickadee*** (1940), a spoof Western, in which they exploited their unique comic personae. West, with her ample hourglass figure, was a sashaying parody of a sex symbol and the mistress of sexual innuendo, and one of the few comediennes to make it big in the movies. Her racy wisecracks in *She Done Him Wrong* and *I'm No Angel* (both 1933) resulted in the formation of the Motion Picture Production Code. West responded by resorting to double-entendre to make her comedy a little less direct.

The Marx Brothers broke into cinema in 1929 with ***The Cocoanuts***, but they had been performing on stage long before that. Four of the brothers – Groucho, Harpo, Chico, and Zeppo – had been in vaudeville since childhood, and by the 1920s, had become one of the most popular theatrical acts in the US. Uninhibited and irrepressible, they conveyed a sense of spontaneity as they disrupted everything around them with their unique brand of surreal, madcap humour. Although there were originally five brothers in the act, three soon took centre stage. Groucho's witticisms, Harpo's dumb show, and Chico's massacre of the English language combined several traditions of comedy. An anarchic spoof on warfare, ***Duck Soup*** (1933), directed by Leo McCarey, is considered by many to be their finest picture. ***Love Happy*** (1949) was the last film they worked on together.

Groucho Marx was a potent influence on Woody Allen (see p.182). Another was Bob Hope, who, in 1940, teamed up with Bing Crosby and Dorothy Lamour to make seven hilarious *Road To...* pictures.

Screwball comedy

Screwball comedy was a unique creation of Hollywood in the 1930s. Its main elements were irreverent humour, fast-paced action and dialogue, and eccentric characters – generally the idle rich.

LAUREL AND HARDY

English-born Stan Laurel (1890–1965) and American Oliver Hardy (1892–1957) are the most famous and best-loved comedy team ever. They are at their hilarious best in more than 60 short films that they made together from 1927, such as ***The Music Box*** (1932), in which they try to deliver a piano up a huge flight of stairs. Their bowler hats and suits are symbols of their pretentions to middle-class respectability, but their innocence, Stan's clumsiness, Ollie's delusions of grandeur, and their constant squabbling mark them out as overgrown children.

Stan and Ollie established their complementary characters early on, with Hardy's famous glare at the camera, and baffled Laurel scratching his head and crying.

The improbable plots commonly focused on the battle of the sexes. An archetypal film is Gregory La Cava's ***My Man Godfrey*** (1936), which tells of a man (William Powell) from a shantytown who becomes butler to a wealthy family, straightens out their lives, and marries their scatterbrained daughter (Carole Lombard). Other screwball comedy gems were Frank Capra's ***It Happened One Night*** (1934, the first film to win all five major Oscars), with Claudette Colbert as a runaway heiress and Clark Gable as a hard-boiled reporter; Mitchell Leisen's ***Easy Living*** (1937) and ***Midnight*** (1939); and Leo McCarey's ***The Awful Truth*** (1937). Howard Hawks directed the madcap ***Bringing Up Baby*** (1938) with Cary Grant and Katharine Hepburn – and a leopard in the title role; and the irreverent, fast-paced ***His Girl Friday*** (1940), also starring Cary Grant. Preston Sturges' social comedies continued in a similar vein into the 1940s, but with the advent of World War II, frivolity and social ridicule seemed inappropriate.

The 1950s saw more sophisticated, harder-edged comedies such as Joseph Mankiewicz's ***All About Eve*** (1950) and several Katharine Hepburn–Spencer Tracy films in which they took the battle of the

Film poster, 1933

The Marx Brothers demonstrate their musical skills in an MGM studio publicity still – Harpo on harp, Chico on piano, and Groucho on trombone.

Film poster, 1949

sexes to a new level, particularly in George Cukor's ***Adam's Rib*** (1949). The latter could be seen as a forerunner of the glossy Rock Hudson–Doris Day movies: ***Pillow Talk*** (1959), ***Lover Come Back*** (1961), and ***Send Me No Flowers*** (1964), and other romantic comedies of the 1960s and beyond. The formula for these "rom-coms" (or "chick flicks", as they would be dubbed a few decades later) was"boy meets girl, boy loses girl, boy gets girl". This was a durable formula, as evidenced by later variations, such as Rob Reiner's ***When Harry Met Sally*** (1989), Garry Marshall's ***Pretty Woman*** (1990), Mike Newell's ***Four Weddings and a Funeral*** (1994), James L. Brooks' ***As Good as It Gets*** (1997), and Nancy Meyers' ***Something's Gotta Give*** (2003).

Ealing comedy

Long before British comedies became internationally popular in the 1990s, Britain had made the delightful Ealing comedies from the 1940s to the 1950s. These included Charles Crichton's ***The Lavender Hill Mob*** (1951), and Alexander MacKendrick's ***The Man in the White Suit*** (1951) and ***The Ladykillers*** (1955), all of which starred Alec Guinness. He also played eight different roles in Robert Hamer's ***Kind Hearts and Coronets*** (1949). In 2004, ***The Ladykillers*** was remade by the Coen brothers.

Satire

Parallel to Hollywood romantic comedies were black satires, such as Stanley Kubrick's ***Dr. Strangelove*** (1964) and Robert Altman's ***M*A*S*H*** (1970); the more genial genre spoofs of Mel Brooks' ***Blazing Saddles*** (1974) and ***Young Frankenstein*** (1974); the wacky humour of Jim Abrahams' and the Zucker brothers' ***Airplane!*** (1980) and ***The Naked Gun*** series (1988–91); as well as Mike Myers' deliciously silly ***Austin Powers*** movies (1999–2002) – parodies of the James Bond films.

Although a number of "naughty" French comedies were shown widely in the 1960s, it was ***La Cage aux Folles*** (1978) – Edouard Molinaro's drag queen farce – that broke all box office records in the US for a foreign language film to that date. Hollywood remade it as ***The Birdcage*** (1996), along with a number of other French comedies, such as Coline Serreau's ***Three Men and a Cradle*** (***Trois Hommes et un Couffin***, 1985), which became ***Three Men and a Baby*** (1987). Italian comedy became popular abroad after the success of Mario Monicelli's ***Big Deal on Madonna Street*** (***I Soliti Ignoti***, 1958) about a group of useless crooks trying to carry out a heist. It was remade by Louis Malle in a California setting, as ***Crackers*** (1984), and was the inspiration behind Woody Allen's ***Small Time Crooks*** (2000).

The US comedians that came to the fore in the 1980s and 1990s included Eddie Murphy (***Trading Places***, 1983), Steve Martin (***L.A. Story***, 1991), and Jim Carrey (***The Cable Guy***, 1996). Each, in their own way, continued the genre and displayed a flair for broad, visual comedy rather than elegant, verbal wit.

Michel Serrault camps it up in *La Cage aux Folles* (1978), a French farce set in St Tropez, which was transplanted to Miami in the remake, *The Birdcage* (1996).

WHAT TO WATCH

The General (Clyde Bruckman and Buster Keaton, US, 1927)
Duck Soup (Leo McCarey, US, 1933)
His Girl Friday (Howard Hawks, US, 1940)
The Ladykillers (Alexander Mackendrick, UK, 1955)
The Pink Panther (Blake Edwards, US, 1963)
Annie Hall (Woody Allen, US, 1977)
Airplane! (Jim Abrahams, David Zucker, and Jerry Zucker, US, 1980)
Four Weddings and a Funeral (Mike Newell, UK, 1994)
The Full Monty (Peter Cattaneo, UK, 1997)
Meet the Parents (Jay Roach, US, 2000)
Bridget Jones's Diary (Sharon Maguire, UK, 2001)
The Devil Wears Prada (David Frankel, US, 2006)

Costume Drama

The classic costume drama, or period piece, derives from literary sources. The best examples of the genre are typified by lavish costumes and design that succeed in capturing, in meticulous detail, the ambience of the particular era in which they are set.

Becky Sharp (1935) was the first Technicolor feature film and the sixth adaptation of William Makepeace Thackeray's novel *Vanity Fair*. The most visually striking moment in the film was the ball scene, which showed off the women's gorgeous gowns and the soldiers' red uniforms to great effect. Technicolor and costume dramas were made for each other, but the marriage was only consummated in 1939 with ***Gone With the Wind***.

In 1938, Bette Davis had won the Best Actress Oscar for her performance as the spoiled Southern belle Julie Marsden in William Wyler's ***Jezebel*** (1938), set in pre-Civil War New Orleans. In one scene, Davis arrives at a ball – at which unmarried girls traditionally wear white – dressed in a scarlet gown, to scandalize the assembled company. The impact of this single splash of colour was brilliantly suggested by Ernest Haller's black-and-white photography.

« **Reese Witherspoon** as Becky Sharp in Mira Nair's 2004 adaptation of William Makepeace Thackeray's ***Vanity Fair***.

Melodrama

Gainsborough Pictures in England made a series of melodramatic period pieces in the 1940s with Margaret Lockwood, James Mason, Phyllis Calvert, and Stewart Granger. Examples include Leslie Arliss' ***The Man in Grey*** (1943) and ***The Wicked Lady*** (1945). Two decades later, Tony Richardson's bawdy Oscar-winning version of Henry Fielding's *Tom Jones* (1963) captured a similar spirit. In the 1980s, James Ivory made refined costume dramas, adapted from the novels of Henry James and E.M. Forster.

WHAT TO WATCH

- ***Jezebel*** (William Wyler, US, 1938)
- ***Les Enfants du Paradis*** (Marcel Carné, France, 1945)
- ***Senso*** (Luchino Visconti, Italy, 1954)
- ***Barry Lyndon*** (Stanley Kubrick, UK, 1975)
- ***Dangerous Liaisons*** (Stephen Frears, US, 1988)
- ***Howards End*** (James Ivory, UK, 1992)
- ***Sense and Sensibility*** (Ang Lee, UK/US, 1995)
- ***Bright Star*** (Jane Campion, Various, 2009)

Across the world

Unusually, Martin Scorsese entered Ivory territory with ***The Age of Innocence*** (1993). Other leading directors who made rare ventures into the genre were Stanley Kubrick with ***Barry Lyndon*** (1975); Ingmar Bergman with ***Fanny and Alexander*** (1982); Peter Greenaway with ***The Draughtsman's Contract*** (1982); Stephen Frears with ***Dangerous Liaisons*** (1988); and Mike Leigh with ***Topsy-Turvy*** (1999). In Italy, Luchino Visconti made two historical romances: ***Senso*** (1954) and ***The Leopard*** (1963). In the 1990s, France turned out a string of them, including Jean-Paul Rappeneau's ***Cyrano de Bergerac*** (1990) and ***The Horseman on the Roof*** (1995), and Patrice Chéreau's ***La Reine Margot*** (1994).

Jane Austen mania

The 1990s saw a renewed interest in Jane Austen. Roger Michell's ***Persuasion*** (1995), Ang Lee's ***Sense and Sensibility*** (1995), Douglas McGrath's ***Emma*** (1996), Patricia Rozema's ***Mansfield Park*** (1999), and Joe Wright's ***Pride & Prejudice*** (2005) were made, as well as an Indianized version, Gurinder Chadha's ***Bride & Prejudice*** (2004).

Cult

The term "cult movie" denotes any film that, for a reason unallied to its intrinsic artistic quality, has attracted obsessive devotion from a group of fans. The expression "so bad it's good" is often used to describe many cult movies.

In the final scene of *The Wicker Man* (1973), police sergeant Howie, played by Edward Woodward, is dragged inside the wicker statue of a man and set on fire, as a ritual sacrifice.

Considered one of the worst film directors of all time, Edward D. Wood has gathered a cult following. So cheap were Wood's films that the spaceships in *Plan 9 from Outer Space* (1958) were represented by spinning hubcaps and paper plates.

Reefer Madness (1936) was a propaganda film made by a religious group to warn of the dangers of marijuana. The movie follows a group of dope peddlers who turn clean-cut teenagers into raving lunatics by giving them a puff of "the demon weed". *Reefer Madness* remained in obscurity for nearly 40 years until its re-release in 1972. It became a camp hit, especially among the pot-smoking youth – the very people it had aimed to alarm.

The Rocky Horror Picture Show (1975), combining the conventions of science fiction, horror movies, and musicals, with elements of transvestism and homosexuality, attracted fans, dressed as characters from the film, to midnight screenings. Russ Meyer's "nudie-cutie" films also gained a cult following, especially *Faster, Pussycat! Kill! Kill!* (1965).

The poster for *Attack of the 50ft. Woman* (1958) shows Allison Hayes turned into a giant; she wreaks havoc and eventually crushes her cheating husband to death.

Gaining more of a following among gay audiences was John Waters' *Pink Flamingos* (1972), starring drag superstar Divine.

Cultists revel in films with ludicrous titles, such as *Santa Claus Conquers the Martians* (1964) or *Attack of the 50ft. Woman* (1958). A more mainstream film would occasionally catch people's imagination, such as Rob Reiner's *This Is Spinal Tap* (1984) and Bruce Robinson's acidly witty *Withnail and I* (1987).

WHAT TO WATCH

- *Plan 9 from Outer Space* (Edward D. Wood, US, 1958)
- *Faster, Pussycat! Kill! Kill!* (Russ Meyer, US, 1965)
- *Pink Flamingos* (John Waters, US, 1972)
- *The Wicker Man* (Robin Hardy, UK, 1973)
- *The Rocky Horror Picture Show* (Jim Sharman, UK, 1975)
- *Withnail and I* (Bruce Robinson, UK, 1987)
- *Fight Club* (David Fincher, US/Germany, 1999)

Disaster

The heyday of the disaster movie was the 1970s, the decade in which this sub-genre of action movies reached its zenith. A string of films were released, featuring stellar casts threatened by earthquakes, sinking ships, fires, air crashes, tidal waves, and other catastrophes.

The success of ***Airport*** (1970) – in which an airliner comes under a bomb threat – spawned three sequels and the spoof ***Airplane!*** (1980). It also initiated a cycle of disaster movies that included ***Earthquake*** (1974), a film made in Sensurround, a process that gave audiences the sensation of a minor tremor at certain climactic moments.

Taking advantage of this vicarious enjoyment of others in peril and of the latest special effects was producer Irwin Allen, dubbed "The Master of Disaster". He produced ***The Poseidon Adventure*** (1972), in which Gene Hackman, Shelley Winters, and Ernest Borgnine, among others, try to escape from a capsized luxury liner; and ***The Towering Inferno*** (1974), in which Paul Newman and Steve McQueen battle to rescue people from a burning 138-storey hotel.

These films actually formed part of a second wave of disaster movies. The first included ***San Francisco*** (1936), ***In Old Chicago*** (1937), and ***The Rains Came*** (1939) – an earthquake, a fire, and a flood feature as the respective climaxes of each movie – unlike the films of the 1970s, where the disasters were central to the plot. The genre faded after Allen followed his triumphs with the risible ***The Swarm*** (1978), in which Michael Caine battles killer bees, and ***Beyond The Poseidon Adventure*** (1979), featuring Caine again, now trying to loot the ship.

There was a revival of disaster movies in the mid-1990s with ***Independence Day*** (1996), ***Titanic*** (1997), ***Armageddon*** (1998), and ***The Day After Tomorrow*** (2004), all benefitting from the arrival of computer-generated imagery (CGI).

WHAT TO WATCH

Airport (George Seaton, US, 1970)

The Poseidon Adventure (Ronald Neame, US, 1972)

The Towering Inferno (John Guillermin, US, 1974)

Independence Day (Roland Emmerich, US, 1996)

Titanic (James Cameron, US, 1997)

Jake Gyllenhaal stars in ***The Day After Tomorrow*** (2004), Roland Emmerich's big-budget warning about the effects of global warming on the planet.

Documentary

The documentary, or non-fiction film, goes back to the very beginning of cinema history. Since undergoing a renaissance and becoming more popular than ever at the beginning of the 21st century, the genre could be considered the most enduring of all film forms.

Man with a Movie Camera (1929), Dziga Vertov's experimental film, portrays life in the former Soviet Union.

John Grierson, the leading force behind the British documentary movement in the 1930s, defined this type of film as "the creative treatment of actuality".

Documentaries dominated cinema in its early years, but after 1908, they became secondary to fiction films. It was not until immediately after the Russian Revolution (1917) that they began to be taken more seriously, when propaganda pictures were sent across the vast country on "agitprop" (agitation and propaganda) trains to educate the masses about Communism. Film-maker Dziga Vertov edited a series of "agitprop" films called ***Kino-Pravda*** (Cinema Truth) between 1922 and 1925. These were created from newsreel sequences to which he added slow or reverse motion, animation, texts, and still photographs.

In contrast to the didactic Russian films were American Robert Flaherty's ethnological documentaries, such as ***Nanook of the North*** (1922). The future directors of ***King Kong*** (1933), Merian C. Cooper and Ernest B. Schoedsack, directed two exotic adventure-travel movies: ***Grass*** (1925), following the people of a Persian tribe during their annual migration, and ***Chang*** (1927), the story of a Thai family's struggle to survive life with a herd of elephants. In Germany, Walter Ruttmann's ***Berlin: Symphony of a Great City*** (1927), an impressionistic view of a day in the German capital, was shot using cameras hidden in a removal van and in suitcases, to catch people unawares. Vertov used all the techniques of the cinema at his disposal to make ***Man with a Movie Camera*** (1929), a filmed poem of a Soviet city. These experimental movies were part of an effort to distance documentaries from the style of fiction films.

Impoverished fisherman Colman "Tiger" King and his family struggle to survive in Robert J. Flaherty's ***Man of Aran*** (1934).

Social comment

In Western Europe and the US, documentaries highlighted social and environmental problems. In the UK, the Crown Film Unit developed under Grierson, who believed that cinema should have a social purpose. The unit produced some of the most outstanding documentaries of the 1930s, including Alberto Cavalcanti's ***Coal Face*** (1935); and Basil Wright and Harry Watt's ***Night Mail*** (1936), both of which included W.H. Auden's verse and Benjamin Britten's music.

In the US, Pare Lorentz's ***The River*** (1938) showed the effects of soil erosion in the Mississippi Basin. The film won the Best Documentary award at the Venice Film Festival, beating Leni Riefenstahl's ***Olympia*** (1938), a movie about the 1936 Berlin Olympics. Dutch-born Joris Ivens' ***The Spanish Earth*** (1937), with narration written and spoken by Ernest Hemingway, was one of the several films that supported the Republican cause during the Spanish Civil War (1936–39). The outbreak of World War II took both fiction and documentary film-makers, on both sides, into the field of propaganda. The end of the war saw a drop in the output of documentary films in the West. Firstly, they had become too closely associated with wartime propaganda, and secondly, television documentaries were gaining prominence. It took more than 15 years for the crisis to pass.

WHAT TO WATCH

Man with a Movie Camera (Dziga Vertov, USSR, 1929)

Night and Fog (Alain Resnais, France, 1955)

Don't Look Back (D.A. Pennebaker, US, 1967)

The Sorrow and the Pity (Marcel Ophüls, France, 1969)

Bowling for Columbine (Michael Moore, US, 2002)

Capturing the Friedmans (Andrew Jarecki, US, 2003)

The Story of the Weeping Camel (Byambasuren Dava and Luigi Falorini, Germany, 2003)

March of the Penguins (Luc Jacquet, France, 2005)

An Inconvenient Truth (Davis Guggenheim, US, 2006)

Films of truth

In late 1950s England, Free Cinema – a movement that began with a series of shorts describing mostly working-class people and places – launched the careers of Lindsay Anderson, Tony Richardson, and Karel Reisz. In France, Alain Resnais' career began with several remarkable short art films, including ***Van Gogh*** (1948), ***Guernica*** (1950), and ***Night and Fog*** (1955), a devastating documentary about Nazi concentration camps. Georges Franju's powerful ***Blood of the Beasts*** (***Le Sang des Bêtes***, 1949) showed the daily slaughter of animals in an abattoir juxtaposed with everyday life in Paris. Other film-makers who have contributed to the *cinéma verité* (the cinema of truth) movement include Chris Marker and Jean Rouch. The latter held that the camera's intervention stimulated people to greater spontaneity.

In the US, Direct Cinema was developed in the early 1960s, by a group of film-makers, notably Richard Leacock, D.A. Pennebaker, and the Maysles brothers, Albert and David. Like *cinéma verité* film-makers, exponents of Direct Cinema also believed that the camera should unobtrusively record the "truth".

Fred Wiseman, a leading exponent of Direct Cinema, eavesdropped on many institutions in films such as ***High School*** (1968), ***Juvenile Court*** (1973), and ***Welfare*** (1975). Pennebaker's ***Don't Look Back*** (1967) – a behind-the-scenes look at Bob Dylan's British concert tour – started a trend for "rockumentaries". In this vein, Michael Wadleigh's ***Woodstock*** (1970) stands out, and won the Oscar for Best Documentary Feature.

Reportage

From the late 1960s, there was a gradual move away from *cinéma verité* and the recording of reality, towards historical reporting and investigative exposés. These included Marcel Ophüls' four-and-half-hour ***The Sorrow and the Pity*** (1969), which builds up a complex picture of France under the Occupation. Ophüls' ***Hotel Terminus: The Life and Times of Klaus Barbie*** (1988) was a disturbing portrait of the "Butcher of Lyon", while Claude Lanzmann's ***Shoah*** (1985) gave an insight into the Holocaust. Errol Morris' investigation into a 1976 murder, ***The Thin Blue Line*** (1988), helped free an innocent man from death row, and his ***Fog of War*** (2003) put in the confessional the man who was the US Defence Secretary during the Vietnam conflict. No less serious were Michael Moore's examinations of America's dark side: ***Roger and Me*** (1989), ***Bowling for Columbine*** (2002), and ***Fahrenheit 9/11*** (2004).

Documentaries now compete with fiction films at the box office. ***Être et Avoir*** (2002), the story of an inspirational rural school teacher in France; ***Spellbound*** (2002), about children competing in the US National Spelling Bee; and ***Super Size Me*** (2004), Morgan Spurlock's take on fast-food and obesity in the US, were all international commercial hits.

March of the Penguins (2005), a nature documentary from France, portrays the annual journey of emperor penguins across Antarctica.

Nicolas Philibert's *Être et Avoir* (2002) is a delightful portrait of George Lopez, a dedicated rural schoolmaster. He is seen here with the impish Jojo.

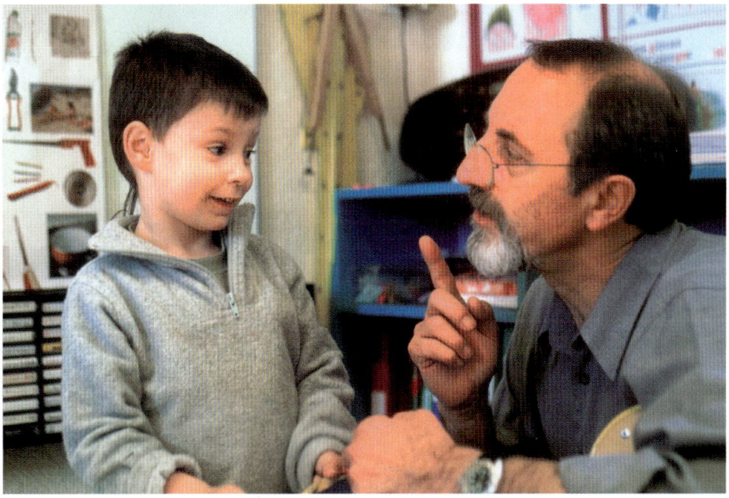

Epic

Narratives in the epic tradition surpass the ordinary in scale and reach heroic proportions. This applies to the film genre too. Epic movies typically feature vast panoramas, with hundreds of extras, and are likely to be historical or Biblical stories containing spectacular scenes.

The first film to be worthy of the title of epic was *Cabiria* (1914), a huge spectacle made in Italy. It followed the adventures of a slave girl during the Second Punic War in about 200BCE. Its great success in America inspired D.W. Griffith to embark on his large-scale productions – *The Birth of a Nation* (1915) and *Intolerance* (1916). However, it was Cecil B. DeMille who became most associated with epics, with a series of films that started with *The Ten Commandments* (1923), and went on to his 1956 remake of the same film. Fred Niblo's *Ben-Hur* (1925) featured a spectacular sea battle and a breathtaking chariot race (replicated in William Wyler's 1959 version of the film).

Politics and epics

Sometimes, epic films had a topicality. In the USSR, Sergei Eisenstein and Dmitri Vasilyev's *Alexander Nevsky* (1938), made under threat of Nazi invasion, told of how the hero defended Holy Russia in the 13th century against brutal Teutons. The film inspired Laurence Olivier's *Henry V* (1944), made when Britain was preparing to launch an invasion of German-occupied France.

In the 1940s, MGM head Dore Schary was eager to adapt Henryk Sienkiewicz's novel about Roman dictator Nero to film. He wanted to equate Nero with modern dictators. However, the hit US$8-million movie *Quo Vadis* was not made until 1951.

In the celebrated 20-minute chariot race in *Ben-Hur* (1959), 8,000 extras watched Charlton Heston in the title role, on an 18-acre set.

Akira Kurosawa's epic *Kagemusha* (1980) follows a thief who poses as a clan leader to confuse his enemy. It was the most expensive Japanese movie of the time.

Filling the screen

It was apt that the first feature film in CinemaScope (see p.34) was ***The Robe*** (1953), a Biblical epic that began a renaissance of epics that filled the vast screen. Among the biggest and best were Howard Hawks' ***Land of the Pharaohs*** (1955), King Vidor's ***War and Peace*** (1956), Stanley Kubrick's ***Spartacus*** (1960), and Anthony Mann's ***El Cid*** (1961). From 1958, Italy made several "sword and sandal" movies with famous bodybuilders, such as Steve Reeves, who played Hercules and other mythological heroes.

WHAT TO WATCH

- *The Birth of a Nation* (D.W.Griffith, US, 1915)
- *Alexander Nevsky* (Sergei M. Eisenstein and Dmitri Vasilyev, USSR, 1938)
- *The Robe* (Henry Koster, US, 1953)
- *The Ten Commandments* (Cecil B. DeMille, US, 1956)
- *Ben-Hur* (William Wyler, US, 1959)
- *Spartacus* (Stanley Kubrick, US, 1960)
- *Doctor Zhivago* (David Lean, US, 1965)
- *Gladiator* (Ridley Scott, US, 2000)
- *Kingdom of Heaven* (Ridley Scott, Various, 2005)

Epic costs

At a cost of around US$40 million, ***Cleopatra*** (1963) took more than four years to shoot in Rome, nearly bankrupting Twentieth Century Fox in the process. Yet studios were still willing to invest in epics. Director David Lean made the leap from small black-and-white British pictures to long, lavish films, such as ***Doctor Zhivago*** (1965). Akira Kurosawa's impressive ***Kagemusha*** (1980) was completed only with the assistance of his American producers. Michael Cimino's ***Heaven's Gate*** (1980) was the biggest flop of all time, costing United Artists US$44 million and earning only US$1.5 million at the box office. A new cycle of epics kicked off with Mel Gibson's ***Braveheart*** (1995), and continued with Ridley Scott's ***Gladiator*** (2000) starring Russell Crowe and Wolfgang Petersen's ***Troy*** (2004) with Brad Pitt, both of which included computer-generated effects.

Cleopatra (1963) was panned by the critics and avoided by film-goers, but made its money back.

Film Noir

"Film noir" is a term that French film critics originally applied to the dark, doom-laden, black-and-white Hollywood crime dramas of the 1940s – such as ***The Maltese Falcon*** (1941) – which were seen in French cinemas for the first time after World War II.

The roots of film noir can be seen in the German expressionist films of the 1920s and 1930s, such as Robert Wiene's ***The Cabinet of Dr. Caligari*** (1920) and Fritz Lang's ***M*** (1931). The style and subject matter were also influenced by certain French films of the 1930s, including Jean Renoir's ***La Chienne*** (1931) and ***La Bête Humaine*** (1938). Both were remade by Fritz Lang as noirs in Hollywood, as ***Scarlet Street*** (1945) and ***Human Desire*** (1954) respectively.

Noir in American society

The low-key lighting, off-centre camera angles, and shadowy, claustrophobic atmosphere were imported to the US by emigré film-makers, such as Lang, Robert Siodmak (***Phantom Lady***, 1944), Jacques Tourneur (***Out of the Past***, 1947), Otto Preminger (***Fallen Angel***, 1945), Billy Wilder (***Double Indemnity***, 1944), and Edgar Ulmer (***Detour***, 1945), all of whom made some of the best film noirs. The style may have originated in Europe, but the subject matter was found in urban America and was inspired by hard-boiled crime writers, including James M. Cain, Raymond Chandler, Dashiell Hammett, and Cornell Woolrich.

Jane Greer plays a *femme fatale* who has caught Robert Mitchum in her web in ***Out of the Past*** (1947), which was released in the UK as ***Build My Gallows High***.

WHAT TO WATCH

- ***Double Indemnity*** (Billy Wilder, US, 1944)
- ***Fallen Angel*** (Otto Preminger, US, 1945)
- ***The Big Sleep*** (Howard Hawks, US, 1946)
- ***Kiss Me Deadly*** (Robert Aldrich, US, 1955)
- ***Touch of Evil*** (Orson Welles, US, 1958)
- ***Chinatown*** (Roman Polanski, US, 1974)
- ***L.A. Confidential*** (Curtis Hanson, US, 1997)
- ***Sin City*** (Frank Miller and Robert Rodriguez, US, 2005)

CHIAROSCURO

The word *chiaroscuro* comes from the Italian *chiaro* (bright) and *oscuro* (dark). It was first used to refer to the use of light and shade in paintings. The bold contrast between light and shade in cinematography gave film noirs their look and atmosphere. The effect is seen here in a scene from *The Killers* (1946), featuring Burt Lancaster and Ava Gardner.

Robert Siodmak's *The Killers* (1946) was partly based on a short story by Ernest Hemingway. Burt Lancaster made his screen debut in the film, as Ole "Swede" Andersen.

Film noir developed during and after World War II, in the context of post-war anxiety and cynicism. The almost exclusively male anti-heroes of the genre, many of whom were private eyes, shared this malaise. They were disillusioned loners roaming through dark alleyways, rundown hotels, cheerless bars, and gaudy nightclubs. The detectives, the police, and the villains were all as corrupt and mercenary as each other.

Hard-boiled anti-heroes

Alan Ladd made a name for himself as the baby-faced killer in *This Gun for Hire* (1942), his first film opposite vampish Veronica Lake. The couple teamed up again in *The Glass Key* (1942), based on Dashiell Hammett's novel, and *The Blue Dahlia* (1946), scripted by Raymond Chandler. Chandler's cynical private eye, Philip Marlowe, was portrayed most memorably by Humphrey Bogart in Howard Hawks' *The Big Sleep* (1946).

Chandler also co-wrote the script for *Double Indemnity*, the archetypal noir, in which an insurance salesman (Fred MacMurray) is led into fraud and murder by the amoral and seductive Barbara Stanwyck. Many film noirs centre around a weak man whose life is ruined when he gets caught in a web of passion, deceit, and murder, by a beautiful and charming – but unscrupulous and double-dealing – *femme fatale*.

Film poster, 1944

Post-noir and neo-noir

By the early 1950s, the classic period of film noir had ended, but there were isolated examples of the genre still being made, such as Robert Aldrich's *Kiss Me Deadly* (1955) and Orson Welles' *Touch of Evil* (1958).

In the 1960s, Jean-Pierre Melville kept film noir alive in France with his crime thrillers. Some years later, a number of post- and neo-noirs appeared in the US.

Notable among these were Robert Altman's *The Long Goodbye* (1973); Roman Polanski's *Chinatown* (1974); Lawrence Kasdan's *Body Heat* (1981); the Coen brothers' *Blood Simple* (1984); and Curtis Hanson's *L.A. Confidential* (1997). All of these movies paid homage to film noirs of the past.

Clive Owen (left) roughs up Benicio Del Toro in *Sin City* (2005).

Gangster

The gangster movie came into being as a distinct genre in Prohibition America of the 1920s, when alcohol was banned and racketeers flourished. The crime films of the late 1920s and 1930s were updated to dramatic effect in the mob movies of the 1970s and 1990s.

Film poster, 1931

Although the gangster film came into its own only after the introduction of sound – guns blazing, cars screeching, and fast-paced, tough, and slangy dialogue – urban crime had provided material for this genre from film's earliest days. One of the first was D.W. Griffith's 17-minute ***The Musketeers of Pig Alley*** (1912), set in a New York slum. Raoul Walsh, a former assistant to Griffith, made his first feature film ***Regeneration*** (1915), about a New York street gang. Later, in Germany, Fritz Lang's ***Dr. Mabuse The Gambler*** (1922), about a master criminal who tries to take over the world, portended the coming of Hitler. The first true gangster films, however, were Josef von Sternberg's ***Underworld*** (1927, with George Bancroft); and Lewis Milestone's ***The Racket*** (1928), both of which dealt with organized crime. Sternberg followed up with two more crime films starring Bancroft – ***The Dragnet*** (1928) and ***Thunderbolt*** (1929), his first film with sound. Rouben Mamoulian's ***City Streets*** (1931), with Gary Cooper, featured the first sound flashback.

New realism

It was the cycle of gangster movies produced by Warner Bros. that achieved a new realism. Some were based on real incidents and living hoodlums. Mervyn LeRoy's ***Little Caesar*** (1931), depicting the rise and fall of a gang boss, was closely modelled on Al Capone. The final line, "Mother of Mercy, is this the end of Rico?" spoken by the dying Edward G. Robinson, was just the beginning of a Hollywood crime wave – 50 gangster movies were made in 1931 alone. ***Little Caesar*** made Robinson a star. James Cagney achieved the same status for William Wellman's ***Public Enemy*** (1931), which includes the celebrated scene in which Cagney shoves half a grapefruit into Mae Clarke's face.

There were complaints that these films endowed gangsters with a certain kind of glamour. When Howard Hawks' ***Scarface*** (1932) was released, it immediately ran into trouble with the censors. Some of the violent scenes had to be cut and the subtitle "Shame of the Nation" added. One of the great classics of the genre, ***Scarface*** starred Paul Muni as a brutish, childish, and arrogant racketeer. Brian De Palma directed a violent remake in 1983.

In 1934, the puritanical Production Code was enforced, stating that "crime will be shown to be wrong and that the criminal life will be loathed and that the law will at all times prevail". Villains could no longer be protagonists. Gangster films were, however, Hollywood's most profitable movies. So the studios switched to making law enforcement officers the heroes. Cagney and Robinson changed sides, though the movies were still about gangsters, and no less violent.

William Wyler's ***Dead End*** (1937) and Michael Curtiz's ***Angels With Dirty Faces*** (1938) showed just what a bad influence a gangster can have on children. The stars of these films, Humphrey Bogart and James Cagney, faced each other in Raoul Walsh's ***The Roaring Twenties*** (1939), the documentary-style culmination of the Hollywood gangster cycle.

James Cagney stars as "Rocky" Sullivan, a hoodlum who proves to be a bad influence on the Dead End Kids in *Angels With Dirty Faces* (1938).

The end of the era

World War II saw the demise of the gangster movie, which reappeared in the 1940s in the guise of film noir (see pp.98–99). Henry Hathaway's ***Kiss of Death*** (1947) introduced Richard Widmark to the screen as a giggling psychopathic killer. Walsh and Cagney

Joe Pesci (centre left) plays a brutal gangster in Martin Scorsese's ***GoodFellas*** (1990). His ruthlessness impresses small-time crook Ray Liotta (left).

were reunited in ***White Heat*** (1949), in which the latter played a murderer with a mother complex. Roger Corman picked up the genre in the late 1950s and 1960s with ***Machine-Gun Kelly*** (1958), starring Charles Bronson; and ***The St. Valentine's Day Massacre*** (1967). In France, Jacques Becker's influential ***Hands off the Loot!*** (***Touchez pas au Grisbi***, 1954), starring the magisterial Jean Gabin in the role of an ageing gangster, was a precursor to Jean-Pierre Melville's crime dramas of the 1960s. In 1960, both Jean-Luc Godard and François Truffaut paid homage to the American gangster picture, in ***Breathless*** (***A bout de souffle***) and ***Shoot the Pianist*** respectively.

Akira Kurosawa did the same in Japan with two adaptations of Ed McBain cop novels: ***The Bad Sleep Well*** (1960) and ***High and Low*** (1963). There were also the *yakuza* (Japanese organized crime) films, such as Seijun Suzuki's ***Tokyo Drifter*** (1966), Kinji Fukasaku's ***Battles Without Honour and Humanity*** (1973), and Takeshi Kitano's ***Fireworks*** (***Hana-Bi***, 1997).

In the US, Arthur Penn's ***Bonnie and Clyde*** (1967) and Francis Ford Coppola's ***The Godfather*** (1972) gave a new direction to the genre, while ***Mean Streets*** (1973), featuring a group of small-town hoods, established Martin Scorsese's reputation. Scorsese went on to make ***GoodFellas*** (1990), ***Casino*** (1995), and ***Gangs of New York*** (2002); the last had street gang warfare in 19th-century New York as its subject.

Other directors – Sergio Leone (***Once Upon a Time in America***, 1984), Warren Beatty (***Bugsy***, 1991), and the Coen brothers (***Miller's Crossing***, 1990) – made successful gangster films; in the UK, Guy Ritchie started a trend of British crime movies with ***Lock, Stock and Two Smoking Barrels*** (1998). Quentin Tarantino made the most impact on the genre, with ***Reservoir Dogs*** (1992) and ***Pulp Fiction*** (1994). Both recalled early Warner Bros. heist classics such as John Huston's ***The Asphalt Jungle*** (1950).

WHAT TO WATCH

- ***Little Caesar*** (Mervyn Leroy, US, 1931)
- ***Public Enemy*** (William Wellman, US, 1931)
- ***Angels With Dirty Faces*** (Michael Curtiz, US, 1938)
- ***Bonnie and Clyde*** (Arthur Penn, US, 1967)
- ***The Godfather*** (Francis Ford Coppola, US, 1972)
- ***GoodFellas*** (Martin Scorsese, US, 1990)
- ***Pulp Fiction*** (Quentin Tarantino, US, 1994)
- ***Snatch*** (Guy Ritchie, UK, 2000)
- ***Gangs of New York*** (Martin Scorsese, US, 2002)
- ***Road to Perdition*** (Sam Mendes, US, 2002)

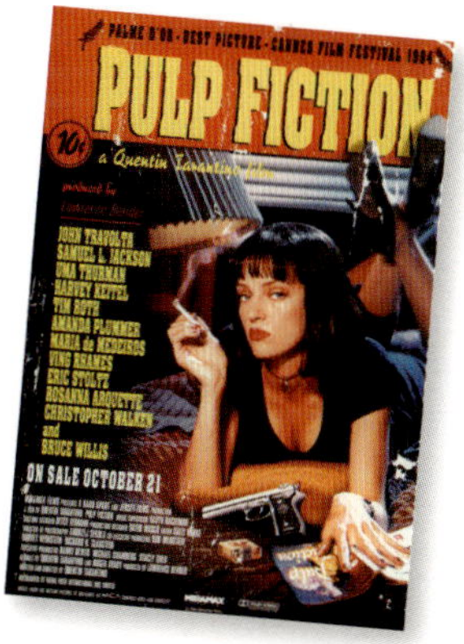

Film poster, 1994

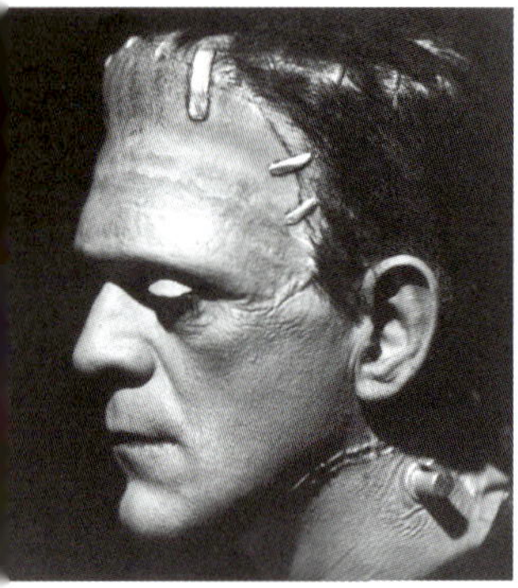

Boris Karloff stars as the monster in James Whale's *Frankenstein* (1931), a performance that was both touching and poetic. The striking make-up was devised by Jack Pierce.

Horror

Horror movies tap into our deepest fears and anxieties, and what is suggested is often more frightening than what is revealed. The German expressionist films of the 1920s, influenced by the English Gothic novel, were among the first examples of the genre.

The high watermark of Hollywood horror was the 1930s. The films of the period were informed by a crystallization of influences, which included Mary Shelley's *Frankenstein*, Bram Stoker's *Dracula*, and Robert Louis Stevenson's *Dr. Jekyll and Mr. Hyde*; German expressionist films like ***The Cabinet of Dr. Caligari*** (1920) and ***Nosferatu*** (1922); and the emigration of European film-makers to Hollywood from the mid-1920s. However, the two most influential films (both 1931) were directed by an American, Tod Browning, and an Englishman, James Whale. Browning's ***Dracula***, featuring Bela Lugosi's chilling performance, and Whale's ***Frankenstein***, with Boris Karloff, set the style for a cycle of horror films, mainly from Universal Studios.

Classic chillers

Browning had previously made eight horror movies with Lon Chaney. Whale was to contribute two more classic horrors to the genre: ***The Old Dark House*** (1932) and ***The Bride of Frankenstein*** (1935). The former was another strand of the horror genre – the haunted-house movie, one of the first being ***The Cat and The Canary*** (1927), directed by German-born Paul Leni. Universal also created a new creature in ***The Werewolf of London*** (1935) and ***The Wolf Man*** (1941), the latter with the hulking Lon Chaney Jr., who was to reprise the role three more times.

WHAT TO WATCH

- ***Nosferatu*** (F.W. Murnau, Germany, 1922)
- ***The Bride of Frankenstein*** (James Whale, US, 1935)
- ***Cat People*** (Jacques Tourneur, US, 1942)
- ***The Night of the Living Dead*** (George A. Romero, US, 1968)
- ***The Exorcist*** (William Friedkin, US, 1973)
- ***Halloween*** (John Carpenter, US, 1978)
- ***Ring*** **(*Ringu*)** (Hideo Nakata, Japan, 1998)
- ***The Blair Witch Project*** (Daniel Myrick and Eduardo Sánchez, US, 1999)

Arguably the best of the ***Dr. Jekyll and Mr. Hyde*** films was Rouben Mamoulian's 1931 version (the fifth) starring Fredric March. The next year also saw the release of Danish Carl Dreyer's ***Vampyr***, which had an eerie, dream-like quality.

During the 1940s, the real horrors of World War II made monster movies seem innocuous in comparison. The chillers produced by Val Lewton at RKO relied on a suggestion of horror

rather than its depiction. Each scene in Jacques Tourneur's ***Cat People*** (1942) and ***I Walked with a Zombie*** (1943), and Mark Robson's ***The Seventh Victim*** (1943) was invested with an underlying fear of the supernatural.

Misako Uno (left) is haunted by a spirit (Takako Fuji), in director Takashi Shimizu's ***The Grudge 2*** (2006).

Low-budget scares

In the 1950s and 1960s, Britain's Hammer Studios brought all the notorious monsters back to life in gory Technicolor. They made stars of Christopher Lee and Peter Cushing in a number of ***Dracula*** and ***Frankenstein*** films. Also in England in the 1960s, Roger Corman produced a series of garish adaptations of Edgar Allen Poe's short stories, most of which featured Vincent Price's ghoulish hamming. Following Corman's low-budget independent example was George A. Romero, whose horror movies were full of slavering zombies, from ***Night of the Living Dead*** (1968) to ***Land of the Dead*** (2005). In the 1960s and 1970s, Italy also produced a stream of startling, baroque horror flicks directed by Mario Bava and Dario Argento.

The 1970s saw a number of gory horror films, including Tobe Hooper's exploitative ***The Texas Chainsaw Massacre*** (1974) and William Friedkin's hit, ***The Exorcist*** (1973). John Carpenter's ***Halloween*** (1978), Sean Cunningham's ***Friday the 13th*** (1980), and Wes Craven's ***A Nightmare on Elm Street*** (1984), all featured terrorized teens and spawned endless sequels, which were invariably inferior. ***The Blair Witch Project*** (1999) showed what could be achieved with a tiny budget. The protagonists of the movie filmed on two video cameras as if it were a real documentary (see p.55).

The one country that has produced more horror films than any other is Japan, which has almost redefined the genre. The most successful of Japanese horror films was Hideo Nakata's ***Ring*** (***Ringu***, 1998), about a video tape that shocks to death those who watch it. The film was remade in the US in 2002 as ***The Ring***.

Old favourites, such as ***The Mummy***, which first terrified film-goers in 1932, continue to be revisited. The 1999 version of the film benefits from the use of CGI technology.

Frances Dee features in Jacques Tourneur's ***I Walked with a Zombie*** (1943), an example of RKO's horror output of the 1940s. The atmosphere and lighting of the movie contributed greatly to its disturbing tone.

Film poster, 1931

Martial Arts

The popularity of martial arts movies grew in the early 1970s due to the West's growing interest in Eastern philosophy and the star presence of Bruce Lee. In recent years, the genre has been rediscovered through films such as ***Hero*** (2002).

Jackie Chan, a fan of both Buster Keaton and Bruce Lee, successfully combines physical comedy with action.

Martial arts movies typically include a series of brilliantly choreographed fights in which the protagonist is outnumbered by enemies armed with knives or clubs, and defeats them with his or her bare hands. The plots are usually simple affairs of good versus evil.

The most well-known actor in this field was Bruce Lee, whose reputation is based on only four films – *Fists of Fury* (1971); *The Chinese Connection* (1972); *The Way of the Dragon* (1972), which he wrote and directed himself; and *Enter the Dragon* (1973), in which he and two others manage to free hundreds of prisoners from an island fortress over which an evil warlord holds sway. *Enter the Dragon* was Lee's last completed film, before his mysterious death at the age of 32. It was given the Hollywood treatment and made a fortune for Warner Bros.

From the 1980s, a plethora of martial arts movies appeared, such as John G. Avildsen's *The Karate Kid* (1984), and those with Jean-Claude Van Damme ("the muscles from Brussels"), Chuck Norris, Steven Seagal, and Jackie Chan, whose comic take on the genre earned him the nickname "the Buster Keaton of kung fu". Jet Li, often called Bruce Lee's true successor, began a new wave of kung fu movies in China in the 1990s, such as *Once Upon a Time in China* (1991), directed by Tsui Hark.

WHAT TO WATCH

- *Fists of Fury* (Wei Lo, Hong Kong, 1971)
- *The Chinese Connection* (Wei Lo, Hong Kong, 1972)
- *Enter the Dragon* (Robert Clouse, Hong Kong/US, 1973)
- *The Karate Kid* (John G. Avildsen, US, 1984)
- *Once Upon a Time in China* (Tsui Hark, Hong Kong, 1991)
- *Crouching Tiger, Hidden Dragon* (Ang Lee, Taiwan/Hong Kong/US, 2000)
- *Hero* (Zhang Yimou, China/Hong Kong, 2002)

The martial arts movie *Crouching Tiger, Hidden Dragon* (2000), with its outstanding special effects, became the highest grossing foreign-language film ever released in America.

Bruce Lee prepares for action in *Enter the Dragon* (1973), which was the first American-produced martial arts film. It made a legend of Lee and inspired a generation of film-makers.

Melodrama

In between the male-oriented war films, Westerns, and action movies that Hollywood turned out in the 1930s and 1940s, there was "the woman's picture" or melodrama. The genre continued successfully into the 1950s and 1960s, with a slightly more feminist slant.

The term "melodrama" is often used to refer to Hollywood tearjerkers whose plots revolve around a woman who is the victim of adultery, unrequited love, or a family tragedy. The heroine goes on to overcome these difficulties or, at least, learns to cope with them. British dramas were often too restrained to become melodramas, though David Lean's heart-breaking ***Brief Encounter*** (1945), about an illicit, seemingly unconsummated affair, comes close.

Among the American directors who instigated these high-class soap operas were Frank Borzage, Edmund Goulding, and John M. Stahl. Borzage's forte was sentimental romance, especially with the sweet and innocent-looking Janet Gaynor (***Seventh Heaven***, 1927; ***Street Angel***, 1928) and the delicate, tragic Margaret Sullavan in four movies, including ***Little Man, What Now?*** (1934), about young lovers fighting against adversity.

Goulding, at Warner Bros., provided Bette Davis with some of her best and most typical melodramas, including ***Dark Victory*** (1939), in which she goes blind before dying radiantly. Stahl pulled out all the stops for ***Leave Her to Heaven*** (1945), a lurid tale of a woman (Gene Tierney) whose jealousy ruins all those around her. He also directed three elegant "weepies": ***Magnificent Obsession*** (1935), ***Imitation of Life*** (1934), and ***When Tomorrow Comes*** (1939), all remade (the latter as ***Interlude***, 1957) by Douglas Sirk, whose films of the 1950s are considered the peak of Hollywood melodrama.

WHAT TO WATCH

- *Imitation of Life* (John M. Stahl, US, 1934)
- *Stella Dallas* (King Vidor, US,1937)
- *Now, Voyager* (Irving Rapper, US, 1942)
- *Mildred Pierce* (Michael Curtiz, US, 1945)
- *Brief Encounter* (David Lean, UK, 1945)
- *The Life of Oharu* (Kenji Mizoguchi, Japan, 1952)

Trevor Howard bids Celia Johnson goodbye on the platform where they first met, in David Lean's ***Brief Encounter*** (1945), written by Noël Coward.

Directors Rainer Werner Fassbinder (Germany) and Pedro Almodóvar (Spain) both embraced the flamboyant style and plot absurdities of the Sirkian soaps, while commenting on them. In 2002, Todd Haynes made the perfect Sirk pastiche, ***Far from Heaven***.

Many of these melodramas depended on the leading lady. Barbara Stanwyck (King Vidor's ***Stella Dallas***, 1937), Bette Davis (Irving Rapper's ***Now, Voyager***, 1942), and Joan Crawford (Michael Curtiz's ***Mildred Pierce***, 1945) reigned supreme among the soap queens, all three sacrificing themselves for others in the films mentioned and in many others. While India (Nargis Dutt), France (Arletty), Greece (Melina Mercouri), and Italy (Anna Magnani) all produced their own stars, arguably the greatest actress in the melodrama genre was Kinuyo Tanaka of Japan. She featured in 14 of Kenji Mizoguchi's films, including ***The Life of Oharu*** (1952) and ***Sansho, the Bailiff*** (1954) – period films that transcended the genre.

Film poster, 1939

Musical

Born with the coming of sound, the movie musical had its base in vaudeville and opera. With its brazen blending of fantasy and reality, the musical provided audiences with an accessible and immediate escape from life, first in the Great Depression, and then beyond.

Dance director Busby Berkeley's water sprites perform *By a Waterfall*, a typically extravagant number from the film *Footlight Parade* (1933).

In *The Pirate* (1948), Judy Garland says, "I know there is a real world and a dream world and I shan't confuse them". However, that is exactly what this and other musicals set out to do, and this unreality gave directors, cameramen, and designers the most creative scope within the commercial structure of Hollywood. Musicals could also circumvent censorship more easily than other genres. Scantily dressed women and sexual innuendo went almost unnoticed by the censors when within the seemingly harmless confines of the musical. The studio system of the 1930s,1940s, and 1950s enabled these lavish dreams to take shape. Each major studio stamped its product with distinguishing aesthetic trademarks, emphasized by their own particular stars, dance directors, designers, and orchestrators.

European style

In the late 1920s and early 1930s, European artists and technicians flooded Hollywood, bringing with them a cosmopolitan style and approach. Their music-theatre background was opera and operetta. They knew little of the American tradition of vaudeville, the inspiration behind so many "backstage" musicals; and they did not perceive America as a glamorous enough setting for musical comedy.

Paris was the glittering backdrop of three musicals that German-born Ernst Lubitsch made for Paramount – the most European of the studios – which starred Jeanette MacDonald and Maurice Chevalier. Chevalier's Gallic charm and MacDonald's Anglo-Saxon reserve and self-mockery made a seductive, piquant combination. *The Love Parade* (1929), with its lavish settings, songs integrated into the scenario, and sexual innuendo, set a pattern for screen operettas. At MGM, Lubitsch directed Chevalier and MacDonald again in *The Merry Widow* (1934), while Russian-born Rouben Mamoulian directed the duo in the witty and stylish *Love Me Tonight* (1932).

Backstage musicals

Coming from the American vaudeville tradition, *The Broadway Melody* (1929) pioneered the backstage musical, which was to dominate the genre, on and off, for decades to come. It was also the first all-talking, all-singing, all-dancing movie, and the first film with sound to win an Oscar for Best Picture. The plots of backstage musicals revolved around the problems of putting on a show. They followed the auditions, the rehearsals, the bickering, the wisecracking chorus girls, the out-of-town tryouts, the financial difficulties, and the final, spectacular production, which often featured a youngster taking over the lead at the last moment and achieving instant stardom. Unlike in operettas, people only sang and danced within the confines of the show. Another formula was to dispense with plot altogether in favour of a string of statically filmed numbers. The first of these was ***The Hollywood Revue of 1929*** (1929), in which Arthur Freed and Nacio Herb Brown's song, *Singin' in the Rain*, was first heard.

MGM paid three extravagant tributes to Broadway impresario Florenz Ziegfeld: ***The Great Ziegfeld*** (1936), which features a gigantic revolving wedding cake; ***Ziegfeld Girl*** (1941), which, with clever editing, shows Judy Garland on top of the same cake; and ***Ziegfeld Follies*** (1946), which featured MGM's biggest stars of the period, including Fred Astaire and Gene Kelly.

Lucille Ball, bedecked in plumes of feathers, cracks a whip at a posse of girls dressed as black cats, performing a feline dance in ***Ziegfeld Follies*** (1946).

The cast of *On the Town* (1949) included Frank Sinatra and Gene Kelly.

Great dancers

Astaire has been the greatest dancer in the history of cinema so far. He remains unsurpassed in invention, virtuosity, and elegance. Although he tried various cinematic forms, they never hindered the purity of his dancing, either solo or with his many dancing partners, the most famous of whom was Ginger Rogers. The two first teamed up in ***Flying Down to Rio*** (1933), after which they danced together through eight more RKO musicals – all light-hearted comedies of errors set against sophisticated, cosmopolitan settings – till 1939. Astaire then moved with ease into MGM's Technicolor musicals.

Cyd Charisse plays the tantalizing gangster's moll and Fred Astaire is a private eye in the *Girl Hunt* ballet from ***The Band Wagon*** (1953).

As a dancer, choreographer, and director, Gene Kelly became one of the most creative forces in the 1950s, the heyday of the musical. He experimented with slow motion, multiple images, animation, and trick photography to extend the appeal of dancing. He showed off his varied dancing skills in the 18-minute ballet that ends Vincente Minnelli's ***An American in Paris*** (1951) and in the exuberant title number of ***Singin' in the Rain*** (1952), a film that was co-directed by Kelly and Stanley Donen.

What distinguished the films that burst forth from MGM by directors such as Donen, Kelly, and Minnelli was the integration of musical numbers into the film's narrative theme. In these features, song, dance, and music no longer punctuated the story, but actually worked to advance the plot. Minnelli's sumptuous ***Gigi*** (1958) was among the very last musicals especially written for the screen, apart from the stream of colourful Elvis Presley vehicles in the 1960s.

Screen adaptations

In the early days of the musical, studios lavished fortunes on celluloid versions of Broadway shows in the hope of repeating their success, but these bore little resemblance to the stage originals.

More faithful adaptations began in 1950, with MGM's ***Annie Get Your Gun***. ***Guys and Dolls*** (1955), ***Oklahoma!*** (1955), ***The King and I*** (1956), ***South Pacific*** (1958); and in the 1960s, ***West Side Story*** (1961), ***My Fair Lady*** (1964), and ***The Sound of Music*** (1965) followed. However, after ***Hello, Dolly*** (1969) flopped, the musical – like the Western – became a rare phenomenon. The genre saw a limited revival in the 1970s, with Bob Fosse's ***Cabaret*** (1972), which captured the essence of Berlin in the early 1930s, and ***Saturday Night Fever*** (1977) and ***Grease*** (1978), the films in which John Travolta made his name.

Musicals abroad

The Hollywood musical had some influence on the few notable musicals made outside the US. In the Soviet Union in the 1930s, Grigori Aleksandrov made four Hollywood-style musicals, the best known being ***Jazz Comedy*** (1934). Jacques Demy's ***The Young Girls of Rochefort*** (1967) was a direct nod to the MGM musical – Gene Kelly was persuaded to feature – but his ***The Umbrellas of Cherbourg*** (1964), in which all the dialogue was sung, was intrinsically French.

Until the mid-1960s, British musicals were mostly genteel affairs that had little impact outside the UK. That changed with US-born Richard Lester's Beatles' films – ***A Hard Day's Night*** (1964) and ***Help!*** (1965) – followed by Carol Reed's Oscar-winning ***Oliver!*** (1968), Ken Russell's ***The Boy Friend*** (1971), and Alan Parker's ***Bugsy Malone*** (1976). Other examples were few and far between until Parker's ***Evita*** (1996). Interest in the American musical was retained in Baz Luhrmann's visually extravagant ***Moulin Rouge*** (2001) and in further reproductions of Broadway hits, such as Rob Marshall's ***Chicago*** (2002) and Susan Stroman's ***The Producers*** (2005). Sadly, musicals written directly for the screen, which made it a cinematic genre independent of the theatre, have become almost obsolete.

WHAT TO WATCH

- ***Le Million*** (René Clair, France, 1931)
- ***42nd Street*** (Lloyd Bacon, US, 1933)
- ***The Merry Widow*** (Ernst Lubitsch, US, 1934)
- ***Top Hat*** (Mark Sandrich, US, 1935)
- ***Meet Me in St. Louis*** (Vincente Minnelli, US, 1944)
- ***Singin' in the Rain*** (Gene Kelly, Stanley Donen, US, 1952)
- ***Gigi*** (Vincente Minnelli, US, 1958)
- ***West Side Story*** (Robert Wise, Jerome Robbins, US, 1961)
- ***Cabaret*** (Bob Fosse, US, 1972)
- ***Grease*** (Randal Kleiser, US, 1978)
- ***Dirty Dancing*** (Emile Ardolina, US, 1987)
- ***Moulin Rouge!*** (Baz Luhrmann, Australia/US, 2001)
- ***Hairspray*** (Adam Shankman, US/UK, 2007)

Catherine Zeta Jones plays murderous, vampish flapper Velma Kelly in Rob Marshall's *Chicago* (2002), an adaptation of Bob Fosse's jazz-stage Broadway musical.

Propaganda

Produced with the intention of persuading viewers of a particular belief or ideology, propaganda films have been used by governments around the world since the early 20th century. Though documentary is the most popular form, drama is also used to convey a "message".

Westfront 1918 (1930), directed by G.W. Pabst, focuses on the lives of four World War I soldiers. The film highlights the reality of life at the front.

The manipulative power of film was recognized from the earliest days of cinema; part of its effectiveness came from the mistaken belief that the camera cannot lie. Propaganda films came of age during World War I, when every major belligerent power commissioned official films showing its enemy in an unfavourable light.

Film poster, 1943

Political aims

Vladimir Lenin, the head of the Soviet state, realized at the beginning of the Russian Revolution of 1917 that film was the most important of all the arts because it could educate the masses – many of whom were illiterate – to support Bolshevik aims. Almost all the great silent Soviet films of the 1920s, by Sergei Eisenstein, V.I. Pudovkin, and Alexander Dovzhenko, as well as Dziga Vertov's *Kino-Pravda* (literally Cinematic Truth) newsreels (see p.94), were made for propaganda purposes. At the same time, the films were revolutionary in form. Between the wars, many British documentaries, such as *Housing Problems* (1935), explored social evils. In the US, the state tried to sell the New Deal – the reform of the economy during the Great Depression – to the public with Pare Lorentz's *The Plow that Broke the Plains* (1936). In Germany, *Kuhle Wampe* (1932), directed by Slatan Dudow, focused on the effects of unemployment, while G.W. Pabst's *Westfront 1918* (1930) showed the horror of life in the trenches.

> "Cinema is **not an extension** of revolutionary action. Cinema is and must be **revolutionary action in itself**."

Cuban film-maker Santiago Álvarez

Film poster, 1967

However, after the Nazis took over the film industry in 1934, anti-Semitic films serving the government's policies became *de rigueur*. ***The Triumph of the Will*** (1935), Leni Riefenstahl's documentary film of the Nuremberg Rally of 1934, earned her the reputation of being Germany's foremost ideological propagandist.

World War II and beyond

During World War II, British director Humphrey Jennings made documentaries about the effect of the war on ordinary people. His ***London Can Take It!*** (1940) and ***Listen To Britain*** (1942) did much to influence public opinion in America. When the US entered the war in 1941, a stream of anti-Nazi dramas were produced, with titles such as ***Hitler's Madman*** (Douglas Sirk, 1943) and ***Hitler's Children*** (Edward Dmytryk, 1943). Tarzan, Sherlock Holmes, and even Donald Duck (who appeared in Walt Disney's ***Der Fuehrer's Face***, 1943) were recruited into battle against the enemy. Frank Capra, John Huston, William Wellman, William Wyler, and John Ford served in the American Office of War Information, and contributed to the war effort, significantly in Capra's ***Why We Fight*** (1942–45). During the Cold War, the US Information Service's anti-Soviet documentaries, and the crude fiction films that replaced Nazis with Communists, had little effect in the liberal climate of the 1960s and 1970s. Some of the most effective propaganda films were, in fact, anti-American, such as ***Hanoi, Tuesday 13th*** (1967), a short by Santiago Álvarez.

WHAT TO WATCH

The Triumph of the Will
(Leni Riefenstahl, Germany, 1935)

The Plow that Broke the Plains
(Pare Lorentz, US, 1936)

Der Fuehrer's Face
(Jack Kinney, US,1943)

In *To Whom Does the World Belong?* (1932), children from Berlin's tent city look up to see an unemployed young man about to throw himself off a building. The film was banned by the Nazis.

Science Fiction and Fantasy

In science fiction and fantasy films, imaginary worlds and scenarios are constructed – often with the aid of special effects – to enable the improbable to become possible. Themes within these films include alien life forms, space and time travel, and futuristic technology.

» **Johnny Depp** plays a naive man-made boy in ***Edward Scissorhands*** (1990), Tim Burton's tragi-comic satire, hatched from an idea that the director had as a child.

Jean Cocteau, who directed the magical ***Beauty and the Beast*** (***La Belle et la Bête***, 1946), said that "the cinema is a dream we all dream at the same time". This is especially true of science fiction (sci-fi) and fantasy films. Victor Fleming's ***The Wizard of Oz*** (1939) separates reality and fantasy by showing Dorothy's dream domain in glorious Technicolor and her home in monochrome. Fantasy adventures go beyond the limitations of our minds to an imagined, but not always preferable, world. Similarly, the worlds that science fiction creates are often warped.

Many fantasy adventures are about displacement, where characters find themselves in a strange, sometimes hostile environment. Examples include Nicolas Roeg's ***The Man Who Fell to Earth*** (1976), Steven Spielberg's ***E.T.: The Extra-Terrestrial*** (1982), Tim Burton's ***Edward Scissorhands*** (1990), and the ***Chronicles of Narnia*** series (2005–).

» **In *The Wizard of Oz*** (1939) – an Academy award-winning movie – Dorothy embarks upon a journey with the Scarecrow, Tinman, and Lion, during which they encounter the Wicked Witch of the West.

Early sci-fi

Audiences still delight in films from the pre-digital days of cinema. The space travel genre was started by George Méliès' ***A Trip to the Moon*** (1902), based on Jules Verne's story (see p.14). Méliès went on to film more of Verne's visionary novels, many of which – such as *Twenty Thousand Leagues Under the Sea* and *A Journey to the Centre of the Earth* – were filmed and refilmed over the years.

Russian cinema's first venture into the territory of science fiction was Yakov Protazanov's ***Aelita*** (1924), a comedy-drama featuring two Russians who land on Mars and organize a Soviet-style revolution against the autocratic Queen Aelita. However, it would be many years before Russia returned to the genre, with Andrei Tarkovsky's ***Solaris*** (1972) and ***Stalker*** (1979), both of which are technologically convincing despite having minimal special effects. In France, René Clair's first film, ***The Crazy Ray*** (1923), tells of a mad scientist who, with the aid of a magic ray (an effect created with stop-motion photography), causes people to freeze in different positions. After the influential ***Metropolis*** (1927), Fritz Lang embarked on ***The Woman in the Moon*** (1929), about a scientist who believes the moon is rich in gold and tries to corner the market. Raoul Walsh's ***The Thief of Bagdad*** (1924), starring Douglas Fairbanks, set new Hollywood standards for special effects that still astonish, despite Alexander Korda's impressive 1940 Technicolor remake. Fairbanks climbs a magic rope, braves the Valley of Monsters, and sails over rooftops on a magic carpet.

Sci-fi writers

The 1930s and 1940s were not very rich in science fiction or fantasy movies. However, there were three superlative adaptations of H.G. Wells novels: James Whale's ***The Invisible Man*** (1933), in which Claude Rains made his first screen (dis)appearance;

William Cameron Menzies' ***Things to Come*** (1936), about an apocalyptic world war; and Lothar Mendes' ***The Man Who Could Work Miracles*** (1936), in which the gods grant a clerk the power to do what he wishes. Wells also provided the source material for ***The War of the Worlds*** (1953) – remade by Spielberg in 2005 – and ***The Time Machine*** (1960). Both were produced by Hungarian-born special effects expert George Pal, whose ***Destination Moon*** (1950) began a stream of Hollywood sci-fi movies in the 1950s.

WHAT TO WATCH

- ***Metropolis*** (Fritz Lang, Germany, 1927)
- ***The Wizard of Oz*** (Victor Fleming, US, 1939)
- ***The Time Machine*** (George Pal, US, 1960)
- ***2001: A Space Odyssey*** (Stanley Kubrick, US)
- ***Solaris*** (Andrei Tarkovsky, Russia, 1972)
- ***Star Wars*** (George Lucas, US, 1977)
- ***The Matrix*** (Larry and Andy Wachowski, US, 1999)
- ***Avatar*** (James Cameron, US, 2009)
- ***Inception*** (Christopher Nolan, US, 2010)

Robert Wise's ***The Day the Earth Stood Still*** (1951), an anti-war sci-fi classic, features an alien who warns that unless nuclear weapons are destroyed, his race will annihilate Earth.

Unlike the low-budget sci-fi that dominated the 1950s, Stanley Kubrick's ***2001: A Space Odyssey*** (1968) revolutionized space travel films with its technology. The screenplay by Arthur C. Clarke was adapted from one of his own short stories. Other science fiction writers whose novels have been adapted to film include Ray Bradbury (***Fahrenheit 451***, 1966), Stanislaw Lem (***Solaris***, 1972), and Isaac Asimov (***I, Robot***, 2004). Many of the novels and short stories of Philip K. Dick have also been made into films, including ***Blade Runner*** (1982), ***Minority Report*** (2002), and ***The Adjustment Bureau*** (2011).

Time travel became popular in the 1980s with Terry Gilliam's ***Time Bandits*** (1981) – the first in a fantasy trilogy with ***Brazil*** (1985) and ***The Adventures of Baron Munchausen*** (1988); James Cameron's ***The Terminator*** series (1984); and Robert Zemeckis's ***Back to the Future*** (1985). These films became paradigms for future sci-fi and fantasy movies.

Film poster, 1956

The T-1000 terminator (Robert Patrick) is sent from the future to assasinate John Connor, the leader of the future human resistance in ***Terminator 2: Judgment Day*** (1991).

Jedi Padawan Obi-Wan Kenobi and Jar Jar Binx undertake a voyage to meet Queen Amidala in *Star Wars: Episode I - The Phantom Menace* (1999).

Monster movies

In Japan, a decade after the horrors of Hiroshima and Nagasaki, ***Godzilla*** (1954) was the first of a series of Godzilla movies, in which many of the creatures were the result of nuclear radiation. The films were influenced by ***The Beast from 20,000 Fathoms*** (1953), about a dinosaur revived by an atomic blast; countless imitations followed. The monster was animated by Ray Harryhausen, the most celebrated of all special effects (SFX, see p.72) men, whose crowning achievement was Don Chaffey's ***Jason and the Argonauts*** (1963).

Special effects

To quote the motto of the ***Star Trek*** series, sci-fi and fantasy films "boldly go where no man has gone before" and so, are more reliant on special effects than any other genre. With ***Star Wars*** (1977), the art of special effects entered a new age. Computer-generated imagery (CGI) soon dominated most American blockbusters of this genre from the 1980s, often becoming their *raison d'être*. Ironically, the Wachowski brothers' ***The Matrix*** (1999), which depended heavily on CGI, is a cautionary tale about computers taking over the world. Steven Spielberg made magic with ***Jurassic Park*** (1993), in which a wealthy entrepreneur secretly builds a theme park on a remote island, featuring living dinosaurs created from prehistoric DNA. James Cameron effectively used CGI in immersive 3-D technology to transport the audience to Pandora, an exotic alien world, in his Oscar-winning movie ***Avatar*** (2009).

Jake Sully (Sam Worthington) plays a paraplegic marine sent on a mission to the moon Pandora in James Cameron's *Avatar* (2009). The movie won Oscars for Best Art Direction, Cinematography, and Visual Effects.

Serial

The serial was a multi-episode, usually action-adventure, film. It was shown in cinemas in weekly instalments and each chapter ended on a cliffhanger. It is the only obsolete cinematic genre, though some of its features are evident in television soap operas and mini-series.

From the earliest days of film, serials were an important ingredient of cinema programmes. ***The Adventures of Kathlyn*** (1913) was the first true serial, but a year later, its director Louis Gasnier caused a sensation with ***The Perils of Pauline*** (1914), starring the most famous "serial queen", Pearl White. She played the title character and endured all sorts of indignities from villains, such as being tied to a railway line.

In France, Louis Feuillade was directing serials such as ***Fantômas*** (1913–14), the story of a master criminal. His greatest triumph was ***Les Vampires*** (1915–16), which had a dream-like quality admired by general public and surrealists alike. In Germany, Fritz Lang made his reputation with ***The Spiders*** (1919–20), featuring the use of mirrors, hypnosis, underground chambers, and arch criminals.

In the US, 28 serials were made in 1920 alone. With the coming of sound, the main studios started producing serials of better quality. These included Universal's ***Flash Gordon*** (from 1936) with Larry "Buster" Crabbe in the title role, battling his nemesis Ming the Merciless (Charles Middleton). It was the most expensive serial ever made – at US$350,000, three times the average serial budget. Crabbe also starred in ***Buck Rogers Conquers the Universe*** (1939).

Other hit serials of the 1930s were ***Dick Tracy***, ***Zorro***, ***The Lone Ranger***, and ***Hawk of the Wilderness***. During World War II, ***Captain America***, ***Superman***, and ***Batman*** all faced German or Japanese villains. In the 1950s, mainly due to the advent of television, the production of serials began to diminish. The Western serial ***Blazing the Overland Trail*** (1956) was the last ever produced.

WHAT TO WATCH

The Perils of Pauline (Louis Gasnier, US, 1914)

Flash Gordon (Frederick Stephani, US, 1936)

The Lone Ranger (John English and William Witney, US, 1938)

"Buster" Crabbe's most famous role was as Flash Gordon, whose adventures in outer space thrilled audiences through three serials in 1936, 1938, and 1940.

Series

Series may be sequels (*The Godfather: Part II*), prequels (the *Star Wars* saga), or films with different plots but the same characters (the *Indiana Jones* cycle). The convention of putting numerals after film titles, as in *Spider-Man 2* (2004), did not begin until the 1970s.

Harrison Ford (right) as the eponymous hero and his archeologist father, Sean Connery, are bound together, in Steven Spielberg's *Indiana Jones and the Last Crusade* (1989), Jones' third adventure.

Before the 1970s, feature film sequels were rare, yet favourite characters kept on reappearing in numerous films. One of the first was Tarzan, who initially swung into view in 1918, played by Elmo Lincoln in *Tarzan of the Apes*. Several other silent Tarzans appeared before Johnny Weissmuller's famous yodelling call was heard in *Tarzan the Ape Man* (1932). Weissmuller, a former US Olympic swimming champion, went on to make 19 Tarzan movies over the next 16 years.

Series made up a significant part of Hollywood's B picture output from the 1930s. Among the longest running were *Andy Hardy* (1938–58), *Sherlock Holmes* (1939–46), *Dr. Kildare* (1938–47), *Charlie Chan* (1931–49), and various movies featuring a gang of lovable juvenile delinquents: *The Dead End Kids*, *The East Side Kids*, and *The Bowery Boys* (1938–58). Notable series from the 1960s onwards included *The Pink Panther* and *Planet of the Apes*.

From Sean Connery to Daniel Craig, actors across the ages have played James Bond.

The French-Italian co-production *Don Camillo* (1951–65), about a parish priest in conflict with a Communist mayor, was a major international hit. In England, the broad *Carry On...* farces ran from 1958–78, while the *James Bond* films began with *Dr. No* in 1962, making it the longest continuing series in the English language. The ingredients of the Bond recipe remain virtually unchanged to this date.

Among the highest grossing series in cinema history are *The Lord of the Rings* (2001–03) and *Harry Potter* (2001–11), both adapted from novels. However, in terms of numbers, the Japanese series *Zatoichi* (1962–2003) remains unbeaten. Its hero – a blind swordsman – featured in 27 films.

WHAT TO WATCH

- *Charlie Chan* (Various, US, 1931-49)
- *Don Camillo* (Various, France/Italy, 1951–65)
- *Zatoichi* (Various, Japan, 1962–2003)
- *James Bond* (Various, UK, 1962–)
- *The Lord of the Rings* (Peter Jackson, New Zealand/US, 2001–03)
- *Harry Potter* (Various, UK/US 2001–11)
- *The Chronicles of Narnia* (Various, UK/US 2005–)

Teen

In the 1950s, producers began to recognize a market for youth-oriented films, the number of which grew steadily until a dramatic increase in the 1980s. Often set in a school, these movies invariably showed teens trying to attract the opposite sex and escape adult control.

Film poster, 1959

Teenagers were usually patronized and ridiculed in films made before the 1950s. An example was the extremely popular ***Andy Hardy*** series of the 1930s and early 1940s, which starred Mickey Rooney as a happy-go-lucky adolescent getting into scrapes.

The growing teen audience of the 1950s began to identify with new stars like Marlon Brando (***The Wild One***, 1953) and James Dean (***Rebel Without a Cause***, 1955). In the next decade, a series of "beach party" movies came out, while Roger Corman's biker and LSD films appealed to a hipper youth audience. In the 1970s, George Lucas' seminal ***American Graffiti*** (1973) sparked off other "rites-of-passage" pictures. Then came the so-called "Brat Pack", a group of young actors associated with the films of writer-director John Hughes, including ***The Breakfast Club*** (1985) and ***Pretty in Pink*** (1986), the latter directed by Howard Deutch.

Although most teen stars fade from view as they (and their fans) mature, a few have gone on to productive careers, including Demi Moore, Rob Lowe, and James Spader. Actors such as Drew Barrymore and Scarlett Johansson have established themselves as true 21st-century stars. However, Miley Cyrus is already beating a path for the next generation...

WHAT TO WATCH

- ***Rebel Without a Cause*** (Nicholas Ray, US, 1955)
- ***American Graffiti*** (George Lucas, US, 1973)
- ***The Breakfast Club*** (John Hughes, US, 1985)
- ***Mean Girls*** (Mark Waters, US, 2004)

Judd Nelson, Emilio Estevez, Ally Sheedy, Molly Ringwald, and Anthony Michael Hall star in John Hughes' Brat Pack flick, ***The Breakfast Club*** (1985).

Thriller

Thrillers are gripping yarns of suspense, in which the tension is created by placing one or more characters in a threatening situation from which they have to escape. This type of film can cross several genres to produce action, science fiction, and even Western thrillers.

Cary Grant is chased by a mysterious, crop-dusting plane that suddenly appears from nowhere, in *North by Northwest* (1959), one of Alfred Hitchcock's most celebrated set pieces.

In *North by Northwest* (1959), Alfred Hitchcock, "The Master of Suspense", perfected one of the fundamental thriller types: the picaresque pursuit. This is usually a mystery, involving spies or terrorists, in which the protagonist is the pursued or the pursuer, attempting to solve a crime or prevent a disaster. Among the number of films that could be called Hitchcockian are Carol Reed's *The Third Man* (1949), Stanley Donen's *Charade* (1963), and *Arabesque* (1966), and several thrillers by Brian De Palma, particularly *Obsession* (1976).

Another Hitchcockian theme is the "woman-in-peril" psychological thriller, as epitomized by *Psycho* (1960). Other potent examples are *Gaslight* (1940 and 1944), in which a man drives his wife slowly insane to gain an inheritance; Anatole Litvak's *Sorry, Wrong Number* (1948), in which an invalid (Barbara Stanwyck) overhears, on the phone, a plot to murder her; Terence Young's *Wait Until Dark* (1967), in which Audrey Hepburn plays a blind woman terrorized by gangsters; and Phillip Noyce's *Dead Calm* (1989), in which Nicole Kidman battles a crazed castaway on a yacht.

Film poster, 1966

The 1970s saw a number of post-Watergate conspiracy thrillers, including Alan Pakula's *The Parallax View* (1974), a no-holds-barred look at a political assassination cover-up. The conspiracy thriller reappeared in the 1990s, with films such as Phillip Noyce's *Patriot Games* (1992) and *Clear and Present Danger* (1994), both of which starred Harrison Ford. It continued with Doug Liman's *The Bourne Identity* (2002) and its sequels, starring Matt Damon, and Fernando Meirelles' *The Constant Gardener* (2005).

WHAT TO WATCH

The Third Man (Carol Reed, UK, 1949)

Psycho (Alfred Hitchcock, US, 1960)

The Silence of the Lambs (Jonathan Demme, US, 1991)

The Constant Gardener (Fernando Meirelles, UK/Germany, 2005)

The Girl Who Played With Fire (Daniel Alfredson, Various, 2009)

Underground

The term "underground" as a film genre originated in the US towards the end of the 1950s. It applied to experimental film-making, which was rooted in the European avant-garde but was strongly connected to the American Beat movement that emerged at the time.

In the 1940s, experimental film-making began in the US, encouraged by European artists and film-makers, including Oskar Fischinger and New York-based Hans Richter and Marcel Duchamp.

Maya Deren's ***Meshes of the Afternoon*** (1943) was one of the first independent underground films. Dealing with a suicide, it is famous for its four-stride sequence: from beach to grass to mud to pavement to rug. In the early 1950s, younger directors like Stan Brakhage emerged, working in a similar mode. Their films are often described as "psychodramas".

In 1955, brothers Jonas and Adolfas Mekas started the magazine *Film Culture,* which was crucial to new American cinema. Jonas Mekas' ***Guns of the Trees*** (1961) was one of several feature-length films inspired by the French New Wave.

Towards the end of 1960, the New American Cinema Group was formed, favouring films that were "rough, unpolished but alive". Like many such films, Jack Smith's ***Flaming Creatures*** (1963) embraced Hollywood even as it defied its narrative traditions by using clips of "tits'n'sand" movies.

The mode for campness was exploited by Andy Warhol in movies such as ***Blow Job*** (1963). A year later, Kenneth Anger's gay biker film ***Scorpio Rising***, starring Nelson Leigh, Ernie Allo, and Bruce Byron, was released, and it became a seminal movie in US underground cinema.

Michael Snow attempted to redefine our way of seeing by exploring new time and space concepts in films such as ***Wavelength*** (1967).

WHAT TO WATCH

Meshes of the Afternoon (Maya Deren, US, 1943)

Wavelength (Michael Snow, Canada/US, 1967)

Flesh (Paul Morrissey, US, 1968)

Maya Deren stars in her own ***Meshes of the Afternoon*** (1943), a study of feminine angst. The film rejects the traditional narrative structure in favour of a dream logic.

Film poster, 1927

War

Battle scenes and war have been the subject of films since the beginning of cinema, but as a genre, war movies came of age during World War I. Often, they take an anti-war stance, but equally, they can be made to stir up popular support and even serve as propaganda.

War films emerged as a major film genre after the outbreak of World War I. The most significant was D.W. Griffith's ***Hearts of the World*** (1918), which used documentary material and a studio reconstruction of a French village occupied by "beastly Huns" led by a ruthless German officer (Erich von Stroheim).

Charlie Chaplin's ***Shoulder Arms*** (1918), set partly in the trenches, was released only a few weeks before the armistice, drawing howls of protest. Yet, it was Chaplin's biggest triumph up to that time, proving that comedy could provide a much-needed release from tragic events.

After the armistice, war films all but ceased. Exceptions included Abel Gance's ***J'Accuse*** (1919), which he described as "a human cry against the bellicose din of armies". Rex Ingram's ***The Four Horsemen of the Apocalypse*** (1921), which made Rudolph Valentino a star, had a strong anti-war message. However, it was also so anti-German that some thought it promoted hatred between nations, and the film was banned in Germany and withdrawn from circulation for years.

War films were revived in the mid-1920s, with King Vidor's ***The Big Parade*** (1925), Raoul Walsh's ***What Price Glory?*** (1926), and William Wellman's ***Wings*** (1927), the first film to win the Best Picture Oscar. When sound was first introduced, cinemas were flooded with war films, and in 1930 alone, there appeared Howard Hawks' ***The Dawn Patrol***, Howard Hughes' ***Hell's Angels***, James Whale's ***Journey's End***, and Lewis Milestone's ***All Quiet on the Western Front***, a portrayal of the German perspective. In Germany itself, G.W. Pabst's ***Westfront 1918*** (1930) depicted the futility of life in the trenches. However, as the memories of the war and the mood of anti-militarism that marked these films began to fade, the subject became less popular. Jean Renoir's ***La Grande Illusion*** (1937), the first war film after some years, was a moving anti-war statement that did not actually include any fighting.

Hawks' ***Sergeant York*** (1941), based on the true story of World War I's most decorated US soldier (played by Oscar winner Gary Cooper), was

A soldier stands in the war cemetery, before the dead of World War I rise up from their graves to accuse the living, in Abel Gance's *J'Accuse* (1919).

WHAT TO WATCH

J'Accuse (Abel Gance, France, 1919)
Paths of Glory (Stanley Kubrick, US, 1957)
Apocalypse Now (Francis Ford Coppola, US, 1979)
Das Boot (Wolfgang Petersen, Germany, 1981)
Full Metal Jacket (Stanley Kubrick, US, 1987)
Saving Private Ryan (Steven Spielberg, US, 1998)
No Man's Land (Danis Tanovic, Bosnia, 2001)
The Hurt Locker (Kathryn Bigelow, US, 2008)

The Hurt Locker (2008), a film about the Iraq War, was directed by Kathryn Bigelow, who made history by becoming the first woman to win an Oscar for Best Director.

intended to inspire American audiences as the country emerged from isolation to join the fight against the Axis powers.

World War II has always been the most popular period for war genre film-makers because the issues seemed more straightforward than in most wars. After the US entered the war, Hollywood turned out a stream of flag-waving action features, as did the UK. British films like Noël Coward's ***In Which We Serve*** (1942) and Carol Reed's ***The Way Ahead*** (1944) were deemed more realistic but more class-conscious than their US counterparts.

Unlike the usual war saga, Wellman's ***The Story of G.I. Joe*** (1945) concentrated on the fatigue and anxiety that the common soldier suffered. The heroics were left to Errol Flynn and John Wayne, who were depicted winning the war almost single-handedly.

After World War II

Post-war films were allowed to be a little more critical of the military establishment. Mark Robson's ***Home of the Brave*** (1949) courageously took on the subject of racism in the US army, while few punches were pulled in ***Attack!*** (1956), Robert Aldrich's powerful indictment of life in the military.

Japan, which had made jingoistic films during the war, now concentrated on pacifist themes. Kon Ichikawa's ***The Burmese Harp*** (1956), is a cry of anguish for the victims of World War II. The next year saw Stanley Kubrick's bitterly ironic and moving World War I drama, ***Paths of Glory***. In contrast, the 1960s saw a number of war epics celebrating Allied victories, such as ***The Longest Day*** (1962), ***The Battle of the Bulge*** (1965), and ***The Battle of Britain*** (1969).

Robert Altman's iconoclastic ***M*A*S*H*** (1970), although set in Korea, was plainly a reference to the Vietnam War. The only US film on the subject made during the Vietnam War was ***The Green Berets*** (1968), a gung-ho action movie starring John Wayne. It was only in the 1970s that this conflict was properly explored in movies. The most effective of these films were Michael Cimino's ***The Deer Hunter*** (1978), Francis Ford Coppola's ***Apocalypse Now*** (1979), Oliver Stone's ***Platoon*** (1986), and Stanley Kubrick's ***Full Metal Jacket*** (1987).

However, film-makers constantly returned to World War II for inspiration. From Germany came Wolfgang Petersen's ***Das Boot*** (1981), which followed the efforts of a U-boat crew to survive; and ***Stalingrad*** (1993). Russia, which had earlier made such remarkable films like Grigori Chukhrai's ***The Ballad of a Soldier*** (1959) and Andrei Tarkovsky's ***Ivan's Childhood*** (1962), continued the tradition with Elem Klimov's powerful ***Come and See*** (1985). In America, there was an 18-year gap between Sam Fuller's tough, symbolic ***The Big Red One*** (1980) and other distinguished World War II dramas, such as Terrence Malick's ***The Thin Red Line*** and Steven Spielberg's ***Saving Private Ryan***, with its 30-minute opening sequence of a soldier's eye view of battle.

The 1991 Gulf War was examined in Edward Zwick's ***Courage Under Fire*** (1996) and David O. Russell's ***Three Kings*** (1999). No matter which conflict is portrayed, the eternal truths of war lend a similarity to all war movies.

Peter Weir's *Gallipolli* (1981) is set during World War I.

Western

The Western is not only the oldest of all film genres, but it is the only home-grown American cinematic form. From the 1920s to the early 1960s, it was the Western's popularity that consolidated Hollywood's dominance in the global film market.

Film poster, 1903

The historical setting of films belonging to this genre is traditionally between the 1850s and the 1890s, a period that saw events such as the gold rushes in California and Dakotas, the American Civil War, the building of the trans-continental railway, the Indian wars, the opening up of the cattle ranges and the subsequent range wars, and the steady spread westwards of homesteaders, farmers, and immigrants. This was also the period that witnessed the virtual extermination of the buffalo and of the majority of the indigenous Native American tribes. However, some Westerns go back to the time of America's colonial era or forward to the mid-20th century. The geographical location is usually west of the Mississippi river, north of the Rio Grande river, and south towards the border with Mexico.

The most fundamental theme of the Western is the civilizing of the wilderness – the taming of nature, lawbreakers, and "savages" (usually Native Americans). Among the iconic elements are remote forts and vast ranches, and the small-town saloon, jail, and main street – where the inevitable showdown between hero and villain takes place. However, many of the best Westerns also have a psychological complexity that stretches beyond the simplistic good versus evil premise, towards the dimensions of Greek tragedy.

The birth of the Western

Before the beginning of cinema in 1895, there were the popular Wild West shows of "Buffalo Bill" Cody, Zane Grey's frontier stories, Owen Wister's *The Virginian* – the first modern Western novel, published in 1902 – and dime novels about the exploits of heroes on both sides of the law: Wyatt Earp, Doc Holliday, Wild Bill Hickok, Calamity Jane, Bat Masterson, the James brothers, and Billy the Kid. As the newspaperman says in John Ford's ***The Man Who Shot Liberty Valance*** (1962), "When the legend becomes fact, print the legend." So by the time of the first narrative screen Western, Edwin S. Porter's ***The Great Train Robbery*** (1903), the legends of the West were already embedded in popular culture.

That ten-minute film launched the career of "Broncho Billy" Anderson, who became the first Western hero. Other stars followed, the most famous being W.S. Hart and Tom Mix. Also in the early 1900s, D.W. Griffith was making Westerns, mainly featuring red devils thirsty for the blood of whites, such as the two-reeler ***The Battle of Elderbush Gulch*** (1913). The next year, Cecil B. DeMille's ***The Squaw Man*** became the first feature shot entirely in Hollywood. More crucial to the growth of the genre was James Cruze's ***The Covered Wagon*** (1923), a two-and-a-half-hour-long reconstruction of one of the greatest 19th-century treks across America. Its success led to an increase in the production of Westerns, and allowed John Ford to make the far superior and longer ***The Iron Horse*** (1924).

WHAT TO WATCH

- ***Stagecoach*** (John Ford, US, 1939)
- ***The Man From Laramie*** (Anthony Mann, US, 1955)
- ***The Searchers*** (John Ford, US, 1956)
- ***The Magnificent Seven*** (John Sturges, US, 1960)
- ***The Man who Shot Liberty Valance*** (John Ford, US, 1962)
- ***The Wild Bunch*** (Sam Peckinpah, US, 1969)
- ***Once Upon a Time in the West*** (Sergio Leone, Italy/US, 1968)
- ***Unforgiven*** (Clint Eastwood, US, 1992)
- ***True Grit*** (Joel and Ethan Coen, US, 2010)

John Ford's *Stagecoach* (1939) was a milestone in the history of the Western and was the first to be shot in Utah's Monument Valley.

Clint Eastwood stars as "Blondie" in ***The Good, the Bad and the Ugly*** (1966), the third and last of Sergio Leone's Spaghetti Westerns in which he starred.

A golden age

Westerns were enhanced by the coming of sound, but the golden age began with John Ford's ***Stagecoach*** (1939), beautifully shot in the now familiar Monument Valley, Utah. It raised the genre to artistic status, stamped Ford as one of the great directors of Westerns, and ensured John Wayne's rise from B-movie obscurity to A-list stardom.

Most of the leading Hollywood directors made Westerns, including German-born Fritz Lang with ***The Return of Frank James*** (1940), ***Western Union*** (1941), and ***Rancho Notorious*** (1952); and Hungarian-born Michael Curtiz with ***Dodge City*** (1939), ***Virginia City*** (1940), and ***Santa Fe Trail*** (1940), all three starring Errol Flynn.

In this rich period, Ford made his resplendent Cavalry trilogy: ***Fort Apache*** (1948), ***She Wore a Yellow Ribbon*** (1949), and ***Rio Grande*** (1950) – romantic visions of the Old West with John Wayne at their centre. Wayne also starred in Howard Hawks' ***Red River*** (1948), in which his muscular macho security was contrasted with Montgomery Clift's nervy angularity, creating a special tension. Hawks went on to make three more fine Westerns with Wayne, the best being ***Rio Bravo*** (1959).

Anthony Mann's five films starred a new, tougher actor, James Stewart. His ***Bend of the River*** (1952) and ***The Man from Laramie*** (1955) were among the most distinguished Westerns of the 1950s. Others include Budd Boetticher's taut Westerns that starred Randolph Scott, including ***Seven Men from Now*** (1956); Henry King's ***The Gunfighter*** (1950); Fred Zinnemann's ***High Noon*** (1952); George Stevens' ***Shane*** (1953); William Wyler's ***The Big Country*** (1958); and Delmer Daves' ***Broken Arrow*** (1950) and Robert Aldrich's ***Apache*** (1954) – two of the few films in which Native Americans were treated sympathetically.

In Howard Hawks' *Red River* (1948), the patriarch (John Wayne) and his adopted son (Montgomery Clift, in his first film) have an uncomfortable relationship.

The decline of the genre

In 1950, Hollywood produced 130 Westerns. A decade later, this was down to 28. There are several explanations for this decline: the increase in Western television series, which replaced the many B-Western features produced for the cinema; the fact that the ideology that formed the Western was becoming outmoded in the new, permissive society; and the rise of the more violent Spaghetti Westerns, which brought stardom for Clint Eastwood. These Italian-produced films were influenced in plot and tone by Japanese samurai films, as was John Sturges' ***The Magnificent Seven*** (1960), a transplanting of Akira Kurosawa's ***Seven Samurai*** (1954).

The genre was kept alive by Sam Peckinpah's nostalgic but harsh views of the Old West and revisionist Westerns such as Arthur Penn's ***Little Big Man*** (1970). However, studios considered the Western a moribund genre, hence Kevin Costner's long battle to make ***Dances with Wolves*** (1990). His patience paid off when it won seven Academy Awards, including Best Picture. Two years later, Clint Eastwood's ***Unforgiven*** also won the Best Picture Oscar. In a modern twist to the genre, the award-winning ***Brokeback Mountain*** (2005) features a ranch hand and a cowboy in love.

Director and star Kevin Costner carries an injured Mary McDonnell in ***Dances with Wolves*** (1990), in which Costner is adopted by a Sioux tribe.

Jake Gyllenhaal and Heath Ledger star in Ang Lee's ***Brokeback Mountain*** (2005), based on E. Annie Proulx's short story.

World **Cinema**

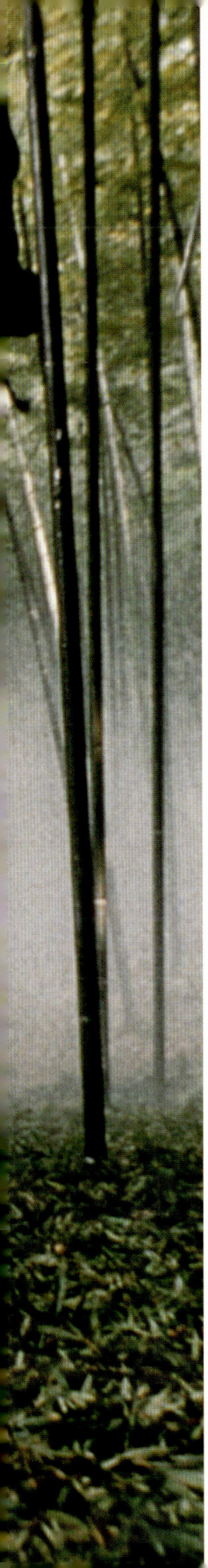

In an age of internationalism, cinema has proved the most global of the arts. As more and more people are visiting the Taj Mahal, the Kremlin, and Mount Fuji, audiences are increasingly appreciative of Indian, Russian, and Japanese films, as well as the rich output of many other countries.

In the 1890s, early cinema came into being almost simultaneously in the US, Great Britain, France, and Germany. Within 20 years, cinema had spread to all parts of the globe, developed a sophisticated technology, and become a major industry. Today, both the sheer diversity of world cinema and the number of films produced is staggering. This chapter attempts to cover as many countries and as many significant films as possible but a book of any size cannot hope to include everything. (The omission of countries, such as the Netherlands and some from South-East Asia, is addressed in this introduction.)

In the 1920s, the general public went to see silent movies from many parts of the world. However, a wider appreciation of world cinema by the West only really began after World War II, when Italian, Japanese, German, and French motion pictures were once more available. The increasing awareness of the quality of these films was aided by the recognition given each year by the Academy of Motion Picture Arts and Sciences. Vittorio De Sica's ***Shoeshine*** (1946) was the first to receive a special award in 1947. In 1956, Federico Fellini's ***La Strada*** (1954) became the first winner of the new Academy Award for the Best Foreign Language (as in non-English language) Film.

In the last few decades, it has gradually become recognized that entertainment is not the preserve of Hollywood. Gangster movies, horror films, whodunits, Westerns, war epics, melodramas, musicals, and love stories are produced all over the globe. A glance at the long list of American remakes of "foreign" films will confirm that Hollywood has drawn inspiration from world cinema. Neither is it one-way traffic. There are the film noirs of Jean-Pierre Melville that are based on the American model, and countless quotes in French New Wave films that come from Hollywood movies. Witness the popularity of Spaghetti Westerns and the influence of US movies on German directors Wim Wenders and Rainer Werner Fassbinder.

From its earliest days, Hollywood has benefited from an influx of gifted stars from abroad. From Sweden came Greta Gustafsson (Garbo) and Ingrid Bergman (mother of Isabella Rossellini). From Germany came Maria Magdelena Von Losch (Marlene Dietrich) and from Austria, Hedy Kiesler

« **Bamboo canes** are chopped down with brilliance to form palisade cages and improvised spears, one of the many dazzling, gravity-defying stunts in Zhang Yimou's ***House of the Flying Daggers*** (2004).

The blind toddler is an orphan girl's child in Kurdish-Iranian Bahman Ghobadi's *Turtles Can Fly* (2004) – a devastating picture of the effects of war (in this case the second Gulf War) on children.

(Hedy Lamarr). Italy gave America Sofia Scicolone (Sophia Loren), while Egypt supplied Michel Shalhoub (Omar Sharif). From Brazil came Maria do Carmo Miranda Da Cunha (Carmen Miranda). Over the last few decades, it has become common for actors, such as Burt Lancaster, Donald Sutherland, Nastassja Kinski, Isabella Rossellini, Gérard Depardieu, Charlotte Rampling, Antonio Banderas, Juliette Binoche, Penelope Cruz, Audrey Tatou, and Jackie Chan, to move with ease between English-speaking and foreign-language films.

Directors, too, brought their expertise to Hollywood, including Victor Sjöström (Sweden), Fritz Lang (Germany), Billy Wilder (Austria), Jean Renoir (France), Miloš Forman (Czechoslovakia) to name but a few. One of the first European directors to have a career on two continents was Louis Malle, who directed ***Atlantic City*** (1980) in the United States and then returned to his native France for ***Au Revoir Les Enfants*** (1987). In recent years, there has been even more cross-fertilization: a New Zealander, Peter Jackson, directed ***The Lord of the Rings*** (2001–03); and a Mexican, Alfonso Cuarón, directed ***Harry Potter and the Prisoner of Azkaban*** (2004). However, the supreme example is Taiwanese-born Ang Lee, who has directed movies that range from typically English (***Sense and Sensibility***, 1995) to Asian (***Crouching Tiger, Hidden Dragon***, 2000), and American (***Brokeback Mountain***, 2005).

Brigitte Lin plays a mysterious drug dealer in Wong Kar Wai's ***Chungking Express*** (1994), which has two unconnected stories set in Hong Kong.

Gael García Bernal plays the young Che Guevara with Roderigo de la Serna as Alberto Granado in Brazilian Walter Salles' film ***The Motorcycle Diaries*** (2004).

Dutch director Paul Verhoeven made successful erotic thrillers, such as ***Spetters*** (1980) and ***The Fourth Man*** (1983), in his homeland, before crossing the Atlantic to make major hits such as ***RoboCop*** (1987), ***Total Recall*** (1990), and ***Basic Instinct*** (1992). Other notable directors to come from the Netherlands were documentary film-makers Joris Ivens and Bert Haantra, and Fons Rademakers, who directed ***The Assault*** (1986) – winner of the Best Foreign Film Oscar. From Belgium came André Delvaux, whose films, which merged dream and reality, put him in the tradition of other Belgian artists like René Magritte. Most conspicuous are the Dardenne brothers, Jean-Pierre (born 1951) and Luc (born 1954), whose international reputation has grown over the years with such realistic dramas as ***The Promise*** (1996), ***Rosetta*** (1999), ***The Son*** (2002), and ***The Child*** (2005).

In South-East Asia, Indonesia is mostly known for popular teenage films and musicals. Since 1998, a new generation of film-makers has emerged that includes as many female as male directors, writers, and producers. The majority of Thai films are made for entertainment, mixing comedy, melodrama, and music. Wisit Sasanatieng's ***Tears of the Black Tiger*** (2000) was a successful pastiche of such genres. Pen-Ek Ratanaruang's musical ***Monrak Transistor*** (2001) was another Thai film that did well internationally, as did the bizarre ***Tropical Malady*** (2004), directed by Apichatpong Weerasethakul. Vietnam's most celebrated director is Tran Anh Hung, whose ***The Scent of Green Papaya*** (1993), ***Cyclo*** (1995), and ***The Vertical Rays of the Sun*** (2000) were released worldwide. In the Philippines, Lino Brocka gained recognition internationally when his films ***Insiang*** (1976), ***Jaguar*** (1979), and ***Bona*** (1980) won acclaim at the Cannes Film Festival.

As a result, it could be said that the centre of film has shifted from its traditional bases in the US and Europe to Asia and beyond.

Aoua Sangare stars in ***Yeleen*** (***Brightness***, 1987), Souleymane Cisse's magical film from Mali that draws on African ritual with elemental imagery of water, fire, and earth.

Africa

There are three distinct areas of film production on the African continent, all rising out of centuries of colonialism, and mostly divided linguistically into films in Arabic, French, and English. Recent years have seen an increase in big-budget hits seen by Western audiences.

A young man returns home from Europe in Abderrahmane Sissako's ***Waiting for Happiness*** (2002), a rare film to come from Mauritania.

Many African nations did not have a film industry before they became independent of colonial rule in the 1960s and 1970s. Since then, cinema has begun to flourish and productions have attracted international attention. France has been a major provider of financial resources for African film-makers, many of whom have received training at cinema schools in Europe.

From the 1930s, Arab cinema became synonymous with Egyptian cinema. Soon to become the pre-eminent genre, the Egyptian musical made its first appearance in 1932 with ***The Song of the Heart***, directed by Italian Mario Volpi. However, the production of films made in North Africa as a whole remained very low until well after World War II. It was only with the emergence of director Youssef Chahine that Egyptian cinema began to be taken seriously internationally. He would alternate between big-budget productions, such as ***Alexandria... Why?*** (1978) and ***Adieu Bonaparte*** (1985); and patently political films, such as ***The Sparrow*** (1973), about Egypt's Six-Day War against Israel. His film ***Cairo Station*** (1958) focused on the dispossessed. Chahine's films and Shadi Abdelsalam's ***The Night of Counting the Years*** (1969), about the robbing of mummies' tombs, all stood out from the commercial dross of the Egyptian film industry.

In the Maghreb, Algeria's first films about independence reflected the struggle for liberation, the most famous being Gillo Pontecorvo's

WHAT TO WATCH

The Money Order (Ousmane Sembene, Senegal, 1968)

The Night of Counting the Years (Shadi Abdelsalam, Egypt, 1969)

Xala (Ousmane Sembene, Senegal, 1975)

Chronicle of the Burning Years (Mohammed Lakhdar-Hamina, Algeria, 1975)

Alexandria... Why? (Youssef Chahine, Egypt, 1978)

Man of Ashes (Nouri Bouzid, Tunisia, 1986)

Yeelen (Souleymane Cissé, Mali, 1987)

Yaaba (Idrissa Ouadragoa, Burkina Faso, 1989)

The Silences of the Palace (Moufida Tlatli, Tunisia, 1994)

Waiting for Happiness (Abderrahmane Sissako, Mauritania, 2002)

The Battle of Algiers (1966), an Italian-Algerian co-production. Mohammed Lakhdar-Hamina's *Chronicle of the Burning Years* (1975), which traces the history of Algeria from 1939 to 1954, was among the most expensive productions to come out of the developing world. Algeria, Morocco, and Tunisia have all produced award-winning films over the years, such as Tunisian Moufida Tlatli's *The Silences of the Palace* (1994), both an emotionally powerful look at the role of women in a changing world and a rare movie by a woman film-maker working in a male-dominated Arab country. Senegalese film-maker Ousmane Sembene, the pre-eminent director of sub-Saharan African cinema, has likewise done some pioneering work, thanks to which younger African film directors, such as Souleymane Cissé from Mali and Idrissa Ouedragoa from Burkina Faso, were able to make their mark. FESPACO, the most famous African film festival, held biannually in Ouagadougou, Burkina Faso, since 1969, has been a wonderful shop window for sub-Saharan cinema.

Under the years of apartheid, South Africa produced very little of worth. Many films post-apartheid continued to look back on that period. *Mapantsula* (1988) by Oliver Schmitz, and Graham Hood's Oscar-winning *Tsotsi* (2005), about black-on-black violence, look at the present day.

Ousmane Sembene, born in 1923, is the director of a number of acclaimed films, and is considered the father of black African cinema.

Tsotsi (2005), which follows the life of a violent gang leader in Johannesburg, South Africa, won Best Foreign Language Film at the 2006 Academy Awards.

The Middle East

Although the cinema of this region has been dominated by films from North Africa, particularly Egypt and the Maghreb, there have been significant films made in the Middle East, many based on the political tensions in the area.

Free Zone (2005) stars Natalie Portman as an American woman in Jordan trying to establish her identity in the dramatic conditions of the country.

In Lebanon, before the long civil war started in 1975, cinema attendance was the highest in the Arab world (though the country produced few features of its own). Syria and Iraq made a number of strong documentaries, but like their neighbours, turned out few feature films.

However, at the beginning of the 21st century, the tragic situation in the Middle East, particularly the tensions between Israel and Palestine, gave rise to some of the best films to come from that area. Palestinian writer-director Elia Suleiman's *Divine Intervention* (2002) uses black humour to examine the situation at an Israeli-Palestinian checkpoint. *The Syrian Bride* (2004), by Israeli director Eran Riklis, is also set in no-man's land, in an arid area between checkpoints at the Israeli and Syrian borders. The first feature by Palestinian director Tawfik Abu Wael, *Thirst* (2004) is a beautifully composed film about an Arab family living in an abandoned village in a dusty corner of Israel.

Amos Gitai, the Israeli director best known internationally, made *Free Zone* (2005), in which three women – an American, an Israeli, and a Palestinian – become travelling companions in a remote area of Jordan. The controversial Foreign Film Academy Award nominee, *Paradise Now* (2005) traces 24 hours in the lives of two Palestinian suicide-bombers. Director Hany Abu-Assad is a Palestinian born in Israel, and he made the story an exciting thriller, while at the same time perceptively revealing the minds of these "martyrs".

Hany Abu-Assad's *Paradise Now* (2005) tells of two friends recruited for a suicide bombing in Tel Aviv.

WHAT TO WATCH

- *Divine Intervention* (Elia Suleiman, Palestine, 2002)
- *The Syrian Bride* (Eran Riklis, Palestine, 2004)
- *Thirst* (Tawfik Abu Wael, Palestine, 2004)
- *Paradise Now* (Hany Abu-Assad, Palestine, 2005)

Iran

In the 1990s, the cinema of Iran entered the world stage with the gradual thaw in the country's strictly controlled popular culture. What was revealed was a most original and vibrant national cinema.

Iran, under its various authoritarian regimes, had produced only a few notable films over the years. However, in the 1960s, a handful of Iranian films began to be seen abroad. Among the first was Dariush Mehrjui's ***The Cow*** (1968), about a farmer who loses his beloved cow, assumes the animal's identity, and slides into madness. This minutely observed study of village life and its sparse style presaged later Iranian movies.

After the Islamic Revolution of 1979, cinema was condemned for its perceived Western values. Nevertheless, in 1983, a Cinema Foundation was established to encourage domestic film-making. As a result of this support, new directors such as Mohsen Makhmalbaf and Abbas Kiarostami emerged with a number of cinematic masterpieces. There followed many more, including Jafar Panahi, Majid Majidi, Marzieh Meshkini, Babak Payami, and Makhmalbaf's daughter Samira, who, at 18, directed her first feature, ***The Apple*** (1998), which launched her as a leading figure in world cinema.

WHAT TO WATCH

- ***The Cow*** (Dariush Mehrjui, 1968)
- ***The White Balloon*** (Jafar Panahi, 1995)
- ***Taste of Cherry*** (Abbas Kiarostami, 1997)
- ***The Children of Heaven*** (Majid Majidi, 1997)
- ***Blackboards*** (Samira Makhmalbaf, 2000)
- ***The Day I Became a Woman*** (Marzieh Meshkini, 2000)
- ***Secret Ballot*** (Babak Payami, 2001)
- ***Kandahar*** (Mohsen Makhmalbaf, 2001)
- ***Turtles Can Fly*** (Bahman Ghobadi, 2004)

Despite the rigid restrictions imposed by the fundamentalist Islamic regime, the majority of Iranian cinema – which is one of the most subtly feminist in the world – has managed to find ingenious ways of making profound statements about the human condition.

Women in their colourful but imprisoning burqas make a journey across Afghanistan in Mohsen Makhmalbaf's hotly topical ***Kandahar*** (2001).

Eastern Europe

The histories of Poland, Hungary, and former Czechoslovakia in the 20th century, and of their film industries, follow certain similar patterns – independence followed by Nazi subjugation, then repressive Communism, liberalization, a hardening of the regime, and freedom.

Kanal (1957), a film about the 1944 Warsaw uprising, shows how Polish partisans were pursued and trapped in the sewers by Nazi soldiers.

The first film studio in Poland was built in Warsaw in 1920, two years after the country's independence. In 1929, a group of avant-garde film-makers formed START, a society for devotees of artistic film. The best known of these directors, Aleksander Ford, became a key figure in Polish cinema. His most important "socially useful" films were ***The Street Legion*** (1932) and ***People of the Vistula*** (1936).

During World War II, film-making was still permitted in countries under German occupation, except in Poland, for fear of a subtle use of patriotic references. The devastation of the war forced the film industry to begin from scratch. The majority of post-war films tended to deal with the Nazi occupation, the horrors of the ghetto, and the heroes of the resistance. Aleksander Ford's ***Border Street*** (1948) was one of the first of a cluster of Polish films that emerged from the rubble of the war. It follows several families, from different social classes in pre-war Warsaw, whose lives are changed by the tragic events of the period. Ford's ***Five Boys from Barska Street*** (1953), the first major Polish film in colour, was about juvenile delinquency. The assistant on the film was Andrzej Wajda, whose first feature film, ***A Generation*** (1955), was to give a very different view of Polish youth. ***Kanal*** (1957) and ***Ashes and Diamonds*** (1958) completed Wajda's war trilogy and brought Polish cinema to the world's attention as never before.

The late 1950s and 1960s were fertile times for Polish cinema, which produced Andrzej Munk's ***Eroica*** (1957); Jerzy Kawalerowicz's ***Mother Joan of the Angels*** (1961), set in a 17th-century convent and one of the first Polish films seen in the West not dealing with a war theme; Roman Polanski's ***Knife in the Water*** (1962); Wojciech Has' ***The Saragossa Manuscript*** (1965); and Jerzy Skolimowski's ***Walkover*** (1965). Many of these directors were graduates of the excellent film school in Lodz. However, after 1968, as in neighbouring Hungary and former Czechoslovakia, political repression and censorship limited freedom of expression, and cinema suffered as a result.

Zygmunt Malanowicz and Jolanta Umecka embrace in Roman Polanski's first feature, ***Knife in the Water*** (1962).This absurdist drama of sexual rivalry and generation gap received an Oscar nomination and brought Polanski immediate fame.

In the mid-1970s, in the face of censorship, a new trend called the Cinema of Moral Concern surfaced, characterized by sensitivity to ethical problems and a focus on the relationship between the individual and the state. Examples are Andrzej Wajda's ***Man of Marble*** (1976), Krzysztof Zanussi's satires ***Camouflage*** (1977) and ***The Constant Factor*** (1980), Agnieszka Holland's ***Provincial Actors*** (1979), and Krzysztof Kieslowski's ***No End*** (1984).

Klaus Maria Brandauer (right) plays an actor who sells his soul when working under the Nazis in István Szabó's Oscar-winning film ***Mephisto*** (1981).

Hungary

During its brief period under Communism in 1919, Hungary became the first country to nationalize its film industry, several months ahead of the Soviet Union. However, when Horthy's fascist government came into power in 1920, it was put back into private ownership. Alexander Korda, Mihaly Kertesz (Michael Curtiz), Paul Fejos, and film theoretician Béla Balázs, all of whom had made valuable contributions to Hungarian film, were forced to leave the country. The quality of films was at its lowest during Hungary's alliance with the Axis powers during World War II. The first important post-war success was Géza von Radványi's ***Somewhere in Europe*** (1947), which marked the return of Balázs as a screenwriter and led to the re-nationalization of the film industry. In the late 1950s, helped by the setting up of the Balázs Béla Studio, a younger generation of film-makers made their mark: Miklós Jancsó (***The Round-Up***, 1965), István Szabó (***Father***, 1967), and István Gaál (***The Falcons***, 1970). Gaál's film draws an impressive analogy between the taming of wild birds and a way of life that requires blind obedience. Pal Gábor's ***Angi Vera*** (1979), which eloquently conveys the repressive

In Miklós Jancsó's *The Round-Up* (***Szegénylegények***, 1965), a group of peasants is tortured in an attempt to find the leader of a partisan movement.

In *Divided We Fall* (2000), Jan Hrebejk's black comedy, Boleslav Polivka (centre) plays an unlikely hero who hides his Jewish friend – an escapee from a concentration camp – in his house under the nose of a Nazi sympathizer, who also lives in the house.

climate of Stalinist Hungary in the late 1940s, surprised and impressed critics in the West. Márta Mészáros, formerly married to Miklós Jancsó, also made a reputation with her intimist films on the female condition, most particularly her three-part "Diary" (1982–90): ***Diary for My Children***, ***Diary for My Loves***, and ***Diary for My Mother and Father***. Béla Tarr emerged in the 1990s as one of the most remarkable of European directors, with his seven-and-a-half-hour ***Sátántangó*** (1994), and ***Werckmeister Harmonies*** (2000), in which the long take is stretched to its limits.

Czechoslovakia

Czechoslovakia became an independent nation in 1918, but competition from German and US films limited independent Czech cinema for some time. Two films stood out during the end of the silent era: Gustav Machaty's ***Erotikon*** (1929), which achieved much of its erotic effect by symbolic imagery, and Curt Junghan's ***Such is Life*** (1929), which dealt with conditions of working-class life in Prague. However, Machaty's greatest claim to fame was ***Ecstasy*** (1933), in which the nude scenes played by Hedy Kiesler (later Lamarr) caused a furore. The Pope protested when it was shown at the Venice Film Festival, the

WHAT TO WATCH

Knife in the Water (Roman Polanski, Poland, 1962)

The Shop on the High Street (Ján Kadár, Czechoslovakia, 1965)

The Round-Up (Miklós Jansců, Hungary, 1965)

Loves of a Blonde (Miloš Forman, Czechoslovakia, 1965)

Daisies (Vera Chytilová, Czechoslovakia, 1966)

Closely Observed Trains (Jiří Menzel, Czechoslovakia, 1966)

Man of Marble (Andrzej Wajda, Poland, 1976)

The Three Colours trilogy (Krzysztof Kieslowski, Poland, 1993–94)

Divided We Fall (Jan Hrebejk, Czech Republic, 2000)

The Turin Horse (Béla Tarr, Hungary, 2011)

Five-year-old Andrei Chalimon attempts to imitate his musician stepfather in the title role of Jan Sverák's charming Oscar-winning ***Kolya*** (1996).

nude scenes were cut in the US, and Hedy's husband tried to buy up all the prints. Protests apart, the film is, in fact, full of pastoral beauty.

In 1933, the Barrandov studios, one of the best equipped in Europe, opened in Prague. During the war, the Germans took it over, which interrupted any advance in the industry. After the war, the national film school, FAMU, was set up in Prague, and a new generation of directors emerged from it, notably Ivan Passer, Jiří Menzel, Vera Chytilová, and Miloš Forman. Ján Kadár's ***The Shop on the High Street*** (1965) was the first Czech film to win a Foreign Film Oscar, followed by Menzel's ***Closely Observed Trains*** (1966). The Russian invasion of 1968 ended this exciting period of activity. Kadár, Passer, and Forman left for the US. Chytilová, whose ***Daisies*** (1966) was the most anarchic film of the period, was silenced. The animosity towards the Russians is dealt with in ***Kolya*** (1996), in which a Czech finds himself with a Russian stepson, whom he learns to love.

Film censorship was less rigorous in Slovakia: directors, such as Stefan Uher, Dušan Hanák, and Juraj Jakubisko, were able to pursue their careers relatively freely. Since the formation of the Czech Republic and Slovakia in 1993, the film industries have developed their own distinct characters.

The Balkans

Given the political upheavals that this region of Europe has suffered since the advent of cinema, it is not surprising that its film production has been sporadic and often traditionalist. However, in recent years, these countries have produced a number of talented film-makers.

Yugoslavia

In Yugoslavia, the best of the small output of pre-World War II feature films was Mihajlo Popovic's ***With Faith in God*** (1931), a Serbian World War I epic. After 1945, the country's films dealt almost exclusively with the war, as in the popular "partisan" movies. However, it was animation films that made an impact abroad, especially through the work of the Zagreb school, a refreshing alternative to Walt Disney.

The best-known directors are Dusan Makavejev, officially disapproved of at home due to the sexual and political content of his films, and Aleksandar Petrovic, whose ***Three*** (1965) and ***I Even Met Happy Gypsies*** (1967) were nominated for the Best Foreign Film Oscar. Bosnian Emir Kusturica burst onto the scene in 1981, winning awards with each new film.

Bulgaria

In 1915, seven years after gaining independence, Bulgaria produced its first feature film, ***The Bulgarian is Gallant***. It starred and was directed by Vassil Gendov, who also directed Bulgaria's first talkie, ***The Slaves' Revolt*** (1933). During World War II, only propaganda films were allowed and then, under Communist rule, features focused on the Soviet socialist realism model. As with elsewhere in Europe, there was an improvement from the 1960s, with Vulo Radev's ***The Peach Thief*** (1964) being among the first internationally important productions. Metodi Andonov's ***The Goat Horn*** (1972) – remade by Nikolai Volev in 1994 – became the most critically acclaimed Bulgarian film of the time.

Underground (1995), by celebrated Bosnian director Emir Kusturica, is an epic portrait of Yugoslavia from 1941 to the present. Kusturica had earlier won Best Director at Cannes for ***Time of the Gypsies*** (1988).

Anthony Quinn plays Alexis Zorba in ***Zorba the Greek*** (1964), directed by Michael Cacoyannis, one of the few Greek directors to gain international recognition for his work.

Romania

Romania took a long time to build the semblance of a film industry, which has produced about 15 films a year from the 1960s. A breakthrough was made with Liviu Ciulei's ***Forest of the Hanged*** (1964), which won Best Director at Cannes in 1965. This anti-war drama had an understated quality, in contrast to earlier propaganda epics. Lucian Pintilie, arguably the best-known Romanian director, made his first feature, ***Sunday at Six***, in the same year.

Until his death in 1989, Communist despot Nicolae Ceausescu controlled the arts with an iron fist. During his time in power, rigid censorship rules forced directors to employ various metaphors to get their films released, and it was not until 16 years after his death that they could rid themselves of these constraints. Although several New Wave films can be seen as metaphors of Romanian society, they are, at the same time, almost documentary-like observations of it – disturbing works of intense realism, with underlining black humour. The first was Cristi Puiu's ***The Death of Mr. Lazarescu*** in 2005, followed by Catalin Mitulescu's ***The Way I Spent The End of The World***, Corneliu Porumboiu's ***12.08 East of Bucharest***, Radu Muntean's ***The Paper Will Be Blue*** (all 2006); and Cristian Mungiu's ***4 Months, 3 Weeks and 2 Days*** (2007), which won the *Palme d'Or* at Cannes in 2007.

WHAT TO WATCH

- ***A Matter of Dignity*** (Michael Cacoyannis, Greece, 1957)
- ***I Even Met Happy Gypsies*** (Aleksandar Petrovic, Yugoslavia, 1967)
- ***The Goat Horn*** (Metodi Andonov, Bulgaria, 1972)
- ***Yol*** (Yilmaz Güney and Serif Gören, Turkey, 1982)
- ***Underground*** (Emir Kusturica, Yugoslavia, 1995)
- ***Eternity and a Day*** (Theo Angelopoulos, Greece, 1998)
- ***Uzak*** (Nuri Bilge Ceylan, Turkey, 2002)
- ***The Death of Mr. Lazarescu*** (Cristi Puiu, Romania, 2005)
- ***4 Months, 3 Weeks and 2 Days*** (Cristian Mungiu, Romania, 2007)

Greece

Although the first Greek film appeared in 1912, long periods of instability crippled any attempts at forming a film industry – few features were produced until the 1950s. Michael Cacoyannis reached the peak of his popularity with ***Zorba the Greek*** (1964); and since the 1970s, Theo Angelopoulos has achieved iconic status.

Turkey

Omer Lutfi Akad was the D.W. Griffith of Turkish cinema. His feature ***In the Name of the Law*** (1952) marked a departure from the cheap melodramas being made at the time, but it was almost three decades before Yilmaz Güney became the most internationally acclaimed director Turkey has ever produced. However, several of his best films, including ***Yol*** (1982), were directed by proxy as he languished in prison for his left-wing political activities. Since Güney, there has been an impressive string of Turkish films including Yesim Ustaoglu's ***Journey to The Sun*** (1999), Nuri Bilge Ceylan's ***Uzak*** (2002), and Semih Kaplanoglu's ***Angel's Fall*** (2005).

Yol (1982) shows Turkey through the eyes of five prisoners.

Russia

In the 1920s, Russian cinema was the most exciting and experimental in the world, until the heavy hand of Stalinism came down with a vengeance. Despite occasional masterpieces, it would be many years before the country re-emerged to take its place among the great cinematic nations.

A gang of thieves is surprised by Mr. West and his faithful cowboy aide in *The Extraordinary Adventures of Mr. West in the Land of the Bolsheviks* (1924).

There was little of cinematic interest in pre-Revolution Russia as it was impossible to deal with contemporary issues under strict Tsarist censorship. Films depended heavily on adaptations from literature or the theatre, and until World War I, foreign films dominated the Russian market. The leading director was Yakov Protazanov, who directed more than 40 films between 1909 and 1917. He was one of the few members of the old guard to remain in Russia after the revolution in October 1917, going on to make the Soviet Union's first science fiction movie, *Aelita* in 1924.

In their first days of power, the Bolsheviks established a State Commission of Education, which included an important subsection devoted to cinema. As the new Soviet leader, Lenin realized the immense value of film as propaganda, and early Soviet cinema played an important role in getting the revolutionary message across to the people, with "agitprop" trains (see p.94) employed to trawl the vast country. Film schools were set up in Moscow and Petrograd (later Leningrad) in 1918 and the film industry was nationalized a year later. However, because of the Civil War and the blockade of foreign films, film stock, and equipment, it took a few years before Russia could start producing more than a handful of feature films.

Things started to change in 1924 as the economy improved. The Soviet government declared that the state would not interfere in matters of artistic style – even non-naturalistic and avant-garde expression – but that the films should have a revolutionary content. Thus began an exciting and fruitful period of film-making. Lev Kuleshov, one of the first theorists of cinema, put his research at the services of his first feature, the gag-filled satire, *The Extraordinary Adventures of Mr. West in the Land of the Bolsheviks* (1924). Using mobile cameras, quick cutting, and sequences derived from American chase films, the film managed to deride the West's stereotyped view of "mad, savage Russians" while creating its own stereotyped American – the Harold-Lloyd type Mr. West.

Russian experimentation

There followed the silent masterpieces of Sergei Eisenstein, Vsevolod Pudovkin, Alexander Dovzhenko, Boris Barnet, Abram Room, Dziga Vertov, and the directing duo of Leonid Trauberg

WHAT TO WATCH

- *The Battleship Potemkin* (Sergei Eisenstein, 1925)
- *Storm Over Asia* (Vsevolod Pudovkin, 1928)
- *Man with a Movie Camera* (Dziga Vertov, 1929)
- *Earth* (Alexander Dovzhenko, 1930)
- *Ivan the Terrible Parts I and II* (Sergei Eisenstein, 1944/58)
- *The Cranes Are Flying* (Mikhail Kalatozov, 1957)
- *Ballad of a Soldier* (Grigori Chukhrai, 1959)
- *The Colour of Pomegranates* (Sergei Parajanov, 1969)
- *Come and See* (Elem Klimov, 1985)
- *Russian Ark* (Aleksandr Sokurov, 2002)

and Grigori Kozintsev, all bursting with creative enthusiasm. Leading the way was Eisenstein's ***The Strike*** (1925), for which he used the "dynamic montage" – that is, visual metaphors and shock cuts. This reached its peak in ***The Battleship Potemkin*** (1925), with its memorable Odessa Steps sequence (see p.261), and ***October*** (1928).

Taking the same subject as ***October*** (the 1917 Russian Revolution), Pudovkin portrayed a different slant in ***The End of St. Petersburg*** (1927), while Dovzhenko made ***Earth*** (1930), a pastoral symphony dedicated to his native Ukraine. Barnet directed a number of delightfully fresh satirical comedies such as ***The Girl with the Hatbox*** (1927) and ***The House on Trubnaya*** (1928). Abram Room's ***Bed and Sofa*** (1927) used warmth and humour to depict a *ménage-à-trois*. Trauberg and Kozintsev's film, ***The New Babylon*** (1929), set in Paris at the time of the Commune in 1871, brilliantly used montage and lighting to contrast the lives of the rich and the poor. Meanwhile, Vertov continued to make documentaries, culminating in ***Man with A Movie Camera*** (1929).

Tragically, this great period of Russian experimentation came to an end as Stalin tightened his grip. More and more of the best films, especially those of Eisenstein, were attacked for being "bourgeois", due to their use of symbolism and modernistic visual style. By the end of 1932, the slogan "socialist realism", a phrase attributed to Stalin himself, was *de rigueur* in all the arts. Socialist realism was opposed to "formalism", or art that put style above content. Soviet art had to be optimistic, understandable, and loved by the masses. This meant that the experimentation that had made Soviet cinema great was now heavily controlled.

Counterplan (1932), directed by Fridrikh Ermler and Sergei Yutkevich, about the foiling of a sabotage attempt on a steel plant, was, according to one writer, "the first victory of socialist realism in the Soviet cinema".

Nevertheless, in the period before World War II, the Soviet Union did produce some films that can still be enjoyed today, such as the Hollywood-style musicals, ***Jazz Comedy*** (1934) and ***Volga-Volga*** (1938), made by Grigori Aleksandrov, a former colleague of Eisenstein. Mark Donskoy's ***Gorky*** trilogy – ***The Childhood of Maxim Gorky*** (1938), ***My Apprenticeship*** (1939), and ***My Universities*** (1940) – was rich in incident, character, and period detail; it was one of the few masterpieces of socialist realism. Another was Eisenstein's first film with sound, ***Alexander Nevsky*** (1938), with a wonderful score by Sergei Prokofiev.

The death of Stalin

During World War II, the film industry concentrated mainly on morale-boosting documentaries. One of the few features made was Eisenstein's ***Ivan The Terrible*** (1944), which was made in two parts, the first approved by Stalin, but the second banned and not released until 1958. The post-war years represented a low point in Soviet cinema both in quality and quantity. It was only after Stalin's death in 1953, and Khrushchev's famous speech in 1956 (which attacked aspects of Stalinism), that it began to pick up. The result of this "thaw" was a number of films that merited international success. Mikhail Kalatozov's ***The Cranes Are Flying*** (1957), a lyrical love story, won the Best Film award at Cannes, while Grigori Chukhrai's ***Ballad of a Soldier*** (1959), an unrhetorical and moving portrait of everyday life in wartime Russia, won a Special Jury Prize.

This relative freedom of expression continued into the mid-1960s, with some notable films, such as Josef Heifitz's ***The Lady with the Little Dog*** (1959); Kozintsev's ***Hamlet*** (1964); Andrei

Mikhail Kalatozov's *The Cranes Are Flying* (1957) is a beautiful portrayal of love, and the horrors of war.

Innokenti Smoktunovsky stars as the Prince of Denmark (left), with Viktor Kolpakov as the Gravedigger in *Hamlet* (1964).

Two young women confide in each other in Vladimir Menshov's Oscar-winning ***Moscow Does Not Believe in Tears*** (1980).

Tsar Nicholas II and the Russian royal family take tea on the eve of the Revolution, in Aleksandr Sokurov's extraordinary one-take ***Russian Ark*** (2002), filmed entirely in the Hermitage, St. Petersburg.

Tarkovsky's ***Ivan's Childhood*** (1962); and Sergei Parajanov's ***Shadows of Our Forgotten Ancestors*** (1964), before repression set in again. Tarkovsky's ***Andrei Rublev*** (1966) and Parajanov's ***The Colour of Pomegranates*** (1969) were both shelved. Despite some exceptions, including Sergei Bondarchuk's remarkable eight-hour ***War and Peace*** (1966–67), good films were few and far between until the late 1970s when Vladimir Menshov directed ***Moscow Does Not Believe in Tears*** (1980), a romantic comedy-drama that won the Best Foreign Film Oscar in the same year.

The post-Communist era

After the fall of Communism, there was a phase when most Russian films were either kitsch or imitations of American action movies. However, after its initial reaction against the past, Russia once again became one of the leading cinematic countries, with films such as Pavel Chukhrai's ***The Thief*** (1997); Aleksandr Sokurov's ***Russian Ark*** (2002); and Andrei Zvyagintsev's ***The Return***, Aleksei German Jr's ***The Last Train***, and Boris Khlebnikov and Aleksei Popogrebsky's ***Koktebel*** (all 2003).

The breakup of the Soviet Union meant that the former Soviet Republics were able to establish a characteristic cinema, good examples of which are cosmopolitan Georgian director Otar Iosseliani's ***Brigands–Chapter VII*** (1996) and Jamshed Usmonov's ***Angel on the Right*** (Tajikistan, 2002).

The Nordic Countries

Considering the small size of their populations, the cinematic contribution of the Nordic countries, led by Sweden and Denmark, has been phenomenal. From Ingmar Bergman to Lars von Trier, many directors from this part of Europe have been highly influential.

In 1906, Nordisk Film (the oldest existing film company in the world) provided the impetus for the rise of Danish cinema. Some of the early Danish films had "shocking" subjects with such titles as ***The White Slave Trade*** (1910), ***The Morphine Takers*** (1911), and ***Opium Dreams*** (1914). Production dipped after World War I and took a long time to recover, forcing Denmark's most famous directors, Carl Dreyer and Benjamin Christensen, to seek work elsewhere. In Sweden, Dreyer shot ***The Parson's Widow*** (1920) and Christensen made his most famous film, ***Witchcraft through the Ages*** (1922), a semi-documentary movie made using a series of tableaux inspired by artists Hieronymus Bosch and Pieter Bruegel. Dreyer went back to Denmark during World War II, and made one of his best films, ***Day of Wrath*** (1943). However, fearing imprisonment by Nazis for what were seen as allusions to the tyranny of the occupation in the film, he fled to Sweden until after the war. Among the light comedies and soft porn produced in Denmark in the 1950s, only Dreyer's ***Ordet*** (1955), which won the Golden Bear in Berlin, stood out.

Notable Danish films from the 1960s were Palle Kjærulff-Schmidt's *Once There Was a War* (1966), about a boy in Copenhagen during the occupation, and Henning Carlsen's ***Hunger*** (1966), adapted from Knut Hamsun's novel about a penniless writer.

WHAT TO WATCH

- ***The Phantom Carriage*** (Victor Sjöström, Sweden, 1921)
- ***Day of Wrath*** (Carl Dreyer, Denmark ,1943)
- ***Persona*** (Ingmar Bergman, Sweden, 1966)
- ***Babette's Feast*** (Gabriel Axel, Denmark,1987)
- ***Festen*** (Thomas Vinterberg, Denmark, 1998)
- ***The Idiots*** (Lars von Trier, Denmark, 1998)
- ***Songs from the Second Floor*** (Roy Andersson, Sweden, 2000)
- ***O'Horten*** (Bent Hamer, Norway, 2007)
- ***The Girl with the Dragon Tattoo*** (Niels Arden Oplev, Sweden/Denmark/Germany/Norway, 2009)

Pia Degermark stars in the title role of Bo Widerberg's lyrical ***Elvira Madigan*** (1967), set to the strains of Mozart's Piano Concerto No.21. Degermark won Best Actress at Cannes for her role.

Swedish cinema

In Sweden, the Svenska Bio studio was founded in 1907, and two years later, Charles Magnusson joined as production manager. In 1912, he signed up two directors, Victor Sjöström and Mauritz Stiller, who were to transform Swedish cinema. In the same year, Magnusson and Julius Jaenzon co-directed ***The Vagabond's Galoshes***, based on a Hans Christian Andersen fairy tale, which had sequences shot on location in France and the US, and included an early tracking shot.

Mauritz Stiller made sophisticated, ironic sex comedies, such as ***Love and Journalism*** (1916) and ***Erotikon*** (1920), before moving closer to the more sombre Swedish literary tradition with films based on the novels of Selma Lagerlöf. Sjöström, with ***Karin, Daughter of Ingmar*** (1920) and ***The Phantom Carriage*** (1921), and Stiller, with ***Sir Arne's Treasure*** (1919) and Greta Garbo's first feature film, ***The Saga of Gosta Berling*** (1924), gave Sweden a

Bibi Andersson (left) and Liv Ulmann play women who swap identities, in Ingmar Bergman's *Persona* (1966).

reputation for making films of high artistic quality. When Sjöström, Stiller, and Garbo left for Hollywood in the mid-1920s, Swedish cinema suffered. The only director of note in the 1930s was Gustaf Molander, whose most famous film was *Intermezzo* (1936), a weepie in which the young Ingrid Bergman had her first starring role. Producer David O. Selznick saw it and offered Bergman a contract and a Hollywood-style remake of the film two years later. One of the most significant Swedish films of the 1940s was Alf Sjöberg's *Frenzy* (1944), about misunderstood youth. It not only launched 26-year-old Ingmar Bergman – whose first screenplay this was – and teenage actress Mai Zetterling, but instigated the renaissance of Swedish cinema. From his debut film, *Crisis* (1946), Bergman's talent was immediately recognized, and from the 1950s, he personified Swedish cinema. Other directors, such as Arne Mattsson (*One Summer of Happiness*, 1951) and Arne Sucksdorff (*The Great Adventure*, 1953) also gained some recognition abroad.

In the 1960s, a younger generation of directors emerged such as Bo Widerberg, most renowned for the tragic love story, *Elvira Madigan* (1967), and Vilgot Sjöman, who caused a scandal with the sexually explicit *I Am Curious Yellow* (1967) and *I Am Curious Blue* (1968). Mai Zetterling's first two films as director, *Loving Couples* (1964) and *Night Games* (1966), were wickedly sensuous Strindbergian dramas with a feminist twist.

However, Ingmar Bergman continued to cast his shadow. Following his classics of the 1950s, notably *The Seventh Seal* (see p.299) and *Wild Strawberries* (both 1957), he made a series of psychodramas (such as *Persona*, 1966), most of them starring Liv Ullmann. (In 2000, Ullmann would direct *Faithless*, a compelling film about their relationship, written by Bergman.) She also starred in Jan Troell's *The Emigrants* (1971) and *The New Land* (1972), two heartfelt sagas of Swedes who emigrated to the US in the 19th century. In 1959, Ullmann had her first starring role in *The Wayward Girl*. This tale of sexual liberation was the last film by Edith Carlmar, Norway's first female director, who made ten features between 1949 and 1959. In 1957, another Norwegian film had made an impact internationally – Arne Skouen's *Nine Lives* – based on the real-life experience of resistance fighter, Jan Baalsrud.

Finland's film of note in the 1950s was Edvin Laine's *The Unknown Soldier* (1955) – still the country's highest-grossing film ever. Jörn Donner made many films dealing with sexuality. He was Finland's best-known director until the arrival of

Swedish experts arrive to examine the domestic habits of Norwegian bachelors in Bent Hamer's quirky satire *Kitchen Stories* (2003).

Leningrad Cowboys Go America (1989) is a typically idiosyncratic film by Finnish director Aki Kaurismäki. It tells the story of a group of Soviet rock musicians.

the idiosyncratic Aki Kaurismäki, who, in the 1980s, put the country firmly on the cinematic map with ***Leningrad Cowboys Go America*** (1989), ***Drifting Clouds*** (1996), and ***The Man Without a Past*** (2002).

Like Kaurismäki, Fridrik Thor Fridriksson from Iceland is the sole international representative of his country. He started to gain wide recognition in the 1990s with offbeat films like ***Cold Fever*** (1995) and ***Devil's Island*** (1996).

Films from the Baltic countries that were emerging from Soviet domination, tentatively began to be recognized abroad after 2000. These included Kristijonas Vildziunas's ***The Lease*** (Lithuania, 2002), Laila Pakalnina's ***The Python*** (Latvia, 2003), and Jaak Kilmi and René Reinumägi's ***Revolution of Pigs*** (Estonia, 2004).

A creative explosion

The 1980s onwards have been a time of great creativity in the Nordic countries. In Denmark, it began when Danish films won Best Foreign Film Oscars two years in succession: Gabriel Axel's ***Babette's Feast*** (1987) and Bille August's ***Pelle the Conqueror*** (1987). In 1995, Lars von Trier and Thomas Vinterberg jointly formulated the artistic manifesto *Dogme 95*, which turned low-budget film aesthetics into a rich cinematic principle. Among the *Dogme* films to make an impact worldwide were Vinterberg's ***Festen*** (***The Celebration***), von Trier's ***The Idiots*** (both 1998), Søren Kragh-Jacobsen's ***Mifune*** (1999), Lone Scherfig's ***Italian for Beginners*** (2000), and Annette Olesen's ***Minor Mishaps*** (2002).

Notable movies from Sweden include Lukas Moodysson's comedy-drama ***Together*** (2000), Roy Andersson's ***Songs from the Second Floor*** (2000), and Björn Runge's ***Daybreak*** (2003). Norway had hits with Ola Solum's ***Orion's Belt*** (1985), Nils Gaup's ***Pathfinder*** (1987), and Knut Erik Jensen's documentary ***Cool and Crazy*** (2001).

In a remote and austere Danish town, guests enjoy a sumptuous, once-in-a-lifetime meal prepared by a French cook (Stéphane Audran), in ***Babette's Feast*** (1987).

Germany

Despite the considerable contribution that Germany has made to the history of film, there was a wide gap between its greatest period – the Silent Era – and the new dawn of German cinema in the 1970s, almost half a century later.

"Never before and in no other country have images and language been abused so unscrupulously as here. Nowhere else have people suffered such a loss of confidence in images of their own, their own stories and myths, as we have," proclaimed German director Wim Wenders in 1977. Wenders was referring to the fatal legacy of Nazism, which permeated so many German films, whether from the Federal Republic (West Germany) or the Democratic Republic (East Germany). This permeation took place mainly between 1949 and 1989, but also before and after that period.

Much of this is expounded by critic Siegfried Kracauer in his book, *From Caligari to Hitler* (1947), which analyzed the German psyche through the country's films. The book's starting point is Robert Wiene's ***The Cabinet of Dr. Caligari*** (1920, see p.259), which was to become a trademark of German cinema in the 1920s, with its stylized, distorted studio sets, artificial lighting, and shadows.

In *The Golem* (1915), the first of several versions of the old Jewish legend, the clay monster (Paul Wegener) contemplates his victim.

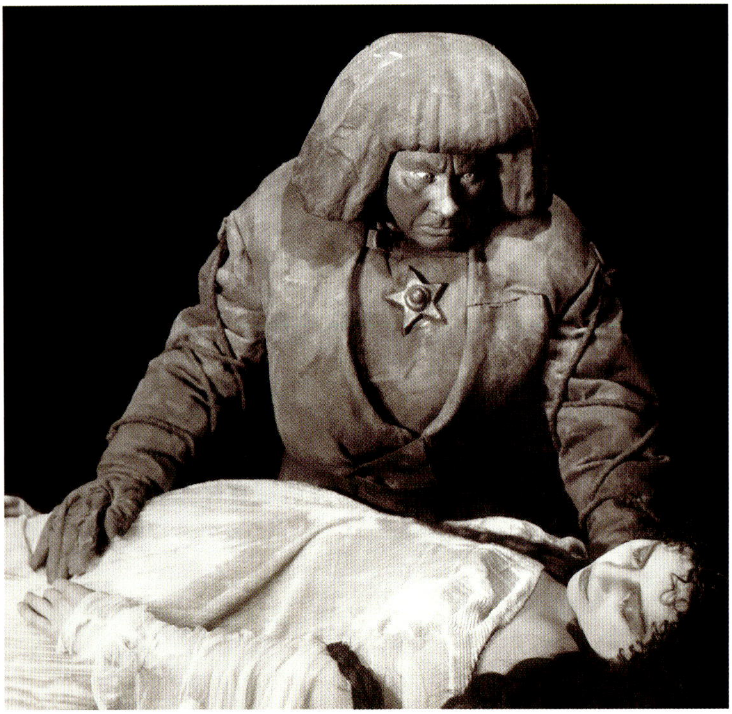

The Silent Age

Before World War I, there were 2,000 cinemas and two large film studios near Berlin. Most German films were farcical comedies and static adaptations from literature and the stage. Nevertheless, there were some films that anticipated the expressionist style of ***Dr. Caligari***, such as the first of the three versions of ***The Student of Prague*** (1913), an early spark that ignited German cinema's love of supernatural subjects, leading in turn to the making of expressionist classics. The film starred Paul Wegener, who sells his reflection to obtain the means to woo the girl of his choice. Wegener also played the role of the monster in ***The Golem*** (1915), which he co-directed with Henrik Galeen.

Film production increased dramatically during World War I because films from enemy countries – the US, France, and England – were not shown in Germany. The renowned company UFA (Universum Film Aktiengesellschaft) was formed in 1917 and remained the dominant force in the industry until the end of World War II. Among the directors who emerged at this time were F.W. Murnau, Paul Leni, Fritz Lang, and Ernst Lubitsch. Murnau's ***Nosferatu*** (1922), Leni's ***Waxworks*** (1924), and Lang's two-part ***Dr. Mabuse the Gambler*** (1922) and ***Metropolis*** (1927) were expressionistic masterpieces. Lubitsch was

WHAT TO WATCH

- ***The Last Laugh*** (F.W. Murnau, 1924)
- ***Pandora's Box*** (G.W. Pabst, 1929)
- ***The Blue Angel*** (Josef von Sternberg, 1930)
- ***M*** (Fritz Lang, 1931)
- ***The Bridge*** (Bernhard Wicki, 1959)
- ***Kings of the Road*** (Wim Wenders, 1976)
- ***The Marriage of Maria Braun*** (Rainer Werner Fassbinder, 1978)
- ***The Tin Drum*** (Volker Schlöndorff, 1979)
- ***Das Boot*** (Wolfgang Petersen, 1981)
- ***Run Lola Run*** (Tom Tykwer, 1998)

also directing lavish historical romances, such as ***Madame Du Barry*** (1919), ***Anne Boleyn*** (1920), and ***Pharaoh's Wife*** (1922).

At the same time, there were the *kammerspiel* (chamber play) films, chiefly Lupu Pick's ***Shattered*** (1921) and Murnau's ***The Last Laugh*** (1924). Two other popular genres also emerged – "street films" such as G.W. Pabst's ***The Joyless Street*** (1925), with 20-year-old Greta Garbo (in her last European film); and "mountain films", which focused on man's battle against Nature. The latter was exemplified by the films of Arnold Fanck, the best being ***The White Hell of Pitz Palu*** (1929). Appearing in four of Fanck's films was director Leni Riefenstahl, whose first feature as a director, ***The Blue Light*** (1932) was a similar "mountain film".

The end of the Golden Age

Before the Golden Age was terminated by Hitler, there were a number of significant sound films: Josef von Sternberg's ***The Blue Angel*** (1930), Pabst's ***Westfront 1918*** (1930) and ***The Threepenny Opera*** (1931), and Leontine Sagan's ***Madchen in Uniform*** (1931), about a lesbian relationship. Fritz Lang's ***M*** (1931), with Peter Lorre as a child killer, and ***Testament of Dr. Mabuse*** (1933) were also produced during this period. The latter, made as Hitler seized power, had the mad villain expressing sentiments too close for Nazi comfort. This provoked Joseph Goebbels, the Minister of Propaganda, to ask Lang to change the last reel. Lang refused to do so and fled the country.

All filming now came under the control of Goebbels, who also purged all Jews from the industry. More than 1,000 films were made under the Nazis, most of them frivolous comedies and musicals, balanced with a number of anti-Semitic propaganda pieces, including ***Jew Süss*** and ***The Eternal Jew*** (both 1940). Other propaganda films were ***Hitlerjunge Quex*** (1933), and Riefenstahl's ***Triumph of the Will*** (1935) and ***Olympia*** (1938). One of the few movies to survive the period was ***The Adventures of Baron Munchausen*** (1943), an elaborate fantasy, superbly photographed in Agfacolor. It was produced to celebrate the 25th anniversary of UFA studios.

After the war, it took just as long to rebuild the film industry as it did to rebuild the now Allied-occupied country. Almost all the production facilities, including UFA and Tobis studios, were in the Russian zone and were taken over by DEFA, the newly formed State film company. Most of the post-war films (known as "rubble films") in both East and West Germany were marked by strong sociological content, in an attempt to come to terms with bitter reality. After the division of Germany in 1949, the two industries developed separately – East Germany made films with a heavy political slant, while West Germany, in contrast, turned out more escapist entertainment.

Emil Jannings features as a proud hotel doorman who loses his job and is reduced to a lavatory attendant in F. W. Murnau's ***The Last Laugh*** (1924).

The astonishing 12-year-old David Bennent plays Oskar in Volker Schlöndorff's Oscar-winning ***The Tin Drum*** (1979), based on an allegorical novel on Nazism.

In Wim Wenders' *Wings of Desire* (1987), an angel (Bruno Ganz) falls in love with a trapeze artist played by Solveig Dommartin.

A slow rebirth

The 1950s was a fallow period for German films, although they produced several stars, such as Romy Schneider, Horst Buchholz, Curd Jürgens, and Maria Schell, all of whom became internationally recognized. The only film of much note was Bernhard Wicki's ***The Bridge*** (1959), about seven schoolboys who, drafted into the dregs of Hitler's army in 1945, are asked to defend a bridge against American tanks, which they do to the death.

Lola (Franka Potente) has twenty minutes to find 100,000 Deutschmarks to stop her boyfriend robbing a grocery store, in Tom Tykwer's fast-paced hit film ***Run Lola Run*** (1998).

In the early 1960s, West German film-maker Alexander Kluge wrote a manifesto demanding subsidies and the setting up of a film school. It paved the way for a new wave of directors including Volker Schlöndorff, Rainer Werner Fassbinder, Werner Herzog, and Wim Wenders. There followed Hans-Jürgen Syberberg, with his attempts to demystify Germany's cultural and historical past; Edgar Reitz, whose ***Heimat*** (made in a series from 1984–2005) mirrored modern German history; and feminist film-makers Margarethe von Trotta and Helma Sanders-Brahms. Wolfgang Petersen's ***Das Boot*** (1981), Oliver Hirschbiegel's ***Downfall*** (2004), and Wolfgang Becker's ***Good Bye Lenin!*** (2003) dealt with recent German history.

As the Nazi period – a subject that dominated the country's films from the 1960s – recedes into the past, a new, more confident German cinema has emerged, typified by Tom Tykwer's ***Run Lola Run*** (1998), which cleverly covers the same time span in three different ways; Hans Weingartner's ***The Edukators*** (2004), about a group of anarchists; and German-born Turk Fatih Akin's ***Head-On*** (2004), a cry of rage on behalf of Turkish immigrants.

France

No other country, except the US, has contributed so much to the technical and artistic development of film than France. In fact, it could be argued that France has an even more enviable record, consistently producing films of both commercial and artistic merit.

Though there is still a dispute as to which country invented cinema, what is certain is that the Lumière brothers of France were the first to exploit it commercially. They first showed their films to the general public in Paris on 28 December 1895, the date generally acknowledged as marking the birth of cinema. Not long after this, film producers Léon Gaumont and Charles Pathé, realizing the commercial potential of the new medium, began to build their movie empires. Alice Guy-Blaché, in charge of production at Gaumont, became the first woman director with ***La Fee Aux Choux*** (***The Good Fairy and the Cabbage Patch***, 1896).

Some of the earliest French films, besides the magic cinematic tricks of Georges Méliès, were reproductions of classic plays that typically consisted of a series of tableaux. Early stars included legendary stage actress Sarah Bernhardt who starred in ***Queen Elizabeth*** (1912), which was distributed successfully in the US. However, the most famous French name there was that of elegant comedian Max Linder, who influenced Charlie Chaplin and other great comics of the silent screen. At the same time, Louis Feuillade was making his serials: ***Fantômas*** (1913–14), about a diabolical criminal, and ***Les Vampires*** (1915–16).

Louis Feuillade's *five-episode Fantômas* (1913–14) puts an arch criminal and master of disguise (René Navarre) in a variety of tricky situations.

World War I disrupted French film production, allowing American cinema to become more dominant in Europe. After the war, the French developed it as an art form. Film theoretician Ricciotto Canudo referred to cinema as "The Seventh Art" and one of the first serious critics, Louis Delluc, an important director in his own right, coined the word *cinéaste* (film-maker). The *Prix Louis Delluc* has been awarded annually since 1937 to the best French movie of the year. Germaine Dulac directed ***The Seashell and the Clergyman*** (1928), which was probably the first surrealist film, while Dulac's ***The Smiling Madame Beudet*** (1923) is recognized as the first feminist movie. Other firsts include the use of slow motion in Jean Epstein's ***The Fall of the House of Usher*** (1928), and the blurred image (*flou*) in Marcel L'Herbier's ***El Dorado*** (1921). Abel Gance was a towering figure in French cinema, and was already using split-screen techniques in ***J'accuse!*** (1919) – long before his masterpiece ***Napoléon*** (1927).

The coming of sound

From the 1930s, Jean Renoir, Marcel Pagnol, and Sacha Guitry relished using dialogue, while René Clair made musicals. This period was characterized by "poetic realism" as seen in the work of Marcel Carné (***Le Jour se Lève***, 1939), Jean Renoir (***La Bête Humaine***, 1938), and

WHAT TO WATCH

Napoléon (Abel Gance, 1927)
L'Atalante (Jean Vigo, 1934)
La Grande Illusion (Jean Renoir, 1937)
Le Jour se Lève (Marcel Carné, 1939)
Diary of a Country Priest (Robert Bresson, 1951)
Hiroshima Mon Amour (Alain Resnais, 1959)
Jules et Jim (François Truffaut, 1962)
Weekend (Jean-Luc Godard, 1967)
La Haine (Mathieu Kassovitz, 1995)
The Taste of Others (Agnès Jaoui, 2000)
The Class (Laurent Cantet, 2008)
A Prophet (Jacques Audiard, 2009)
Of Gods and Men (Xavier Beauvois, 2010)

Jean Gabin (centre) plays a gangster hiding from the authorities, in Julien Duvivier's *Pépé le Moko* (1937).

Julien Duvivier (*Pépé le Moko*, 1937); all three films starred the charismatic Jean Gabin. The German occupation of France in 1940 sent Renoir, Clair, Duvivier, and German-born Max Ophüls into self-exile in Hollywood.

Carné remained in France, however, as did Jean Cocteau, Jacques Becker, Claude Autant-Lara, Henri Clouzot, and Robert Bresson. All made escapist films that avoided propaganda and the censor. After Liberation, Cocteau, Clouzot, Becker, and Bresson made some of their best work, while Renoir, Clair, and Ophüls made welcome returns. In 1946, the Centre National du Cinéma Français (CNC) was set up. One of its first actions was to protect the French film industry against the influence of foreign films – particularly American – by limiting the number shown. It also helped finance independent productions, many of which reflected the social and political climate of the post-war years, with a return to realism and film noir – the master of which was Jean-Pierre Melville.

Marcel Carne's ***Les Enfants du Paradis*** (1945) is a tale of ill-fated love.

However, in the 1950s, the veteran directors still dominated. Some, such as Marcel Carné, who had made the internationally acclaimed *Les Enfants du Paradis* (1945) during the occupation, saw their reputations gradually decline. Many succumbed to the lure of commercial cinema, turning out lavish but uninspired colour movies, often in lucrative co-productions with Italy.

There was also a literary tradition pursued by Claude Autant-Lara, who adapted Stendhal, Maupassant, and Dostoevsky to the screen. The French stars of the 1950s were, to a great extent, the French stars of the 1930s and 1940s – Jean Gabin, Fernandel, Edwige Feuillère, Gérard Philipe, Danielle Darrieux, and Pierre Fresnay.

The first rumblings of discontent were given influential expression in 1948 by Alexandre Astruc, in an article called *The Birth of the New Avant-Garde: Le Camera Stylo*. Astruc fulminated against the assembly-line method of producing movies, which the French industry had inherited from Hollywood, and where front-office interference ensured that maverick films were tailored to fit tried-and-tested formulas.

Cahiérs du Cinéma

In 1951, critic André Bazin founded *Cahiérs du Cinéma*, the most influential film magazine. Several young critics on the magazine decided to take practical action in their battle against traditional, literary French films, or *cinéma de papa*, by making movies themselves, taking advantage of the subsidies brought in by the Gaullist government. The leading figures of this movement, which soon became known as the "French New Wave", were François Truffaut, Jean-Luc Godard, Alain Resnais, Claude Chabrol, Jacques Rivette, Eric Rohmer, and Louis Malle. This core group of directors initially collaborated and assisted each other, helping in the development of a common and distinct use of form, style, and narrative. This made their work instantly recognizable, and their influence is still felt across the film world.

In the 1980s, three young directors – Jean-Jacques Beinex, Luc Besson, and Leos Carax – gave a new, "postmodern" face to French cinema, deriving their aesthetics for their cool thrillers from commercials and pop videos. Women have also been among the first rank of French directors. After Agnès Varda and Marguerite Duras had become established, there followed Yannick Bellon, Nelly Kaplan, Coline Serreau, Diane Kurys, and Claire Denis; and excellent new French films and directors continue to emerge today. Examples include social satires (Laurent Cantet's ***Human Resources***,1999 and ***Time Out***, 2001); sophisticated comedies (Agnès Jaoui's ***The Taste of Others***, 2000 and ***Look at Me***, 2004); personal dramas (François Ozon's ***Five Times Two***, 2004 and ***Time to Leave***, 2005); films of urban decay (Mathieu Kassovitz's ***La Haine***, 1995); sexual explorations (Catherine Breillat's ***Romance***, 1999 and Gaspard Noé's ***Irreversible***, 2002); and romantic comedies (Jean-Pierre Jeunet's ***Amélie***, 2001).

Jacques Tati as Monsieur Hulot finds it difficult to enter the ultra-modern house of his brother-in-law (Jean-Pierre Zola) in ***Mon Oncle*** (***My Uncle***, 1958).

Claude Laydu, in the title role of Robert Bresson's poignant *Diary of a Country Priest* (1951), plays a man isolated and assailed by self-doubt.

Italy

Italy has had a profound influence on cinema style, particularly within three periods: pre-World War I with mammoth epics; the immediate post-World War II of the neorealists (see box, p.286); and from 1960 to the mid-1970s, with the "second film renaissance" led by Federico Fellini.

Cabiria (1914), Giovanni Pastrone's pioneering epic, required huge sets and took six months to shoot in studios and on location.

In 1905, the first Italian studios were built. They were owned by two of the largest production companies, Cines and Itala, both of which made successful costume dramas. At Cines, Mario Caserini directed *Giovanna d'Arco* (1908) and Ubaldo Maria del Colle made *The Last Days of Pompeii* (1913); while at Itala, Giovanni Pastrone made *The Fall of Troy* (1911) and, most significantly, *Cabiria* (1914). The latter, which tells of the adventures of a Sicilian slave girl rescued by the muscular Maciste, took more than six months to shoot and contained technical innovations such as dolly and crane shots. Its success in the US inspired D.W. Griffith and Cecil B. DeMille to embark on large-scale productions. These early spectacles would be the prototypes for "peplum" ("sword and sandal") epics, popular in the 1950s.

World War I and competition from the US put an end to big production spectacles, and all the studios had closed down by 1922. Ironically, it was Mussolini's Fascist regime that revived Italian cinema. The film school, Centro Sperimentale di Cinematografia, was founded in 1935, and Cinecittà Studios (soon to be known as "Hollywood on the Tiber") was opened by Mussolini.

Although Italian cinema in the 1930s was dominated by "White Telephone" films (superficial tales of the wealthy) and propaganda films that looked back on the glory that was Rome, such as *Scipione l'Africano* (1937), there were some notable exceptions. Mario Camerini's *What Scoundrels Men Are!* (1932), the first Italian film to be shot entirely on location, and Alessandro Blasetti's *Four Steps in the Clouds* (1942), anticipated neorealism by using humble characters and ordinary backgrounds.

Sophia Loren stars in Vittorio De Sica's *Two Women* (1960) for which she gained the rare honour of winning a Best Actress Oscar for a foreign-language film.

The neorealist movement

Luchino Visconti's *Ossessione* (1943, see p.282), is regarded by many as the first neorealist movie. This label was applied to any post-Liberation film that dealt with the working class, and was shot on location, whether with actors or a non-professional cast. One of the key figures of the movement was Cesare Zavattini, who wrote scripts for almost all of Vittorio De Sica's films from 1944–73, including *Bicycle Thieves* (1948, see p.286) and *The Garden of the Finzi-Continis* (1970). Although the world praised Italian neorealist films, they only made up a small percentage of production. After the war, Italian audiences preferred escapist entertainment, such as comedies starring Toto and Alberto Sordi.

By 1950, Italian neorealism began to decline, though De Sica's *Umberto D.* (1952) and *The Roof* (1956) continued the tradition, and some younger

Amarcord (1973), Federico Fellini's semi-autobiographical, affectionate, and often dream-like memoir of Rimini, his home town, has a lovely climactic wedding celebration.

directors, such as Pier Paolo Pasolini in his first film ***Accattone*** (1961), showed its influence, as did some films from countries as diverse as Brazil and Iran. Roberto Rossellini, whose ***Rome, Open City*** (1945) and ***Paisà*** (1946) are among the best examples of neorealism, began to move away from the style, with spiritual melodramas starring Ingrid Bergman; and both Visconti and De Sica abandoned many of the principles of neorealism. The 1950s was the time of "peplum" movies and frivolous vehicles for international stars, such as Silvana Mangano, Gina Lollobrigida, and Sophia Loren.

The 1960s heralded a golden age of Italian cinema. The watershed year was 1960, which saw the release of Federico Fellini's ***La Dolce Vita*** (see p.305), Luchino Visconti's ***Rocco and His Brothers***, Michelangelo Antonioni's ***L'Avventura*** (see p.307), and Vittorio De Sica's ***Two Women***. Then came a flood of remarkable films from these four masters as well as from Pasolini, Bernardo Bertolucci (***The Conformist***, 1970, see p.315), Marco Bellocchio, Ermanno Olmi, Ettore Scola, Francesco Rosi, and the Taviani brothers. At the same time, Sergio Leone and others were making "Spaghetti Westerns" (see pp.122–25), injecting new life into the genre. There was also Italian horror cinema, whose leading practitioners were Mario Bava and Dario Argento.

Following a lull in the 1980s, the industry was given a boost by a wave of films by new directors. At the forefront of this were Giuseppe Tornatore with ***Cinema Paradiso*** (1988, see p.330), Gabriele Salvatores with ***Mediterraneo*** (1991), and Roberto Benigni with ***Life is Beautiful*** (1997). All won Best Foreign Film Oscars. There were many other films of quality that kept interest in Italian cinema alive, notably Gianni Amelio's ***Open Doors*** (1990) and ***The Keys to the House*** (2004), ***Il Postino*** (1994) by Michael Radford, Nani Moretti's ***The Son's Room*** (2000), and Marco Tullio Giordana's ***The Best of Youth*** (2003).

WHAT TO WATCH

- *The Flowers of St. Francis* (Roberto Rossellini, 1950)
- *Umberto D.* (Vittorio De Sica, 1952)
- *La Notte* (Michelangelo Antonioni, 1961)
- *The Leopard* (Luchino Visconti, 1963)
- *The Gospel According to St. Matthew* (Pier Paolo Pasolini, 1964)
- *Amarcord* (Federico Fellini, 1973)
- *1900* (Bernardo Bertolucci, 1976)
- *Cinema Paradiso* (Giuseppe Tornatore, 1988)
- *Il Postino* (Michael Radford, 1994)
- *The Best of Youth* (Marco Tullio Giordana, 2003)
- *Gomorrah* (Matteo Garrone, 2008)
- *Vincere* (Marco Bellocchio, 2009)

Jasmine Trinca and Luigi Lo Cascio star in the 383-minute *The Best of Youth* (2003).

United Kingdom

Despite overwhelming competition from US films, British cinema has managed to survive in the shadow of its perceived rival in Hollywood. Creating films with a distinctly British flavour, it continues to export its talented directors and stars.

One of the first British production companies was founded as early as 1898, by an American, Charles Urban. Cecil Hepworth was one of the first English directors to realize the potential of the medium, his most famous film being ***Rescued by Rover*** (1905), a seven-minute thriller made on a budget of £8. Two directors of the Silent Era who stood out were George Pearson and Maurice Elvey.

Cecil Hepworth's *Rescued by Rover* (1905) tells the story of a collie dog who rescues a baby abducted by gypsies.

Some soon-to-be important figures began making films in the 1920s: producer Michael Balcon, who would be the main force behind the films produced at Ealing Studios; Alfred Hitchcock (see p.210), who was already gaining a reputation as a master of suspense with films such as ***The Lodger*** (1927); Victor Saville, who later directed three musicals with Britain's top musical-comedy star Jessie Matthews in the 1930s; and Herbert Wilcox, who made several films during the 1930s and 1940s.

To counteract the dominance of American films, a British quota system was introduced in 1927, under which exhibitors were obliged to show a 5 per cent quota of British films, increasing to 20 per cent by 1935. This led to an increase in the production of British films, but also had the adverse effect of encouraging cheap and inferior films, known as "quota quickies".

The first British talkie was ***Blackmail*** (1929), directed by Alfred Hitchcock, who would go on to make some of the best British films of the 1930s. Alexander Korda, a Hungarian emigré, formed the production company London Films and built Denham Studios. He directed ***The Private Life of Henry VIII*** (1933), which broke US box office records and gave Charles Laughton the first Best Actor Oscar for a British film.

During World War II, there were some excellent morale-boosting features and documentaries by directors such as Humphrey Jennings (***London Can Take It!***, 1940); Carol Reed (***The Way Ahead***, 1944); David Lean and Noël Coward (***In Which We Serve***, 1942); Michael Powell and Emeric Pressburger (***The Life and Death of Colonel Blimp***, 1943); and Laurence Olivier, who made ***Henry V*** (1944) a patriotic pageant. Olivier also acted with Vivien Leigh in three films, including ***Fire Over England*** (1937).

Vivien Leigh and Laurence Olivier, the most glamorous couple in British cinema, are seen here in their first of three films together, ***Fire Over England*** (1937).

After the war, entertainment was richly provided by the Ealing comedies (see p.90). However, war films such as Michael Anderson's ***The Dam Busters*** and Guy Hamilton's ***The Colditz Story*** (both 1955) continued to be made. In the late 1950s, younger film-makers began to feel that British films did not address contemporary issues. The change came about with Jack Clayton's ***Room at the Top*** (1959), which treated class and sex with a refreshing frankness. A series of "kitchen sink" films of working-class life followed, outstanding among which were Karel Reisz's ***Saturday Night and Sunday Morning*** (1960, see p.306), Tony Richardson's ***A Taste of Honey*** (1961), John Schlesinger's ***A Kind of Loving*** (1962), and Lindsay Anderson's ***This Sporting Life*** (1963). These soon gave way to more escapist "Swinging London" films, and the cycle of James Bond movies, beginning with ***Dr. No*** (1962).

Swinging London

London became the world's most fashionable capital and many foreign directors made films there. Among them were Michelangelo Antonioni (***Blow-Up***, 1966), Roman Polanski (***Repulsion***, 1965), François Truffaut (***Fahrenheit 451***, 1966), and Stanley Kubrick, who settled in England. Two American-born directors apart from Kubrick – Richard Lester (two Beatles films: ***A Hard Day's Night***, 1964, and ***Help!***, 1965) and Joseph Losey (***The Servant***, 1963, and ***Accident***, 1967) – also made an impact.

Quality began to decline in the 1970s, to be revived in the 1980s by Hugh Hudson's ***Chariots of Fire*** (1981) and Richard Attenborough's ***Gandhi*** (1982), both of which won Best Picture Oscars; Bill Forsyth's ***Gregory's Girl*** (1981); Peter Greenaway's ***The Draughtsman's Contract*** (1982); and Terry Gilliam's ***Brazil*** (1985). From the early 1990s onwards, there have been a number of commercial and critical successes, including Mike Newell's romantic comedy, ***Four Weddings and a Funeral*** (1994), starring Hugh Grant; Danny Boyle's crime drama ***Trainspotting*** (1996); Peter Cattaneo's social comedy ***The Full Monty*** (1997); Guy Ritchie's gangster movie ***Lock, Stock and Two Smoking Barrels*** (1998); and Stephen Daldry's drama ***Billy Elliot*** (2000), about a boy torn between his love for ballet and the prejudices of his father. Other notable films are Stephen Frears' crime thriller ***Dirty Pretty Things*** (2002); Kevin Macdonald's award-winning documentary ***Touching The Void*** (2003); and the period drama ***The King's Speech*** (2010), directed by Tom Hooper, which won Academy Awards for Best Original Screenplay, Best Actor, Best Director, and Best Picture.

WHAT TO WATCH

- ***The Lady Vanishes*** (Alfred Hitchcock, 1938)
- ***Brief Encounter*** (David Lean, 1945)
- ***Odd Man Out*** (Carol Reed, 1947)
- ***Black Narcissus*** (Michael Powell and Emeric Pressburger, 1947)
- ***Whisky Galore*** (Alexander Mackendrick, 1949)
- ***The Servant*** (Joseph Losey, 1963)
- ***If....*** (Lindsay Anderson, 1968)
- ***Local Hero*** (Bill Forsyth, 1983)
- ***Brazil*** (Terry Gilliam, 1985)
- ***Billy Elliot*** (Stephen Daldry, 2000)
- ***Touching the Void*** (Kevin Macdonald, 2003)
- ***The King's Speech*** (Tom Hooper, 2010)

Film poster, 1996

In *The King's Speech* (2010), Oscar-winner Colin Firth portrays Britain's King George VI, who battled against a stammer.

Spain

For 36 years, under Franco's repressive regime, it was almost impossible for Spain to create a vibrant film industry and for talented film-makers to express themselves freely. However, after Franco, Spanish films became among the best in the world.

Luis Buñuel's third and last film made in Spain, ***Tristana*** (1970) starred Catherine Deneuve, and was set in the Spain of the 1920s.

Any chance that Spain would have had to develop its small film industry in the early 20th century was dashed by the military dictatorship of Primo de Rivera from 1923–30. The arrival of sound coincided with the election of a democratic government in 1931, and an attempt was made to build up a film industry. Several studios were constructed and the first big production and distribution company, CIFESA, was founded in 1934. However, many gifted film-makers, most notably Luis Buñuel, went to Hollywood to work on Spanish-language versions of American films. Before that, Buñuel had made ***Land Without Bread*** (1933), the first of only three films he was to make in his native country. A stark documentary on the poverty of peasants in a barren area of Spain, it so effectively revealed this social evil that it was promptly banned by the government.

Government dominance

After the Spanish Civil War, when the Nationalists came to power, they immediately brought the film industry under government control, imposing strict moral and political guidelines. The fact that José Luis Sáenz de Heredia's fascistic ***Raza*** (1942), which is based on an autobiographical novel by General Franco, is regarded as one of the outstanding Spanish films of the 1940s says a lot about Spanish cinema of the period. However, in the next decade, despite restrictions, a distinctive type of cinema emerged, led by Juan Antonio Bardem and Luis García Berlanga. They co-directed ***This Happy Pair*** (1953), about a young couple's financial struggles. Berlanga's ***Welcome Mr. Marshall!*** (1953) is a sardonic look at the effect of the possibility of American aid on a small Spanish town. Despite cuts, ***El Verdugo*** (***Not on Your Life,*** 1963) contains social criticism spiked with gallows humour. Bardem's ***Death of a Cyclist*** (1955), a bitter comment on contemporary Spain, won the *Grand Prix* at Cannes. Bardem also bravely produced ***Viridiana*** (1961), which marked Buñuel's return to Spain after 29 years. The film's savage attack on the mentality and rituals of the Catholic church led to it being banned outright in Spain. Buñuel returned to the country in slightly more liberal times to make ***Tristana*** (1970).

Italian director Marco Ferreri directed three films in Spain in the 1960s, the best being ***The Wheelchair*** (1960), a black comedy in the Buñuel vein. Carlos Saura was the first Spanish director to deal with the Spanish Civil War and its aftermath. Saura's films contain an oblique criticism of Franco's regime and analyse the bourgeoisie, the church, the army, and sexual taboos. ***The Hunt*** (1966) was the first of many films to star his future wife, Geraldine Chaplin. Saura's later films, such as ***Cria Cuervos*** (1976) and ***Elisa, My Life*** (1977), have a shifting

WHAT TO WATCH

- ***Welcome Mr. Marshall!*** (Luis García Berlanga, 1953)
- ***Death of a Cyclist*** (Juan Antonio Bardem, 1955)
- ***Viridiana*** (Luis Buñuel, 1961)
- ***The Spirit of the Beehive*** (Victor Erice, 1973)
- ***Cria Cuervos*** (Carlos Saura, 1976)
- ***Tierra*** (Julio Medem, 1996)
- ***Talk to Her*** (Pedro Almodóvar, 2002)
- ***The Sea Inside*** (Alejandro Amenábar, 2004)

chronology and an obsession with childhood. These two films starred the remarkable child actress Ana Torrent, who had made her mark in Victor Erice's ***The Spirit of the Beehive*** (1973), about an 8-year-old girl who becomes obsessed with Boris Karloff's good-bad monster in James Whale's ***Frankenstein*** (1931). This impressive debut feature can be read partly as an allegorical account of a country living under the shadow of an authoritarian regime. Erice completed only three films in a career spanning nearly three decades, the other two being ***El Sur*** (1983), about a young girl's relationship with her father, and ***Quince Tree of the Sun*** (1992), one of the best films on the creative process of art.

In *The Spirit of the Beehive* (1973), Ana (Ana Torrent) hands an apple to a fugitive whom she relates to the monster in the 1931 film, ***Frankenstein***.

A new dawn of creativity

José Luis Borau's ***Furtivos*** (1975), which exposes the harsh reality of Franco's Spain, opened two months before the death of the Generalissimo. It was the first film to be distributed in Spain without a licence from the censors. However, the expected burst of creativity in the new era had to wait until Pedro Almodóvar came on the scene in the 1980s with his outrageously camp melodramas. His movie ***All About My Mother*** (1999) won a Best Foreign Film Oscar, as did Fernando Trueba's ***Belle Epoque*** (1992) and Alejandro Amenábar's ***The Sea Inside*** (2004). Other first-class directors are Bigas Luna (***Jamón, Jamón***, 1992, and ***The Tit and The Moon***, 1994); Julio Medem (***Tierra***, 1996, and ***Sex and Lucia***, 2001); and Mexican-born Guillermo del Toro (***The Devil's Backbone***, 2001). Trueba (***Two Much***, 1995) and Amenábar (***The Others***, 2001) have made the trip to Hollywood, while actors who have become famous in the US include Javier Bardem, Penélope Cruz, and Antonio Banderas. Veteran directors such as Carlos Saura and Mario Camus, whose ***The Holy Innocents*** (1984) is one of the best Spanish films in the last few decades, continue to remain active.

Fernando (Jorge Sanz), a deserter from the army during the Spanish Civil War, has to decide between three women, daughters of his best friend, in ***Belle Epoque*** (1992).

Portugal

Portugal has never had a large indigenous film industry, making only an average of ten films annually. However, the country has attracted foreign film-makers and produced a great director in Manoel de Oliveira, who has put Portuguese cinema on the map.

João César Monteiro plays the manager of an ice-cream parlour, who fantasizes about his young female employees in ***God's Comedy*** (1995), which he also directed.

In the late 1920s, under the influence of various European avant-garde movements, Portugal produced a number of remarkable films: José Leitão de Barros's ***Maria do Mar*** (1930), Jorge Brum do Canto's beautiful documentaries, and especially Manoel de Oliveira's ***Working on the Douro River*** (1931), a series of images of the fishermen and workers in the director's home town of Oporto. In 1942, Oliveira made his first feature, the neorealistic (see box, p.286) ***Aniki Bóbó***, about the adventures of street urchins growing up in the slums of Oporto. He did not make another feature for 21 years, after which he would make one film a year into his nineties, creating a synthesis of literary, theatrical, musical, and visual material. Perhaps his most accessible film is ***Abraham's Valley*** (1993), a sensual and understated version of *Madame Bovary*.

Other Portuguese directors of stature include António de Macedo (***Sunday Afternoon***, 1966); Fernando Lopes (***On The Edge of the Horizon***, 1993); João Botelho (***A Portuguese Goodbye***, 1986, and ***Hard Times***, 1988); Paulo Rocha (***River of Gold***, 1998, and ***The Heart's Root***, 2000); and Teresa Villaverde (***Três Irmãos***, 1994). A notable figure was João César Monteiro, who starred in and directed ***God's Comedy*** (1995), which won the Special Jury Prize at the Venice Film Festival. Monteiro himself appeared in many of his own long, observant, and often bizarre films.

Leonor Silveira plays the sensuous Ema in Manoel de Oliveira's ***Abraham's Valley*** (1993), based on the novel by Agustina Bessa-Luís.

WHAT TO WATCH

- ***Hard Times*** (João Botelho, 1988)
- ***Abraham's Valley*** (Manoel de Oliveira, 1993)
- ***God's Comedy*** (João César Monteiro, 1995)
- ***River of Gold*** (Paulo Rocha, 1998)
- ***O Delfim*** (Fernando Lopes, 2002)

Canada

Canada's close proximity to the US and the cultural gulf between its French- and English-speaking population has not prevented the development of an identifiable film industry, especially in the field of animation. The nation's cinematic output has been particularly successful since the early 1970s.

Nick Stahl (left) plays Dodge and Joshua Close plays Oliver in Jacob Tierney's ***Twist*** (2003), a gay take on Charles Dickens' *Oliver Twist*, set in the hustler district of Toronto.

The Canadian Pacific railway set up a film unit as early as 1900, but it was only in 1939, when the National Film Board of Canada was established under John Grierson to counteract Hollywood's dominance, that Canadian films began to make an impression worldwide. The NFB built up a strong animation department, where Norman McLaren was able to experiment with the art form. Michael Snow was prominent in avant-garde circles with his "abstract" films.

After World War II, Francophone Canadians began making films, many of which were *cinema verité* (see box, p.311) documentaries influenced by French director Jean Rouch. Among the leading figures in Canada were Pierre Perrault and Michel Brault. Gradually, French Canadian directors became the prime force in the Canadian film industry. Claude Jutra (***My Uncle Antoine***, 1971), Gilles Carle (***The True Nature of Bernadette***, 1972), and especially Denys Arcand, made their mark in the 1970s. Arcand, known as "the Godfather of the New Canadian cinema", has continued to make trenchant satires on Quebec society, in ***Jesus of Montreal*** (1989) and ***The Barbarian Invasions*** (2003). It was easier and more likely that Anglophone directors, like Ted Kotcheff and Norman Jewison, could work in Hollywood. However, two English Canadian directors, David Cronenberg and Atom Egoyan, despite having worked abroad, remain resolutely Canadian in their different idiosyncratic ways.

Marie-Josée Croze plays Nathalie, who tries to offer comfort to a man dying of cancer, in Denys Arcand's bleak and funny ***The Barbarian Invasions*** (2003).

WHAT TO WATCH

- ***My Uncle Antoine*** (Claude Jutra, 1971)
- ***The True Nature of Bernadette*** (Gilles Carle, 1972)
- ***The Apprenticeship of Duddy Kravitz*** (Ted Kotcheff, 1974)
- ***The Decline of the American Empire*** (Denys Arcand, 1986)
- ***I've Heard the Mermaids Singing*** (Patricia Rozema, 1987)
- ***Dead Ringers*** (David Cronenberg, 1988)
- ***Jesus of Montreal*** (Denys Arcand, 1989)
- ***Exotica*** (Atom Egoyan, 1994)
- ***The Sweet Hereafter*** (Atom Egoyan, 1997)
- ***The Barbarian Invasions*** (Denys Arcand, 2003)
- ***Twist*** (Jacob Tierney, 2003)

Central America

Mexico has always been the leading producer of feature films in Latin America. Post-Revolution Cuba, which once produced more than 10 features a year, has gradually turned to digital film-making – the only solution for poor film-producing countries in Central America.

A poor couple, Pedro Armendáriz and Maria Elena Marqués, find a very valuable pearl in Emilio Fernández's ***La Perla*** (1947), based on a book by John Steinbeck.

Until Sergei Eisenstein's *¡Que Viva Mexico!* (1932), Mexican audiences were exposed only to popular melodramas, crude comedies, and Spanish-language versions of Hollywood films. Eisenstein's visit to Mexico inspired directors such as Emilio Fernández and cameraman Gabriel Figueroa, and the number of Mexican-made films grew.

Fernández's ***Maria Candelaria*** (1944), which was shot by Figueroa and starred renowned Hollywood actor Dolores del Rio, won Best Film at Cannes. Spanish exile Luis Buñuel made most of his films in Mexico from 1946 to 1960, perhaps the best being ***Los Olvidados*** (***The Young and the Damned***, 1950). Figueroa, who shot most of Buñuel's Mexican films, also worked with John Ford (***The Fugitive***, 1947) and John Huston (***The Night of the Iguana***, 1964). During World War II, movie production in Mexico tripled. Argentina and Spain were run by fascist governments and so Mexico became the world's largest producer of Spanish-language films in the 1940s. Although Mexico's government was reactionary, it encouraged the production of films that it thought would help to articulate a true Mexican identity, in contrast to the view portrayed by Hollywood.

Indigenous cinema suffered through the 1960s and 1970s, until government sponsorship of the industry and the creation of State-supported film helped create *Nuevo Cine Mexicano* (New Mexican Cinema) in the 1990s. Alfonso Arau's ***Like Water for Chocolate*** (1992) paved the way for Alejandro Gonzáles Iñárritu's ***Amores Perros*** (2000) and Alfonso Cuarón's ***Y Tu Mamá También*** (2001).

Film poster, 2001

Cuban cinema

In pre-Revolution Cuba, films were mostly light musicals and comedies. Shortly after Castro took power in 1959, the Cuban Institute of Cinematic Art and Industry was set up to control film production and distribution. One of its founders was Tomás Gutiérrez Alea, who made some of Cuba's finest films. Humberto Solás reinvented the historical epic with ***Lucía*** (1968); and Santiago Álvarez, imprisoned more than once under Batista's regime, made weekly newsreels. Using this footage, with stills, and cartoons, and other devices, he became a leading maker of short agitprop documentaries in the 1960s. The Vietnam war gave him the material for ***Hanoi, Tuesday 13th*** (1967) and ***LBJ*** (1968).

The Cuban Revolution attracted foreign directors such as Chris Marker (***¡Cuba Si!***, 1961) and Agnès Varda (***Salut les Cubains***, 1963) to Cuba. One of the most remarkable films made there was Mikhail Kalatozov's propagandist ***I Am Cuba*** (1964). Wim Wenders' Oscar-nominated ***Buena Vista Social Club*** (1999), a documentary about the ageing, home-grown musicians of the title, was shot in Havana.

Haiti, although it does not have a film industry to speak of, has been the subject of a number of documentaries. It is also the setting for several feature films, from Jacques Tourneur's fanciful ***I Walked with a Zombie*** (1943) to Laurent Cantet's ***Vers le Sud*** (2005), a film about sexual tourism.

WHAT TO WATCH

- ***Maria Candelaria*** (Emilio Fernández, Mexico, 1944)
- ***La Perla*** (Emilio Fernández, Mexico, 1947)
- ***Los Olvidados*** (Luis Buñuel, Mexico, 1950)
- ***I Am Cuba*** (Mikhail Kalatozov, Soviet Union/Cuba, 1964)
- ***Memories of Underdevelopment*** (Tomás Gutiérrez Alea, Cuba, 1968)
- ***Lucía*** (Humberto Solás, Cuba, 1968)
- ***Like Water for Chocolate*** (Alfonso Arau, Mexico, 1992)
- ***Amores Perros*** (Alejandro Gonzáles Iñárritu, Mexico, 2000)
- ***Y Tu Mamá También*** (Alfonso Cuarón, Mexico, 2001)
- ***Pan's Labyrinth*** (Guillermo del Toro, Mexico, 2006)

In *Lucía* (1968), Raquel Revuelta stars in the title role – one of three women from different epochs, each demonstrating a woman's changing role in a macho society.

South America

Politics have never been far away from South American cinema. The 1960s saw a new wave of political protest movies, and by the end of the 20th century, this had broadened into mainstream success, particularly for Argentinian and Brazilian directors.

In ***Antonio das Mortes*** (1969), Glauber Rocha's political allegory, the titular assassin ends up siding with the peasants to fight against the brutal landowners.

Film-making in South America was extremely parochial and unsophisticated during the Silent Era, when local products were eclipsed by foreign films. Sound helped to advance the Argentinian and Brazilian film industries, however. During the 1930s, Argentina rivalled Mexico in the Latin-American market with its "gaucho" and tango movies, the most successful directed by José A. Ferreyra and starring tango singer Libertad Lamarque.

In Brazil, the large number of illiterate people meant the studios had to produce films with sound quickly. One of the earliest was ***Alô, Alô, Brasil*** (1935), a musical that launched Carmen Miranda's career. The most important figure in early Brazilian cinema was Humberto Mauro, who tried to elevate the poor quality of local production with serious features such as ***Ganga Bruta*** (1933), probably the first great Brazilian film. In the 1940s, film production in Brazil was down to its lowest level. At this time, Alberto Cavalcanti returned to his native land after a successful cosmopolitan career (particularly at Ealing Studios in England) to become head of production at the Vera Cruz film company. The first Brazilian movie to become internationally known, Lima Barreto's poetic Robin Hood-type adventure ***O Cangaceiro*** (***The Bandit***, 1953), was made under Cavalcanti's aegis.

Cinema languished in Argentina during the Peronist era (1946–55), until Leopoldo Torre Nilsson emerged to become one of the most famous of all Argentinian directors. The son of prolific director Leopoldo Torres Rios, Torre Nilsson began working with his father at the age of 15, and was a scriptwriter and assistant on many of his father's films. His own movies, most of them adaptations from the novels of his wife, Beatriz Guido, broke away from the staple Argentinian product of superficial comedies and melodramas. ***House of the Angel*** (1957), ***The Fall*** (1959), and ***The Hand in the Trap*** (1961) are studies of a bourgeoisie repressed by a suffocating Catholic Church and its effect on adolescents. The Gothic claustrophobia of these films echoes the work of Spanish director Luis Buñuel without the biting irony. ***Summerskin*** (1961) and ***The Terrace*** (1963) show teenagers creating a world of their own, away from the stifling mansions of their parents. Unfortunately, by the mid-1960s, Torre Nilsson found it increasingly difficult to make the films he wanted because of the political and economic climate of his country.

WHAT TO WATCH

- ***The Hand in the Trap*** (Leopoldo Torre Nilsson, Argentina, 1961)
- ***Barren Lives*** (Nelson Pereira dos Santos, Brazil, 1963)
- ***Antonio das Mortes*** (Glauber Rocha, Brazil, 1969)
- ***The Hour of the Furnaces*** (Fernando Solanas/Octavio Getino, Argentina, 1970)
- ***The Battle of Chile*** (Patricio Guzmán, Chile, 1975/79)
- ***The Official Story*** (Luis Puenzo, Argentina, 1985)
- ***Central Station*** (Walter Salles, Brazil, 1998)
- ***City of God*** (Fernando Meirelles, Brazil, 2002)
- ***The Secret in Their Eyes*** (Juan José Campanella, Argentina, 2010)

The New Wave and liberation

Brazilian film finally matured in the 1960s with *Cinema Nôvo*, a New Wave movement of young political film-makers. The main figures were Glauber Rocha (***Black God White Devil***, 1964), Ruy Guerra (***The Guns***, 1964), Carlos Diegues (***Ganga Zumba***, 1963), and Nelson Pereira Dos Santos (***Barren Lives***, 1963). Produced under repressive conditions following the military coup in 1964, ***Antonio das Mortes*** (1969) was Rocha's last radical cry from Brazil before almost 10 years in exile.

In Argentina, a group of film-makers set up the independent *Grupo Cine Liberacion*. A leading figure was Fernando Solanas. His ***The Hour of the Furnaces*** (1968), a three-part masterpiece co-directed with Octavio Getino, presents a dazzling array of interviews, intertitles, songs, poems, footage from other films, and new material, bearing witness to the negative effects of neo-colonialism. This devastating film, made clandestinely, ends with a two-minute close-up of the dead Che Guevara (to whom the film is dedicated, along with "all who died fighting to liberate Latin America"). The film was partly responsible for new and rigorous censorship laws.

In the same year, Miguel Littin's ***The Jackal of Nahueltoro*** (1969) was released. It was one of the best films to come out of Chile in the creative period just before and during the presidency of Salvador Allende. Based on a real case, it tells the story of an illiterate peasant murderer, who is taught to read and understand social values upon arrival in prison, only to be executed by a firing squad. Patricio Guzmán's ***The Battle of Chile*** (1975–79), a powerful documentary on the events leading up to the overthrow of the Allende government by the CIA and the forces of General Pinochet, was smuggled out of the country into Cuba, where it took over four years to edit. The events of the bloody military coup in Chile on 11 September 1973, are seen through the eyes of two young boys in Andrés Wood's ***Machuca*** (2004).

A former teacher, Dora (Fernanda Montenegro), waits with Josué (Vinícius de Oliveira) in a quest to find the boy's father, in ***Central Station*** (1998).

Glauber Rocha's *Black God White Devil* (1964) tells of a self-styled black saint, who gains a following in the sertão – the parched land of north-east Brazil.

Gael García Bernal (front), as the young Che Guevara, rides with Rodrigo De la Serna, who plays Alberto Granado in Walter Salles' ***The Motorcycle Diaries*** (2004).

Latin resurgence

The 1980s saw a renaissance of Argentinian cinema. ***Funny Dirty Little War*** (1983), Hector Olivera's black comedy of Peronist militants in the early 1970s, is a fast, furious, and funny political satire. Luis Puenzo's moving ***The Official Story*** (1985) is about the fate of the children of the Disappeared – the thousands of Argentinian citizens who vanished without a trace during the "Dirty War" (1976–83). This courageous film won the Best Foreign Film Oscar. The previous year, María Luisa Bemberg's ***Camila***, an indictment of oppression during the dictatorship of 1847, was seen as a criticism of modern Argentina.

Carlos Sorin made the fascinating ***A King and His Movie*** (1986), about the difficulties of a director trying to make a historical film in Argentina. He followed this with the gently humorous road movie ***Historias Minimas*** (2002), and the canine comedy, ***Bombón: El Pero*** (2004). Among the other first-rate Argentinian films of this later period were Fabián Bielinsky's ***Nine Queens*** (2000) and Pablo Trapero's cop thriller ***El Bonaerense*** (2002). Other recent successes include Trapero's semi-documentary ***Familia Rodante*** (2004) and Lucrecia Martel's ***The Holy Girl*** (2004).

In Brazil, director Hector Babenco followed his searing exposure of homeless children (***Pixote***, 1981) with the prison drama ***Carandiru*** in 2003. The other well-known Brazilian director, Walter Salles, had hits with ***Central Station*** (1998) and ***The Motorcycle Diaries*** (2004), while Fernando Meirelles triumphed in 2002 with ***City of God***. In a lighter vein, Andrucha Waddington's ***Me, You, Them*** (***E Tu Eles***, 2000), tells the story of a strong woman and her three husbands, all living together. Other countries not known for film production had successes, too, such as Juan Pablo Rebella and Pablo Stoll's ***25 Watts*** (2001) and ***Whisky*** (2004), from Uruguay; Barbet Schroeder's ***Our Lady of the Assassins*** (2000), from Columbia; and Rodrigo Bellott's ***Sexual Dependency*** (2003), from Bolivia, which uses a split screen throughout.

Carlos Sorin's *Bombón: El Pero* (2004) follows the life of an out-of-work mechanic (Juan Villegas) whose life is transformed when he is given a pedigree dog.

China, Hong Kong, and Taiwan

Until the 1980s, China, the world's most populous nation, produced relatively few internationally known films, whereas its neighbours, Hong Kong and Taiwan, were renowned for their martial arts movies. Today, China has become a cinematic force to be reckoned with.

Zheng Junli's landmark film ***Crows and Sparrows*** (1949) was released only after the Civil War.

China was one of the slowest countries in Asia to develop its own film industry, and many of its first films were derived from staged opera productions or light comedies. Although they attracted large local audiences, these films were rarely widely distributed. One problem was language. The main studios were in Shanghai, and when talking pictures arrived, the films were made in Mandarin rather than the local dialect, and few members of the audience could understand them. Small companies in Hong Kong then started making films in Cantonese, which were distributed in China. The first Chinese film to be acclaimed internationally was Cai Chusheng's ***Song of the Fishermen*** (1934), about the daily hardships faced by fishermen on the River Yangtze.

When Japan invaded Shanghai in 1937, many film-makers left for Hong Kong or Taiwan. Others followed the government into exile in Chungking. The Japanese took over the studios in order to produce propaganda films, and very few Chinese pictures were made. After the war, left-wing groups produced the best films, such as Zheng Junli's ***Crows and Sparrows*** (1949), about a corrupt landlord and his tenants who fight for their rights. One of the last great films to come out of of pre-Communist China, it was a landmark in its move towards a style not far from Italian neorealism (see box, p.286).

Films of the cultural revolution

The first film to be produced after the People's Republic of China was established in 1949 was the Soviet-Chinese documentary, ***Victory of the Chinese People*** (1950) directed by Sergei Gerasimov. Xie Jin emerged as the brightest of the Chinese directors in the early 1960s with ***The Red Detachment of***

A young woman (Gong Li) studies the barrels in her middle-aged husband's wine distillery in ***Red Sorghum*** (1987), Zhang Yimou's story of passion and murder.

Women (1960), based on the classic Chinese ballet, and ***Two Stage Sisters*** (1965). Both films revealed a vivid sense of colour, composition, and inventive camera angles. The finely crafted ***Two Stage Sisters***, although anti-Capitalist and pro-feminist, contained many elements of Hollywood melodrama. It was one of the last films made before the Cultural Revolution, during which Xie Jin was accused of "bourgeois humanism" and imprisoned for some years, only able to return to film-making in the late 1970s.

WHAT TO WATCH

- ***Two Stage Sisters*** (Xie Jin, China, 1965)
- ***A Touch of Zen*** (King Hu, Taiwan, 1969)
- ***The Way of the Dragon*** (Bruce Lee, Hong Kong, 1972)
- ***Yellow Earth*** (Chen Kaige, China, 1984)
- ***City of Sadness*** (Hsiou-hsien Hou, Taiwan, 1989)
- ***Ju Dou*** (Zhang Yimou and Yang Fengliang, Japan/China, 1990)
- ***Raise the Red Lantern*** (Zhang Yimou, China, 1991)
- ***Yi Yi*** (Edward Yang, Taiwan, 2000)
- ***Crouching Tiger, Hidden Dragon*** (Ang Lee, Taiwan, 2000)
- ***Still Life*** (Jia Zhang Ke, China, 2006)

A mere six films were made during the Cultural Revolution, all of them crude propaganda, but visually striking; most were revised versions of previously filmed Peking operas. ***The White-Haired Girl*** (1970) and ***Red Detachment of Women*** (1971) were supervised by Mao Zedong's wife, former film actress and dancer, Jiang Qing.

After the Cultural Revolution, film production picked up, and films made were highly critical of that period. Xie Jin's ***Legend of Tianyun Mountain*** (1980), presented a bleak picture of a young girl pressurized by the Red Guard to leave her intellectual lover for political reasons. Wu Tian-ming's ***Life*** (1984) was the first in a series of films that depicted a person's struggle to retain some individuality. Wu belonged to The Fifth Generation – directors who graduated from the Beijing Film Academy in the 1970s. The most famous of these were Chen Kaige and Zhang Yimou, whose first films respectively, ***Yellow Earth*** (1984) and ***Red Sorghum*** (1987), made them the most widely known mainland Chinese directors ever. Chen's ***Farewell My Concubine*** (1993) was the first Chinese film to win the *Palme d'Or* at Cannes. Notable movies from other Fifth Generation directors include Huang Jianxin's ***The Black Cannon Incident*** (1986), a witty satire on bureaucracy, and Tian Zhuangzhuang's ***Horse Thief*** (1986), filmed in Tibet.

Hong Kong

In Hong Kong, where most of the population spoke Cantonese, film production reached its peak in 1960 with over 200 films being produced that year, so much so that the former British colony claimed to be "The Hollywood of the East". The mixture of musicals, detective films, and soft porn gave way, in the late 1960s, to new-style martial arts films, which brought in huge profits from abroad – most of it going to the Shaw Brothers' film company. The first kung fu (simply meaning "technique" or "skill") film to get a general release in the West was Jeong Chang-hwa's ***Five Fingers of Death*** (1972).

Bruce Lee, in his first starring role, displays his karate skills in ***The Big Boss*** (1971) – the film that literally kick-started kung fu mania.

Taiwan

The first big swordplay hit was the Taiwanese production of ***Dragon Inn*** (1967). The director King Hu, who worked in Taiwan, went on to make ***A Touch of Zen*** (1969) – an exciting three-hour epic, set during the rule of the Ming dynasty, and one of the finest examples of the genre. Chang Cheh reinvented the swordplay film with a trilogy: ***The One-Armed Swordsman*** (1967), ***Return of the One-Armed Swordsman*** (1969), and ***The New One-Armed Swordsman*** (1971) – all three were quintessential tales of heroic bloodshed. Meanwhile, Golden Harvest, a production company started by Raymond Chow, broke the Shaw Brothers monopoly with Bruce Lee "chop-socky" hits, starting with ***The Big Boss*** (1971). After Lee's premature death at the age of 32 in 1973, prolific director Chang Cheh continued the tradition, taking fight choreography to new heights. His films influenced other directors, such as John Woo and Liu Jialiang, and made many Hong Kong stars famous, including Ti Lung.

Although Taiwan was associated with kung fu movies, several directors made political and social dramas in a more cryptic style, the best known being Hou Hsiao-Hsien, whose work was similar to that of Japan's Yasujiro Ozu. Today, the most internationally celebrated Taiwanese director is Ang Lee, whose work ranges from an updated version of the Chinese *wu xia* (samurai-style) tradition of storytelling involving myth, swords and magic (***Crouching Tiger, Hidden Dragon***, 2000) to Hollywood hits such as ***Brokeback Mountain*** (2005).

Three heroes (Hsu Feng, Shih Chun, and Tien Peng) await their enemies in King Hu's martial arts classic ***A Touch of Zen*** (1969).

Korea

Although Korean films now loom large in the world cinema landscape, with international hits such as Park Chan-wook's ***Sympathy for Lady Vengeance*** (2005), it is only since the mid-1990s that the films have established a distinctive character and been truly visible.

The fact that Korea was under Japanese rule from 1903 to 1945 did not help the establishment of a film industry, although a number of silent Korean movies were made. In 1937, when Japan invaded China, the Korean film industry was converted into a propaganda machine. However, after World War II, despite the country regaining its independence, it was soon divided into the Communist North and the Capitalist South.

Two of the most important Korean films appeared in the 1960s: Kim Ki-young's ***The Housemaid*** (1960) and Yu Hyun-mok's ***Aimless Bullet*** (1961). Both were dark, domestic melodramas that dealt with family life and survival in the years following the end of the Korean War (1950–53).

In 1962, the Motion Picture Law mandated that film companies must produce at least 15 films per year. Korean studios made more; however, few were seen outside the country. The leading director of the period was Shin Sang-ok, whose ***My Mother and Her Guest*** (1961), told through the eyes of a young girl who wants her widowed mother to marry again, is considered a masterpiece. Sang-ok and his wife were kidnapped from their native South Korea in the late 1970s and held for several years in the North to make movies for Kim Jong Il, the son of the North Korean leader. The couple were granted asylum in the US in 1986.

After a fallow period, there were some signs of revival in the 1980s when Im Kwon-taek's films began to appear at festivals. He had made dozens of movies since 1962, and his breakthrough came with ***Mandala*** (1981), a film about Buddhist monks. Another of his films, ***Adada*** (1987), reflects the marginalized position of women in traditional Korean society. ***Seopyeonje*** (1993) is the story of a family of roaming *pansori* (a sort of Korean folk opera) and the singers' struggles in post-war Korea. This film became an unexpectedly huge hit in Korea. In 2002, Im Kwon-taek won the Best Director award at Cannes for his magnificent ***Chihwaseon***, about the life of a 19th-century Korean painter. In the same year, Lee Chang-dong's astonishing ***Oasis*** (2002), about a love affair between a social misfit and a girl with cerebral palsy, won several awards.

In 1996, Hong Sang-soo made his debut with the award-winning ***The Day a Pig Fell into the Well***, which weaves four characters'experiences into a single story. The same year saw the debut of controversial director Kim Ki-duk, whose violent films such as ***The Isle*** (2000) and ***Address Unknown*** (2001) were balanced by the serene ***Spring, Summer, Fall, Winter... and Spring*** (2003). Other recent successes include Kang Je-gyu's thriller ***Shiri*** (1999) and Park Chan-wook's ***Vengeance*** trilogy – ***Sympathy for Mr. Vengeance*** (2002), ***Oldboy*** (2003), and ***Sympathy for Lady Vengeance*** (2005). Two films by women, Lee Jeong-hyang's ***The Way Home*** (2002) and Jeong Jae-eun's ***Take Care of My Cat*** (2001), have also been at the forefront of Korean cinema.

WHAT TO WATCH

- ***The Day a Pig Fell into the Well*** (Hong Sang-soo, 1996)
- ***Shiri*** (Kang Je-Gyu, 1999)
- ***Chihwaseon*** (Im Kwon-taek, 2002)
- ***The Way Home*** (Lee Jeong-hyang, 2002)
- ***Oasis*** (Lee Chang-dong, 2002)
- ***Spring, Summer, Fall, Winter... and Spring*** (Kim Ki-duk, 2003)
- ***Secret Sunshine*** (Lee Chang-dong, 2007)

Chihwaseon (2002) traces the life of an artist (Choi Min-Sik) known for his addiction to alcohol and women.

Japan

Japan has been making high-quality films since the beginnings of cinema, but they remained virtually unknown in the West for over half a century. Since the 1950s, however, Japanese cinema has become very successful, both critically and commercially.

For most of its history, Japanese cinema was divided into two categories: *gendai-geki* – films in a contemporary setting – and *jidai-geki* – period films that were usually set in the Togukawa era (1603–1868), before the country opened up to Western influence. A sub-genre was *shomin-geki* ("home dramas") – movies about families, of which directors Yasujirô Ozu and Yasujirô Shimazu were the most consistent practitioners.

At first, two theatrical traditions were carried over to the cinema: the *onnagata* (males in female roles), and the *benshi* (an actor who stood at the side of the screen and narrated the film). However, as films became more realistic, the *onnagata* looked out of place and, with the coming of sound, the *benshi* also became redundant.

Following an earthquake in 1923, which devastated Tokyo and destroyed its film studios, Japan had to rely on foreign imports for some years. Gradually the industry recovered, though foreign audiences were still largely unaware of Japanese films. An exception was Teinosuke Kinugasa's ***Crossways*** (1928). Its fragmentary close-ups, claustrophobic atmosphere of angst, and dark, stylized décor, were reminiscent of German expressionism, though the director had apparently not seen any German films up to that time.

The first Japanese talkie was Heinosuke Gosho's ***The Neighbour's Wife and Mine*** (1931), a delightful slice-of-life comedy. However, as Japan became increasingly militaristic, more and more right-wing propaganda films were being made. Humanists, such as Kenji Mizoguchi, avoided government propaganda, and later he would direct twin masterpieces: ***Osaka Elegy*** and ***Sisters of the Gion*** (both 1936), stories of exploited women in contemporary Japan.

Wartime Japan

All Japanese cinema came under state power in 1939 and film production slowed down. However, some of the great directors continued to make films in their own way. Ozu made ***There Was a Father*** (1942), one of his most affecting films. The most popular war film was Kozaburo Yoshimura's ***The Story of Tank Commander Nishizumi*** (1940), which was not afraid to show the weakness and hardships that were associated with war.

Sisters of the Gion (1936) is director Kenji Mizoguchi's depiction of two geisha sisters.

American occupation

Under American occupation, a number of *jidai-geki* films were made in order to avoid censorship of contemporary issues. Despite the flood of American films and the problems of industrial disputes, Toho, the largest studio, did become established, along with relatively new directors such as Akira

WHAT TO WATCH

- ***The Life of Oharu*** (Kenji Mizoguchi, 1952)
- ***Seven Samurai*** (Akira Kurosawa, 1954)
- ***Equinox Flower*** (Yasujirô Ozu, 1958)
- ***An Actor's Revenge*** (Kon Ichikawa, 1963)
- ***Boy*** (Nagisa Ôshima, 1969)
- ***Vengeance Is Mine*** (Shohei Imamura, 1979)
- ***Tampopo*** (Juzo Itami, 1985)
- ***Hana-bi*** (Takeshi Kitano, 1997)
- ***After Life*** (Hirokazu Koreeda, 1998)
- ***Spirited Away*** (Hayao Miyazaki, 2001)
- ***Still Walking*** (Hirokazu Koreeda, 2008)
- ***Caterpillar*** (Koji Wakamatsu, 2010)

In Akira Kurosawa's *Seven Samurai* (1954), farmers recruit seven unemployed samurai to protect their village from bandits.

Kurosawa and Keisuke Kinoshita – who directed ***Carmen Comes Home*** (1951), the first Japanese colour film. The breakthrough came when Kurosawa's ***Rashomon*** (1950, see p.291) won the *Grand Prix* award at Venice in 1951, thus opening up the floodgates of Japanese films to the West. Among the most celebrated of that time were: ***Seven Samurai*** (Akira Kurosawa, 1954), ***Tokyo Story*** (Yasujirô Ozu, 1953), and ***Ugetsu Monogatari*** (Kenji Mizoguchi, 1953). Others were Kon Ichikawa's anti-war films: ***The Burmese Harp*** (1956) and ***Fires on the Plain*** (1959); and Masaki Kobayashi's ***The Human Condition*** (1959–61), an impressive and harrowing trilogy of socially conscious films.

Audience members watch the performance of an *onnagata* (female impersonator) in Kon Ichikawa's ***An Actor's Revenge*** (1963), a study of opposites – love/hate, illusion/reality, masculinity/femininity.

During the same period, Ishirô Honda created ***Godzilla*** (1954), which led to a whole stream of movies featuring threatening prehistoric monsters and mutants, formed as a result of radioactivity caused by nuclear bombs. The dubbing in the West was atrocious, but the special effects were spectacular.

The 1960s saw Japanese cinema mature creatively, beginning with Kaneto Shindo's ***The Island*** (1960), a tale – told beautifully in widescreen, without dialogue – about the hard life of a peasant family. Masaki Kobayashi's ***Harakiri*** (1962) remained true to the traditions of period film, while managing to criticize the rigid codes of honour that are basic to their subject. Kobayashi's ***Kwaidan*** (1964), one of the most expensive Japanese films up to that date, tells four tales of the supernatural using haunting imagery derived from Japanese art.

Among the new wave of Japanese directors, many of whom explored eroticism and violence, were Shohei Imamura (***The Insect Woman***, 1963 and ***The Pornographer***, 1966); Hiroshi Teshigahara (***Woman in the Dunes***, 1964); Yoshishige Yoshida (***Eros plus Massacre***, 1969); and Nagisa Ôshima (***Death by Hanging***, 1968). It was Ôshima who took the sexual revolution still further with his ***Ai No Corrida*** (1976).

1980 and beyond

Old hands like Kurosawa, who made his two great spectacles ***Kagemusha*** (1980) and ***Ran*** (1985), and Imamura, whose ***Ballad of Narayama*** (1983) was adjudged the Best Film at Cannes, continued to have success. Of the younger generation, Juzo Itami was the bright new meteor of Japanese cinema in the 1980s, with his comic satires of Japanese culture: ***Tampopo*** (1985), ***A Taxing Woman*** (1987), and ***A Taxing Woman's Return*** (1988), all starring his wife Nobuko Miyamoto.

At the turn of the 21st century, Japanese films kept on winning prizes at festivals and attracting large audiences. A dominant figure was Takeshi Kitano, whose films range from violent *yakuza* (gangster) movies (***Hana-bi***, 1997 and ***Brother***, 2000) to period films (***Zatoichi***, 2003) and sentimental comedies (***Kikujiro***, 1999). Credited as "Beat" Takeshi, he has also acted in many films, including his own. In Kinji Fukasaku's ***Battle Royale*** (2000), in which a school forces its pupils to slaughter one another on an island, Takeshi plays the role of a sadistic headmaster.

Japan has also produced some of the most effective horror films, many of which have been adapted by Hollywood. Hideo Nakata's ***Ringu*** (1998) – Japan's most successful horror film to date – led to a sequel, a prequel, and an American remake

Koji Yakusho plays a gangster who invades the ramen (noodle) bar owned by Nobuko Miyamoto in director Juzo Itami's gastronomic comedy, *Tampopo* (1985).

in 2002. Another Hollywood remake was ***The Grudge*** (2004), originally made by the same director, Takashi Shimizu, as the chiller ***Ju-On*** (2000). Also frightening, but more subtle, are the supernatural crime movies directed by Kiyoshi Kurosawa (no relation to Akira), such as ***Pulse*** (2001).

Other violent films included Takashi Miike's ***Audition*** (1999). In a different vein are Hirokazu Koreeda's films that explore memory and loss, such as ***Nobody Knows*** (2004), and Hayao Miyazaki's charming ***Spirited Away*** (2001), which won the Oscar for the Best Animated Feature – a reflection of the rise in the huge popularity of Japanese anime films, first awoken in the West by ***Akira*** (1988).

In Shinichiro Watanabe's *Cowboy Bebop* (2001), the bounty-hunting crew is out to catch the culprit behind a terrorist attack.

India

India is the world's largest producer of films – in the 1990s, the country made more than 800 films annually. It is the only country that has a bigger audience for indigenous films than imported ones. It also boasts one of the biggest international audiences.

Film poster, 1975

Indian films mean different things to different people. For the majority, they mean "Bollywood" (a conflation of Bombay, the old name for Mumbai, and Hollywood), and for others, they mean exquisite art movies as exemplified by the work of Satyajit Ray. The films of Bollywood tended to be rigidly formulaic Hindi-language musicals, comedies, or melodramas. In the 1990s, Bollywood musicals, the staple of the Indian film industry, became more and more popular among non-Indians in the West – mainly for their kitsch qualities. Although they came into being with the coming of sound, some of the plots were already apparent in the popular silent films.

The most prominent of the early silent film director-producers was Dadasaheb Phalke, who introduced the mythological film, peopled by gods and goddesses of the Hindu pantheon. All the roles were played by men, as women were forbidden to act during the early 20th century. However, Phalke was ruined by the introduction of sound which, in a country with 18 major languages and more than 800 different dialects, inevitably resulted in the fragmentation of the industry and its dispersal into different language markets.

Mumbai, the original centre of the industry, continued to dominate by concentrating on films in Hindi, the most widely-spoken Indian language.

Sunil Dutt plays the rebellious son in *Mother India* (1957), Mehboob Khan's classic tragic epic of rural life.

WHAT TO WATCH

Devdas (Bimal Roy, 1955)
Pather Panchali (Satyajit Ray, 1955)
Mother India (Mehboob Khan, 1957)
Charulata (Satyajit Ray, 1964)
Bhuvan Shome (Mrinal Sen, 1969)
Sholay (Ramesh Sippy, 1975)
Nayagan (Mani Ratnam, 1987)
Salaam Bombay! (Mira Nair, 1988)
Bandit Queen (Shekhar Kapur, 1994)
Dilwale Dulhaniya Le Jayenge (Aditya Chopra, 1995)
Kannathil Muthamittal (Mani Ratnam, 2002)
Shwaas (Sandeep Sawant, 2004)
Harishchandrachi Factory (Paresh Mokashi, 2009)
Peepli Live (Anusha Rizvi, 2010)

In the south, Chennai (formerly Madras) developed its own massive industry with films in Tamil. Hindi and Tamil films constituted the majority of Indian cinema, both dominated by a Hollywood-style star system. Among minority language cinema, Bengali films gained prominence, thanks mainly to Satyajit Ray's influence in the 1950s. The first talkie was Ardeshir Irani's *Alam Ara* (1931), with dialogue in both Urdu and Hindi. It contained several song and dance numbers and its huge financial success led to films adopting a formula – stories set around songs.

At the same time, almost imperceptibly, Hindi cinema developed a tradition of socially aware films. Founded in 1934, the Bombay Talkies studio produced a number of such movies. However, it was only in the 1950s that Indian films began to be shown around the world. Among the first were *Aan* (1952), the first Indian feature in Technicolor, and *Mother India* (1957), both directed by Mehboob Khan. The latter starred Nargis (see p.105), and was nominated for a Best Foreign Film Oscar. Bimal Roy's *Do Bigha Zameen* (1953), about the bitter issue of caste, won the *Prix International* at Cannes.

Influence on world cinema

When Jean Renoir came to Kolkata (formerly Calcutta) in 1950 to shoot ***The River*** (1951), he was assisted by Satyajit Ray. Renoir encouraged Ray to fulfil his dream of making a film based on *Pather Panchali*, a novel by Bibhutibhushan Banerjee that deals with Bengali village life. With the majority of money coming from the West Bengal government, Ray was able to make ***Pather Panchali*** in 1955, the first film in his ***Apu*** trilogy. Aside from Renoir's importance to Ray, the influence of ***The River*** cannot be overestimated. It was one of the first films from the West to show India other than as an exotic background to Kipling-style colonial adventures. It was only after this film that Fritz Lang visited India in 1956 to make ***Taj Mahal***, later abandoned. James Ivory also made several films there, including ***Shakespeare-Wallah*** (1965) and ***Heat and Dust*** (1983). Another European director to be influenced was Louis Malle (***Phantom India***, 1969).

The success of Ray's films proved that it was possible to work outside the commercial system. Those who benefited from this newly independent cinema included Marxists Mrinal Sen and Ritwik Ghatak, who developed a new kind of social cinema in opposition to Ray's European humanism.

Sen, often called the "Bengali Godard", attacked poverty and exploitation in Indian society. "I wanted to make disturbing and annoying films, not artistic ones," he said. His ***The Royal Hunt*** (1976) and ***And Quiet Rolls the Dawn*** (1979) are powerful political parables that look at the complexities of the country. Meanwhile, Ghatak's best-known films – ***Meghe Dhaka Tara*** (1960), ***Komal Gandhar*** (1961), and ***Subarnarekha*** (1965) – make up a trilogy based in Kolkata that addresses the subject of refugees.

In contrast, in Mumbai, Hrishikesh Mukherjee laid the foundation of a genuine middle-class cinema, with ***Anand*** (1970). The film tells the story of a terminally ill man who, determined to remain cheerful, brings about positive changes in the lives of those around him. Meanwhile, Bollywood movies were improving in quality, both technically and artistically. Ramesh Sippy's ***Sholay*** (1975), starring one of the greatest Bollywood actors, Amitabh Bachchan, is one of the most successful Hindi films of the 1970s.

In the 1980s, Indian "art cinema" was not so visible. However, in 1988, Mira Nair's ***Salaam Bombay!***, became a huge international success.

Satyajit Ray (centre), worked extensively with cinematographer Subrata Mitra on ten films.

Made in record time and for little money, it was an impressively assembled mosaic of Mumbai's street life, its harsh cruelties and fleeting pleasures. Other critically acclaimed Indian films in recent years have been Shekhar Kapur's ***Bandit Queen*** (1994), an examination of caste discrimination, human suffering, and the role of women in India's changing culture; Deepa Mehta's ***Fire*** (1996), which references Indian mysticism and the epic poetry of the *Ramayana* as well as late-20th-century feminism; and Sudhir Mishra's hard-hitting ***Hazaaron Khwaishein Aisi*** (2005), about three college students in the 1970s, and how the political and social upheaval of the times changes their lives.

India is the world's largest producer of feature films, most of them musicals, the soundtracks of which are released before the movie is. Since the 1980s, the sale of music rights has generated income for the film industry equivalent to the distribution revenues.

Chanda Sharma as Sweet Sixteen, plays a beautiful Nepali virgin who has been sold into prostitution in Mira Nair's realistic drama ***Salaam Bombay!*** (1988).

Australia and New Zealand

Since the 1970s, Australian films have increasingly come to the world's attention, while Peter Jackson, director of ***The Lord of the Rings***, put New Zealand and its beautiful scenery on the map with his big-budget trilogy.

Mel Gibson continues in his role as a vengeful futuristic cop in *Mad Max 2* (1981).

Australia has been making homegrown movies ever since *The Story of the Kelly Gang* (1906), believed to be the world's first feature-length film at 66 minutes. However, in the beginning there was little incentive to make Australian movies because of the American and British exports. When World War I cut Australia off from European film imports, it began to turn out its own cheap productions, melodramas, and "black blocks farces"– broad comedies of rural families.

Phillip Noyce's *Rabbit-Proof Fence* (2002) follows three young aboriginal girls in 1931 attempting to make a 1,500 mile trek home.

There was little attempt at art cinema, an exception being Raymond Longford's *The Sentimental Bloke* (1919), Australian cinema's first international success. Most other films transplanted Hollywood formulas, particularly the Western, to Australia.

By 1936, only four countries in the world were entirely "wired for sound": the US, the UK, Australia, and New Zealand. The best-known Australian director from the early sound era was Charles Chauvel (1897–1959), who made two successful war films: ***40,000 Horsemen*** (1941) and ***The Rats of Tobruk*** (1944). Ken G. Hall's wartime documentary, ***Kokoda Front Line!*** (1942), brought Australia its first Oscar. However, until the 1970s, Australian films meant films made in Australia by foreigners. For Ealing Studios, Harry Watt made Aussie Westerns such as ***The Overlanders*** (1946) and ***Eureka Stockade*** (1949), which began the trend for making British films in Australia. Among these directors were Stanley Kramer (***On the Beach***, 1959), Fred Zinnemann (***The Sundowners***, 1960), and Tony Richardson (***Ned Kelly***, 1970).

In 1973, the Australian Film Development Corporation (AFDC) came into being, and quickly bore fruit. The directors who emerged were Bruce Beresford (***The Getting of Wisdom***, 1977), Peter Weir (***Picnic at Hanging Rock***, 1975), Fred Schepisi (***The Devil's Playground***, 1976), Phillip Noyce (***Newsfront***, 1978), Gillian Armstrong (***My Brilliant Career***, 1979), and George Miller (***Mad Max***, 1979). All went on to have parallel careers in Hollywood. Of the next generation, Baz Luhrmann is the most celebrated. His first feature, ***Strictly Ballroom*** (1992), won many awards and became one of Australia's most profitable films ever.

Although he worked mostly overseas, perhaps the first well-known New Zealand director was animator Len Lye, who invented the technique called "direct film", or painting designs on film stock without using a camera. Jane Campion is another high-profile New Zealand director, whose ***An Angel at My Table*** (1990) launched her international career. While Campion, Roger Donaldson, and Geoff Murphy used their first films to enter Hollywood, Peter Jackson managed to lure the studios to Wellington in order to shoot his ***The Lord of the Rings*** trilogy (2001–03).

WHAT TO WATCH

Picnic at Hanging Rock
(Peter Weir, Australia, 1975)

The Getting of Wisdom
(Bruce Beresford, Australia, 1977)

Newsfront
(Phillip Noyce, Australia, 1978)

My Brilliant Career
(Gillian Armstrong, Australia, 1979)

Mad Max
(George Miller, Australia, 1979)

Crocodile Dundee
(Peter Faiman, Australia, 1986)

An Angel at My Table
(Jane Campion, New Zealand, 1990)

Heavenly Creatures
(Peter Jackson, New Zealand, 1994)

The Lord of the Rings trilogy
(Peter Jackson, New Zealand, 2001, 2002, and 2003)

Happy Feet
(George Miller, Australia, 2006)

Australia
(Baz Luhrmann, Australia, 2008)

Paul Mercurio and Tara Morice win the Australian Pan Pacific Ballroom Dancing Championship in Baz Luhrmann's hit, ***Strictly Ballroom*** (1992).

A-Z of **Directors**

The definition of a director's function has been accepted only recently. Long considered just an anonymous member of a team, generally subordinate to the producer, the director is now pre-eminent in the perception of a film. Today, most film-lovers are familiar with a director's role. They know their names and even recognize their distinctive styles.

In the early days, the public was generally unaware of a director's name. People went to see movies on the strength of the stars and the subject. Gradually, certain directors became known because they made themselves visible. For instance, Cecil B. DeMille often introduced his films in trailers and Alfred Hitchcock made brief appearances in his films. This made them recognizable, and encouraged the public to associate them with a certain genre – in this case, the epic and the thriller respectively. It was the influential French magazine *Cahiers du Cinéma* that formulated the auteur theory in the mid-1950s. Its writers argued that a film, though a collective medium, always had the signature of the director on it, and that directors should be viewed in the light of thematic consistency. This formulation shed light on those directors, especially in the Hollywood studio system, who had never been considered within the "cinema as art" school of criticism, such as Vincente Minnelli, Howard Hawks, Nicholas Ray, and Otto Preminger. The theory was taken up by critics globally and the director was finally given his due as the principal creator of a film, if not the "onlie begetter".

With the growth of film studies courses in universities, and the increased sophistication of audiences, many movie-goers are familiar with the names of such great directors of the past as Sergei Eisenstein, Ingmar Bergman, and Akira Kurosawa. Today, one hears audiences referring to the latest Spielberg movie rather than the latest Tom Hanks film.

Currently, there are directors emerging from obscurity, renowned ones adding to their filmographies, and new talent being discovered. This A–Z of Directors has been made as up-to-date as possible. It includes the young, the old, the quick, and the dead; international independent geniuses, Hollywood greats, cult figures, and underground and experimental film-makers. The overall aim has been to include directors whose work has been widely shown globally, either in commercial cinemas or art houses. The profiles are an attempt to give readers enough objective information to be able to assess the type, quality, content, and style of each director's work, and then to discover or rediscover them for themselves.

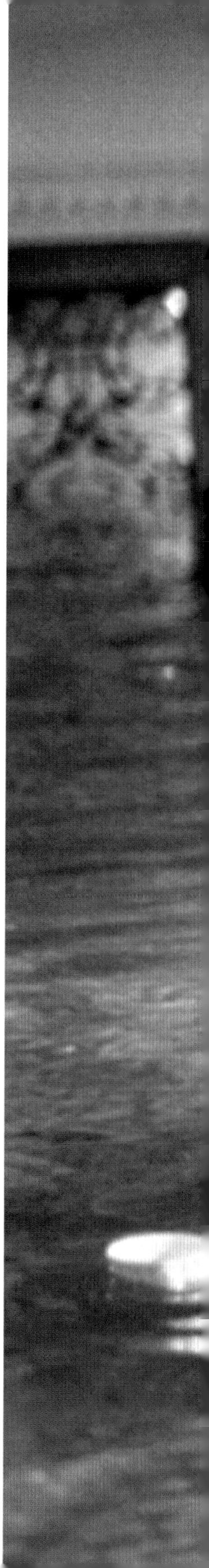

James Cameron and his crew are seen here shooting *Titanic* (1997), which won 11 Academy Awards, including Best Director.

PANAFLEX

Film poster, 1986

Woody **Allen**

BORN 1935

NATIONALITY American

CAREER 1969– **FILMS** 42

GENRE Comedy, Drama

Films directed by the prolific Woody Allen have amused adult audiences over many years. In the best of them, however, there is pain lurking beneath the comic surface.

Before directing films, Woody Allen was a stand-up comic whose subject matter was his own obsessions – his relationships with women and his analyst, and death – which he elaborated on in his films. His first five movies were constructed as closely linked revue sketches, although in ***Love and Death*** (1976), a witty pastiche of 19th-century Russian literature, he paid more attention to form. ***Annie Hall*** (1977) was a breakthrough film, successfully showing a complex relationship (based on his own with Diane Keaton), while ***Manhattan*** (1979) is a stunning black-and-white paean to New York, the city he loves. There is an autobiographical element in many of his films, most intense in ***Husbands and Wives*** (1992), during the filming of which he broke up with Mia Farrow, his real-life partner. Among his wittiest comedies are ***Take the Money and Run*** (1969), ***Bananas*** (1971), ***Sleeper*** (1973), ***Broadway Danny Rose*** (1984), and ***The Purple Rose of Cairo*** (1985). Allen's admiration for Ingmar Bergman is clear in ***Interiors*** (1978), his first "serious" movie. Other homages to Bergman include ***A Midsummer Night's Sex Comedy*** (1982) and ***Deconstructing Harry*** (1997). He used Bergman's favourite cameraman Sven Nykvist on ***Crimes and Misdemeanors*** (1989) and cast Max von Sydow, who acted in many Bergman films, in ***Hannah and Her Sisters*** (1986). ***Sweet and Lowdown*** (1999) and ***Stardust Memories*** (1980) were inspired by Federico Fellini. ***Match Point*** (2005) was a box-office hit and for Allen, "arguably maybe the best film" he'd made. Although in the 1990s, his work lost some of its resonance, Allen has managed to speak to a small but loyal audience of intelligent fans.

WHAT TO WATCH

- *Sleeper* (1973)
- *Love and Death* (1976)
- *Annie Hall* (1977)
- *Manhattan* (1979)
- *Broadway Danny Rose* (1984)
- *The Purple Rose of Cairo* (1985)
- *Hannah and Her Sisters* (1986)
- *Crimes and Misdemeanors* (1989)
- *Husbands and Wives* (1992)
- *Match Point* (2005)
- *Vicky Cristina Barcelona* (2008)

Scarlett Johansson plays the seductive Nola Rice, here with director Woody Allen on the set of ***Match Point*** (2005), the first film Allen made in the UK.

Pedro **Almodóvar**

BORN 1949

NATIONALITY Spanish

CAREER 1974– **FILMS** 19

GENRE Underground, Melodrama

Pedro Almodóvar's outrageous and provocative films have made him the most internationally acclaimed Spanish film-maker since the death of oppressive military leader Franco in 1975.

"My films represent the new mentality...in Spain after Franco died...because now it is possible to make a film like *Law of Desire*." Despite its homoerotic sex scenes, *Law of Desire* (1987) was heralded as a model for Spain's future cinema. Almodóvar's forté is in incorporating elements of underground and gay culture into mainstream forms with wide crossover appeal, thus redefining perceptions of Spanish cinema and Spain itself. His first feature film, ***Pepi, Luci, Bom and Lots of Other Girls*** (1980), was made in 16mm and blown up to 35mm for public release. Although his breakthrough export success was ***Women on the Verge of a Nervous Breakdown*** (1988), he hit his stride in Spain with *What Have I Done to Deserve This?* (1984). In *Matador* (1986), he explores the link between violence and eroticism, while in *High Heels* (1991), *All About My Mother* (1999), *Talk to Her* (2002), and *Bad Education* (2004), he shows a warmth towards his characters.

Cecilia Roth, as the heroine of *All About My Mother* (1999), is seen against a poster advertising the appearance of her son's idol (Marisa Parades) in *A Streetcar Named Desire*.

WHAT TO WATCH

- *What Have I Done to Deserve This?* (1984)
- *Law of Desire* (1987)
- *Women on the Verge of a Nervous Breakdown* (1988)
- *High Heels* (1991)
- *All About My Mother* (1999)
- *Talk to Her* (2002)
- *Bad Education* (2004)
- *Volver* (2006)

Victoria Abril, one of Pedro Almodóvar's leading ladies in the early 1990s, takes direction on the set of *High Heels* (1991).

Film poster, 1976

Robert **Altman**

BORN 1925 **DIED** 2006

NATIONALITY American

CAREER 1951–2006 **FILMS** 36

GENRE Satirical comedy, Drama

With an individualism that gained him the reputation of being a difficult man for producers to work with, Robert Altman tried something different with each film. Unusual by US standards, he refused to make formulaic pictures.

After four forgettable movies, Altman was offered *M*A*S*H* (1970) – after 14 other directors turned it down. Its iconoclasm struck a chord in a US disenchanted with the Vietnam War. The director later subverted traditional Hollywood genres with revisionist Westerns such as *McCabe & Mrs. Miller* (1971), in which the hero (Warren Beatty) is a pimp; while *Buffalo Bill and the Indians* (1976) reveals William Cody (Paul Newman) as a phoney.

Altman liked to use the same actors, often getting performers to improvise their dialogues. He adeptly mapped out areas in which a group of people are brought together for a purpose. This allowed him to manipulate 24 characters in *Nashville* (1975), 40 in *A Wedding* (1978), and a huge cast in *Short Cuts* (1993) and *Gosford Park* (2001).

The experimental use of sound is a crucial feature of Altman's films. Examples include simultaneous conversations and loudspeaker announcements in *M*A*S*H*, the 8-track sound system in *California Split* (1974), and the absence of a music score in *Thieves Like Us* (1974). After the relative failure of *Popeye* (1980), and being fired from *Ragtime* (1981), Altman was forced to work mostly in television. However, in 1992 he became the darling of Hollywood again with *The Player*.

WHAT TO WATCH

- *M*A*S*H* (1970)
- *McCabe and Mrs. Miller* (1971)
- *Nashville* (1975)
- *The Player* (1992)
- *Short Cuts* (1993)
- *Gosford Park* (2001)
- *A Prairie Home Companion* (2006)

Theo **Angelopoulos**

BORN 1935

NATIONALITY Greek

CAREER 1970– **FILMS** 13

GENRE History, Politics, Epic, Drama

An exploration of an inner journey, *Eternity and a Day* (1998) shows how time becomes a central concern for terminally ill Alexandre (Bruno Ganz).

In 1975, after the seven-year military dictatorship in his country ended, Theo Angelopoulos emerged on the international scene with some of the most ambitious Greek films to date.

A portrayal of official incompetence that subtly undermines the "Colonels' regime", *Days of '36* (*Meres Tou '36*, 1972) is the first of a trilogy, followed by *The Travelling Players* (*O Thiasos*, 1975) and *The Hunters* (*Oi Kynigoi*, 1977), all allegories of 20th-century Greek politics. In later films, Angelopoulos used more widely known actors: Marcello Mastroianni in *The Beekeeper* (*O Melissokomos*, 1986), Harvey Keitel in *Ulysses' Gaze* (*To Vlemma tou Odyssea*, 1995), and Bruno Ganz in *Eternity and a Day* (*Mia aioniotita kai mia mera*, 1998). Featuring slow pans and long takes, the films are rewarding metaphysical road movies. Other films of note are *Landscape in the Mist* (*Topio stin omichli*, 1988) and *The Weeping Meadow* (*Trilogia: To livadi pou dakryzei*, 2004), the first of a projected trilogy (followed by *The Dust of Time*, 2008) that is stylistically breathtaking and vividly descriptive.

WHAT TO WATCH

- *The Travelling Players* (1975)
- *Landscape in the Mist* (1988)
- *Eternity and a Day* (1998)
- *The Weeping Meadow* (2004)

Michelangelo **Antonioni**

BORN 1912 **DIED** 2007

NATIONALITY Italian

CAREER 1950–2004 **FILMS** 17

GENRE Psychological drama

The long tracking shots, set pieces, attention to design and architecture, and the relationship between the characters and their environment are hallmarks of Michelangelo Antonioni's meditations on contemporary angst.

Antonioni's elegant first feature, ***Story of a Love Affair*** (***Cronaca di un Amore***, 1950), reveals a personal stamp, but his style reached its maturity with ***L'Avventura*** (1960), which redefined the perception of time and space in cinema. This film was followed by ***La Notte*** (1961) and ***L'Eclisse*** (1962) to form a trilogy that examined themes of alienation. In ***Il Deserto Rosso*** (1964), Monica Vitti portrays Giuliana, a housewife who is driven mad by the industrial landscape she is surrounded by. Antonioni used deep reds and greens to reflect her neurosis, while brighter colours appear during her flights of fantasy. In his next four films, the director cast his eye outside Italy: on China with a documentary, ***Chung Kuo – Cina*** (1972); on "Swinging Sixties" London in ***Blow-Up*** (1966), with a fashionable photographer at the film's centre; on liberated American youth in ***Zabriskie Point*** (1970), which ends spectacularly with a materialistic civilization exploding; and on arid North Africa in ***The Passenger*** (***Professione: Reporter***, 1975).

Back in Italy and reunited with Vitti, his lover with whom he made four films, Antonioni made ***The Oberwald Mystery*** (***Il Mistero di Oberwald***, 1981), one of the first major pictures to be shot on video. He worked on video for the next few years, although ***Identification of a Woman*** (***Identificazione di una donna***, 1982) was shot on film. In 1985, he had a stroke that partially paralysed him. Despite this, he made ***Beyond the Clouds*** (***Al di là delle nuvole***, 1995) – based on his short stories.

WHAT TO WATCH

- ***L'Avventura*** (1960)
- ***La Notte*** (1961)
- ***L'Eclisse*** (1962)
- ***Il Deserto Rosso*** (1964)
- ***Blow-Up*** (1966)
- ***The Passenger*** (1975)

Jack Nicholson plays a reporter in ***The Passenger*** (1975), a film that questions notions of reality and illusion.

Ingmar **Bergman**

BORN 1918 **DIED** 2007

NATIONALITY Swedish

CAREER 1946–1982 **FILMS** 40

GENRE Psychological, Metaphysical drama

Ingmar Bergman was a pastor's son and his films were filled with religious imagery, paradoxically expressing a godless, loveless universe. His *oeuvre* can be seen as the autobiography of his psyche.

Dividing his directing between the stage and the screen, Bergman often introduced the theatre into his films as a metaphor for the duality of personality. At least five of his films take place on an island, a circumscribed area like the stage. The subject of his early work is the struggle of adolescents against an unfeeling adult world. The transient, sun-soaked Swedish summer days, the only period of happiness before the encroachment of a winter of discontent, are captured glowingly in ***Summer Interlude*** (***Sommarlek***, 1951) and ***Summer with Monika*** (***Sommaren med Monika***, 1953). An operetta-like comedy of manners, ***Smiles of a Summer Night*** (***Sommarnattens leende***, 1955) was the culmination of this first period. ***The Seventh Seal*** (***Det sjunde inseglet***), set in cruel medieval times, and ***Wild Strawberries*** (***Smultronstället***), both 1957, consolidated Bergman's international reputation, as did ***The Face*** (***Ansiktet***, 1958) – a Gothic tale. The trilogy on the silence of God: ***Through a Glass Darkly*** (***Såsom i en spegel***, 1961), ***Winter Light*** (***Nattvardsgästerna***, 1963), and ***The Silence*** (***Tystnaden***, 1963), moved Bergman into a more angst-ridden world.

Although women have always been central to his work, it is with ***Persona*** (1966) that the female face in close-up became his field of vision. A succession of psychodramas followed, including the emotionally charged ***Cries and Whispers*** (***Viskningar och rop***, 1972). In ***Autumn Sonata*** (***Höstsonaten***, 1978), the director points an accusing finger at parental neglect, while ***Fanny and Alexander*** (***Fanny och Alexander***, 1982) is a magical evocation of childhood. He announced this film as his final feature and, although he continued to direct for television and theatre, it was a superlative climax to his 36 years as one of cinema's most profound artists.

WHAT TO WATCH

- *Summer Interlude* (1951)
- *Smiles of a Summer Night* (1955)
- *The Seventh Seal* (1957)
- *Wild Strawberries* (1957)
- *The Face* (1958)
- *Cries and Whispers* (1972)
- *Autumn Sonata* (1978)
- *Fanny and Alexander* (1982)

» **Isak** (Erland Josephson) and Helena Ekdahl (Gunn Wallgren) share a moment of intimacy in *Fanny and Alexander* (1982), Bergman's most autobiographical film.

Bernardo **Bertolucci**

BORN 1940

NATIONALITY Italian

CAREER 1962– **FILMS** 15

GENRE Epic, Political, Psychological drama

The son of a well-known poet, and winner of a prestigious poetry prize himself, Bernardo Bertolucci believes that "cinema is the true poetic language", a claim justified by many of his wide-ranging films.

Bertolucci directed his first film ***The Grim Reaper*** (***La Commare Secca***, 1962) at the age of 22. In his second, ***Before the Revolution*** (***Prima della Rivoluzione***, 1964), he began to explore important themes in his work: father-son relationships and political-personal conflict – themes also seen in ***The Spider's Stratagem*** (***Strategia del Ragno***, 1970). ***The Conformist*** (***Il Conformista,*** 1970) successfully brought together his Freudian and political concerns in pre-war Italy. However, it was ***Last Tango in Paris*** (1972) that gained him worldwide notoriety, mainly because of the loveless sex scenes between Paul, a middle-aged American (Marlon Brando), and a young Frenchwoman, Jeanne (Maria Schneider).

With ***1900*** (1976), a film about class struggle, Bertolucci turned away from the introspection of his previous films. ***The Tragedy of a Ridiculous Man*** (***La Tragedia di un uomo ridicolo***, 1981), an ambiguous view of terrorism, failed to please the public and the critics; but ***The Last Emperor*** (1987), the first Western film to be made entirely in China and covering 60 years of the country's history (1906–67), won nine Oscars, including Best Director, Best Picture, and Best Cinematography. ***The Sheltering Sky*** (1990), set in Africa; ***Little Buddha*** (1993); and ***The Dreamers*** (2003) are other Bertolucci films of note.

WHAT TO WATCH

- ***Before the Revolution*** (1964)
- ***The Conformist*** (1970)
- ***Last Tango in Paris*** (1972)
- ***1900*** (1976)
- ***The Last Emperor*** (1987)
- ***The Dreamers*** (2003)

Bertolucci directs Debra Winger and John Malkovich in ***The Sheltering Sky*** (1990), in which an American couple travel across North Africa to find meaning in their relationship.

Luc **Besson**

BORN 1959

NATIONALITY French

CAREER 1983– **FILMS** 9

GENRE Thriller, Science fiction

Even into his forties, Luc Besson was the *enfant terrible* of French cinema, getting his inspiration from comic books, Hollywood blockbusters, and pop videos.

Besson's first contribution to the French movement *Cinema du Look* in which style overrides content, was the flashy ***Subway*** (1985), set in a vividly imagined Paris metro that is inhabited by social misfits. The breathtaking ***The Big Blue*** (***Le Grand Bleu***, 1988), about two deep-sea divers, was a more personal project – Besson's parents were diving instructors. Both ***Nikita*** (1990), a homage to the American action movie, and ***Léon*** (1995), set in New York, are thrillers but also explore personal growth and morality. Besson's work reached its climax in the stylish science fiction, ***The Fifth Element*** (1997) – with its spectacular special effects – about evil aliens out to destroy mankind. In contrast, the exquisite black-and-white film ***Angel-A*** (2005) is set in a hauntingly vacant Paris.

WHAT TO WATCH

- ***The Big Blue*** (1988)
- ***Nikita*** (1990)
- ***Léon*** (1995)
- ***The Fifth Element*** (1997)

Film poster, 1997

Robert **Bresson**

BORN 1901 **DIED** 1999

NATIONALITY French

CAREER 1943–1983 **FILMS** 13

GENRE Metaphysical drama

Although Robert Bresson made only 13 films in 40 years, his *oeuvre* is impressively consistent: austere, uncompromising, and elliptical.

Claude Laydu and Nicole L'Admiral star in *Diary of a Country Priest* (1951), the first truly Bressonian film in its use of non-professional actors, natural sound, and pared-down images.

Of his insistence on using only non-professional actors in his films, Bresson declared: "Art is transformation. Acting can only get in the way." However, in his first two films, *Angels of the Streets* (*Les Anges du Péché*, 1943) and *Ladies of the Park* (*Les Dames du Bois de Boulogne*, 1945) – both about the redemption of women – he used professional actors. *A Man Escaped* (*Le Vent Souffle où il Veut*, 1956), a testament to courage, is about a French resistance fighter, while *Balthazar* (*Au Hasard Balthazar*, 1966), about the life of a donkey, is one of Bresson's most lyrical films. Many of his movies, such as *The Trial of Joan of Arc* (*Procès de Jeanne d'Arc*, 1962), end in death. In 1969, with *A Gentle Creature* (*Une Femme Douce*), he started using colour, and a more overt sensuality was noticeable. *The Devil, Probably* (*Le Diable Probablement*, 1977) brought the theme of pollution – literal and figurative – into Bresson's enclosed world.

WHAT TO WATCH

- *Ladies of the Park* (1945)
- *Diary of a Country Priest* (*Journal D'un Cure de Campagne*, 1951)
- *A Man Escaped* (1956)
- *Balthazar* (1966)
- *L'Argent* (1983)

Tod **Browning**

BORN 1880 **DIED** 1962

NATIONALITY American

CAREER 1915–1939 **FILMS** 47

GENRE Horror

Film poster, 1925

The eerily atmospheric horror movies Tod Browning made with actors Lon Chaney and Bela Lugosi are the director's hallmark.

In 1918, Browning signed with Universal where he made 17 movies, including two in which Chaney had small roles. After Chaney became a star, the actor persuaded MGM to hire Browning. Together, the pair made eight horror films, great vehicles for Chaney – the "man with a thousand faces". After the actor's death in 1930, Browning moved back to Universal to make *Dracula* (1931) with Lugosi. In the same genre are the campy *Mark of the Vampire* (1935) and the inventive *The Devil-Doll* (1936). In a way, *Freaks* (1932) is an anti-horror movie as it urges audiences not to be repulsed by the monsters. This masterpiece was banned for 30 years until rehabilitated at the Venice Film Festival, a few weeks before Browning's death.

WHAT TO WATCH

- *The Unholy Three* (1925)
- *The Blackbird* (1926)
- *The Unknown* (1927)
- *West of Zanzibar* (1928)
- *Dracula* (1931)
- *Freaks* (1932)
- *The Devil-Doll* (1936)

Luis **Buñuel**

BORN 1900 **DIED** 1983

NATIONALITY Spanish

CAREER 1929–1977 **FILMS** 34

GENRE Surrealist drama, Comedy

Born with the 20th century, Luis Buñuel never wavered in his ideas and vision, establishing himself as perhaps the most mordantly comic and subversive of all the great directors.

In response to a bourgeois family upbringing and a Jesuit school education, Buñuel entered adulthood fervently anti-middle class and anti-clerical.

His first two films, ***An Andalusian Dog*** (***Un Chien Andalou***, 1929) and ***Age of Gold*** (***L'Age d'Or***, 1930), both made under the influence of André Breton's *Surrealist Manifesto*, contained many themes – Catholicism, the bourgeoisie, and rationality – that would reappear in his later films. After ***Land Without Bread*** (***Las Hurdes***, 1933) – a stark documentary about the contrast between peasant poverty and the wealth of the Church – was banned in Spain, Buñuel did not make another film for 15 years.

In 1947, he moved to Mexico and made ***The Young and the Damned*** (***Los Olvidados***, 1950), a powerful, detached view of a cruel world of juvenile delinquents. Despite directing about a dozen cheap films for the home market, he managed to make gems like ***Torments*** (***El***, 1953), ***Robinson Crusoe*** (1952), and ***Wuthering Heights*** (***Abismos de pasión***, 1953). ***Viridiana*** (1961), the first film in 29 years that he made in his native land, is a savage comedy about Catholic mentality and rituals – again banned in Spain. Nevertheless, because of the film's critical success, Buñuel was welcomed back into the centre of world cinema. ***The Exterminating Angel*** (***El Ángel exterminador***, 1962), made in Mexico, is a parable about guests at a sumptuous party who find it physically impossible to leave. In ***The Discreet Charm of the Bourgeoisie*** (***Le charme discret de la bourgeoisie***, 1972), the wealthy are unable to get anything to eat. Two other masterpieces are ***Diary of a Chambermaid*** (***Le journal d'une femme de chambre***, 1964), a cynical take on Octave Mirbeau's novel, and the witty, erotic, and subversive ***Belle de Jour*** (1967).

Silvia Pinal plays novice nun Viridiana, who fights a losing battle to remain true to her moral ideals and faith in ***Viridiana*** (1961), which won the Best Film award at Cannes.

WHAT TO WATCH

- *An Andalusian Dog* (1929)
- *Age of Gold* (1930)
- *The Young and the Damned* (1950)
- *Nazarin* (1958)
- *Viridiana* (1961)
- *The Exterminating Angel* (1962)
- *Diary of a Chambermaid* (1964)
- *Belle de Jour* (1967)
- *Tristana* (1970)
- *The Discreet Charm of the Bourgeoisie* (1972)

Catherine Deneuve plays Severine Serizy and Michel Piccoli plays Henri Husson in ***Belle de Jour*** (1967), in which Severine is a middle-class wife who leads a double life, playing out the fantasies of the rich.

Frank **Capra**

BORN 1897 **DIED** 1991

NATIONALITY American

CAREER 1926–1961 **FILMS** 37

GENRE Comedy, Melodrama, Drama

From 1936 onwards, Frank Capra's films evoked the American Dream, through which any honest, decent, and patriotic American could overcome corruption and disappointment to prove the power of the individual.

Film poster, 1937

Capra began his movie career as a gag writer for comedian Harry Langdon. After directing movies at First National, he went to Columbia, where he made madcap comedies such as *Platinum Blonde* (1931), *American Madness* (1932), and *It Happened One Night* (1934), which won five Academy Awards and turned Columbia from a "Poverty Row" studio into a major one. He also made Barbara Stanwyck a star at Columbia with four movies, including *The Bitter Tea of General Yen* (1933). An early masterpiece was *Lady for a Day* (1933), filled with wonderful New York street characters. Capra's autobiography states that an unknown man came to him in 1935 and told him to use his gifts for God's purpose. Following this advice, he lost the sensuality and anarchy in his films and replaced his central female characters with idealistic boy-scout heroes. The result was sentimental social comedies that were deemed "Capra-esque". *Mr. Deeds Goes to Town* (1936) and *Meet John Doe* (1941) with Gary Cooper, and *You Can't Take It with You* (1938), *Mr. Smith Goes to Washington* (1939), and *It's a Wonderful Life* (1946), with James Stewart, glorify the little man's fight for what is right and decent. Politically naïve as they are, the films have comic pace and invention, splendid sets, as in *Lost Horizon* (1937), and outstanding performances.

WHAT TO WATCH

- *Platinum Blonde* (1931)
- *The Bitter Tea of General Yen* (1933)
- *Lady for a Day* (1933)
- *It Happened One Night* (1934)
- *Mr. Deeds Goes to Town* (1936)
- *You Can't Take It with You* (1938)
- *Mr. Smith Goes to Washington* (1939)
- *It's a Wonderful Life* (1946)

James Stewart plays the eponymous hero in *Mr. Smith Goes to Washington* (1939). The quintessential everyman is seen here with Clarissa Saunders (Jean Arthur).

Jean (Jean Gabin) and Nelly (Michèle Morgan), play doomed lovers who meet in a misty French seaside city, in *Port of Shadows* (1938).

Marcel **Carné**

BORN 1909 **DIED** 1996

NATIONALITY French

CAREER 1936–1974 **FILMS** 20

GENRE Poetic realism, Costume drama

In Marcel Carné's ***Hôtel du Nord*** (1938), Raymonde (Arletty), observing her dingy surroundings, cries, "Atmosphere! Atmosphere!". There are many such dialogues in his best films, which, mostly written by Jacques Prévert and shot by Alexandre Trauner, were beautifully crafted, written, and played.

After assisting Belgian director Jacques Feyder on four of his greatest films between 1933 and 1935, Carné directed Feyder's wife, Françoise Rosay, in ***Jenny*** (1936). This was co-scripted by poet Jacques Prévert, with whom Carné was to collaborate on six further films over the next decade. ***Bizarre Bizarre*** (***Drôle de Drame***, 1937), an eccentric comedy thriller set in an imaginary Victorian London, was followed by ***Port of Shadows*** (***Le Quai des Brumes***, 1938), the film that created the melancholic "poetic realism" associated with the director and his screenwriters. The slant-eyed Michèle Morgan together with the doomed Jean Gabin trying to grab happiness in a fog-bound port are images typically associated with the world-weariness in pre-war France. ***Daybreak*** (***Le Jour se Lève***, 1939), one of the most celebrated of the Carné–Prévert poetic realist films, made memorable use of the dark set and the small room in which Gabin, wanted for murder, has barricaded himself. The Nazi occupation of France forced Carné to make "escapist" films such as ***The Devil's Envoys*** (***Les Visiteurs du Soir***, 1942) – a medieval fairy tale – and ***Children of Paradise*** (***Les Enfants du Paradis***, 1945), a rich evocation of 19th-century Paris. ***Gates of the Night*** (***Les Portes de la Nuit***, 1946), which marked the end of the Carné–Prévert partnership, failed to take into account the optimistic post-war mood in France, and flopped at the box office. Carné attempted to capture old glory with Jean Gabin in ***La Marie du Port*** (1950), and ***The Adultress*** (***Thérèse Raquin***, 1953), but he was a spent force and his reputation, despite some youth films such as ***Youthful Sinners*** (***Les Tricheurs***, 1958), was swept away by the French New Wave (see pp.42–43).

Film poster, 1938

WHAT TO WATCH

- *Bizarre Bizarre* (1937)
- *Port of Shadows* (1938)
- *Daybreak* (1939)
- *The Devil's Envoys* (1942)
- *Children of Paradise* (1945)

A gangster's moll (Gena Rowlands) and Phil (John Adames) are chased by crooks in *Gloria* (1980).

John **Cassavetes**

BORN 1929 **DIED** 1989

NATIONALITY American

CAREER 1959–1989 **FILMS** 12

GENRE Drama

Actor-director John Cassavetes is remembered as the godfather of American independent film-makers. Although his breakthrough film *Shadows* (1959) was not the first US movie made outside the system, it became a rallying point for future generations.

The searing domestic drama *Faces* (1968), which was self-financed, had a great impact when first released. It played for a year in New York and earned Oscar nominations for its cast of unknowns.

Cassavetes was often labelled an improvisational film-maker, but his movies were almost entirely scripted. Yet, the director had a preference for documentary-style camerawork and was obsessed with human interaction. His wife Gena Rowlands became his muse, appearing in *Minnie and Moskowitz* (1971), *A Woman Under the Influence* (1974), *Opening Night* (1977), *Gloria* (1980), and *Love Streams* (1984).

WHAT TO WATCH

- *Shadows* (1959)
- *Faces* (1968)
- *Minnie and Moskowitz* (1971)
- *Gloria* (1980)

Claude **Chabrol**

BORN 1930 **DIED** 2010

NATIONALITY French

CAREER 1958–2009 **FILMS** 53

GENRE Crime

Stephane Audran (right) and Bernadette Lafont are the bored Parisian shopgirls longing for better lives in Chabrol's *Les Bonnes Femmes* (1960).

Credited with starting *La Nouvelle Vague* or the French New Wave film movement (see pp.42–43), the prolific Claude Chabrol created an *oeuvre* of ironic black comedies, and endless variations on the theme of infidelity and murder.

Murder, often seen as an inevitable act, is at the heart of most of Chabrol's films. He mocked the complacency of bourgeois marriage in his movies, which often came with the added spice of Stephane Audran (his second wife) in the role of the victim or as the cause of murder. Whatever seethes under the surface of his characters – guilt, jealousy, or crime – the niceties of life go on. Large meals at home or in a restaurant became his signature scenes. Although Chabrol had always been happy in the mainstream, it was his *Le Beau Serge* (1958), made on location in his own village, that is considered the first film of the New Wave. After Audran, Chabrol found, in Isabelle Huppert, the ideal actress to portray his perverse heroines with a taste for murder.

WHAT TO WATCH

- *The Cousins* (*Les Cousins*, 1959)
- *The Good Time Girls* (*Les Bonnes Femmes*, 1960)
- *The Unfaithful Wife* (*La Femme Infidèle*, 1969)
- *The Hatter's Ghost* (*Les Fantômes du Chapelier*, 1982)
- *The Ceremony* (*La Cérémonie*, 1995)
- *Nightcap* (*Merci Pour le Chocolat*, 2000)

Chaplin, artist extraordinaire, is seen here behind the camera for ***The Gold Rush*** (1925). Said to be his favourite film, it has a famous scene showing the poor hero reduced to eating his shoes.

Charlie **Chaplin**

BORN 1889 **DIED** 1977

NATIONALITY British

CAREER 1921–1967 **FILMS** 11

GENRE Comedy, Drama

Born in the Victorian slums of Lambeth in London, Charlie Chaplin died in Switzerland as the wealthy Sir Charles. He became one of the most famous men in the world on the strength of over 60 silent shorts made before 1920, and only a handful of unforgettable features.

In 1913, Chaplin, the son of music hall performers, went to Mack Sennett's Keystone Studios in Hollywood where he featured in dozens of short slapstick comedies. In *Kid Auto Races at Venice* (1914), he appeared for the first time as the Little Tramp, a character he was to play until 1936. Chaplin was soon directing and writing all his own films, gradually breaking away from the crude techniques of the Sennett comedies. He introduced pathos and a detailed social background into more structured and ambitious farces such as *Easy Street* (1917) and *The Immigrant* (1917). His first feature, *The Kid* (1921), was set in the London slums. *A Woman of Paris* (1923) starred Edna Purviance – his leading lady in almost 30 comedies – as a high-class prostitute. Although critically acclaimed, the feature failed at the box office. The next three films were Chaplin's greatest: ***The Gold Rush*** (1925), ***The Circus*** (1928), and ***City Lights*** (1931), and all managed to shift, Dickens-like, from satire to pathos to comedy.

Feeling that talkies would weaken his global appeal, Chaplin resisted dialogue for 13 years. In *Modern Times* (1936), his voice is heard for the first time – singing gibberish. *The Great Dictator* (1940), his first real talkie, has many comic set-pieces as well as being an attack on Hitler. Chaplin continued to experiment with styles in *Monsieur Verdoux* (1947) and *Limelight* (1952), which contains a stunning music hall sequence.

WHAT TO WATCH

- *The Kid* (1921)
- *A Woman of Paris* (1923)
- *The Gold Rush* (1925)
- *The Circus* (1928)
- *City Lights* (1931)
- *Modern Times* (1936)
- *The Great Dictator* (1940)

Film poster, 1921

René **Clair**

BORN 1898 **DIED** 1981

NATIONALITY French

CAREER 1924–1965 **FILMS** 23

GENRE Comedy, Fantasy, Musical

The films of René Clair have the same reputation for gaiety as Paris, the city in which he was born. In the 1920s, he created some of the most original films of early French cinema.

Entr'acte (1924) – a 20-minute surrealistic but playful film shot in the city and featuring modernist artists such as Marcel Duchamp – earned Clair the reputation of being a member of the avant-garde. His adaptation of Eugène Labiche's 19th-century farce, *The Italian Straw Hat* (*Un Chapeau de Paille d'Italie*, 1928), in which he substituted many of the play's verbal jokes with visual ones, was made with clockwork precision. His first film with sound, *Under the Roofs of Paris* (*Sous les Toits de Paris*, 1930) – one of the very first French talkies – uses songs, sound effects, and street noises (created in the studio).

The musical comedies *The Million* (*Le Million*, 1931) and *Freedom for Us* (*À Nous la Liberté*, 1931) influenced Hollywood musicals in the use of related action and songs, while the latter's satire on the dehumanizing effects of mass production inspired Chaplin's *Modern Times* (1936). Just before the war, Clair left France to work abroad. Whether in Britain (*The Ghost Goes West*, 1935) or in the US (*I Married a Witch*, 1942), he continued to direct in his carefree way. His post-war films include *Beauty and the Devil* (*La Beauté du Diable*, 1950) and, his first film in France for over a decade, *Silence is Golden* (*Le Silence est d'Or*,1947) – a regretful look at silent cinema. Clair's gentle irony is evident in the comedy *Summer Manoeuvres* (*Les Grandes Manoeuvres*, 1955), his first film in colour.

Film poster, 1932

WHAT TO WATCH

- *The Italian Straw Hat* (1928)
- *Under the Roofs of Paris* (1930)
- *The Million* (1931)
- *Freedom for Us* (1931)
- *The Last Billionaire* (*Le Dernier Milliardaire*, 1934)
- *The Ghost Goes West* (1935)
- *It Happened Tomorrow* (1944)
- *Night Beauties* (*Les Belles de Nuit*, 1952)
- *Summer Manoeuvres* (1955)

Henri-Georges **Clouzot**

BORN 1907 **DIED** 1977

NATIONALITY French

CAREER 1942–1968 **FILMS** 14

GENRE Thriller

Mainly because of ill health, Henri-Georges Clouzot made only 14 films, most of them exceptionally dark in character, with a fine observation of human frailty.

Clouzot's second film, *The Raven* (*Le Corbeau*, 1943), about the effect poison-pen letters have on a French village, took a bleak view of provincial life. In 1953, he made the successful *The Wages of Fear* (*Le Salaire de la Peur*), about four men transporting dangerous nitro-glycerine in trucks. *Diabolique* (*Les Diaboliques*, 1955) is a chilling tale of murder set in a school. An intriguing documentary, *The Picasso Mystery* (*Le Mystère Picasso*, 1956) brilliantly captures the painter at work. *The Truth* (*La Verité*, 1960) is an awkward coming together of the New Wave (see pp.42–43) actress Brigitte Bardot with the "old guard".

Christina (Véra Clouzot) looks on as Nicole (Simone Signoret) prepares to kill her husband by mixing poison in his whisky bottle in *Diabolique* (1955).

WHAT TO WATCH

- *The Raven* (1943)
- *Quay of the Goldsmiths* (*Quai des Orfèvres*, 1947)
- *The Wages of Fear* (1953)
- *Diabolique* (1955)
- *The Picasso Mystery* (1956)

Jean **Cocteau**

BORN 1889 **DIED** 1963

NATIONALITY French

CAREER 1930–1960 **FILMS** 6

GENRE Avant-garde, Fantasy

Poet, novelist, playwright, film director, designer, painter, stage director, and ballet producer – the versatile Jean Cocteau directed six films that make up part of his work in other art forms.

For Cocteau, films were another form of poetry. He made his first film when he was 41 and already famous. *The Blood of a Poet* (*Le Sang D'un Poète*, 1930) contains all the signs and symbols of his personal mythology evident in his novels, poems, and drawings. The haunting, witty *Orpheus* (*Orphée*, 1950) is a perfect marriage between Greek myth and Cocteau's own ideas. It elaborates on the theme of the poet caught between the worlds of the real and the imaginary, as is the heroine in *Beauty and the Beast* (*La Belle et la Bête*, 1946). *Testament of Orpheus* (*Le Testament d'Orphée*, 1960) is a poetic, semi-autobiographical evocation of the director's work.

WHAT TO WATCH

- *The Blood of a Poet* (1930)
- *Beauty and the Beast* (1946)
- *Orpheus* (1950)
- *The Testament of Orpheus* (1960)

Film poster, 1946

Joel and Ethan **Coen**

BORN 1954 (Joel), 1957 (Ethan)

NATIONALITY American

CAREER 1984– **FILMS** 15

GENRE Film noir, Comedy, Drama

When the Coen brothers first burst onto the film scene with *Blood Simple* in 1984, they immediately established their credentials as true descendents of the masters of American film noir, while putting their own distinctive, often quirky stamp on their films.

Blood Simple helped to ignite the indie film movement of the mid-1980s. Despite having their movies financed and distributed by major studios, the Coen brothers have remained true independents. Nominally, Joel directs and Ethan produces, but as Joel has said, "We really co-direct the movies. We could just as easily take the credit 'produced, written, and directed' by the two of us."

Crime is the core of their films, but intrinsically they are fables of good versus evil. Most are film noirs disguised as horror (*Blood Simple*), farce (*Raising Arizona*, 1987), gangster movie (*Miller's Crossing*, 1990), psychological drama (*Barton Fink*, 1991), police thriller (*Fargo*, 1996), black comedy (*The Big Lebowski*, 1998), social drama (*O Brother, Where Art Thou?*, 2000), and Western (*No Country for Old Men*, 2007). *The Man Who Wasn't There* (2001) is their most direct homage to 1940s film noir, while *True Grit* (2010) is their take on the Western in a contemporary style. However different they are on the surface, each film contains elements of the other: horror edging into comic-strip farce, violence into slapstick, and vice versa.

WHAT TO WATCH

- *Blood Simple* (1984)
- *Raising Arizona* (1987)
- *Barton Fink* (1991)
- *Fargo* (1996)
- *The Big Lebowski* (1998)
- *No Country for Old Men* (2007)
- *A Serious Man* (2009)
- *True Grit* (2010)

John Turturro, Tim Blake Nelson, and George Clooney star in ***O Brother, Where Art Thou?*** (2000), an easy-going comedy about escaped convicts.

» **Francis Ford Coppola** (right) is seen here with Joe Mantegna on the set of *The Godfather: Part III* (1990), in which Mantegna plays Joey Zasa, a rival of the Corleones.

Francis Ford **Coppola**

BORN 1939

NATIONALITY American

CAREER 1962– **FILMS** 21

GENRE Gangster, War, Drama

In his rollercoaster career, not only has Francis Ford Coppola always been torn between two extremes of film-making – the massive epic form, and the small, intimate film – but has fluctuated between mammoth hits as well as failures.

It was Coppola who led the way for other "movie brat" directors, such as Martin Scorsese, George Lucas, and Steven Spielberg, to emerge from film schools and storm into Hollywood in the 1970s. Coppola first worked as writer and assistant director to Roger Corman, who enabled him to direct his first movie, *Dementia 13* (1963). *You're a Big Boy Now* (1966), a lively comedy about a young man's sexual education, was very much a movie by a 26-year-old of the mid-1960s. In 1969, Coppola opened his own studio, American Zoetrope, after the unhappy experience of making the musical *Finian's Rainbow* (1968) for Warner Bros. *The Conversation* (1974), made for Zoetrope, is a post-Watergate thriller about a professional eavesdropper (Gene Hackman) being under surveillance himself. *The Godfather* (1972) made Coppola one of the world's most bankable directors, while *The Godfather: Part II* (1974) won six Oscars, and is one of the few sequels that is considered better than the original.

With *Apocalypse Now* (1979), Coppola succeeded in his desire to "give its audience a sense of the horror, the madness, the sensuousness, and the moral dilemma of the Vietnam War". The film, costing US$31 million, took three-and-a-half years to complete and five years to break even. The failure of *One From the Heart* (1982), a US$27-million musical romance, led Coppola to scale down his ambitions with two teen films, *The Outsiders* and *Rumble Fish* (both 1983), the casts of which now read like a Who's Who for the Brat Pack. *Tucker: The Man and His Dream* (1988), about an entrepreneur's pursuit of a dream, then followed. Coppola returned to familiar territory with *The Godfather: Part III* (1990), concluding a saga that started off as "just another gangster picture" and ended up being one of the great achievements of post-war American cinema.

Film poster, 1979

WHAT TO WATCH

- *The Godfather* (1972)
- *The Conversation* (1974)
- *The Godfather: Part II* (1974)
- *Apocalypse Now* (1979)
- *The Outsiders* (1983)
- *Tucker: The Man and His Dream* (1988)
- *The Godfather: Part III* (1990)

George Cukor

BORN 1899 **DIED** 1983

NATIONALITY American

CAREER 1930–1981 **FILMS** 49

GENRE Comedy, Musical, Drama

The name George Cukor on movie titles conjures up the image of a sophisticated dinner party where elegant people meet, and the conversation is pitched at the right level – neither vulgar nor highbrow.

Cukor's career had a shaky start when he was taken off an early film *One Hour with You*, (1932). The same thing happened in 1939, when he was taken off *Gone With the Wind*. At MGM, however, he distinguished himself with productions such as *Dinner at Eight* (1933), *David Copperfield* (1935), and *Romeo and Juliet* (1936). He soon gained the reputation of a "woman's director", and the titles of many of his films reflect this: *Little Women* (1933); *The Women* (1939), with an all-female cast; *Camille* (1936); *Two-Faced Woman* (1941); *A Woman's Face* (1941); *Les Girls* (1957); and *My Fair Lady* (1964), for which he won his only Academy Award. His favourite actress was Katharine Hepburn, whom he directed in *A Bill of Divorcement* (1932), *Holiday* (1938), *The Philadelphia Story* (1940), and *Sylvia Scarlett* (1935). Later, Cukor moved to harder-edged comedies such as *Adam's Rib* (1949), *Pat and Mike* (1952), and *Born Yesterday* (1950). Cukor reached his peak in the 1950s with *A Star is Born* (1954), in which his use of lighting, colour, and costumes surpassed all other musicals on the CinemaScope screen.

WHAT TO WATCH

- *Dinner at Eight* (1933)
- *Little Women* (1933)
- *Sylvia Scarlett* (1935)
- *David Copperfield* (1935)
- *Camille* (1936)
- *Holiday* (1938)
- *The Women* (1939)
- *The Philadelphia Story* (1940)
- *Adam's Rib* (1949)
- *A Star is Born* (1954)
- *My Fair Lady* (1964)

Film poster, 1964

Michael Curtiz

BORN 1888 **DIED** 1962

NATIONALITY Hungarian (American)

CAREER 1912–1962 **FILMS** 163

GENRE Drama

Representing the archetypal studio director of Hollywood's golden era, Michael Curtiz, under contract to Warner Bros. for 27 years, turned out more than 150 films of every genre.

During the 1930s and 1940s, Curtiz, who had made many films in Hungary and Austria, was the studio's ideal director, filming with economy, fluency, and pace. He made over a dozen pictures with Errol Flynn, including some of the star's best swashbucklers, such as *The Adventures of Robin Hood* (1938). He directed James Cagney in *Angels with Dirty Faces* (1938) and *Yankee Doodle Dandy* (1942), for which Cagney won his only Oscar. Joan Crawford, too, won her sole Academy Award under Curtiz's guidance for *Mildred Pierce* (1945). In *Life With Father* (1947), he explores comedy, while his unmistakable touch is also seen in *Casablanca* (1942).

WHAT TO WATCH

- *Kid Galahad* (1937)
- *The Adventures of Robin Hood* (1938)
- *Angels with Dirty Faces* (1938)
- *Casablanca* (1942)

Clarence (William Powell) and Vinnie (Irene Dunne), are seen here with their sons, played by Johnny Calkins, Martin Milner, Jimmy Lydon, and Derek Scott in *Life With Father* (1947).

Cecil B. **DeMille**

BORN 1881 **DIED** 1959

NATIONALITY American

CAREER 1914–1956 **FILMS** 72

GENRE Epic, Western, Comedy, Melodrama

A name that evokes the image of a larger-than-life showman is Cecil B. DeMille – the director who made extravagant Biblical epics. However, his films covered much wider ground during Hollywood's "Golden Age".

Charlton Heston plays Moses in *The Ten Commandments* (1956); DeMille's grandiose remake featured a cast of thousands and gigantic sets.

After a few Westerns, including ***The Squaw Man*** (1914), one of the first major films produced in Hollywood, DeMille brought Metropolitan Opera soprano Geraldine Farrar from New York to play the eponymous heroine in ***Carmen*** (1915). In 1918, the director made a series of risqué domestic comedies, six of them starring Gloria Swanson. These were followed by ***The Ten Commandments*** (1923), which parallels the Biblical story with a modern one. Sex and religion were bedfellows in the films ***The King of Kings*** (1927), ***The Sign of the Cross*** (1932), and ***The Crusades*** (1935). His only musical, ***Madam Satan*** (1930), featured a bizarre party sequence on a Zeppelin. The milk bath in ***Cleopatra*** (1934) with Claudette Colbert highlighted his obsession with bathtub scenes.

DeMille's best period was from 1937 to 1947, during which he directed ***The Plainsman*** (1936), ***North West Mounted Police*** (1940), and ***Unconquered*** (1947), all of which starred Gary Cooper. Lively, unsubtle, and patriotic celebrations of the pioneers of America, they extolled strength, perseverance, and forthright manliness. DeMille saw himself as a pioneer too, and he would narrate many of his films in a grandiloquent manner, returning to the Bible with ***Samson and Delilah*** (1949). When receiving praise for the climactic destruction of the temple, DeMille claimed modestly, "Credit is due to the *Book of Judges*, not me". The director was attracted to the circus, and ***The Greatest Show on Earth*** (1952) was his first film set in contemporary times since 1934. Before he died, he was planning to make ***Be Prepared***, an epic story of the boy-scout movement.

WHAT TO WATCH

- *The Cheat* (1915)
- *The Ten Commandments* (1923)
- *Cleopatra* (1934)
- *The Plainsman* (1936)
- *Union Pacific* (1939)
- *Reap the Wild Wind* (1942)
- *Unconquered* (1947)
- *Samson and Delilah* (1949)
- *The Greatest Show on Earth* (1952)
- *The Ten Commandments* (1956)

Vittorio De Sica is seen here standing behind his cameraman at an outdoor shoot of *Umberto D.* (1952), a poignant, lyrical tale about an old man's struggle to retain his dignity in the face of poverty.

Vittorio **De Sica**

BORN 1901 **DIED** 1974

NATIONALITY Italian

CAREER 1940–1974 **FILMS** 25

GENRE Drama, Melodrama, Comedy

The neorealist (see pp.154–55) films of Vittorio De Sica changed the face of Italian cinema. The director claimed that "my films are a word in favour of the poor and unhappy and against the indifference of society towards suffering".

A successful stage and film actor throughout the 1920s and 1930s, De Sica directed four light comedies before making a sudden breakthrough with the dramatic, humane, and sharply realistic ***The Children Are Watching Us*** (***I Bambini ci Guardano***, 1944), one of the first Italian neorealist films. It was De Sica's first important collaboration with the writer Cesare Zavattini, who worked on many of his films. They both believed in the camera's responsibility to observe real life as it is lived without the traditional compromises of entertaining narratives.

De Sica proved himself a sensitive director of children again in ***Shoeshine*** (***Sciuscià***, 1946), set in Rome during the Allied occupation and dealing with the main theme of the neorealists – poverty in post-war Italy. The film had non-professional actors in real locations. It was an international sensation, and the first non-English language film to win an honorary Academy Award. Yet, De Sica had to raise the money himself for ***Bicycle Thieves*** (***Ladri di Biciclette***, 1948), his most famous film. ***Miracle in Milan*** (***Miracolo a Milano***, 1951), set in a shanty town where the poor get all they desire, prefigured the work of Federico Fellini and Pier Paolo Pasolini. Following ***Umberto D.*** (1952), an ode to his father, De Sica returned to comedy. However, ***Two Women*** (***La Ciociara***, 1960), which gained Sophia Loren a Best Actress Academy Award, is a stark tale of a mother and her daughter trying to survive in Italy in 1943. His next notable film was ***The Garden of the Finzi-Continis*** (***Il Giardino dei Finzi Contini***, 1970), about Italy's involvement in the Holocaust. It won the Academy Award for Best Foreign Film.

WHAT TO WATCH

- *Shoeshine* (1946)
- *Bicycle Thieves* (1948)
- *Miracle in Milan* (1951)
- *Umberto D.* (1952)
- *Two Women* (1960)
- *The Garden of the Finzi-Continis* (1970)

Film poster, 1948

Film poster, 1943

Carl **Dreyer**

BORN 1889 **DIED** 1968

NATIONALITY Danish

CAREER 1919–1964 **FILMS** 15

GENRE Drama

In the relatively few films he made over 50 years, Carl Dreyer used deceptively simple means to achieve powerful effects and a cool emotional intensity.

One of Dreyer's first mature works, ***Mikael*** (1924), is close to German expressionism (see box, p.259), while the feminist ***Master of the House*** (***Du skal ære din hustru***, 1925) is more naturalistic – yet they both have a formal beauty that is also seen in ***The Passion of Joan of Arc*** (***La Passion de Jeanne d'Arc***, 1928), his ground-breaking silent film. ***The Vampire*** (***Vampyr***, 1932) makes other horror films look insignificant. ***Day of Wrath*** (***Vredens dag***, 1943), which follows a witch-hunt in 17th-century Denmark, was thought to be an allegory for occupied Denmark. ***The Word*** (***Ordet***, 1955), which tells of a miraculous resurrection in a rural household, is an extraordinary expression of spiritual optimism. ***Gertrud*** (1964), his last film, was made after a ten-year break from directing. It radiates a deep and affecting atmosphere of serenity.

WHAT TO WATCH

- *Master of the House* (1925)
- *The Passion of Joan of Arc* (1928)
- *The Vampire* (1932)
- *Day of Wrath* (1943)
- *The Word* (1955)
- *Gertrud* (1964)

Clint **Eastwood**

BORN 1930

NATIONALITY American

CAREER 1971– **FILMS** 32

GENRE Western, Thriller, Action, Drama

After making his name as an actor in the 1950s and 1960s, Clint Eastwood emerged as a director in the early 1970s, gaining admiration for his range of movies, particularly his personal Westerns.

In Italy during the mid-1960s, three Sergio Leone Spaghetti Westerns launched Clint Eastwood's film-acting career. Back in the US, he made five movies for Don Siegel in which he continued to play loners, notably the diffident detective Harry Callahan in ***Dirty Harry*** (1971). There are elements of Leone and Siegel in his own films as actor-director. Siegel's influence is evident in his first feature, ***Play Misty for Me*** (1971), a misogynistic thriller; and Leone's is seen in ***High Plains Drifter*** (1973), a moody, stylishly self-conscious Western. Eastwood soon came into his own with his self-mocking Westerns, often revealing flaws in his macho image. ***The Outlaw Josey Wales*** (1976), ***Bronco Billy*** (1980), ***Pale Rider*** (1985) – his most classic Western – and the Academy Award-winning ***Unforgiven*** (1992), are the summation of his career in this genre. He showed his versatility in cop movies: ***Sudden Impact*** (1983), ***The Rookie*** (1990), and ***Mystic River*** (2003); biopics: ***Bird*** (1988), and ***White Hunter, Black Heart*** (1990); love stories: ***The Bridges of Madison County*** (1995); and a boxing drama, ***Million Dollar Baby*** (2004).

WHAT TO WATCH

- *Play Misty for Me* (1971)
- *The Outlaw Josey Wales* (1976)
- *Bird* (1988)
- *Unforgiven* (1992)
- *Mystic River* (2003)
- *Million Dollar Baby* (2004)
- *Flags of Our Fathers* (2006)
- *Letters From Iwo Jima* (2006)
- *Invictus* (2009)

A devastated Jimmy (Sean Penn) learns of his daughter's murder in *Mystic River* (2003); Eastwood's standout direction makes this multi-layered film hauntingly real.

Sergei **Eisenstein**

BORN 1898 **DIED** 1948

NATIONALITY Russian

CAREER 1925–1944 **FILMS** 8

GENRE Propaganda, Avant-garde, Epic

One of the undisputed geniuses of cinema, Sergei Eisenstein was not only a leading practitioner of his art, but its principal theorist. Despite strict Soviet government guidelines, he was able to set his personal stamp on the seven features he was allowed to complete.

In Eisenstein's first film, *Strike* (*Stachka*, 1925), many of his stylistic devices were already in evidence: caricature, visual metaphors, and shock cutting – a factory boss uses a lemon squeezer as police move in on striking workers; shots of a slaughterhouse are cut in as the police mow them down. What Eisenstein defined as "dynamic montage" (rapid cutting) is used to devastating effect in the "Odessa Steps" sequence in *The Battleship Potemkin* (*Bronenosets Potyomkin*, 1925).

The "intellectual montage", based on Eisenstein's editing technique, at which the audience must not only react emotionally but be shocked into thinking, was perfected in *October* (*Oktyabr*, 1927). The number of shots – 3,200 – was more than double those of *Potemkin*. The emotional and rhythmic composition shows the storming of the Winter Palace, the dismemberment of the Tsar's statue, and a dead white horse sliding off a drawbridge into the river. The film completed his Russian Revolution trilogy, through which several motifs reappear – especially that of turning wheels representing change: *Strike* ending in defeat, *The Battleship Potemkin* in partial triumph, and *October* in ultimate victory. *October* displeased those in power, who felt that Eisenstein was unwise to experiment with a film whose subject matter was as sensitive as that of the revolution. He tried to appease the party with *The General Line* (*Staroye i Novoye*, 1928), but could not restrain his ironic humour, such as in the mock marriage of a cow and a bull, and when the milk hovers for a moment in a cream-separator before it splatters orgasmically onto a woman's face.

In 1931, left-wing American novelist Upton Sinclair agreed to finance *Que Viva Mexico* (1931). It was originally intended as a four-part semi-documentary on Mexican life and history, but Eisenstein overran the time and budget. The money was withdrawn, and he never got to edit the material he had shot. Today the film exists in various re-edited forms and its baroque images, tinged with eroticism, make the viewer regret the loss.

Charged with "formalism" in the unfinished *Bezhin Meadow* (*Bezhin Lug*, 1936), Eisenstein recanted by making the patriotic spectacle *Alexander Nevsky* (*Aleksandr Nevskiy*, 1938), a richly enjoyable epic with stirring images and a dramatic use of Prokofiev's music, especially in the famous "Battle of the Ice" sequence. Taking his imagery from grand opera, Japanese *kabuki* theatre, and Shakespearean and Russian icons, Eisenstein embarked on the three parts of *Ivan the Terrible* (*Ivan Groznyy I, II*, 1944–1946), but only two were completed. Stalin approved Part I, but as Ivan's character became more complex, he turned against it, perhaps recognizing something of himself. Part II was not shown until 10 years after both Eisenstein's and Stalin's deaths. *Ivan the Terrible* is the peak of Eisenstein's work, fulfilling his ambitions of achieving a synthesis of all the arts.

Eisenstein (third left) directs the cast of *Ivan the Terrible Part II* (1958) during the winter of 1943 in Kazakhstan.

Film poster, 1925

WHAT TO WATCH

- *Strike* (1924)
- *The Battleship Potemkin* (1925)
- *October* (1927)
- *The General Line* (or *The Old and the New*, 1928)
- *Alexander Nevsky* (1938)
- *Ivan the Terrible Part I* (1944)
- *Ivan the Terrible Part II* (1946, released 1958)

Rainer Werner **Fassbinder**

BORN 1945 **DIED** 1982

NATIONALITY German

CAREER 1969–1982 **FILMS** 23

GENRE Melodrama

Almost a one-man film industry, Rainer Werner Fassbinder made dozens of films over a period of 12 years: a surprising, consistent, entertaining, probing, and lively output.

With friends from the Munich Action Theatre Group, Fassbinder began making movies in 1969, rapidly becoming a part of the new generation of young directors putting German cinema back on the map after 30 years. Often starring his favourite actress Hanna Schygulla, Fassbinder's films reveal a heartless, avaricious post-war Germany. The characters tend to be frustrated by the barrenness of urban existence, sometimes turning to violence, as in *The Third Generation* (*Die Dritte Generation*, 1979), which focuses on a Berlin terrorist group. One of the many Fassbinder films to use Douglas Sirk's Hollywood melodramas as its prime model, *Fear Eats the Soul* (*Angst essen Seele auf*, 1974) borrows the plot from *All That Heaven Allows* (1955) and shows a lonely ageing woman having an affair with a younger Arab man. Women are generally at the centre of his movies, and *The Marriage of Maria Braun* (*Die Ehe der Maria Braun*, 1979), *Lola* (1981), and *Veronika Voss* (*Die Sehnsucht der Veronika Voss*, 1982) all portray women trying to survive in an ironically evoked Germany. A more flamboyant style is used in these recreations of an era than the static camera set-ups of the director's earlier films. Sexuality, as a means for the strong to manipulate the weak, is a frequent motif, whether he shows heterosexuality – *Effi Briest* (1974) and *Lili Marleen* (1981) – or homosexuality – *The Bitter Tears of Petra von Kant* (*Die Bitteren Tränen der Petra von Kant*, 1972) and *Fox* (*Faustrecht der Freiheit*, 1975).

In his short life, Fassbinder made more than 40 productions, including television and stage work. He also wrote, edited, photographed, and produced many of his films.

Hanna Schygulla and Margit Carstensen star in the beautifully visualized *The Bitter Tears of Petra von Kant* (1972), based on Fassbinder's own play about desire and power.

WHAT TO WATCH

- *The Merchant of Four Seasons* (1971)
- *The Bitter Tears of Petra von Kant* (1972)
- *Fear Eats the Soul* (1974)
- *Effi Briest* (1974)
- *Fox* (1975)
- *Mother Küsters' Trip To Heaven* (1975)
- *In a Year of 13 Moons* (1978)
- *The Marriage of Maria Braun* (1979)
- *Lola* (1981)
- *Veronika Voss* (1982)

Federico **Fellini**

BORN 1920 **DIED** 1993

NATIONALITY Italian

CAREER 1950–1990 **FILMS** 19

GENRE Comedy, Drama

A magnificent ringmaster, Federico Fellini created a world that was rather like a circus, peopled by grotesque or innocent clowns.

For 12 years following his arrival in Rome from Rimini, Fellini wrote film scripts, many for Roberto Rossellini. Unlike Rossellini, however, Fellini was never a neorealist (see box, p.286), and established his own mythology when he started directing. He said, "If the cinema didn't exist I might have become a circus director", and it could also be said that if the circus did not exist, he might not have become a film director. The circus as metaphor (and reality) plays an important role in his films. In ***La Strada*** (1954), Giulietta Masina (Fellini's wife) plays an innocent clown, mistreated by a travelling strongman (Anthony Quinn). The film, the first to win the Academy Award for Best Foreign Language Film, made Fellini internationally known. He used Masina's Chaplinesque persona as the "innocent" prostitute in ***Nights of Cabiria*** (***Le Notti di Cabiria***, 1957). Marcello Mastroianni plays Fellini's alter ego in ***La Dolce Vita*** (1960) and in ***8½*** (1963), the title referring to the number of Fellini's films (including collaborations). This calculated self-portrait remains a compendium of every Fellini theme and stylistic device. An autobiographical aspect is also evident in ***I Vitelloni*** (1953), ***Roma*** (1972), and ***Amarcord*** (1973).

WHAT TO WATCH

- *I Vitelloni* (1953)
- *La Strada* (1954)
- *La Dolce Vita* (1960)
- *8½* (1963)
- *Julietta of the Spirits* (*Giulietta degli Spiriti*, 1965)
- *Roma* (1972)
- *Amarcord* (1973)
- *Fellini's Casanova* (1976)

Film poster, 1960

Robert J. **Flaherty**

BORN 1884 **DIED** 1951

NATIONALITY American

CAREER 1922–1949 **FILMS** 6

GENRE Documentary

Considered by many to be the father of the documentary film, Robert J. Flaherty conveyed the importance of primitive societies and the balance between man and nature in his silent era films.

Flaherty lived with the Inuit for 16 months in order to make his first full documentary feature, ***Nanook of the North*** (1922). After the film's success, Paramount asked him to make a "Nanook" of the South Seas, and he spent two years in the Samoan Islands making ***Moana*** (1926), filming an Eden where noble tribes hunted, fished, and cooked.

Gainsborough Studios gave him free rein on ***Man of Aran*** (1934), and he spent a full two years off the coast of Ireland living with the Aran islanders, documenting their harsh daily lives. ***The Land*** (1942), although incomplete, marked a departure for the director and he swapped exotic communities for more familiar landscapes. The film prepared the ground for ***Louisiana Story*** (1948), a poetic slice of Americana on the Louisiana bayou.

WHAT TO WATCH

- *Nanook of the North* (1922)
- *Moana* (1926)
- *Man of Aran* (1934)
- *Louisiana Story* (1948)

Joseph Boudreaux is a young Cajun boy, with a pet raccoon, in ***Louisiana Story*** (1948), which explores man's relationship with the environment.

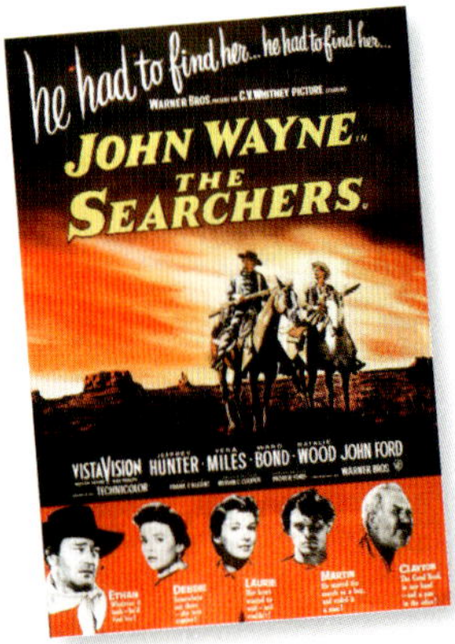

Film poster, 1956

John **Ford**

BORN 1895 **DIED** 1973

NATIONALITY American

CAREER 1917–1966 **FILMS** 123

GENRE Western, Drama

It was John Ford (Sean Aloysius O'Feeney) who, more than anyone else, gave the Western an epic stature. He created a personal, recognizable world that is an essential part of American culture.

The Westerns made by Ford are romantic visions of the Old West. They are mythical views of America's past, where men are heroes, defending the lives of women and children in the community, fort, or homestead. The births, deaths, funerals, weddings, and dances are punctuated by songs and drunken brawls. It was from 1939, with ***Stagecoach***, that the true Ford Western emerged. His few ventures out of America included two films set in Ireland: ***The Informer*** (1935), an atmospheric drama that takes place during the Irish Rebellion, and ***The Quiet Man*** (1952), a romance. These, and ***How Green Was My Valley*** (1941), set in Wales, won him Academy Awards for Best Director.

WHAT TO WATCH

- *Stagecoach* (1939)
- *Young Mr. Lincoln* (1939)
- *The Grapes of Wrath* (1940)
- *Fort Apache* (1948)
- *The Searchers* (1956)
- *The Man Who Shot Liberty Valance* (1962)

In the 1930s, Ford used Henry Fonda's noble, youthful character to great effect as the epitome of American idealism, in ***Young Mr. Lincoln*** (1939) and in ***The Grapes of Wrath*** (1940), for which he won another Oscar. During World War II, he made morale-boosting documentaries, then returned to Westerns. Among the best were ***My Darling Clementine*** (1946), starring Fonda, and ***She Wore a Yellow Ribbon*** (1949), with John Wayne, the leading light of the "Ford Stock Company" (as the group of actors most regularly used by Ford was known). ***The Searchers*** (1956) was the culmination of Ford's frontier movies, and ***The Man Who Shot Liberty Valance*** (1962) was the last Western he made with Wayne. Despite the substantial budget he had for it, he shot the film in black-and-white, probably to evoke a sense of nostalgia.

Milos **Forman**

BORN 1932

NATIONALITY Czech (American)

CAREER 1963– **FILMS** 14

GENRE Biopic, Comedy, Costume drama

The Czech films of Milos Forman reveal a gently mocking humour and a keen eye for the minutiae of human behaviour, qualities he brought to bear on his American movies.

Tom Hulce plays Mozart in *Amadeus* (1984); Forman's compelling portrait of the legendary composer is filled with rich details, powerful drama, and a wonderful score.

WHAT TO WATCH

- *Loves of a Blonde* (1965)
- *The Firemen's Ball* (1967)
- *One Flew Over the Cuckoo's Nest* (1975)
- *Amadeus* (1984)
- *Man on the Moon* (1999)

Using mostly non-professional actors, and a *cinema verité* technique (see box, p.311), Forman gave ***Black Peter*** (***Cerný Petr***, 1964) and ***Loves of a Blonde*** (***Lásky jedné plavovlásky***, 1965), a comic freshness. ***The Firemen's Ball*** (***Horí, má panenko***, 1967), a satire on petty bureaucracy, led to conflict with the Czech authorities who saw it as a political allegory. Before the Russian invasion, he left for the US, where he made ***One Flew Over the Cuckoo's Nest*** (1975). It won five Oscars, including Best Film and Best Director. ***Amadeus*** (1984), a visual and aural treat shot mostly in the former Czechoslovakia, won eight Academy Awards.

In the first version of *J'Accuse* (1919), Gance's anti-war film, wounded soldiers are welcomed home from the World War I battlefields by the civilian population.

Abel **Gance**

BORN 1889 **DIED** 1981

NATIONALITY French

CAREER 1911–1971 **FILMS** 29

GENRE Epic, Costume drama, Melodrama

One of cinema's great pioneers before the arrival of sound, Abel Gance reached his artistic apogee with the epic masterpiece ***Napoléon*** (1927), in which he used camera techniques that were far ahead of their time.

At the start of his career, Gance experimented with various techniques. In ***The Folly of Doctor Tube*** (***La Folie Du Docteur Tube***, 1915), he used a subjective camera and distorting mirrors for effect. ***J'Accuse*** (***I Accuse***, 1919; remake 1938), Gance's pacifist statement in which a triangular relationship becomes a microcosm for the horrors of war, was actually shot during World War I with real soldiers under fire. It begins with infantrymen forming the letters of the title and ends with dead soldiers rising from their graves. This final scene is then contrasted, in a split-screen sequence, with a victory parade to the Arc de Triomphe. For ***The Wheel*** (***La Roué***, 1923), an ambitious production, he used rapid montage techniques – long before Sergei Eisenstein's experiments with editing. These new methods were showcased in his most impressive movie, ***Napoléon*** (1927), a dazzling biopic of Napoléon Bonaparte.

Sadly, Gance's romantic visual imagination was constrained with the coming of sound. Many of his later films are routine melodramas, although he sometimes used the same ideas and sequences from his silent movies, such as ***The Tenth Symphony*** (***La Dixième Symphonie***, 1918). Poignant and paradoxical is the sequence in ***The Life and Loves of Beethoven*** (***Un Grand Amour de Beethoven***, 1936) when the great composer loses his hearing, portrayed by silent shots of violins, birds, and bells. The loss of sound for Beethoven was as agonizing as the coming of sound was for Gance.

WHAT TO WATCH

- ***The Tenth Symphony*** (1918)
- ***J'Accuse*** (***I Accuse***) (1919)
- ***The Wheel*** (1923)
- ***Napoléon*** (1927)
- ***The Life and Loves of Beethoven*** (1936)

Jean-Luc **Godard**

BORN 1930

NATIONALITY French

CAREER 1960– **FILMS** 42

GENRE Drama, Political drama, Satire

Ferdinand (Jean-Paul Belmondo) takes a break after a bizarre car chase, one among a series of wild adventures he shares with Marianne (Anna Karina) in *Pierrot le Fou* (1965).

Always striving to go beyond films into other arts and politics, Jean-Luc Godard has formulated a truly revolutionary film language free from the dominant bourgeois culture in the West.

Breathless (*À Bout de Souffle*, 1960), Godard's first feature, established him as one of the stars of the French New Wave (see pp.42–43). His second, *The Little Soldier* (*Le Petit Soldat*, 1963), portrays an ambivalent view of the Algerian war. *My Life to Live* (*Vivre sa Vie*, 1962) uses a Brechtian device of episodes with texts, quotations, and interviews, giving it a documentary tone. Godard employs colour symbolically in *Pierrot le Fou* (1965), a stunning study of violence and relationships. In *Two or Three Things I Know About Her* (*Deux ou Trois Choses que Je sais d'Elle*, 1967), "her" alludes to Paris, a city that has always inspired him. *Weekend* (1967) is a devastating critique on modern French society. Godard broke away from commercial cinema to shoot a series of ciné-tracts in 16mm and video, but returned to more accessible film-making with *Tout va Bien* (1972). From 1980, a more mature Godard emerged, with his movies becoming contemplative, poetic essays on contemporary issues that challenged audiences to think differently.

WHAT TO WATCH

Breathless (1960)

My Life to Live (1962)

Contempt (*Le Mépris*, 1963)

Band of Outsiders (*Bande á Part*, 1964)

Alphaville (1965)

Two or Three Things I Know About Her (1967)

Weekend (1967)

New Wave (*Nouvelle Vague*, 1990)

In Praise of Love (*Eloge de l'Amour*, 2001)

Our Music (*Notre Musique*, 2004)

Anna Karina plays Natacha von Braun and Eddie Constantine plays Lemmy Caution, an American secret agent, in *Alphaville* (1965), a film set in a futuristic city and shot with minimal lighting.

On the set of *Intolerance* (1916), Griffith, with loud hailer in hand, directs the cast of one of the film's four tales – the modern American story.

D.W. **Griffith**

BORN 1875 **DIED** 1948

NATIONALITY American

CAREER 1908–1931 **FILMS** 35

GENRE Epic, Melodrama, Costume drama

With his epic Civil War drama, ***The Birth of a Nation*** (1915), D.W. Griffith did much to convince the world that cinema is as valid an art form as any other.

The son of a Confederate soldier, Griffith started directing at Biograph Studios in 1908. Biograph was the first studio to shoot a movie in Hollywood – Griffith's ***In Old California*** (1910). With Billy Bitzer (the photographer of nearly all his films), Griffith turned out hundreds of one- and two-reelers, learning his craft as he went along. By 1911, he had used close-ups, changed camera set-ups within one scene, and developed cross-cutting. Despite its reactionary attitudes, ***The Birth of a Nation*** remains a remarkable film in which all the technical innovations of his early work reached maturity. In order to pacify those critics put off by the racist elements in the film, Griffith's next project was the epic ***Intolerance*** (1916), containing four separate stories to illustrate his theme. Throughout this period, the director struggled to free himself from studio control, and a result of this was United Artists, which he co-founded in 1919 with Charlie Chaplin, Douglas Fairbanks, and Mary Pickford.

He made some of his most endearing movies with the waif-like Lillian Gish – his favourite actress – notably ***Broken Blossoms*** (1919), ***True Heart Susie*** (1919), ***Way Down East*** (1920), and ***Orphans of the Storm*** (1921). However, due to his narrow views, and the emergence of new directors and of sound, Griffith lost his popular appeal and his influence. His first talkie, ***Abraham Lincoln*** (1930), failed and he led an obscure existence until his death in 1948.

WHAT TO WATCH

- ***The Birth of a Nation*** (1915)
- ***Intolerance*** (1916)
- ***True Heart Susie*** (1919)
- ***Broken Blossoms*** (1919)
- ***Way Down East*** (1920)
- ***Orphans of the Storm*** (1921)

Film poster, 1930

Howard **Hawks**

BORN 1896 **DIED** 1977

NATIONALITY American

CAREER 1926–1970 **FILMS** 41

GENRE Western, Comedy, Action

Since Howard Hawks' assured narrative style and handling of most genres was not immediately obvious as "art", he was not appreciated as a true auteur and a candidate for Hollywood immortality until years after his death.

Many of the director's own personal interests feature in his films. A pilot in World War I, he brought authenticity to his four films about flying: *The Dawn Patrol* (1930), *Ceiling Zero* (1936), *Only Angels Have Wings* (1939), and *Air Force* (1943). A former designer and race-car driver, he re-created the excitement of the track in *The Crowd Roars* (1932) and *Red Line 7000* (1965). Energetic sportsmanship also inspired him to make *Hatari!* (1962) and *Man's Favourite Sport* (1964). Some of these films focus on the camaraderie of men who risk their lives, but it was the battle of the sexes and gender role-swapping that preoccupied him in his screwball comedies *Twentieth Century* (1934), *Bringing Up Baby* (1938), *His Girl Friday* (1940), and later in *I Was a Male War Bride* (1949). Particularly remarkable was the sublime sexual interplay between Humphrey Bogart and Lauren Bacall in *To Have and Have Not* (1944) and *The Big Sleep* (1946), and the stunning opening number of *Gentlemen Prefer Blondes* (1953). Notable in Hawks' films is the pairing of John Wayne with Montgomery Clift in *Red River* (1948), with Dean Martin in *Rio Bravo* (1959), and with Robert Mitchum in *El Dorado* (1966).

John Wayne, Hawks' favourite actor, plays Colonel Cord McNally, a Union Army officer who travels with his men to Texas in search of justice in *Rio Lobo* (1970).

Lauren Bacall plays Vivien and Humphrey Bogart stars as private detective Philip Marlowe in *The Big Sleep* (1946), a hard-boiled thriller adapted from Raymond Chandler's novel.

WHAT TO WATCH

- *Scarface* (1932)
- *Twentieth Century* (1934)
- *Bringing Up Baby* (1938)
- *Only Angels Have Wings* (1939)
- *His Girl Friday* (1940)
- *To Have and Have Not* (1944)
- *The Big Sleep* (1946)
- *Red River* (1948)
- *Rio Bravo* (1959)

In *Fitzcarraldo* (1982), the manual hauling of a 320-ton steamship over steep hills in the Peruvian jungle was accomplished without special effects, and is one of film's most astonishing scenes.

Werner **Herzog**

BORN 1942

NATIONALITY German

CAREER 1967– **FILMS** 25

GENRE Epic, Documentary

Known for going to any lengths to make a film, Werner Herzog (Werner Stipetic) is drawn to bizarre characters and situations set in stunningly photographed exotic surroundings.

Herzog's first feature, ***Signs of Life*** (***Lebenszeichen***, 1968), takes place during World War II on a Greek island where a German soldier recovering from wounds refuses to obey orders. This theme foreshadowed later preoccupations with outsiders refusing or unable to conform to society. ***Fata Morgana*** (1971), shot in the desolate Sahara desert, is an "outsider" film par excellence, while ***Even Dwarfs Started Small*** (***Auch Zwerge haben klein angefangen***, 1970), set on an island populated by dwarfs, depicts the problematic nature of the liberation of the spirit. ***The Enigma of Kaspar Hauser*** (***Jeder für sich und Gott gegen alle***, 1974), about a wild boy who appeared from nowhere in the early 19th century, also appealed to Herzog's fascination with social misfits. His greatest success was ***Aguirre, Wrath of God*** (***Aguirre, der Zorn Gottes***, 1972). Shot in the Peruvian Andes, it was the first of several films about obsessive heroes played by schizophrenic Klaus Kinski. The odd relationship between Kinski and Herzog became the subject of the director's documentary, ***My Best Fiend*** (***Mein liebster Feind***, 1999), and ***Fitzcarraldo*** (1982) is about a turbulent trip by Kinski and Herzog into more untamed regions, this time the Amazonian jungle, where Brian, the main character, is determined to build an opera house. "If I should abandon this film", Herzog said when conditions became difficult, "I should be a man without dreams... I live my life or end my life with this project".

WHAT TO WATCH

- ***Signs of Life*** (1967)
- ***Fata Morgana*** (1971)
- ***Aguirre, Wrath of God*** (1972)
- ***The Enigma of Kaspar Hauser*** (1974)
- ***Fitzcarraldo*** (1982)
- ***My Best Fiend*** (1999)
- ***Grizzly Man*** (2005)
- ***Encounters at the End of the World*** (2007)
- ***The Bad Lieutenant: Port of Call – New Orleans*** (2009)

Film poster, 1979

Paul Newman (second from left) discusses direction with Alfred Hitchcock (second from right) on the set of *Torn Curtain* (1966).

Alfred **Hitchcock**

BORN 1899 **DIED** 1980

NATIONALITY British

CAREER 1926–1976 **FILMS** 56

GENRE Thriller, Horror, Film noir

For decades, Alfred Hitchcock was the only film director whose name and face were as famous as those of a film star. "Hitch" was dubbed the "Master of Suspense", putting his own unique stamp on the thriller genre.

Hitchcock entered the film industry in 1920 as a designer of silent-film titles, rising to art director, scriptwriter, and assistant director. He directed nine silent films, including *The Lodger* (1927), in which he first explored his favourite theme of the innocent in danger. The movie marked his first appearance in front of the camera in a cameo, which became a feature of all his subsequent films.

The lure of Hollywood

In 1929, while *Blackmail* was in production, sound was introduced to cinema. The 30-year-old Hitchcock quickly demonstrated his understanding of this new technology. At one point in the film, he created a sound montage in which the word "knife" echoes over and over again in the guilty girl's mind. A number of superb comedy-thrillers followed, such as *The Man Who Knew Too Much* (1934) and *The Lady Vanishes* (1938). In 1940, Producer David O. Selznick invited him to Hollywood to direct a movie based on Daphne du Maurier's novel *Rebecca*. Hitchcock's first American film had a British cast headed by Laurence Olivier and Joan Fontaine. *Rebecca* (1940) was a triumph, winning the Oscar for Best Picture and launching his long career in the US.

Psychology, plot, and pursuit

Hitchcock claimed not to care about the morality, subject, or message of his films, but only the manner in which the story was told. The obvious Catholicism in movies such as *I Confess* (1953) and the blatant psychology of *Spellbound* (1945), *Psycho* (1960), and *Marnie* (1964) were merely plot devices.

The pleasure of the director's films lies elsewhere – for example, in the picaresque pursuit of *Saboteur* (1942), in which a man must prove his innocence while being chased by both police and criminals. Then there's the underlying sense of menace that emanates from unexpected places, evident in *The Birds* (1963). Hitchcock also had the remarkable ability to surprise his audiences. In *Psycho*, for example, he audaciously kills off his leading lady (Janet Leigh) halfway through the film.

He demonstrated an extravagant sense of location, as shown with the shooting that coincides with a clash of cymbals during a concert in *The Man Who Knew Too Much* (1934 and 1956); the climactic chase on Mount Rushmore in *North by Northwest* (1959); and the strangulation in London's Covent Garden market in *Frenzy* (1972). From 1956 to 1966, all Hitchcock's films were set to Bernard Herrmann's distinctive pulsating music, particularly effective in *Vertigo* (1958), which many consider his masterpiece.

WHAT TO WATCH

- *The 39 Steps* (1935)
- *The Lady Vanishes* (1938)
- *Shadow of a Doubt* (1943)
- *Strangers on a Train* (1951)
- *Rear Window* (1954)
- *Vertigo* (1958)
- *North by Northwest* (1959)
- *Psycho* (1960)
- *The Birds* (1963)
- *Marnie* (1964)

John **Huston**

BORN 1906 **DIED** 1987

NATIONALITY American

CAREER 1941–1987 **FILMS** 37

GENRE Various

The films of John Huston express his wide-ranging, typically masculine interests, but beneath the tough exterior, a tenderness and a romantic idealism is revealed.

Son of actor Walter Huston and father of Anjelica and Danny – both actors too – John Huston led a varied life as painter, boxer, horseman, hunter, actor, and writer, before becoming a director. *The Maltese Falcon* (1941), starring his favourite actor Humphrey Bogart, was his assured debut and is widely considered the first film noir. He directed his father and Bogart in *The Treasure of the Sierra Madre* (1948), a saga of human greed. Greed is also the theme of *Key Largo* (1948), with Bogart and Lauren Bacall, and of *Beat the Devil* (1953), which parodies *The Maltese Falcon* and Bogart's persona. Most of his heroes are fiercely independent loners, such as Toulouse-Lautrec (*Moulin Rouge*, 1952), Captain Ahab (*Moby Dick*, 1956), Freud (in the 1962 film of the same name), the defeated boxers in *Fat City* (1972), and the preacher in *Wise Blood* (1979). *The Misfits* (1961), starring Clark Gable, Montgomery Clift, and Marilyn Monroe among others, is a film about losers. Fatalism and irony pervade Huston's best movies, which are rich in character and plot and told in an incisive narrative style – one of the best examples being *The Asphalt Jungle* (1950). He made two excursions into the African jungle with *The African Queen* (1951), starring the unlikely pairing of Bogart and Katharine Hepburn, and *The Roots of Heaven* (1958), a film about doomed elephants. Huston's final film, *The Dead* (1987), based on a short story by James Joyce and filmed in Ireland where the director had made his home, was a poignant valediction.

WHAT TO WATCH

- *The Maltese Falcon* (1941)
- *The Treasure of the Sierra Madre* (1948)
- *Key Largo* (1948)
- *The Asphalt Jungle* (1950)
- *The African Queen* (1951)
- *Beat the Devil* (1953)
- *The Misfits* (1961)
- *Reflections in a Golden Eye* (1967)
- *Fat City* (1972)
- *The Dead* (1987)

Film poster, 1950

Tim Holt, Walter Huston, and Humphrey Bogart (clockwise from left) are prospectors united by greed in *The Treasure of the Sierra Madre* (1948), for which Huston won the Best Director Oscar.

Miklós **Jancsó**

BORN 1921

NATIONALITY Hungarian

CAREER 1958– **FILMS** 27

GENRE Political drama

The films of Miklós Jancsó, from the mid-1960s to the mid-1970s, are brilliantly choreographed dramas. Jancsó traces the fight for Hungarian independence and socialism using emblems and symbolism.

In *Beloved Electra* (1974), Jancsó's take on the Greek myth, Electra (Mari Törocsik) takes part in a ritual with women in white, while awaiting her brother's return.

Jancsó's very personal style blossomed in *The Round-Up* (*Szegénylegények*, 1966). This film contains many of the devices and themes that he has used in his later movies. Set on a desolate plain in Hungary, some time after the collapse of the 1948 revolution against the Austrian rule, *The Round-Up* powerfully depicts the conflict between the political oppressor and the oppressed. Jancsó's films are subtly choreographed, with the camera fluidly tracking the movements of characters, emphasizing their relationship to the landscape. Colour, especially red, is used symbolically in *The Confrontation* (*Fényes Szelek*, 1969), *Agnus Dei* (*Égi Bárány*, 1971), and *Red Psalm* (*Még Kér a Nép*, 1972). These films are hymns of despair as well as celebrations of freedom, illustrated by Jancsó's masterful long takes and extended sequence shots.

WHAT TO WATCH

- *My Way Home* (1965)
- *The Round-Up* (1966)
- *The Red and the White* (1968)
- *The Confrontation* (1969)
- *Agnus Dei* (1971)
- *Red Psalm* (1972)
- *Beloved Electra* (1974)

Elia **Kazan**

BORN 1909 **DIED** 2003

NATIONALITY American

CAREER 1945–2003 **FILMS** 19

GENRE Drama, Cult

All of Elia Kazan's films have strong social themes, a keen sense of location, and superb performances. Although Kazan betrayed his friends at the McCarthy hearings in 1952 (see p.31), his reputation as one of the finest directors in the US has never wavered.

Having worked in the theatre and at the Actors Studio, Kazan had great respect for actors, allowing them to develop their work during shooting. This trust inspired some great performances, including those by Marlon Brando in *On the Waterfront* (1954) and Jo Van Fleet in *Wild River* (1960). Kazan made Brando a star with *A Streetcar Named Desire* (1951), "discovered" James Dean (*East of Eden*, 1955), and gave debut screen roles to Jack Palance (*Panic in the Streets*, 1950), Lee Remick (*A Face in the Crowd*, 1957), and Warren Beatty (*Splendor in the Grass*, 1961). He worked closely with Tennessee Williams in *A Streetcar Named Desire* and *Baby Doll* (1956), and with John Steinbeck in *Viva Zapata* (1952) and *East of Eden*.

Film poster, 1955

WHAT TO WATCH

- *A Streetcar Named Desire* (1951)
- *On the Waterfront* (1954)
- *East of Eden* (1955)
- *A Face in the Crowd* (1957)
- *Wild River* (1960)
- *Splendor in the Grass* (1961)

Abbas **Kiarostami**

BORN 1940

NATIONALITY Iranian

CAREER 1974– **FILMS** 19

GENRE Drama

The fact that Iranian cinema is considered one of the best in the world is partly due to Abbas Kiarostami, whose films play brilliantly with audiences' perceptions of cinema.

Abbas Kiarostami had been making films for almost two decades before ***Where is the Friend's Home?*** (***Khane-ye Doust Kodjast?***, 1987), a gently humorous film on a child's loyalty, became an international success. ***And Life Goes On...*** (***Zendegi va Digar Hich***, 1992) follows a film director, after an earthquake, searching for the children who featured in one of his films. ***Through the Olive Trees*** (***Zire Darakhatan Zeyton***, 1994), written and directed by Kiarostami, is about the filming of ***And Life Goes On...*** Kiarostami's trademark – people driving over long distance – reaches perfection in ***Taste of Cherry*** (***Ta'm e Guilass***, 1997). The film shows a middle-aged man bent on suicide, who drives up and down asking passers-by to bury him in a grave he has already dug. The car motif recurs in ***Ten*** (2002), which follows ten conversations that take place in a car being driven through Tehran's streets. Kiarostami has said, "I don't invent material. I just watch and take it from the daily life of people around me". However, his realism is carefully constructed.

Set in Siah Dareh, a remote Kurdish village, ***The Wind Will Carry Us*** (1999) is a parable about outsiders who pretend to search for a treasure in the village cemetery.

WHAT TO WATCH

- *Where is the Friend's Home?* (1987)
- *And Life Goes On...* (1992)
- *Through the Olive Trees* (1994)
- *Taste of Cherry* (1997)
- *The Wind Will Carry Us* (*Bad Ma Ra Khahad Bord*, 1999)
- *Ten* (2002)

Krzysztof **Kieslowski**

BORN 1941 **DIED** 1996

NATIONALITY Polish

CAREER 1976–1993 **FILMS** 9

GENRE Drama

Through his rather sardonic examinations of the conflict between the state and its citizens, Krzysztof Kieslowski has come to represent the "cinema of moral unrest" in Poland.

Politically active in the struggle for a more democratic Poland, Kieslowski expresses many of his ideas obliquely in his features. Nevertheless, his ironic humanism was not appreciated by the authorities and two of his films were suppressed: ***Blind Chance*** (***Przypadek***, made in 1981), which examines the effect of arbitrary fate on the life of a student; and ***No End*** (***Bez Konca***, made in 1985), which shows the ghost of a dead lawyer watching his family survive without him. It was on their release in 1986, followed by two shorts made as part of a TV series, ***The Decalogue*** (***Dekalog***, 1989–90), that he was extolled abroad. ***A Short Film About Killing*** (***Krótki Film o Zabijaniu***, 1988) is a powerful cry against capital punishment. In ***A Short Film About Love*** (***Krótki Film o Milosci***, 1988), a 19-year-old boy is obsessed with a woman in the apartment facing his own. With the fall of communism, Kieslowski chose to work in France where he directed ***The Double Life of Véronique*** (***La Double Vie de Véronique***, 1991) and the ***Three Colours*** trilogy (1993–94).

WHAT TO WATCH

- *Blind Chance* (1981)
- *A Short Film About Killing* (1988)
- *A Short Film About Love* (1988)
- *The Double Life of Veronique* (1991)
- *Three Colours: Blue* (1993)
- *Three Colours: White* (1994)
- *Three Colours: Red* (1994)

Film poster, 1993

Malcolm McDowell plays Alex, head of a violent teenage gang in *A Clockwork Orange* (1971), Stanley Kubrick's bleak view of a futuristic Britain.

Stanley **Kubrick**

BORN 1928 **DIED** 1999

NATIONALITY American

CAREER 1953–1999 **FILMS** 13

GENRE Various

The scrupulous care with which he chose his subjects, his slow method of working, and his reclusive personality meant that all of Stanley Kubrick's films were eagerly awaited.

Kirk Douglas stars in the epic *Spartacus* (1960), in which a slave leads a revolt against the Roman empire.

Deeply pessimistic and claustrophobic, Kubrick's films deal brilliantly with technical and textual complexities. *Lolita* (1962), based on Vladimir Nabokov's novel about a paedophile, was an acerbic comedy full of "perverse passion". Kubrick's anti-militarism first revealed itself in the bitterly ironic and moving World War I drama *Paths of Glory* (1957) and continued in the black comedy *Dr. Strangelove* (1964). In *Full Metal Jacket* (1987), he powerfully depicts the brutal military training for a pointless war (Vietnam). His futuristic movies develop the theme of dehumanization. In *2001: A Space Odyssey* (1968), man is merely a machine controlled by a machine, while in *A Clockwork Orange* (1971) alienated youths are brainwashed into conformity. Madness is manifest in *The Shining* (1980), and sexual fantasies are explored in his final film, *Eyes Wide Shut* (1999). In contrast, *Barry Lyndon* (1975), inspired by the English landscape and portrait paintings of the 18th century, lovingly recreates the sensibilities of the time.

WHAT TO WATCH

- *Paths of Glory* (1957)
- *Lolita* (1962)
- *Dr. Strangelove* (1964)
- *2001: A Space Odyssey* (1968)
- *A Clockwork Orange* (1971)
- *Barry Lyndon* (1975)
- *Full Metal Jacket* (1987)

Akira **Kurosawa**

BORN 1912 **DIED** 1998

NATIONALITY Japanese

CAREER 1943–1993 **FILMS** 31

GENRE Epic

The best-known Japanese director in the West, Akira Kurosawa has achieved an international popularity. Revered by other film-makers, his films remain faithful to the Japanese tradition, yet at the same time bear a strong similarity to American movies.

There has seldom been more cross-fertilization in the cinema than in the work of Kurosawa. Three of his films have been adapted easily into Hollywood Westerns. ***Rashomon*** (1950), the first Japanese film to be shown widely in the West, became ***The Outrage*** (1964); ***Seven Samurai*** (***Shichinin no Samurai***, 1954) was turned into ***The Magnificent Seven*** (1960); and ***The Bodyguard*** (***Yojimbo***, 1961) into ***A Fistful of Dollars*** (1964). Some of his features pay homage to American cinema, while others have literary sources: ***Hakuchi*** (1951) is based on Fyodor Dostoevsky's *The Idiot*; ***Donzoko*** (1957) on Maxim Gorky's *The Lower Depths*; and ***Kumonosu Jô*** (1957) and ***Ran*** (1985) on William Shakespeare's *Macbeth* and *King Lear* respectively. The films make for easy viewing, although tragic contemporary tales like ***To Live*** (***Ikiru***, 1952), about a man dying of cancer, and ***I Live in Fear*** (***Ikimono no Kiroku***, 1955), a family drama, delve much deeper. Kurosawa's flamboyant samurai adventures mix comedy and rich imagery, as in films such as ***The Hidden Fortress*** (***Kakushi-toride no San-akunin***, 1958), and ***Sanjuro*** (***Tsubaki Sanjûrô***, 1962). Widescreen and colour are used magnificently to frame the epic grandeur of ***Dersu Uzala*** (1975), as well as ***Kagemusha*** (1980) and ***Ran*** (1985), with their glorious red sunsets, vivid rainbows, and multicoloured flags.

WHAT TO WATCH

- *Rashomon* (1950)
- *To Live* (1952)
- *Seven Samurai* (1954)
- *Throne of Blood* (*Kumonosu Jô*, 1957)
- *The Hidden Fortress* (1958)
- *The Bodyguard* (1961)
- *Sanjuro* (1962)
- *Dersu Uzala* (1975)
- *Kagemusha* (1980)
- *Ran* (1985)

In *The Hidden Fortress* (1958), two greedy peasants agree to help a princess cross enemy territory in their desire for gold.

In this magnificent battle scene in *Ran* (1985), Kurosawa's cinematic ode to Shakespeare's *King Lear*, a warlord's lack of judgement leads to death and disaster.

Film poster, 1928

Fritz **Lang**

BORN 1890 **DIED** 1976

NATIONALITY German-American

CAREER 1919–1960 **FILMS** 41

GENRE Film noir

Looking at the world with a grim detachment and a strong moral sense, Fritz Lang worked through two career phases: in Germany (1919 to 1932) and Hollywood (1936 to 1956).

Lang's reputation grew in Germany with serials such as ***Dr. Mabuse: The Gambler*** (*Dr. Mabuse, der Spieler*, 1922). ***Die Nibelungen*** (1924), a German saga in two parts, makes impressive use of stylized studio scenery, while the huge sets of ***Metropolis*** (1927) represent a futuristic city-factory. In his first film with sound, ***M*** (1931), Lang made an ironic social comment on justice, capital punishment, and mob rule – themes he would take up again in his first American film, ***Fury*** (1936). ***Hangmen Also Die!*** (1943) was a fictionalized account of the assassination of Gestapo leader Reinhard Heydrich, in which he projected increasing public outrage against Nazi atrocities. Having fled Nazi Germany, he had to deal with dictatorial producers in Hollywood. MGM tacked on a happy ending to ***Fury*** and Warner Bros. did the same to ***Cloak and Dagger*** (1946). Yet he managed to make splendidly dark films of murder, revenge, and seduction, such as ***The Woman in the Window*** (1944) and ***Scarlet Street*** (1945); ***Clash by Night*** (1952), dealing with post-war dissipation; ***The Big Heat*** (1953) and ***Human Desire*** (1954), both film noirs; and ***Beyond a Reasonable Doubt*** (1956).

WHAT TO WATCH

- *Dr. Mabuse: The Gambler* (1922)
- *Metropolis* (1927)
- *M* (1931)
- *Fury* (1936)
- *Hangmen Also Die!* (1943)
- *The Woman in the Window* (1944)
- *Scarlet Street* (1945)
- *Clash by Night* (1952)
- *The Big Heat* (1953)
- *Human Desire* (1954)

Judy Davis as Adela Quested and Dr. Aziz (Victor Banerjee) ride on an elephant, on a fateful visit to the Malabar caves in *A Passage to India* (1984).

David **Lean**

BORN 1908 **DIED** 1991

NATIONALITY British

CAREER 1942–1984 **FILMS** 16

GENRE Epic, Costume drama

After making several films in the 1940s, epitomizing the best of British cinema, David Lean made five international blockbusters. Since then, he became associated with film-making on a grand scale.

Lean co-directed his first film, ***In Which We Serve*** (1942), with Noël Coward, before going on to make three more films with him: ***This Happy Breed*** (1944), ***Blithe Spirit*** (1945), and ***Brief Encounter*** (1945). The last, based on a one-act play by Coward (who wrote the screenplay) is one of the most telling juxtapositions of the romantic and the mundane in film. The script (balancing passionate narration with clipped dialogue), the performances of Trevor Howard and Celia Johnson, and the fluid camerawork make it one of Lean's greatest films. His fine screen adaptations of Charles Dickens, ***Great Expectations*** (1946) and ***Oliver Twist*** (1948), feature brilliant photography (by Guy Green), design, and acting. Lean's expertise can be seen in his three films with Ann Todd, especially ***The Sound Barrier*** (1952). His films on a larger scale – ***The Bridge on the River Kwai*** (1957), ***Lawrence of Arabia*** (1962), ***Doctor Zhivago*** (1965), ***Ryan's Daughter*** (1970), and ***A Passage to India*** (1984) – won a total of 23 Academy Awards.

WHAT TO WATCH

- *In Which We Serve* (1942)
- *Brief Encounter* (1945)
- *Great Expectations* (1946)
- *Oliver Twist* (1948)
- *Hobson's Choice* (1954)
- *The Bridge on the River Kwai* (1957)
- *Lawrence of Arabia* (1962)
- *Doctor Zhivago* (1965)
- *A Passage to India* (1984)

In *Jungle Fever* (1991), Lee's searing study of attitudes to race and the drug culture, Halle Berry makes her big-screen debut in the role of a crack addict.

Spike **Lee**

BORN 1957

NATIONALITY American

CAREER 1983– **FILMS** 20

GENRE Political drama

The most significant turning point in black cinema was the emergence of Spike Lee, whose movies explore a hitherto unknown range of themes from a black perspective.

It was black directors like Melvin Van Peebles, Gordon Parks, and Sidney Poitier in the 1970s who paved the way for Lee in the following decade. However, whiles their films cater mainly to black audiences, Lee's movies appeal to a wider spectrum of society, tackling potentially explosive subjects such as interracial sexual relations and drugs (*Jungle Fever*, 1991), black music (*Mo' Better Blues*, 1990), and black politics (*Malcolm X*, 1992), in mainstream cinema. Lee's first feature, *She's Gotta Have It* (1986), was influenced by the French New Wave directors, and is about a sexually liberated young woman's relationship with three lovers. Costing only US$170,000, it was a huge box office success. Lee's preoccupation with cultural identity was manifest in *Do the Right Thing* (1989), a film set in an Italian pizza parlour on a sweltering day in Brooklyn, where racial tensions are about to explode. In one controversial scene, characters shout racial and ethnic epithets directly to the camera. With a radical approach, a brilliantly constructed set, complex sound design, and vibrant cinematography, Lee showed full mastery of the medium. The film's success allowed him to direct *Malcolm X* after he condemned Warner Bros.' initial decision to hire Norman Jewison for the job. This film, about the iconic African-American political activist, proved that Lee could fuse a popular form with significant social commentary on a large scale.

WHAT TO WATCH

- *She's Gotta Have It* (1986)
- *Do the Right Thing* (1989)
- *Jungle Fever* (1991)
- *Malcolm X* (1992)
- *Crooklyn* (1994)
- *Clockers* (1995)

Denzel Washington shone in his Oscar-nominated role in *Malcolm X* (1992), Lee's biopic on the controversial nationalist leader.

Emil Jannings plays Louis XV and Pola Negri plays the king's mistress in *Madame Dubarry* (1919) – a film that launched both the director and actress into stardom.

Ernst **Lubitsch**

BORN 1892 **DIED** 1947

NATIONALITY German (American)

CAREER 1918–1947 **FILMS** 47

GENRE Comedy

Bringing continental manners and hedonism into puritan America, Ernst Lubitsch established his own style of elegance, wit, incisiveness, and cynicism, perfectly suited to the varied themes he worked on, which came to be called the "Lubitsch Touch".

Lubitsch's features in Germany include a number of ironic historical romances such as *Madame Dubarry* (1919) with Pola Negri. His Hollywood career began with scintillating silent comedies, including *Lady Windermere's Fan* (1925). His musicals with Maurice Chevalier and Jeannette McDonald, as well as comedies *Trouble in Paradise* (1932) and *Design for Living* (1933), treated the audience as sophisticates – rare in commercial cinema. At the end of the 1930s, Lubitsch came up with a number of very entertaining romantic comedies: *Angel* (1937), starring a sparkling Marlene Dietrich; *Ninotchka* (1939), a witty tale of how a stern Russian commisar (Greta Garbo) is seduced by wicked, capitalist ways; and *The Shop Around the Corner* (1940), a charming comedy of errors starring James Stewart. Under the shadow of war, Lubitsch came up with one of Hollywood's great comedies, *To Be or Not to Be* (1942), which took on the Nazi occupation of Poland – of all subjects.

Film poster, 1937

WHAT TO WATCH

- *Trouble in Paradise* (1932)
- *Design for Living* (1933)
- *The Merry Widow* (1934)
- *Desire* (1936)
- *Angel* (1937)
- *Ninotchka* (1939)
- *The Shop Around the Corner* (1940)
- *To Be or Not to Be* (1942)

David **Lynch**

BORN 1946

NATIONALITY American

CAREER 1977– **FILMS** 11

GENRE Horror, Thriller

Over the decades, David Lynch has accumulated a huge following of those willing to enter his bizarre and labyrinthine dream world.

His first feature, *Eraserhead* (1977) was shot in black-and-white, almost entirely at night. A disturbing nightmare of a film, ripped from the womb of surrealist art and German expressionist (see box, p.259) cinema, it appeals equally to intellectuals and horror-movie fans, like much of his work. *The Elephant Man* (1980), a far more conventional film, evokes pity for the hideously deformed Victorian man, John Merrick (played by John Hurt, who wears layers of make-up). Perhaps his most representative film is *Blue Velvet* (1986), which contains elements of satire, crime, and horror – features that are even more evident in the cryptic psychological thriller *Mulholland Drive* (2001). Lynch's most uncharacteristic film is *The Straight Story* (1999), which traces the slow progress of a man travelling hundreds of miles on a lawnmower.

WHAT TO WATCH

- *Eraserhead* (1977)
- *The Elephant Man* (1980)
- *Blue Velvet* (1986)
- *Twin Peaks* (1992)
- *The Straight Story* (1999)
- *Mulholland Drive* (2001)

Film poster, 1977

Louis **Malle**

BORN 1932 **DIED** 1995

NATIONALITY French

CAREER 1956–1994 **FILMS** 21

GENRE Drama

Moving from France to the US with ease, Louis Malle was a "will-o'-the-wisp" director, like the title of one of his films, *Le Feu Follet* (1963). He specialized in difficult or taboo subjects. "I'm always interested in exposing a theme, a character, or situation which seems to be unacceptable", Malle explained.

His subjects included adultery, in *The Lovers* (*Les Amants*, 1958); incest, in *Murmur of the Heart* (*Le Souffle au Coeur*, 1971); and child prostitution, in *Pretty Baby* (1978). In *My Dinner with André* (1981), he filmed 110 minutes of two people having a dinner conversation. *Lacombe Lucien* (1974) was one of the first French films to reveal some of the least savoury aspects of life in France under the Nazi occupation – its "hero" is a young labourer who becomes a Nazi collaborator. *Au Revoir Les Enfants* (1987) is the culmination of Malle's themes – French collaboration with the Nazis, close mother-son relationships, and an unsentimental view of children.

WHAT TO WATCH

- *The Lovers* (1958)
- *Murmur of the Heart* (1971)
- *Lacombe Lucien* (1974)
- *Pretty Baby* (1978)
- *Atlantic City* (1980)
- *Au Revoir Les Enfants* (1987)

Gaspard Manesse and Raphael Fejto star in *Au Revoir Les Enfants* (1987), based on Malle's own childhood.

Film poster, 1959

Joseph L. **Mankiewicz**

BORN 1909 **DIED** 1993

NATIONALITY American

CAREER 1946–1972 **FILMS** 20

GENRE Comedy, Drama

People Will Talk (1951) is one of the most appropriate titles in Joseph L. Mankiewicz's filmography – the screen was mostly a vehicle for his literate, witty, and satirical screenplays.

Although Mankiewicz's films are dialogue-driven, they are not filmed plays. They have an elegant visual style, and many experiment with narrative form, the story being told from different points of view with an effective use of flashbacks. *A Letter to Three Wives* (1949) is a cleverly constructed tale set in suburban America where three wives, Deborah (Jeanne Crain), Lora (Linda Darnell), and Rita (Ann Sothern) wonder which one of their husbands is running away with the local vamp. The terse comedy is derived as much from the dialogue and acting as the meticulously observed milieu. *All About Eve* (1950), a poison-pen letter to the theatrical world of New York, is a high comedy, with Bette Davis playing the role of the bitching, faded idol Margo Channing to the full. *The Barefoot Contessa* (1954) is equally acerbic about the film industry. An absorbing espionage tale, *5 Fingers* (1952) is told in a semi-documentary style. It stars James Mason, who also made a fine Brutus to Marlon Brando's powerful Mark Antony in *Julius Caesar* (1953), an intelligent adaptation of Shakespeare that avoids the temptation towards Hollywood spectacle – unlike the US$45-million *Cleopatra* (1963). Brando was also excellent in *Guys and Dolls* (1955), both his and Mankiewicz's only musical.

WHAT TO WATCH

- *The Ghost and Mrs. Muir* (1947)
- *A Letter to Three Wives* (1949)
- *All About Eve* (1950)
- *5 Fingers* (1952)
- *Julius Caesar* (1953)
- *The Barefoot Contessa* (1954)
- *Guys and Dolls* (1955)
- *Suddenly, Last Summer* (1959)

Gambler Sky Masterson (Marlon Brando) "corrupts" Save-a-Soul missionary Sarah Brown (Jean Simmons) in the stylish musical *Guys and Dolls* (1955).

Leo **McCarey**

BORN 1898 **DIED** 1969

NATIONALITY American

CAREER 1929–1961 **FILMS** 23

GENRE Comedy, Drama

There were three phases to Leo McCarey's brilliant career as a film director: Laurel and Hardy shorts, zany wisecracking comedies, and sentimental romantic comedies.

Among the Laurel and Hardy shorts that Leo McCarey directed from 1927 to 1931 is *Putting Pants on Philip* (1927), the first film the comedians formally made together as a duo. Between 1932 and 1937, McCarey directed comedians Eddie Cantor (*The Kid From Spain*, 1932), W.C. Fields (*Six of a Kind*, 1934), the Marx brothers (*Duck Soup*, 1933), and Harold Lloyd (*The Milky Way*, 1936), as well as Cary Grant in *The Awful Truth* (1937), one of the best screwball comedies ever made. The third phase of McCarey's career, after 1937, includes *Love Affair* (1939), which he remade as *An Affair to Remember* (1957), a shipboard romance. Both *Going My Way* (1944) and *The Bells of St. Mary's* (1945), were handled with enough manipulative skill to persuade even an atheist to ponder.

Cary Grant stars as Nickie, a wealthy bachelor who falls in love with Terry (Deborah Kerr), an ex-nightclub singer, during a sea voyage in *An Affair to Remember* (1957).

WHAT TO WATCH

- *Duck Soup* (1933)
- *Ruggles of Red Gap* (1935)
- *Make Way for Tomorrow* (1937)
- *The Awful Truth* (1937)
- *Love Affair* (1939)
- *Going My Way* (1944)
- *The Bells of St. Mary's* (1945)
- *An Affair to Remember* (1957)

Jean-Pierre **Melville**

BORN 1917 **DIED** 1973

NATIONALITY French

CAREER 1948–1972 **FILMS** 12

GENRE Gangster, Film noir

It was his enthusiasm for the works of writer Herman Melville that made Jean-Pierre Grumbach change his name. However, it was the American gangster novel and film noir that were the greatest influences on his movies, which, in turn, were to inspire several independent American directors.

Bob the Gambler (*Bob le Flambeur*, 1956) and *Two Men in Manhattan* (*Deux Hommes dans Manhattan*, 1959), Melville's first independent low-budget films, were shot on location in Paris and New York, respectively. His gritty, freewheeling style brought something new to the crime thriller, and the eight films he made inhabit a world of sleazy bars, hotels, and nightclubs where double-crossing and killing are the norm. *The Samurai* (*Le Samouraï*, 1967) follows the last day of a cold-blooded killer (Alain Delon) with a code of honour. Melville was in the French Resistance and three of his films, including the tragic *Army of Shadows* (*L'Armée des Ombres*, 1969), are about France under occupation.

WHAT TO WATCH

- *The Strange Ones* (*Les Enfants Terribles*, 1950)
- *Bob the Gambler* (1956)
- *Doulos: The Finger Man* (*Le Doulos*, 1962)
- *Magnet of Doom* (*L'Ainé des Ferchaux*, 1963)
- *Second Breath* (*Le Deuxième Souffle*, 1966)
- *The Samurai* (1967)
- *Army of Shadows* (1969)

In *Second Breath* (*Le Deuxième Souffle*, 1966), prison escapee Gustave (Lino Ventura) gets involved in one last robbery.

Vincente **Minnelli**

BORN 1910 **DIED** 1986

NATIONALITY American

CAREER 1942–1976 **FILMS** 33

GENRE Musical, Melodrama

Film poster, 1958

The world of Vincente Minnelli is one of beauty, fantasy, brilliant colours, stylish set designs, and elaborate costumes, in which Fred Astaire, Judy Garland, Gene Kelly, Cyd Charisse, and Leslie Caron dance and sing.

Seven of the screen's finest musicals were made by the director for MGM. His debut was the ground-breaking African-American musical ***Cabin in the Sky*** (1943), a film that showcased many of the era's legendary performers. He used Technicolor for the first time in ***Meet Me in St. Louis*** (1944), a touching portrayal of family life in 1903. The movie highlights the songs of a radiant Judy Garland (who married Minnelli in 1945). ***The Pirate*** (1948) has stylized theatrical settings, but the performances by Garland and Gene Kelly prevent the film from being "stagey". Kelly (with Leslie Caron) shines in ***An American in Paris*** (1951), which ends with an audacious 18-minute ballet. ***The Band Wagon*** (1953), with Astaire in his finest screen role, includes a number that sums up Minnelli's musicals: *That's Entertainment*. Of the later CinemaScope movies, only ***Gigi*** (1958) is in the same league. Two of Minnelli's "straight" films, ***The Bad and the Beautiful*** (1952) and ***Lust for Life*** (1956), star Kirk Douglas, as a megalomaniac movie producer in the former, and as Vincent van Gogh in the latter. ***Some Came Running*** (1958) is a lush, small-town melodrama, featuring Shirley MacLaine and Frank Sinatra.

WHAT TO WATCH

- *Meet Me in St. Louis* (1944)
- *The Pirate* (1948)
- *An American in Paris* (1951)
- *The Bad and the Beautiful* (1952)
- *The Band Wagon* (1953)
- *Lust for Life* (1956)
- *Gigi* (1958)
- *Some Came Running* (1958)

Judy Garland sings *The Trolley Song* with Tom Drake and a host of others in ***Meet Me in St. Louis*** (1944) – an early Technicolor extravaganza.

Kenji **Mizoguchi**

BORN 1898 **DIED** 1956

NATIONALITY Japanese

CAREER 1923–1956 **FILMS** 94

GENRE Costume drama

Although the West has seen only about a dozen of Kenji Mizoguchi's films, they are enough to establish him as one of the finest directors of all time.

From 1922 to 1936, Mizoguchi's poverty forced him to make films in which he had no interest, but he gradually developed his own style. His humanist view of the brutality of feudal Japan was mainly concerned with the sufferings of women. He preferred long takes, long shots, and gentle camera movements, delicately avoiding the need for cutting by using slow dissolves and minimal close-ups. The effect of moving away to a medium or long shot at critical moments deepens the sympathy for the characters. His best-known films – *The Life of Oharu* (*Saikaku ichidai onna*, 1952), *Tales of Ugetsu* (*Ugetsu monogatari*, 1953), and *Sansho the Bailiff* (*Sanshô dayû*, 1954) – are poignantly told in beautiful images.

Women of the Night (*Yoru No Onnatachi*, 1948) is an emotional drama about a drug dealer's mistress, who learns that her lover is having an affair with her sister.

WHAT TO WATCH

- *Osaka Elegy* (1936)
- *Sisters of the Gion* (1936)
- *The Story of the Last Chrysanthemums* (1939)
- *Utamaro and his Five Women* (1946)
- *The Life of Oharu* (1952)
- *Ugetsu monogatari* (1953)
- *Sansho the Bailiff* (1954)
- *Street of Shame* (1956)

F.W. **Murnau**

BORN 1888 **DIED** 1931

NATIONALITY German

CAREER 1919–1931 **FILMS** 21

GENRE Drama, Fantasy

F.W. Murnau, along with Ernst Lubitsch, was one of the two great German directors in the US. He was killed in a car crash while on his way to Paramount Studios, leaving five masterpieces behind him.

Murnau's first features were supernatural tales, culminating in *Nosferatu* (*Nosferatu, eine Symphonie des Grauens*, 1922), the first Dracula film. Although expressionistic in manner, *The Last Laugh* (*Der Letzte Mann*, 1924) moved nearer the *Kammerspielfilm* (chamber film), which dealt with ordinary people and events with an element of social criticism. The story of how an old hotel doorman (Emil Jannings) is reduced to a lavatory attendant is told without any intertitles. The camera tracking through the hotel corridors, the subjective shots, and the drunken dream sequences all make words superfluous. Jannings also starred in Murnau's *Tartuffe* (*Herr Tartüff*, 1925) and *Faust* (1926) – studio productions with imagery derived from the Old Masters. In Hollywood, he directed *Sunrise* (1927), the simple story of a farmer who tries to kill his devoted wife. The lighting, the fluidity of the camera, and the blend of German and Hollywood techniques combine to make it a poetic masterpiece. However, the studio imposed a happy ending on the film; two more also suffered from studio interference. Reacting to this, Murnau formed his own company with Robert J. Flaherty and went to the South Seas to make *Tabu* (1931), which won an Oscar for Best Cinematography.

WHAT TO WATCH

- *Nosferatu* (1922)
- *The Last Laugh* (1924)
- *Faust* (1926)
- *Sunrise* (1927)
- *Tabu* (1931)

George O'Brien plays Anses, a farmer, and Janet Gaynor is his wife Indre, in *Sunrise* (1927); the farmer falls in love with a city woman, who suggests that he kills his wife.

Manoel **de Oliveira**

BORN 1908

NATIONALITY Portuguese

CAREER 1942– **FILMS** 40

GENRE Costume drama, Documentary

Manoel de Oliveira is among the most original and profound artists working in the medium, and was never more prolific than after he turned 80, writing and directing one film a year until well into his 90s.

While Portugal was under the dictatorial Salazar regime (1932–68), Oliveira was condemned to years of silence and inactivity. As a result, it was only in his 70s that he was able to fully explore his principal interests of desire, fear, guilt, and perdition, underscored by the very Portuguese sentiment of the "consolation of melancholy". Many of his films are adaptations of literary works, which, while assuming the literary nature of the text, destroy conventional narrative with long and fixed shots or the repetition of such shots in beautifully composed colour images. He has stipulated that his life story, ***Memories and Confessions*** (*Visita ou Memórias e Confissões*, 1982), is only to be released after his death.

WHAT TO WATCH

- *Aniki Bóbó* (1942)
- *Doomed Love* (1979)
- *Francisca* (1981)
- *The Cannibals* (1988)
- *Abraham's Valley* (1993)
- *The Convent* (1995)
- *I'm Going Home* (2001)
- *A Talking Picture* (2003)
- *O Estranho Caso de Angelica* (*The Strange Case of Angelica*, 2010)

Ema (Leonor Silveira) is a sensual beauty who enters into a marriage of convenience in *Abraham's Valley* (1993), a haunting portrait of privilege, passion, and loneliness.

Lola Montès (1955) tells the story of the daring but ruined Lola (Martine Carol), seen here with a circus ringmaster, brilliantly played by Peter Ustinov.

Max **Ophüls**

BORN 1902 **DIED** 1957

NATIONALITY German

CAREER 1930–1955 **FILMS** 23

GENRE Costume drama, Melodrama

Max Ophüls' main preoccupation was the transitory nature of love; his bittersweet, nostalgic films are set in the past with a tracking, circling camera suggesting the passage of time.

At the beginning of ***La Ronde*** (1950), the Master of Ceremonies walks through a film studio onto a *fin-de-siécle* set, changes into an opera cloak, and spins a merry-go-round. He is Ophüls' alter ego and the title – literally meaning "the round" – is a clue to his films, which are like merry-go-rounds moving to the sound of a waltz. A masked dancer sweeps into a dance hall in ***House of Pleasure*** (***Le Plaisir***, 1952), the camera moving with him, and he keeps whirling as the music gets livelier until he falls. In ***Lola Montès*** (1955), the ringmaster cracks his whip at the centre of a huge circus ring as the heroine reminisces, and the camera revolves 360 degrees to reveal her past. Everything comes full circle as multiple couples keep changing partners in ***La Ronde*** and after the earrings are passed from hand to hand in ***Madame de...*** (1953).

After five films in Germany including ***Leiberlei*** (1933), a story about doomed love, Ophüls went to the US. The only film he made there that suggests his European period was ***Letter from an Unknown Woman*** (1948). Returning to Paris in 1949, he made ***La Ronde*** with a terrific French cast; ***House of Pleasure***, based on three Guy de Maupassant stories; ***Madame de...***, a witty confection; and his final film, ***Lola Montès***, the only one in colour and with an extraordinary treatment of space on the CinemaScope screen.

WHAT TO WATCH

- ***Leiberlei*** (1933)
- ***Mayerling to Sarajevo*** (1940)
- ***Letter from an Unknown Woman*** (1948)
- ***La Ronde*** (1950)
- ***House of Pleasure*** (1952)
- ***Madame de...*** (1953)
- ***Lola Montès*** (1955)

In an eerie scene from Ôshima's moody period piece *Empire of Passion* (1978), Gisaburo (Takahiro Tamura), a murdered rickshaw driver, returns as a ghost.

Nagisa **Ôshima**

BORN 1932

NATIONALITY Japanese

CAREER 1959– **FILMS** 26

GENRE Drama

The influence of the French New Wave (see pp.42–43) is felt in Nagisa Ôshima's films – stimulating and provocative metaphors of Japanese social values.

Death by Hanging (*Koshikei*, 1968), which earned international renown, and *Boy* (*Shonen*, 1969) critically dissect Japanese social life. The former deals with a condemned man whose body refuses to die, while the latter relates how a boy's parents train him to get knocked down by cars so they can sue the drivers. Ôshima equates sexual liberation with rebellion in *Diary of a Shinjuku Thief* (*Shinjuku dorobo nikki*, 1969). *In the Realm of the Senses* (*Ai no corrida*, 1976) focuses on obsessive sex between a gangster and a prostitute. *Empire of Passion* (*Ai no borei*, 1978) is equally steamy.

WHAT TO WATCH

- *The Sun's Burial* (*Taiyo no hakaba*,1960)
- *Death by Hanging* (1968)
- *Diary of a Shinjuku Thief* (1969)
- *Boy* (1969)
- *The Ceremony* (*Gishiki*, 1971)
- *In the Realm of the Senses* (1976)
- *Empire of Passion* (1978)
- *Taboo* (*Gohatto*,1999)

Yasujirô **Ozu**

BORN 1903 **DIED** 1963

NATIONALITY Japanese

CAREER 1927–1962 **FILMS** 54

GENRE Drama, Comedy

Describing Yasujirô Ozu's work may make it sound trivial, but within their parameters, his films are rich in humour, emotion, and social insight.

Ozu's work is marked by a certain consistency. He never married, yet, apart from his early films which were light, ironic comedies influenced by Hollywood cinema, he deals with middle-class family relationships, particularly the parent-child generation gap. Stylistically and thematically too, the movies of his mature period are very alike and it was this interplay of characters that absorbed him rather than the plot. After 1930, Ozu never used a dissolve and seldom moved the camera, which remained fixed a little lower than waist level. Each of his sequences is of great formal beauty, often punctuated by short external shots and intensified by music.

WHAT TO WATCH

- *Record of a Tenement Gentleman* (1947)
- *Late Spring* (*Banshun*, 1949)
- *Early Summer* (*Bakushû*, 1951)
- *Tokyo Story* (*Tokyo Monogatari*, 1953)
- *Early Spring* (*Soshun*, 1956)
- *Equinox Flower* (*Higanbana*, 1958)
- *Good Morning* (*Ohayo*, 1959)
- *Late Autumn* (*Akibiyori*, 1960)
- *The End of Summer* (*Kohayagawa-ke no aki*, 1961)
- *An Autumn Afternoon* (*Sanma no aji*, 1962)

Keiji Sada and Yoshiko Kuga take tea in *Good Morning* (1959), which Ozu remade from his own first feature *I Was Born, But...* (1932); both are moving portrayals of childhood.

Georg Wilhelm **Pabst**

BORN 1885 **DIED** 1967

NATIONALITY German

CAREER 1923–1956 **FILMS** 34

GENRE Drama, War

Compelling depictions of human degradation in a corrupt society, G.W. Pabst's films came out of a Germany defined by rapid inflation and the rise of Nazism, and went on to inspire a major shift from expressionism to realism in the German cinema.

Despite the obvious unfairness to Pabst, it is tempting to observe that in all his best films, the actresses stand out rather than the director: 20-year-old Greta Garbo on the brink of prostitution in *Joyless Street* (*Die freudlose Gasse*, 1925); Brigitte Helm as the lonely blind girl in *The Love of Jeanne Ney* (*Die Liebe der Jeanne Ney*, 1927); Lotte Lenya in *The Threepenny Opera* (*Die Dreigroschenoper*, 1931); and, above all, American Louise Brooks in *Pandora's Box* (*Die Büchse der Pandora*, 1929) and *Diary of a Lost Girl* (*Tagebuch einer Verlorenen*, 1929). *Pandora's Box* was a star vehicle for Louise Brooks, with her bobbed black hair framing her pale kittenish face, and her every gesture and expression imbued with eroticism. Her character Lulu – a woman who destroys men – became one of the icons of cinema, and inspired Pabst to produce his finest work, *Diary of a Lost Girl* (1929). This film again explores the social and economic breakdown of post-war Germany, with its brutal depiction of a girls' reform school. Both *Westfront 1918* (1930), Pabst's talkie debut, and *Comradeship* (*Kameradschaft*, 1931) plead the cause of international brotherhood. The former ends with a French soldier clutching a dead German's hand; the latter tells of German miners rescuing their French comrades trapped in a shaft. Though *The Threepenny Opera* is a slightly softened adaptation of the Bertolt Brecht–Kurt Weill musical, it retains plenty of anti-bourgeois bite.

Pabst made three historical films under the Nazis, including *Paracelsus* (1943). As a form of atonement, his later films, notably *The Trial* (*Der Prozeß*, 1948), are attacks on anti-Semitism.

WHAT TO WATCH

- *The Love of Jeanne Ney* (1927)
- *Pandora's Box* (1929)
- *Diary of a Lost Girl* (1929)
- *The Threepenny Opera* (1931)
- *Comradeship* (1931)

Pabst's *Westfront 1918* (1930) gives a bitter, realistic view of the barbed wire and trenches of World War I, seen through the eyes of four young German recruits.

In *Shadows of Forgotten Ancestors* (1965), Ivan Mikolajchuk (centre), here wearing the traditional costume of the Ukrainian Hutsuls, plays a tragic hero.

WHAT TO WATCH

The Stone Flower (1962)
Shadows of Forgotten Ancestors (1964)
The Colour of Pomegranates (1968)
Ashik Kerib (1988)

Sergei **Parajanov**

BORN 1924 **DIED** 1990

NATIONALITY Georgian

CAREER 1954–1988 **FILMS** 9

GENRE Costume drama

Sergei Parajanov's poetic, pictorially breathtaking films explore not only the history and folklore of the great Georgian director's native land, but also his idiosyncratic personal universe. Born in Georgia to Armenian parents, Parajanov was imprisoned in the former Soviet Union for three years in 1974, for various "crimes". *Shadows of Forgotten Ancestors* (*Tini Zabutykh Predkiv*, 1964), reveals his great talent for lyricism and opulence. His love for music, dance, and costumes reached its peak in *The Colour of Pomegranates* (*Sayat Nova*, 1968). The film's eloquent imagery illustrates – in a series of tableaux – the poems of 18th-century Georgian poet Sayat Nova. In *Ashik Kerib* (*Ashug-Karibi*, 1988), each kaleidoscopic episode is ravishing; at the end, a white dove lands on a black camera, fluttering out of the past into the present.

Pier Paolo **Pasolini**

BORN 1922 **DIED** 1975

NATIONALITY Italian

CAREER 1961–1975 **FILMS** 12

GENRE Satire, Drama

Street urchin Perkins (Ninetto Davoli) is an object of ridicule in Pasolini's sexually explicit *The Canterbury Tales* (1972). The film was shot on location in Canterbury in the UK.

Although Pier Paolo Pasolini's uncompromising films are rooted in Italian neorealism (see pp.154–55), they are permeated by ideology and myth.

Pasolini was a well-known novelist, poet, and screenwriter before his first film, *Accatone* (1961). He drew on his knowledge of Rome to realistically depict a derelict urban landscape. *The Gospel According to St. Matthew* (*Il Vangelo Secondo Matteo*, 1964) is a poetic attempt to present Christ as an ordinary Italian peasant. *Oedipus Rex* (*Edipo Re*, 1967), while faithful to Sophocles, has a prologue and epilogue set in modern Rome. Pasolini deals with the middle classes for the first time in *Theorem* (*Teorema*, 1968). *The Decameron* (*Il Decameron*, 1971), *The Canterbury Tales* (*I Racconti di Canterbury*, 1972), and *The Arabian Nights* (*Il Fiore Delle Mille e Una Notte*, 1974) form a trilogy of satires. The final ten minutes of his last film *Salo, or the 120 Days of Sodom* (*Salò o le 120 giornate di Sodoma*, 1975) are among the most memorable in all of cinema.

WHAT TO WATCH

Accatone (1961)
The Gospel According to St. Matthew (1964)
Oedipus Rex (1967)
Theorem (1968)
The Decameron (1971)
The Canterbury Tales (1972)
The Arabian Nights (1974)
Salo, or the 120 Days of Sodom (1975)

Sam **Peckinpah**

BORN 1925 **DIED** 1984

NATIONALITY American

CAREER 1961–1983 **FILMS** 14

GENRE Western

Associated with the rise of graphic screen violence in 1960s Hollywood, Sam Peckinpah's lyrical films portray disenchantment. His Westerns, in particular, are explorations into moral ambiguities.

Born and raised on a ranch in California, he attended military school and went through a spell in the Marines. His films reflect his background – a masculine world where manhood and independence are expressed through violence. Hence the nostalgia for the Old West where men were heroes and women were subordinate. The recurring theme of "unchanged men in a changing land" is introduced in his second film, ***Ride the High Country*** (1962), with Randolph Scott and Joel McCrea as ageing gunfighters. In *The Wild Bunch* (1969), set in 1914, William Holden and his gang try to live as outlaws from another age. ***The Ballad of Cable Hogue*** (1970) is another elegy for the Old West, but with more of Peckinpah's edgy sense of humour. Steve McQueen in ***Junior Bonner*** (1972) feels anachronistic (rather like the director himself) in the new-style West and follows his own moral code, living at the edge of society. Peckinpah's running battle with producers, whom he saw as the bad guys, made him disown ***Major Dundee*** (1965) when they recut it. A longer version, closer to his own cut, was released in 2005.

WHAT TO WATCH

- *Ride the High Country* (1962)
- *Major Dundee* (1965)
- *The Wild Bunch* (1969)
- *The Ballad of Cable Hogue* (1970)
- *Pat Garrett and Billy the Kid* (1973)
- *Bring Me the Head of Alfredo Garcia* (1974)

Billy (Kris Kristofferson, left) and Pat (James Coburn, right), play old friends turned adversaries in the 1973 Western, *Pat Garrett and Billy the Kid*.

Roman **Polanski**

BORN 1933

NATIONALITY Polish

CAREER 1962– **FILMS** 19

GENRE Drama

The turbulent life of Roman Polanski has influenced many of his films. His subjects offer a bleak view of humanity; his stories told with absurdist humour.

Born to Polish parents who died in the Holocaust, Polanski revisited 1940s Poland in the Academy Award-winning film *The Pianist* (2002), his first in his native country since *Knife in the Water* (1962). There is little distinction between nightmare and reality in many of his movies. In *Rosemary's Baby* (1968), Mia Farrow screams, "This is not a dream. It is reality", believing that she has been impregnated by the devil. We witness the "reality" of Catherine Deneuve's breakdown as the walls of her room come alive in ***Repulsion*** (1965). Sex is a regular theme in Polanski's films: sexual rivalry (*Knife in the Water*), sexual humiliation (*Cul-de-Sac*, 1966), and incest (*Chinatown*, 1974). After the murder of his wife Sharon Tate in 1969, he directed a blood-soaked *Macbeth* (1971).

WHAT TO WATCH

- *Knife in the Water* (1962)
- *Repulsion* (1965)
- *Cul-de-Sac* (1965)
- *Rosemary's Baby* (1968)
- *Chinatown* (1974)
- *The Tenant* (1976)
- *The Pianist* (2002)
- *The Ghost Writer* (2010)

Knife in the Water (1962) was Polanski's first feature film.

Michael **Powell**, Emeric **Pressburger**

BORN 1905 (Powell), 1902 (Pressburger)
DIED 1990 (Powell), 1988 (Pressburger)

NATIONALITY British (Powell), Hungarian-British (Pressburger)

CAREER 1939–1972 (Powell), 1942–1956 (Pressburger)

FILMS 18

GENRE Fantasy, Musical, War

The films that carry the unusual credit of "Produced, Written, and Directed by Michael Powell and Emeric Pressburger" are eccentric, extravagant, witty fantasies. They contrast sharply with the realistic approach typical of British cinema at the time.

John Justin, June Duprez, and Sabu star in *The Thief of Baghdad* (1940), an early Powell-Berger-Whelan film.

In 1939, Michael Powell (as director) collaborated with Emeric Pressburger (as scriptwriter) for the first time on *The Spy in Black*, thus beginning one of the closest creative partnerships in cinema history. So close was their working relationship that although Pressburger's contribution was mostly writing and Powell was in charge on the studio floor, they received joint directorial credit on their films from 1939 to 1956. This may account for their curious blend of the very British and the very Middle European. There is a mystical love for England in *A Canterbury Tale* (1944) and for Scotland in *I Know Where I'm Going* (1945), and British patriotism and courage in *One of Our Aircraft is Missing* (1942) and *The Small Back Room* (1948). However, the most sympathetic characters, played by different actors, are Germans in *The Spy in Black* (1939, Conrad Veidt), *The Battle of the River Plate* (1956, Peter Finch), and most controversially, *The Life and Death of Colonel Blimp* (1943, Anton Walbrook). Winston Churchill tried to ban the latter for "ridiculing the army" during wartime.

A Matter of Life and Death (1946), *The Red Shoes* (1948), *The Tales of Hoffman* (1951), and *Oh! Rosalinda* (1955) are closer to the world of Vincente Minnelli's Hollywood musicals (influenced in turn by European design) than to any other British film. Each, however, examines the nature of cinema and its links with theatre, painting, and music. *The Red Shoes*, perhaps the duo's most popular film, is also an allegory of the artist's unswerving dedication to art in the person of Boris Lermontov (Anton Walbrook), the ballet-dancer impresario in the film. Out of the 12 films they made between 1943 and 1956, nine were in sensuous Technicolor (photography by Jack Cardiff or Christopher

WHAT TO WATCH

- *The Life and Death of Colonel Blimp* (1943)
- *A Canterbury Tale* (1944)
- *I Know Where I'm Going* (1945)
- *A Matter of Life and Death* (1946)
- *Black Narcissus* (1947)
- *The Red Shoes* (1948)
- *The Small Back Room* (1948)
- *The Tales of Hoffman* (1951)

Challis) with flamboyant sets and designs (Hein Heckroth and Alfred Junge). Junge's studio sets for *Black Narcissus* (1947) create the atmosphere of a Himalayan convent, where nuns struggle against desire. A heady mixture of religion and eroticism also runs through the wondrously strange *A Canterbury Tale*, in which a man pours glue on the heads of girls who date servicemen.

Powell and Pressburger went their separate ways after the World War II adventure film *Ill Met By Moonlight* (1956). Powell never had the same success alone, although the perverse *Peeping Tom* (1960), about a psychopathic murderer who photographs victims at the moment of death, is rich in levels of interpretation and has gained in reputation over the years. In the 1970s, Powell was "rediscovered" by Martin Scorsese and Francis Ford Coppola who set up projects with him. In 1981, he was appointed as advisor at Coppola's Zoetrope Studios.

Moira Shearer stars as Victoria, a young dancer torn between love and her career, with Leonide Massine in *The Red Shoes* (1948), a romance set in the world of ballet.

James Stewart, Ben Gazarra, and Arthur O'Connell discuss the defence in *Anatomy of a Murder* (1959).

Otto **Preminger**

BORN 1905 **DIED** 19 86

NATIONALITY Austrian-American

CAREER 1931–1980 **FILMS** 37

GENRE Film noir, Thriller

The best films of Otto Preminger, made in the US from 1935, are moody crime melodramas, using a cool, interrogatory method.

Many of Preminger's films are put together like pieces of evidence in a trial at which the characters reveal themselves through their obsessions. In *Laura* (1944), a detective falls in love with a "dead" woman; murders and trials also occur in *Fallen Angel* (1945) and *Whirlpool* (1949). A whole town is put on trial in *The Thirteenth Letter* (1951), and trials are central to *The Court-Martial of Billy Mitchell* (1955), *Saint Joan* (1957), and *Anatomy of a Murder* (1959). These are considered the essential Preminger movies, along with *Daisy Kenyon* (1947), starring Joan Crawford. Preminger battled censorship for *The Moon is Blue* (1953) and *The Man with the Golden Arm* (1955). In the 1960s, he shifted to making blockbusters like *Exodus* (1960) and *Advise and Consent* (1962).

WHAT TO WATCH

- *Laura* (1944)
- *Fallen Angel* (1945)
- *Daisy Kenyon* (1947)
- *The Man with the Golden Arm* (1955)
- *Anatomy of a Murder* (1959)
- *Exodus* (1960)
- *Advise and Consent* (1962)

Film poster, 1962

In this dramatic scene in *Storm Over Asia* (1928), Bair, the Mongolian trapper, is captured by British soldiers.

Vsevolod **Pudovkin**

BORN 1893 **DIED** 1953

NATIONALITY Russian

CAREER 1926–1953 **FILMS** 15

GENRE Epic, Costume drama

At the forefront of the experimental period in Soviet silent cinema, Vsevolod Pudovkin was forced to toe the Communist party line later in his career.

Pudovkin and his contemporary, Sergei Eisenstein, were among the first great theorists of cinema, who put their theories of dynamic montage into practice. A comparison was made when they both directed films on the same subject in the same location at the same time. Pudovkin's *The End of St. Petersburg* (*Konets Sankt-Peterburga*, 1927), which shows the effects of the 1917 revolution on an uneducated peasant boy, is more human and less stylized than Eisenstein's *October* (1928). Pudovkin's first feature film, *Mother* (*Mat*, 1926), is a tightly constructed adaptation of Maxim Gorky's rambling novel. His last silent film, the passionate *Storm Over Asia* (*Potomok Chingis-Khana*, 1928) is about Bair (Valéry Inkijinoff), a Mongolian nomad, who leads his people against the British occupying forces.

WHAT TO WATCH

- *Mother* (1926)
- *The End of St. Petersburg* (1927)
- *Storm Over Asia* (1928)

Nicholas **Ray**

BORN 1911 **DIED** 1979

NATIONALITY American

CAREER 1948–1963 **FILMS** 22

GENRE Film noir, Western, Epic

Even within the context of the Hollywood studio, Nicholas Ray managed to make offbeat movies, focusing on alienated characters, and using dynamic framing and dramatic colours.

A pre-credit sequence in *They Live By Night* (1949), Ray's first feature, introduces us to Cathy and Farley, doomed outlaw lovers, with the subtitle: "This boy, this girl were never properly introduced to the world we live in." This statement applies to most of Ray's characters. Among them are Nick (John Derek), the slum boy on trial for murder in *Knock on Any Door* (1949), Dixon (Humphrey Bogart), the isolated screenwriter with sadistic tendencies in *In a Lonely Place* (1950), and the misanthropic cop Jim (Robert Ryan) in *On Dangerous Ground* (1952). They, together with Jim, Plato, and Judy (James Dean, Sal Mineo, and Natalie Wood) from *Rebel Without a Cause* (1955), and cortisone-addicted Ed (James Mason) from *Bigger Than Life* (1956), are all loners trying to make contact with the world. As Johnny (Sterling Hayden) says in *Johnny Guitar* (1954), "I'm a stranger here myself". Ray's use of colour and choreographed action sequences suggest a musical form. The anthropology in *The Savage Innocents* (1960), the ecology in *Wind Across the Everglades* (1958), and the neuroses of male leads, such as Jeff (Robert Mitchum), the lonely rodeo rider in *The Lusty Men* (1952), make these films unusual for the time. Ray's brooding romantic side was stifled in epics such as *King of Kings* (1961) and *55 Days at Peking* (1963). His final work *Lightning Over Water* (1980) is an account of his battle with brain cancer.

Joan Crawford (centre), with Scott Brady and Ben Cooper, was one of only two women starring in *Johnny Guitar* (1954) – the other was Mercedes McCambridge. The film is a psychological study and a penetrating social commentary.

WHAT TO WATCH

- *They Live By Night* (1949)
- *In a Lonely Place* (1950)
- *Johnny Guitar* (1954)
- *Rebel Without a Cause* (1955)
- *Bigger Than Life* (1956)
- *Wind Across the Everglades* (1958)

Satyajit **Ray**

BORN 1921 **DIED** 1992

NATIONALITY Indian

CAREER 1955–1991 **FILMS** 30

GENRE Drama

Satyajit Ray's films, which deal mainly with the collision between traditional and modern beliefs, reveal the human face of his vast country.

Pather Panchali (*Song of the Road*, 1955), *The Unvanquished* (*Aparajito*, 1956), and *The World of Apu* (*Apur Sansar*, 1959), are known to the world as the *Apu* trilogy. *The Music Room* (*Jalsaghar*, 1959) focuses on an ageing aristocrat trying to cling to bygone days, while in *The Chess Players* (*Shatranj ke Khiladi*, 1977), a 19th-century nawab tries to stem the tide of change. *The Lonely Wife* (*Charulata*, 1964) and *Days and Nights in the Forest* (*Aranyer Din Ratri*, 1970) show the influence of Jean Renoir and Anton Chekhov, but the deceptively simple cinematic effects are the master director's own.

In *The Chess Players* (1977), Nawab Wajid Ali Shah (Amjad Khan) confers with his prime minister (Victor Banerjee) before being ousted from the throne by the British.

WHAT TO WATCH

- *Pather Panchali* (1955)
- *The Unvanquished* (1956)
- *The Music Room* (1959)
- *The World of Apu* (1959)
- *The Big City* (1964)
- *The Lonely Wife* (1964)
- *Days and Nights in the Forest* (1970)
- *Distant Thunder* (1973)
- *The Middleman* (1976)
- *The Chess Players* (1977)

Jean **Renoir**

BORN 1894 **DIED** 1979

NATIONALITY French

CAREER 1925–1970 **FILMS** 35

GENRE Drama, Farce, Musical

Jean Renoir's career span almost matches that of cinema's history, from expressionism (see box, p.259) to neorealism (see box, p.286), with films ranging from film noir to Hollywood movies; from Technicolor period spectacles to fast television techniques.

Renoir entered films in order to make his wife, Catherine Hessling, a star. He displayed her strange stylized acting in his first five silent films. However, only with the coming of sound, which he used brilliantly, did he blossom as a director. He directed Michel Simon in his first three talkies, including *Boudu Saved from Drowning* (*Boudu Sauvé des Eaux*, 1932), in which Simon is the spirit of anarchy trapped in a bourgeois marriage. Renoir's egalitarian cinema has no heroes or villains. The three prisoners of war in *Grand Illusion* (*La Grande Illusion*, 1937) are working class, middle class, and aristocratic, united in brotherhood. In *The Rules of the Game* (*La Règle du Jeu*, 1939), the servants are as important as their masters. In the US during World War II, Renoir managed to preserve his style, even persuading the studios to shoot *The Southerner* (1945) on location.

In Europe, he made three stylish, operetta-like romances about the choice between the theatre and life: *The Golden Coach* (*Le Carrosse d'Or*, 1952); *French Can-Can* (1954); and *Elena and Her Men* (1956). His films are a unique blend of emotions and moods, realism, fantasy, tragedy, and farce.

WHAT TO WATCH

- *Boudu Saved from Drowning* (1932)
- *The Crime of Monsieur Lange* (*Le Crime de Monsieur Lange*, 1936)
- *Grand Illusion* (*La Grande Illusion*, 1937)
- *The Human Beast* (*La Bête Humaine*, 1938)
- *The Rules of the Game* (*La Règle du Jeu*, 1939)
- *The Southerner* (1945)
- *The Golden Coach* (*Le Carrosse d'Or*, 1952)
- *French Can-Can* (1954)
- *Elena and Her Men* (1956)

Film poster, 1937

Alain **Resnais**

BORN 1922

NATIONALITY French

CAREER 1959– **FILMS** 18

GENRE Drama, Romance, War

Film poster, 1961

Alain Resnais' best films mingle memory, imagination, past and present, and desire and fulfilment, treating sound, words, music, and images on an equal basis. In ***Hiroshima Mon Amour*** (1959), a French actress has an affair with a Japanese architect. Set in a rebuilt Hiroshima that is still traumatized by the horror of the atom bomb, images of the actress' past in wartime France flash in her mind. ***Last Year at Marienbad*** (*L'Année Dernière à Marienbad*, 1961) changed the concept of subjective time in cinema. ***Muriel*** (1963), with its indirect reference to the Algerian War, seems more realistic on the surface, but it is as stylized and metaphysical as Resnais' previous films. These three masterpieces were never equalled, although ***The War is Over*** (*La Guerre est finie*, 1966), a portrait of an ageing exile from Franco's Spain now living in France, and ***Providence*** (1977), a nightmare lived by a dying novelist, come close. In the 1980s, Resnais made a number of film adaptations of stage works with his own company of actors.

WHAT TO WATCH

- *Hiroshima Mon Amour* (1959)
- *Last Year at Marienbad* (1961)
- *Muriel* (1963)
- *The War is Over* (1966)
- *Stavisky* (1974)
- *Providence* (1977)
- *Same Old Song* (1997)
- *Les Herbes Folles* (*Wild Grass*, 2009)

Jacques **Rivette**

BORN 1928

NATIONALITY French

CAREER 1960– **FILMS** 23

GENRE Avant-garde, Fantasy

The films of Jacques Rivette are challenging, intellectually enquiring, and long. They are probably the most under-appreciated among the works of the French New Wave (see pp.42–43) directors.

Ironically for a director steeped in cinema, theatre dominates much of Rivette's work, one of the major themes being the "play-within-a-film". He explored this in ***Paris Belongs to Us*** (*Paris Nous Appartient*, 1961), in which a group of amateur actors come together in a deserted Paris to stage a performance of Shakespeare's *Pericles*. Paris, shown realistically but where fantastic things take place, is the constant background to his films. One of his most accessible films is ***Céline and Julie Go Boating*** (*Celine et Julie Vont en Bateau*, 1974), a brilliantly comic meditation on the nature of fiction. Rivette's exploration of the act of creation reaches its apex in ***La Belle Noiseuse*** (1991), which captures with painful lucidity the anguish of Frenhofer (Michel Piccoli), an artist struggling to express himself on canvas.

Camille (Jeanne Balibar), a stage actress, hunts for a missing ring in *Va Savoir* (2001), a witty comedy, which, like many of Rivette's films, is located in a theatrical setting.

WHAT TO WATCH

- *Paris Belongs to Us* (1961)
- *The Nun* (*La Religieuse*, 1966)
- *Mad Love* (*L'Amour Fou*, 1969)
- *Celine and Julie Go Boating* (1974)
- *La Belle Noiseuse* (1991)
- *Jeanne la Pucelle I - Les batailles* (1994)
- *Va Savoir* (2001)
- *The Duchess of Langeais* (2007)

Étienne (Didier Sandre), a professor, is seen here with young Rosine (Alexia Portal) in *An Autumn Tale* (1998), a bittersweet look at love and relationships in midlife.

Eric **Rohmer**

BORN 1920 **DIED** 2010

NATIONALITY French

CAREER 1959–2007 **FILMS** 24

GENRE Comedy

In Eric Rohmer's words, "I'm less concerned with what people do than what is going on in their minds while they're doing it". Although most of his films are dialogue-centric, they are far from being conversation pieces.

The characters in Rohmer's delicious comedies of error are defined by their relationships with the opposite sex. The sumptuous, hedonistic settings and seductive characters are essentially what the conversations, narrations, and diary extracts in the plots are all about. In the *Six Moral Tales* series (1963–72), a man renounces sex with a woman for ethical reasons. In *The Collector* (*La Collectioneuse*, 1966), an intellectual rejects the advances of a promiscuous bikini-clad nymphet. (Young girls were to appear with increasing frequency in Rohmer's films as he got older.) In *My Night at Maud's* (*Ma Nuit chez Maud*, 1969), a man spends a chaste night in bed with Maud, a beautiful woman. Jerome (Jean-Claude Brialy), a diplomat spending the summer at a lake resort, allows himself the exquisite pleasure of embracing a teenager's knee in *Claire's Knee* (*Le Genou de Claire*, 1970), as erotic a moment as any bedroom scene. In Rohmer's second series, called *Comedies and Proverbs* (1981–87), characters are less articulate, but still analyse all their actions. His witty investigations into the illusions of love continued with *Tales of Four Seasons* (1990–98.)

WHAT TO WATCH

- *My Night at Maud's* (*Ma Nuit chez Maude*, 1969)
- *Claire's Knee* (*Le Genou de Claire*, 1970)
- *The Aviator's Wife* (*La Femme de l'Aviateur*, 1981)
- *Pauline at the Beach* (*Pauline à la Plage*, 1983)
- *The Green Ray* (*Le Rayon Vert*, 1986)
- *A Tale of Springtime* (*Conte de printemps*, 1990)
- *A Tale of Winter* (*Conte d'hiver*, 1992)
- *A Summer's Tale* (*Conte d'été*, 1996)
- *An Autumn Tale* (*Conte d'automne*, 1998)
- *Les amours d'Astree et de Celadon* (*The Romance of Astrea and Celadon*, 2007)

Film poster, 1970

Roberto **Rossellini**

BORN 1906 **DIED** 1977

NATIONALITY Italian

CAREER 1940–1977 **FILMS** 24

GENRE Cult, Drama, Horror

Passion and humanity resonate through the films of Roberto Rossellini in the three phases of his career: neorealism (see box, p.286), the Ingrid Bergman melodramas, and the films about saints and historical figures.

Although the term neorealist was first applied to Luchino Visconti's ***Ossessione*** (1943), it was Rossellini's three movies – ***Rome, Open City*** (***Roma, Città Aperta***, 1945) on the Resistance; ***Paisan*** (***Païsà***, 1946) on the Liberation; and ***Germany Year Zero*** (***Germania Anno Zero***, 1948) on post-war turmoil – that established the style. Shot with minimum resources in natural surroundings, the films depict historic events in human terms. Children emerge as the nucleus of suffering: in ***Germany Year Zero***, a young boy, unable to feed his family in occupied post-war Germany, throws himself off a building.

Edmund (Edmund Meschke), in ***Germany Year Zero*** (1948), faces a burnt out Berlin where he must eke out a living. The low-angle shot points to the insurmountable task ahead of him.

In *Stromboli* (1950), Karen (Bergman) realizes she has escaped a POW camp only to be imprisoned in marriage. The theme of displacement in Rossellini's war films is revisited here.

In 1950, Rossellini married Ingrid Bergman and instead of casting her in glamorous roles, he gave her intense ones. Bergman seeks salvation atop a volcano in ***Stromboli*** (1950), tends the poor and the sick in ***The Greatest Love*** (***Europa '51***, 1952), witnesses a miracle in ***Voyage to Italy*** (***Viaggio in Italia***, 1953), and is driven to suicide in ***Fear*** (***La Paura***, 1954) – all are films about marriage in crisis. The sequence was interrupted by ***The Flowers of St. Francis*** (***Francesco, Giullare di Dio***, 1950), about the life of the saint. After divorcing Bergman, Rossellini made historical and religious features, mainly for television. These include biopics on Socrates, Augustine of Hippo, the Medicis, Alcide de Gasperi (Italy's first post-war president), and the feature ***The Rise of Louis XIV*** (***La Prise de Pouvoir par Louis XIV***, 1966). ***The Messiah*** (***Il Messia***, 1975), the story of Christ, was his last film.

WHAT TO WATCH

- ***Rome, Open City*** (1945)
- ***Paisan*** (1946)
- ***Germany Year Zero*** (1948)
- ***Stromboli*** (1950)
- ***The Greatest Love*** (1952)
- ***Voyage to Italy*** (1953)
- ***General della Rovere*** (***Il Generale della Rovere***, 1959)
- ***The Rise of Louis XIV*** (1966)

Martin **Scorsese**

BORN 1942

NATIONALITY American

CAREER 1968– **FILMS** 24

GENRE Gangster, Thriller

The exciting, dark, and obsessive talent of Martin Scorsese is seen at its best in his explorations into the Italian-American identity. He looks into its endemic machismo and violence that often manifests itself in crime. His inventiveness was first noticed as editor and virtual director of ***Woodstock*** (1970), the rockumentary (see p.95). Producer Roger Corman helped him make his first feature, ***Boxcar Bertha*** (1972), an excellent apprentice work with a fine sense of locale.

Early influences

Scorsese spent a bedridden asthmatic childhood with his Sicilian-Catholic family in Little Italy, New York. He gives the impression of being obsessed with his background, although he claims to have exorcised his childhood demons by making ***Mean Streets*** (1973). Filmed in dark tones, the movie inhabits the twilight world of nightclubs, where two crooks, Charlie (Harvey Keitel) and "Johnny Boy" (Robert De Niro), try to survive. The smooth bonhomie between members of the Mafia, the pasta meals, Italian arias, religious and family rituals camouflaging the gun lore seething beneath, were to become familiar elements in Scorsese's thrillers. This milieu was revisited in ***GoodFellas*** (1990), where he refines the examination of these dubious, ironically glamourized, members of the Mob, seen through the eyes of Henry (Ray Liotta), who is attracted to the false aura of power and success. In ***Gangs of New York*** (2002), Scorsese recreates the Manhattan of the mid-19th century, where the predecessors of the "goodfellas" operated, on an epic scale.

Raging Bull (1980) is the story of Jake LaMotta – world middleweight boxing champion from 1949 to 1951. Virtually an anti-biopic – unlike his more conventional ***The Aviator*** (2004) – it tells us nothing of La Motta's past. Rather, it presents us, in splendid black-and-white images, with the male animal's primitive emotions. Scorsese's favourite actor, Robert De Niro, won the Academy Award for Best Actor for the raw energy of his performance. If the New York of ***Taxi Driver*** (1976) is the city of the 1940s film noir, then ***New York, New York*** (1977) shows the wonderful town of 1940s musicals. De Niro convincingly enacted the role of a disturbed would-be comedian in Scorsese's black comedy, ***The King of Comedy*** (1982). ***The Departed*** (2006), a crime drama, won him a Best Director Oscar. Away from the violence that dominates many of his films, Scorsese successfully entered Merchant-Ivory territory with ***The Age of Innocence*** (1993) and courted controversy with ***The Last Temptation of Christ*** (1988).

In response to the criticism that his films contain pointless violence, Scorsese says, "There is no such thing as pointless violence. It's reality, it's real life, it has to do with the human condition. Being involved in Christianity and Catholicism when I was very young, you have that innocence, the teachings of Christ. Deep down you want to think that people are really good – but the reality outweighs that".

An unusual film from Scorsese, ***The Age of Innocence*** (1993) nevertheless depicts his well-traversed theme of a man (Daniel Day-Lewis as Newland) caught between desire (for Ellen, played by Michelle Pfeiffer) and reality.

WHAT TO WATCH

- ***Mean Streets*** (1973)
- ***Taxi Driver*** (1976)
- ***New York, New York*** (1977)
- ***Raging Bull*** (1980)
- ***After Hours*** (1985)
- ***The Colour of Money*** (1986)
- ***The Last Temptation of Christ*** (1988)
- ***GoodFellas*** (1990)
- ***The Age of Innocence*** (1993)
- ***Gangs of New York*** (2002)
- ***The Departed*** (2006)
- ***Shutter Island*** (2010)

Film poster, 2004

Ousmane **Sembene**

BORN 1923 **DIED** 2007

NATIONALITY Senegalese

CAREER 1963– **FILMS** 9

GENRE Comedy-drama

The comedy-dramas of Ousmane Sembane dig deep into African society and its colonial past. The director thought of himself as the modern incarnation of the *griot*, the tribal storyteller.

Village women fetch water in *Moolaadé* (2004) (meaning protection); the movie critically analyses the practice of female circumcision – still performed in parts of Africa.

WHAT TO WATCH

- *The Money Order* (1968)
- *God of Thunder* (1971)
- *Xala* (*The Curse*, 1975)
- *The Camp at Thiaroye* (1989)
- *Moolaadé* (2004)

Sembene's favourite theme was the effect on his country of nearly 400 years of colonial rule. He joined the Free French Forces fighting in Senegal in 1942, and his wartime experiences contributed to the authenticity of two of his films, *God of Thunder* (*Emitai*, 1971) and *The Camp at Thiaroye* (*Camp Thiaroye*, 1989), which reveal aspects of World War II through African eyes. *The Money Order* (*Mandabi*, 1968), was the first feature ever made by an all-African crew in a native African language, Wolof – widely spoken in Senegal. Most of his films are in Wolof, and deliver social messages through wry humour and pathos.

Douglas **Sirk**

BORN 1900 **DIED** 1987

NATIONALITY American

CAREER 1934–1959 **FILMS** 41

GENRE Melodrama, Musical, Drama

Remembered, first and foremost, as the director of four rich Technicolor "women's pictures" of the 1950s, Douglas Sirk (Claus Detlev Sierk) directed comedies, musicals, war films, and Westerns.

Born in Germany of Danish parents, Sirk made ten films in Europe under his real name before going to the US. In Hollywood, he attempted a range of genres, all of them created with impeccable style, paying attention to lighting, sets, and costumes. He directed the suave George Sanders in three atmospheric period pieces – *Summer Storm* (1944), *A Scandal in Paris* (1946), and *Lured* (1947). His forté for soap operatics was first evident in a Barbara Stanwyck film, *All I Desire* (1953), but it burgeoned in the melodramas he made in Technicolor for Universal Pictures, beginning with *Magnificent Obsession* (1954). In the film, Rock Hudson plays Bob Merrick, who becomes an eye-surgeon in order to restore the sight of Helen (Jane Wyman). In *All That Heaven Allows* (1955), a middle-aged widow, Cary (Wyman) marries her much younger gardener Ron (Hudson). In *Written on the Wind* (1956), alcoholism, impotence, and disease are rife in the family of oil tycoon Jasper Hadley. *Imitation of Life* (1959), about the close friendship between Annie (Juanita Moore), a black woman, and Lora (Lana Turner), a white woman, provides a weepy end to the golden age of Sirk's Hollywood melodrama. His inventive use of colour, fluid camerawork, compassion for his characters, and condemnation of a hypocritical society, transcend his soap opera material.

Film poster, 1955

WHAT TO WATCH

- *Has Anybody Seen My Gal?* (1952)
- *Take Me to Town* (1953)
- *All I Desire* (1953)
- *Magnificent Obsession* (1954)
- *All That Heaven Allows* (1955)
- *Written on the Wind* (1956)
- *The Tarnished Angels* (1957)
- *Imitation of Life* (1959)

Spielberg's *Jurassic Park* (1993), based on Michael Crichton's novel *The Lost World*, heralded a special effects revolution.

Steven **Spielberg**

BORN 1946

NATIONALITY American

CAREER 1975– **FILMS** 29

GENRE Adventure, Drama, Science fiction

One of the most famous Hollywood directors, Steven Spielberg has an intuitive sense of the hopes and fears of his audience. This quality combined with his showmanship have made him one of the greats, in the league of Cecil B. DeMille, Frank Capra, and Alfred Hitchcock.

Spielberg's first movies were influenced by Hitchcock's mechanics of suspense. ***Duel*** (1971) is a superior psychological thriller about road paranoia, while ***Jaws*** (1975) terrified viewers about horrors lurking in the ocean. However, he wasn't interested in becoming the "new Hitchcock". Instead, the qualities repeatedly found in his films are childlike innocence and wonder. Two films with these features are about friendly aliens: ***Close Encounters of the Third Kind*** (1977) and ***E.T.: The Extra-Terrestrial*** (1982). These, along with the action-adventure film ***Raiders of the Lost Ark*** (1981) and its two sequels made him one of the most successful directors ever.

Spielberg is unencumbered by pretensions or politics. By the mid-1980s, after forming his own film studio, Dreamworks SKG, he was in a position to film anything he chose. He turned to books: ***The Color Purple*** (1985) by Alice Walker, with its tough subject matter of racism, sexism, and lesbianism in the US of the early 20th century, provided meaningful themes to explore. ***Empire of the Sun*** (1987), based on J.G. Ballard's wartime memoir, is a worthy film, but not a significant advance on the prisoner-of-war movies of previous decades. In ***Schindler's List*** (1993), based on Thomas Keneally's novel, Spielberg explored the persecution of Jews in Nazi Germany. An account of the "Final Solution", it is probably his most important film. ***Saving Private Ryan*** (1998), with Tom Hanks as a US platoon commander in Normandy during World War II, displays the most intense combat scenes Hollywood has produced. Made at virtually the same time as ***Schindler's List*** (Spielberg edited one while shooting the other), ***Jurassic Park*** (1993) looked like his insurance policy: a ground-breaking computer-generated imagery (CGI) spectacle with dinosaurs more lifelike than ever seen before. It was pure showmanship, and another colossal hit, but also a reminder that for all his technique, Spielberg has yet to invest his entertainments with the complexity and depth that, for example, Capra managed in ***It's a Wonderful Life*** (1946), or that proved second nature to Hitchcock. ***Artificial Intelligence: AI*** (2001) is arguably the closest he has come to reconciling the two sides of his work – the cerebral side that wants to be respected and the entertainer who needs to be loved.

WHAT TO WATCH

- *Jaws* (1975)
- *Close Encounters of the Third Kind* (1977)
- *Raiders of the Lost Ark* (1981)
- *E.T.: The Extra-Terrestrial* (1982)
- *Jurassic Park* (1993)
- *Schindler's List* (1993)
- *Saving Private Ryan* (1998)
- *Munich* (2005)
- *Indiana Jones and the Kingdom of the Crystal Skull* (2008)

Film poster, 1932

Josef von **Sternberg**

BORN 1894 **DIED** 1969

NATIONALITY Austrian

CAREER 1925–1957 **FILMS** 22

GENRE Melodrama

The iconographic figure of Marlene Dietrich was created by Josef von Sternberg (Jonas Sternberg). She appeared as the eternal *femme fatale* in seven of his films, which are among the most sensuous, bizarre, exotic, and unnaturalistic films in cinema.

In 1927, von Sternberg made ***Underworld***, one of the few silent films to deal with organized crime, and *The Docks of New York* (1928), which treated urban squalor with poetic realism, achieved by soft, shadowy lighting (von Sternberg's trademark).

In *The Salvation Hunters* (1925), his first film, von Sternberg states, "It is not conditions, nor is it environment – our faith controls our lives!" This is certainly true of his own life.

Born in an impoverished family of Orthodox Jews, von Sternberg spent his childhood in hunger and most of his teens on the streets. This experience is reflected in his film-making, which explores the motivations and faith of his characters. *The Last Command* (1928) – with Emil Jannings as exiled Russian General Dolgorucki who is forced to become an extra in a Hollywood film about the Russian Revolution – sets up a strange double image between the exotic Russian past and the present studio set. Jannings also had a masochistic role as Immanuel Rath, a professor caught in the clutches of cabaret singer Lola, in ***The Blue Angel*** (***Der Blaue Engel***, 1930), the film in which the world discovered Dietrich. Conjured up by make-up, wigs, costumes, and the subtle play of light and shadow, Dietrich next appeared as Amy Jolly in ***Morocco*** (1930), Spy X27 in ***Dishonored*** (1931), Shanghai Lily in ***Shanghai Express*** (1932), Helen Faraday in ***Blonde Venus*** (1932), Catherine the Great in ***The Scarlet Empress*** (1934), and Concha Perez in ***The Devil is a Woman*** (1935), inhabiting fantastic countries in these movies. The partnership between von Sternberg and Dietrich is as iconic as that of, say, Laurel and Hardy, or Gilbert and Sullivan. Nothing he did after he worked with Dietrich equalled these films, although ***The Saga of Anatahan*** (1953) showed what von Sternberg could do with just a simple studio set and lighting.

Von Sternberg (right) talks with cameraman Max Fabian and actors Conrad Nagel, Matthew Betz, and Renée Adorée on the set of ***Exquisite Sinner*** (1926), a film from which he was fired.

WHAT TO WATCH

- *The Blue Angel* (1930)
- *Morocco* (1930)
- *Dishonored* (1931)
- *Shanghai Express* (1932)
- *Blonde Venus* (1932)
- *The Scarlet Empress* (1934)
- *The Devil is a Woman* (1935)
- *The Saga of Anatahan* (1953)

Erich von **Stroheim**

BORN 1885 **DIED** 1957

NATIONALITY Austrian

CAREER 1919–1933 **FILMS** 10

GENRE Costume drama

Only the first two films of the ten directed by Erich von Stroheim were released without studio interference. Yet, despite the vandalism committed on his art, he remains one of cinema's great figures.

Born in Vienna to middle-class parents, Stroheim emigrated to the US and became an American citizen and an actor, adding the "von" to his name, and claiming to be an ex-army officer of noble descent. By playing a succession of brutal Prussian officers, he gained the title of "the man you love to hate". As a director, he was profligate with studio money (for example, he rebuilt a large part of Monte Carlo on the Universal backlot) so that Irving Thalberg, Head of Production, called him a "footage fetishist". But the luxury of the settings was essential to his vision of European decadence in his cynical, witty, erotic Ruritanian romances, rich in social and psychological detail. ***Queen Kelly*** (1929) is a truncated but delirious sado-masochistic masterpiece, starring silent movie diva Gloria Swanson. Even ***The Merry Widow*** (1925), based on Franz Lehár's operetta, has a whiff of decay amidst the romanticism. Unlike his other silent films, ***Greed*** (1924) was filmed almost entirely on location. In its two-and-half-hour version (cut down from ten hours), it remains a masterpiece. Soon after he was prevented from completing his only talkie, ***Walking Down Broadway*** (1933) – re-shot and re-edited by director Alfred Werker – he left for France, where he spent the rest of his life as an actor. He returned to Hollywood briefly to act in Billy Wilder's ***Sunset Boulevard*** (1950).

In *Foolish Wives*, (1922), von Stroheim is Sergius Karamzin, a Don Juan who swindles rich women. Maud George plays Princess Olga, his mistress and partner in crime.

WHAT TO WATCH

- ***Blind Husbands*** (1919)
- ***Foolish Wives*** (1922)
- ***Greed*** (1924)
- ***The Merry Widow*** (1925)
- ***The Wedding March*** (1928)
- ***Queen Kelly*** (1929)

The winner of a huge lottery, Trina (Zasu Pitts) becomes obsessed with the money in ***Greed*** (1924), throwing her own life, and the lives of people around her, into turmoil.

Preston **Sturges**

BORN 1898 **DIED** 1959

NATIONALITY American

CAREER 1940–1955 **FILMS** 13

GENRE Comedy

The US of Preston Sturges is a giddy, corrupt, bustling country, full of eccentrics. The witty lines, visual gags, and comic timing form part of an acerbic view of American life, although his misanthropy is tempered with affection for his characters.

Sullivan's Travels (1941), with Joel McCrea (as John Lloyd Sullivan) and Veronica Lake (as "The Girl"), has a clever script that feels contemporary even today.

Born Edmund Preston Biden (he changed his name to Sturges after his adoptive stepfather), Sturges worked as a screenwriter through the 1930s, and was one of the first directors to write his own scripts (doing so for all his films). He won the Oscar for Best Original Screenplay in 1941 for *The Great McGinty* (1940). In *Sullivan's Travels* (1941), a director of comedies wants a first-hand experience of poverty in order to make a serious drama. Over time, however, he realizes that making people laugh is his greatest triumph. Sturges' own mission to make people laugh was achieved in the screwball comedies *The Lady Eve* (1941) and *The Palm Beach Story* (1942). His satires on American small towns, *The Miracle of Morgan's Creek* (1944) and *Hail the Conquering Hero* (1944), exploit motherhood and patriotism for laughs.

WHAT TO WATCH

- *The Lady Eve* (1941)
- *Sullivan's Travels* (1941)
- *The Palm Beach Story* (1942)
- *The Miracle of Morgan's Creek* (1944)
- *Hail the Conquering Hero* (1944)

Andrei **Tarkovsky**

BORN 1932 **DIED** 1986

NATIONALITY Russian

CAREER 1962–1986 **FILMS** 7

GENRE Drama

Andrei Tarkovsky made some of the most intensely personal and visually powerful statements to have come out of Eastern Europe for decades.

Ignat Daniltsev (Aleksei) walks with his mother (Margarita Terekhova) in *The Mirror* (1975); his reflections as a dying man are poetically juxtaposed with Russian history.

His rich pictorial sense was already in evidence in his first feature, *Ivan's Childhood* (*Ivanovo detstvo*, 1962), the story of an orphan boy working for the partisans during World War II. His mastery of the medium was further confirmed in *Andrei Rublev* (*Andrey Rublyov*, 1966). The film, through its portrayal of the great 15th-century icon painter, issues a rallying cry for the arts in the face of repression by authorities, and is a statement on the role of the artist. This measured, impressive parable of the artist's position in society was not allowed to be screened for some years by the Soviet authorities who felt it was too "dark".

WHAT TO WATCH

- *Ivan's Childhood* (1962)
- *Andrei Rublev* (1966)
- *Solaris* (1972)
- *The Mirror* (1975)
- *Stalker* (1979)
- *The Sacrifice* (1986)

Jacques **Tati**

BORN 1907 **DIED** 1982

NATIONALITY French

CAREER 1949–1973 **FILMS** 6

GENRE Comedy

A brilliant observer of the absurdities of modern life and idiosyncrasies of people, Jacques Tati restored the art of visual comedy, taking it to a different plane.

Unlike the films of Chaplin and Keaton, Tati's comedies are not built around himself. However, he is a memorable comic figure as the tall, socially awkward Monsieur Hulot, whose presence triggers amusing incidents – for example, when he picks his way through a minefield of gadgets. Tati's films have little dialogue, but humour manifests itself in the body language of ordinary people, and in the meticulously organized sound effects. ***Mr. Hulot's Holiday*** (*Les Vacances de Monsieur Hulot*, 1953) shows people on holiday with comic realism, while ***Mon Oncle*** (1958) and ***Playtime*** (1967) deal with the ridiculous aspects of the relationship of humans with machines and architecture.

Jacques Tati, as Monsieur Hulot, saunters by beach huts in a scene from ***Mr. Hulot's Holiday*** (1953).

WHAT TO WATCH

- *Jour de fête* (1949)
- *Mr. Hulot's Holiday* (1953)
- *Mon Oncle* (1958)
- *Playtime* (1967)

Solaris (*Solyaris*, 1972) – remade by Steven Soderbergh in 2002 – is a striking sci-fi film, which manages to be technologically convincing without relying on special effects. Tarkovsky approached a different kind of science fiction in ***Stalker*** (1979), which tells of a nightmarish journey, through a forbidden wasteland, undertaken by the shaven-headed stalker of the title and his two companions. Shot in eerie sepia, the film haunts the mind long after it ends. ***The Mirror*** (*Zerkalo*, 1975) is full of dream-like images evoking memories and fantasies of Tarkovsky's private and public life in the form of a visual poem. His last film was ***The Sacrifice*** (*Offret*, 1986), a post-apocalyptic drama which had an unbroken ten-minute take of a burning house as its climax.

Tarkovsky (left) directs Donatas Banionis who plays Kris Kelvin, a psychologist sent to examine bizarre events aboard a space station, in ***Solaris*** (1972).

In *Dogville* (2003), an allegory offering multiple readings, Grace (Nicole Kidman) is a fugitive who finds shelter in a small town with the help of Tom Edison (Paul Bettany).

Lars von **Trier**

BORN 1956

NATIONALITY Danish

CAREER 1984– **FILMS** 14

GENRE Drama

The most famous Danish director since Carl Dreyer, Lars von Trier has as many fans as he has detractors. However, both would agree that he is an auteur with a strong personality.

Von Trier's debut movie, ***The Element of Crime*** (***Forbrydelsens element***, 1984), was the first part of his "Europe in disintegration" trilogy, completed by ***Epidemic*** (1987) and ***Europa*** (1991). All were shot in a mixture of black-and-white and colour, with an atmosphere of despair.

Breaking the Waves (1996), von Trier's first English-language work – filmed like a home video – and ***Dancer in the Dark*** (2000), a musical about an East European woman who goes to America with her son, were unashamedly melodramatic. ***Dogville*** (2003) and ***Manderlay*** (2005), set in an imaginary US, experimented with minimalist theatrical sets. ***The Idiots*** (***Idioterne***, 1998) set out successfully to shock audiences into accepting people with learning difficulties.

WHAT TO WATCH

- *Epidemic* (1987)
- *Europa* (1991)
- *Breaking the Waves* (1996)
- *The Idiots* (1998)
- *Dancer in the Dark* (2000)
- *Dogville* (2003)
- *Antichrist* (2009)

Julie Christie performs a double role as Clarrise/Linda Montag in *Fahrenheit 451* (1966); the sci-fi parable set in a future dystopia was Truffaut's first work in colour.

François **Truffaut**

BORN 1932 **DIED** 1984

NATIONALITY French

CAREER 1959–1983 **FILMS** 21

GENRE Avant-garde

Enthusiasm, lucidity, and freedom of expression characterize the films of François Truffaut, a leading force in the French New Wave (see pp.42–43). Retaining a certain innocence, his films are snapshots of the French avant-garde.

"Are films more important than life?" asks Jean-Pierre Léaud in ***Day for Night*** (***La Nuit Américaine***, 1973). For Truffaut, the answer must have been in the affirmative. The passion he felt for film-making communicated itself in his movies, which are full of cinematic allusions: ***Shoot the Piano Player*** (***Tirez sur le pianiste***, 1960) pays homage to American film noir, ***Jules and Jim*** (***Jules et Jim***, 1962) alludes to Chaplin and Jean Renoir, and the ***The Bride Wore Black*** (***La Mariée Etait en Noir***, 1968) is inspired by Hitchcock's work. However, Truffaut was no mere imitator – many of his films have an immediacy and freshness uncluttered by ciné culture. This is best seen in his semi-autobiographical series of five films, with Jean-Pierre Léaud playing his alter ego Antoine Doinel. The 12-year-old Doinel is sent to reform school in ***The 400 Blows*** (***Les Quatre Cents Coups***, 1959) – as Truffaut himself was. After a short entitled ***Antoine and Collette*** (1962), the series follows Doinel as he grows older and falls in love in ***Stolen Kisses*** (***Baisers Volés***, 1968), marries and has a child in ***Bed & Board*** (***Domicile Conjugal***, 1970), and divorces and becomes a writer in ***Love on the Run*** (***L'Amour en Fuite***, 1979). These seemingly lightweight films hide Truffaut's pain at the loss of youthful spontaneity and the difficulties of love. He demonstrated a wide range in terms of styles and subjects, from the futuristic nightmare of ***Fahrenheit 451*** (1966) and the 19th-

Agnès **Varda**

BORN 1928

NATIONALITY Belgian

CAREER 1954– **FILMS** 16

GENRE Documentary

In 1955, Agnès Varda, a photographer, made *La Pointe-Courte*, although she claimed to have scarcely ever been to the cinema. The film gained her a reputation as "the mother of the French New Wave" (see pp.42–43). Varda wrote, produced, and directed all her films, both fiction and documentary. *Cléo from 5 to 7* (*Cléo de 5 à 7*, 1962) observes two hours in the life of a spoiled nightclub singer as she waits for the medical verdict on whether she is to live or die. Every trivial incident takes on a new significance for her, and Paris is seen as if for the last (or first) time. ***One Sings, the Other Doesn't*** (***L'Une Chante, l'Autre Pas***, 1977) came out of Varda's involvement with the women's movement in 1970s France. Eight years later, she made ***Vagabond*** (***Sans Toit ni Loi***, 1985), one of her most successful features. In between her fiction films, Varda made imaginative documentaries, which were ciné-poetic essays, including tributes to her late husband, director Jacques Demy.

WHAT TO WATCH

- *Cléo from 5 to 7* (1962)
- *Happiness* (1965)
- *One Sings, the Other Doesn't* (1977)
- *Vagabond* (1985)
- *Jacquot de Nantes* (1991)
- *The Gleaners & I* (2000)
- *Les plages d'Agnes* (*The Beaches of Agnes*, 2008)

Sandrine Bonnaire plays Mona, the outcast in *Vagabond* (1985), which presents her as the epitome of the soul, free of social bondage.

century period of *The Story of Adele H* (*L'Histoire d'Adèle H*, 1975), to France under Nazi occupation in *The Last Metro* (*Le Dernier Métro*, 1980).

On the set of *Love on the Run* (1978), the last in the Antoine Doinel series, Truffaut directs Claude Jade, who plays Doinel's wife Christine.

WHAT TO WATCH

- *The 400 Blows* (1959)
- *Shoot the Piano Player* (1960)
- *Jules and Jim* (1962)
- *Fahrenheit 451* (1966)
- *The Bride Wore Black* (1968)
- *Stolen Kisses* (1968)
- *The Wild Child* (1970)
- *Bed & Board* (1970)
- *Day for Night* (1973)
- *The Green Room* (1978)

King **Vidor**

BORN 1894 **DIED** 1982

NATIONALITY American

CAREER 1919–1959 **FILMS** 53

GENRE Drama, Melodrama, Costume drama

King Vidor's name features in the Guinness Book of World Records as the film-maker with the longest career, spanning 67 years and more than 50 films, and his dominant personality is stamped on many of them.

Film poster, 1937

The Big Parade (1925) was one of the first films to deal with the horrors of World War I. It also began "a series of films depicting episodes in the lives of the average American man and woman". In *The Crowd* (1928), John and Mary (played by James Murray and Eleanor Boardman) are a couple newly arrived in New York, whose high hopes are soon dashed by unemployment and poverty. *Hallelujah!* (1929), Vidor's first film with sound, was an all-black musical, shot on location in Tennessee and Arkansas, that retained the visual poetry of silent cinema. His technical virtuosity is apparent in films as varied as *Stella Dallas* (1937), a melodrama starring Barbara Stanwyck; the Western *Duel in the Sun* (1946), with Jennifer Jones; and the epic *War and Peace* (1956), for which Audrey Hepburn was nominated for several awards.

WHAT TO WATCH

- *The Big Parade* (1925)
- *The Crowd* (1928)
- *Hallelujah!* (1929)
- *The Champ* (1931)
- *Our Daily Bread* (1934)
- *Stella Dallas* (1937)
- *Duel in the Sun* (1946)
- *The Fountainhead* (1949)
- *War and Peace* (1956)

Jean **Vigo**

BORN 1905 **DIED** 1934

NATIONALITY French

CAREER 1933–1934 **FILMS** 2

GENRE Drama

Few other directors with such a short filmography have had such a profound influence on other film-makers as Jean Vigo.

The pillow fight sequence in *Zero for Conduct* (1933) is shot in slow motion; the film showcases Vigo's talent for mixing social commentary with unique imagery.

The son of an anarchist who died in prison in 1917, Jean Vigo (Jean Bonaventure de Vigo Almereyda) inherited his father's anti-authoritarian ideas. In *Zero for Conduct* (*Zéro de Conduite*, 1933), set in a dreadful boarding school, four boys organize an uprising. The film, based on Vigo's own childhood experiences, presents a child's-eye view of authority, with adults seen as perverse, hypocritical, and oppressive members of the establishment. The most celebrated sequence is the dormitory pillow fight that becomes a snowy wonderland of feathers in which a mock Catholic procession is enacted. Its influence on Truffaut and Godard is noticeable and it was a direct inspiration for Lindsay Anderson's *If...* (1968). Vigo died of tuberculosis at 29, soon after the premiere of *L'Atalante* (1934), an exquisite tale of a young man who takes his bride to live on a barge that travels the canals around Paris.

WHAT TO WATCH

- *À propos de Nice* (1930)
- *Zero for Conduct* (1933)
- *L'Atalante* (1934)

Lucilla Morlacchi (as Concetta) and Claudia Cardinale (as Angelica) star in the stunningly shot and designed ***The Leopard*** (1963), which is set in the Italy of the 1800s.

Luchino **Visconti**

BORN 1906 **DIED** 1976

NATIONALITY Italian

CAREER 1942–1976 **FILMS** 14

GENRE Drama, Spectacle

Aristocrat, Marxist, neorealist, theatre and opera director fond of a decadent lifestyle, Luchino Visconti was a man of contradictions, a fact that was reflected in his work.

Despite being a Marxist, Visconti was always attracted by European bourgeois art. "Art is ambiguous. It is ambiguity made science", says a character in *Death in Venice* (*Morte a Venezia*, 1971). Visconti was both repelled by and drawn to a decaying society, depicting it in loving detail. In *The Leopard* (*Il Gattopardo*, 1963), Prince Salina of Sicily reflects sadly on the death of the aristocratic world; Ludwig II of Bavaria (Helmut Berger) in *Ludwig* (1972) fights against the philistines who cannot appreciate Richard Wagner's genius; and in *Death in Venice*, cholera threatens to sweep away the luxury of the Hotel des Bains on the Lido. Although he gained a reputation as a neorealist, only *La Terra Trema* (1948) actually comes close to the neorealist (see box, p.286) ideal in its picture of the wretched conditions of Sicilian fishermen, shot in real locations with local people enacting their stories. It is through the conventions of opera that Visconti worked best, as in the lush Verdian spectacle of *Senso* (1954). *Rocco and his Brothers* (*Rocco e i suoi fratelli*, 1960), which tells of a family who escape the poor South, is Visconti's attempt to return to neorealism, despite the film's operatic dimensions.

WHAT TO WATCH

- *Ossessione* (1942)
- *La Terra Trema* (1948)
- *Senso* (1954)
- *Rocco and his Brothers* (1960)
- *The Leopard* (1963)
- *Death in Venice* (1971)
- *The Innocent* (*L'Innocente*, 1976)

Dirk Bogarde delivers one of his finest performances as Gustav von Aschenbach, an ageing composer who is forced to take a convalescent holiday in *Death in Venice* (1971).

In *Katyn* (2007), Maja Ostaszewska plays Anna, a Polish woman who loses her husband in the Katyn forest massacre.

Andrzej **Wajda**

BORN 1926

NATIONALITY Polish

CAREER 1954– **FILMS** 34

GENRE Costume drama, War

In the 1950s, Andrzej Wajda's war trilogy became the voice of disaffected post-war youth. A generation later, Wajda was once again the voice of a Poland struggling to survive political and economic turmoil.

Wajda's war trilogy – *A Generation* (1955), *Canal* (1957), and *Ashes and Diamonds* (1958) – were bitter, anti-romantic World War II films. Censorship in the 1960s and 1970s, forced him to adapt Polish allegorical novels, but even in these, he subtly alluded to contemporary Poland. When censorship was relaxed, he returned to the political subjects of the immediate past. *Man of Marble* (1977) tells the story of the life of a worker-hero of the 1950s who falls from official favour. Its sequel, *Man of Iron* (1981), was about the struggle for solidarity.

WHAT TO WATCH

A Generation (*Pokolenie*, 1954)
Canal (*Kanal*, 1957)
Ashes and Diamonds (*Popiól i Diament*, 1958)
Innocent Sorcerers (1960)
Siberian Lady Macbeth (1961)
Landscape After Battle (1970)
Man of Marble (*Czlowiek z Marmuru*, 1976)
Man of Iron (*Czlowiek z Zelaza*, 1981)
Danton (1983)
Katyn (2007)
Tatarak (2009)

Orson **Welles**

BORN 1916 **DIED** 1985

NATIONALITY American

CAREER 1941–1975 **FILMS** 14

GENRE Film noir, Drama

Film poster, 1947

The idea that Orson Welles could never direct a film to match the achievement of *Citizen Kane* (1941) still persists. But few Hollywood directors can boast of a finer *oeuvre*.

Had Welles been a conformist, he might have been more successful – but his greatness would have been diminished. *Citizen Kane* (1941), his first full-length feature, went against the conventions of chronological narratives and techniques of film-making. In *F for Fake* (1973), Welles tells anecdotes about art forgers with relish, demonstrating that "Art is the lie that makes us see the truth". Who, then, is a storyteller but a great liar? In the splendid comic poem and historical epic, *Chimes at Midnight* (1965), Falstaff – one of the great liars of literature – is given dignity by Welles' portrayal. In *The Immortal Story* (1968), a wealthy merchant wishes to make a popular sailor's myth come true. Power is a sustaining motif of Welles' work, as evidenced in *Citizen Kane*, *Macbeth* (1948), *Othello* (1952), and *Confidential Report* (1955). A struggle for dominance is central to *The Lady from Shanghai* (1947) and *Touch of Evil* (1958). Even though RKO cut *The Magnificent Ambersons* (1942), the film remains a haunting portrait of a family in decline in the late 19th century.

WHAT TO WATCH

Citizen Kane (1941)
The Magnificent Ambersons (1942)
The Lady from Shanghai (1947)
Macbeth (1948)
Othello (1952)
Confidential Report (1955)
Touch of Evil (1958)
Chimes at Midnight (1965)

William **Wellman**

BORN 1896 **DIED** 1975

NATIONALITY American

CAREER 1923–1958 **FILMS** 76

GENRE Various

Although William Wellman's name is most often associated with action pictures, gaining him a reputation for working mainly with men, he brought his expertise to bear on a range of genres in the best Hollywood manner.

Wellman earned the nickname "Wild Bill" for his impatience with actors, his devil-may-care personality, and his spell as a pilot in World War I. He drew on his wartime experiences for *Men With Wings* (1938), about the pioneers of flight; *Lafayette Escadrille* (1958), with his son playing himself; and *Wings* (1927), the first movie to win an Oscar for Best Picture and one of the best flight films ever. Other than the he-man epics, such as *The Call of the Wild* (1935), *Beau Geste* (1939), and *Buffalo Bill* (1944), there was also *Wild Boys of the Road* (1933), a deeply felt story of young people hopping trains during the Great Depression. His original *A Star Is Born* (1937) says more about Hollywood than its two remakes. *Nothing Sacred* (1937) is a hilarious, fast-paced satire; *Roxie Hart* (1942) is a cynical 1920s spoof (remade as *Chicago*, 2002); and *Magic Town* (1947) is a Capra-esque comedy set in a small US town. Wellman also directed five movies with Barbara Stanwyck. It was thanks to him that Robert Mitchum became a star with the semi-documentary *The Story of G.I. Joe* (1945) and James Cagney found stardom with *The Public Enemy* (1931).

WHAT TO WATCH

- *Wings* (1927)
- *The Public Enemy* (1931)
- *Wild Boys of the Road* (1933)
- *The Call of the Wild* (1935)
- *A Star Is Born* (1937)
- *Nothing Sacred* (1937)
- *Beau Geste* (1939)
- *Roxie Hart* (1942)
- *The Ox-Bow Incident* (1943)
- *The Story of G.I. Joe* (1945)
- *The High and the Mighty* (1954)

Film poster, 1937

Wim **Wenders**

BORN 1945

NATIONALITY German

CAREER 1970– **FILMS** 27

GENRE Drama, Musical

Wim Wenders is deeply aware of America's cultural influence on post-war Germany, and his films, whether made in the US or Germany, reflect this.

"The Yanks have colonized our subconscious", says a German character in *Kings of the Road* (*Im Lauf der Zeit*, 1976), Wenders' complex, subtly comic road movie. His films neither condemn nor wholly embrace this idea. His characters are isolated and emotionally stunted – but when they take to the road, change becomes inevitable. The superbly photographed, leisurely odysseys reach metaphysical dimensions, as in *Paris, Texas* (1984), his greatest international success. He returned to the theme in *Don't Come Knocking* (2005).

Nicholas Ray, the renowned director, plays Derwatt in *The American Friend* (1977), a thriller in which a terminally ill picture framer is forced to become an assasin.

WHAT TO WATCH

- *Alice in the Cities* (1973)
- *Kings of the Road* (1976)
- *The American Friend* (1977)
- *Paris, Texas* (1984)
- *Wings of Desire* (1987)
- *Buena Vista Social Club* (1999)
- *Don't Come Knocking* (2005)

Margaret (Gloria Stuart) and her companions discover the dark secrets of an old mansion inhabited by an odd family in Whale's Gothic pastiche, ***The Old Dark House*** (1932).

James **Whale**

BORN 1889 **DIED** 1957

NATIONALITY British

CAREER 1930–1941 **FILMS** 20

GENRE Horror, Musical

The name of James Whale is almost always linked with Frankenstein's monster, which he brought to life in two horror film classics.

After staging R.C. Sherriff's play, *Journey's End*, on Broadway, Whale was invited to Hollywood in 1930 to depict this World War I drama on film. His triumph came with his third feature, ***Frankenstein*** (1931), for which he chose his compatriot Boris Karloff to play the title role. On the whole, Whale preferred to work with British actors: Charles Laughton in ***The Old Dark House*** (1932), Claude Rains in ***The Invisible Man*** (1933), and Elsa Lanchester in ***The Bride of Frankenstein*** (1935). It is perhaps his "Englishness" that frees his horror films, which are full of self-mocking humour, from the Germanic expressionism (see box, p.259) usually associated with early examples of the genre. He moved smoothly from Frankenstein to Hammerstein with ***Show Boat*** (1936), which was the best of the three versions of this movie. Interest in Whale revived when his life story became the subject of Bill Condon's ***Gods and Monsters*** (1998).

Film poster, 1935

WHAT TO WATCH

- *Frankenstein* (1931)
- *The Old Dark House* (1932)
- *The Invisible Man* (1933)
- *The Bride of Frankenstein* (1935)
- *Show Boat* (1936)

Billy **Wilder**

BORN 1906 **DIED** 2002

NATIONALITY American

CAREER 1933–1981 **FILMS** 26

GENRE Comedy, Romance, Film noir

The films of Billy Wilder, which emphasize the importance of dialogue and the structuring of plots, derive from the satiric Viennese theatre, the witty elegance of Ernst Lubitsch, and the harsher screwball comedies of the 1930s.

Austrian-born Wilder began his Hollywood career writing films for Lubitsch and Mitchell Leisen in the 1930s. A writer, director, and producer, he made highly successful films in varying genres over the course of his long Hollywood career, receiving an incredible eight Academy Award nominations as Best Director (second only to William Wyler who had 12). Wilder was also nominated 12 times for his screenplays, which he usually co-wrote, first with Charles Brackett, and, from 1957, with I.A.L. Diamond.

The "Lubitsch Touch" – the unique style and cinematic trademark of Ernst Lubitsch – is at play in Wilder's directorial debut ***The Major and the Minor*** (1942), in which working girl Susan (Ginger Rogers) pretends to be 12 years old to save on her train fare. The three acerbic comedies set in Germany – ***A Foreign Affair*** (1948) in a Berlin ravaged by war; ***Stalag 17*** (1953) in a prisoner-of-war camp; and ***One, Two, Three*** (1961) in a Berlin divided by the Wall – are also compassionate and extremely

Humphrey Bogart, in an unusual romantic role as the serious Linus, succumbs to the charms of Sabrina (Audrey Hepburn) in ***Sabrina*** (1954).

A scene from *Sunset Boulevard* (1950), Wilder's hard-hitting, cynical take on the vagaries of show business, with Gloria Swanson as Norma and William Holden as Joe Gillis.

funny. ***Some Like It Hot*** (1959), a Prohibition-era gangster spoof, is widely considered to be one of the funniest films ever. In 1944, Wilder moved into the newly emerging genre of film noir with ***Double Indemnity***, a dark and pessimistic thriller portrayed with acid humour. ***The Lost Weekend*** (1945), one of the first films to deal seriously with alcoholism, is another grim and gripping depiction.

Wilder's critically acclaimed films often reveal a romantic's bitterness that comes from disappointment – that life is not perfect, love is thwarted, people can be avaricious and cruel, and the world is not improving. This is sensed in ***Sunset Boulevard*** (1950), the glorious swan song of silent screen star Norma Desmond (Gloria Swanson), who dementedly thinks she is making a comeback. "I'm still big, it's the pictures that got small," she tells Joe Gillis (Holden), a world-weary screenwriter.

There are a number of heartless heroes in his work, such as the sensation-seeking reporter Chuck Tatum (Kirk Douglas) in ***Ace in the Hole*** (1951), the slick insurance agent Walter Neff in ***Double Indemnity*** (1944), and the weak, exploitative businessman J.D. Sheldrake in ***The Apartment*** (1960), both played by Fred MacMurray. Others are Dino, Dean Martin's self-parodic crooner in ***Kiss Me, Stupid*** (1964), and Walter Matthau's crooked lawyer Willie Gingrich in ***The Fortune Cookie*** (1966). Wilder's attitude to them is condemnatory, and his tenderness is reserved for the female characters. Audrey Hepburn portrays all that is good in life as she tries to choose between the Larrabee brothers (Humphrey Bogart and William Holden) in ***Sabrina*** (1954), and when she is painfully smitten by middle-aged playboy Frank Flannagan (Gary Cooper) in ***Love in the Afternoon*** (1957). Marilyn Monroe is depicted as alluring but innocent, saving Richard (Tom Ewell) from adultery in ***The Seven Year Itch*** (1955), and poignantly tells "Josephine" (Tony Curtis in drag) how much she loves Joe (Curtis in trousers) in ***Some Like It Hot***, while Shirley MacLaine is rescued by C.C. Baxter (Jack Lemmon) in ***The Apartment*** (1960). ***Fedora*** (1978), about an ageing and reclusive star, explores a plot similar to that of ***Sunset Boulevard***. Both these films record a changing Hollywood.

WHAT TO WATCH

- *The Major and the Minor* (1942)
- *Double Indemnity* (1944)
- *The Lost Weekend* (1945)
- *Sunset Boulevard* (1950)
- *Ace in the Hole* (1951)
- *Stalag 17* (1953)
- *Sabrina* (1954)
- *Some Like It Hot* (1959)
- *The Apartment* (1960)
- *One, Two, Three* (1961)

Film poster, 1955

Aboard a mysterious imaginary train in *2046* (2004) is an android played by Faye Wong. She is also cast as Wang Jing-wen, the daughter of the landlord in whose building the protagonist (Chow Mo-wan) lives.

Wong Kar Wai

BORN 1958

NATIONALITY Chinese

CAREER 1988– **FILMS** 10

GENRE Avant-garde, Romance

One of the most original directors to emerge at the end of the 20th century, Wong Kar Wai belongs to the Second New Wave of Hong Kong film-makers who have developed an innovative, non-realistic approach to films.

Wong's cinema has dazzling images (usually of Hong Kong) with multi-layered, intricately structured plots. Added to this is mood and atmosphere, with nostalgic popular music on the soundtrack and alienated lovelorn characters. Wong achieved most of his cinematic effects with the assistance of cinematographer Chris Doyle, and actors William Chang, Maggie Cheung, Leslie Cheung, and Tony Leung. He consistently employs parallel narratives, where characters arbitrarily cross paths, a technique at its most extreme in ***Chungking Express*** (*Chung Hing sam lam*, 1994), which shows his mastery over two separate storylines. The Hong Kong of the 1960s is Wong's favourite setting. ***Days of Being Wild*** (*A Fei jingjyuhn*, 1991), set in 1960, explores the fears of the territory's handover to China. His most approachable film, ***In the Mood for Love*** (*Fa yeung nin wa*, 2000), also takes place in the 1960s, while ***2046*** (2004) alternates between the 1960s and an imagined future in 2046. In all these films, he asks audiences to abandon their customary ideas of time and space. The ironically titled ***Happy Together*** (*Chun gwong cha sit*, 1997), about the stormy affair of two men, is one of his few films shot outside China, in Argentina and Taiwan.

In ***My Blueberry Nights*** (2007), Natalie Portman plays an inveterate poker player who loses all of her money.

WHAT TO WATCH

- *Ashes of Time* (1994)
- *Chungking Express* (1994)
- *Fallen Angels* (1995)
- *Happy Together* (1997)
- *In the Mood for Love* (2000)
- *2046* (2004)
- *My Blueberry Nights* (2007)

William **Wyler**

BORN 1902 **DIED** 1981

NATIONALITY American

CAREER 1926–1970 **FILMS** 45

GENRE Drama, Epic, Costume drama, Musical

The films of William Wyler are usually sturdy and tasteful entertainments that probe ethical issues, and a number of them have won Academy Awards.

Coming to Hollywood in 1924, German-born Wyler worked his way up from prop boy to director of dozens of short Westerns, each made in a few days. Following these, he worked painstakingly, earning the nickname "99-take Wyler". His reputation as a film-maker of quality dates from his first encounter with cinematographer Gregg Toland on *These Three* (1936), Wyler's first version of Lillian Hellman's play *The Children's Hour*. (He remade it in 1961 when he was able to mention lesbianism.) Toland's camerawork, especially his deep-focus photography, gave Wyler's films a definition they might not otherwise have had. Producer Samuel Goldwyn helped him with some of his best work, in *Dodsworth* (1936) and *Wuthering Heights* (1939). Other Goldwyn productions are *Dead End* (1937), a social drama about juvenile crime in New York, and *The Little Foxes* (1941), a lush Hellman drama with Bette Davis. Wyler also directed Davis excellently in *Jezebel* (1938) and *The Letter* (1940). *The Best Years of Our Lives* (1946), a moving and revealing portrait of post-war America, follows the lives of three soldiers on their return to civilian life, each representing a different armed service and social class. The film won seven Oscars. Wyler's meticulous style filled the canvases of *Friendly Persuasion* (1956), a tale of a Quaker family forced to take up arms during the American Civil War; *The Big Country* (1958), a vast anti-Western; and the epic *Ben-Hur* (1959).

Film poster, 1946

WHAT TO WATCH

- *Jezebel* (1938)
- *The Little Foxes* (1941)
- *Mrs. Miniver* (1942)
- *The Best Years of Our Lives* (1946)
- *Roman Holiday* (1953)
- *Friendly Persuasion* (1956)
- *The Big Country* (1958)
- *Ben-Hur* (1959)
- *Funny Girl* (1968)

Bette Davis is the tempestuous heroine Julie and Henry Fonda is Preston – an engaged couple about to break up – in the compelling period drama *Jezebel* (1938).

Top **100** **Movies**

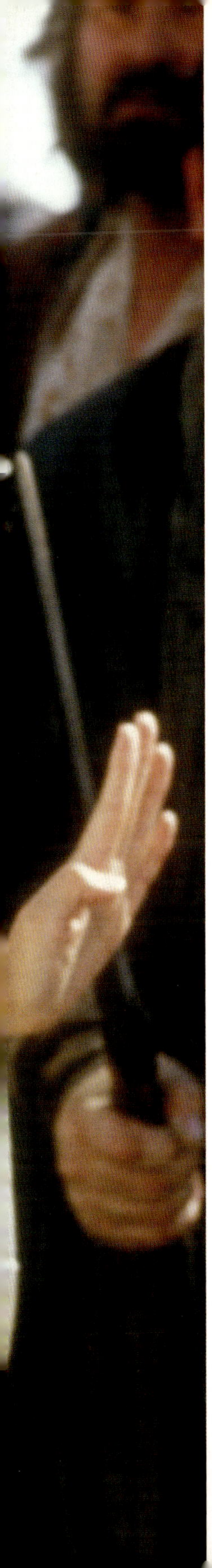

It is never easy to make a definitive list of "must-see" films, since it will always be subjective. However, the movies in this section have delighted, moved, or educated audiences of all ages, all over the world. They have changed our perceptions, and have left an indelible mark on film history.

The choice of movies in this section was guided by various criteria. Although there are a few relatively recent films – up-to-date, instant classics – the majority have been included because they have stood the test of time. Besides those that are part of "the canon" – films that appear regularly on historians' and critics' all-time best lists and are an essential part of any Film Studies course – there are audience favourites as well.

This section features silent masterpieces, from *The Birth of a Nation* (1915) to *The Passion of Joan of Arc* (1928); comedies, from *City Lights* (1931) to *Women on the Verge of a Nervous Breakdown* (1988); and musicals, ranging from *42nd Street* (1933) to *The Sound of Music* (1965). There are horror movies, such as *Nosferatu* (1922); cartoons, from the hand-drawn *Snow White and the Seven Dwarfs* (1937) to the computer-animated *Toy Story* (1995); science fiction films (*Star Wars*,1977, naturally); and Westerns (*Unforgiven*, 1992).

Among the films that are automatically on any list of "greats" are those that, regardless of personal likes and dislikes, have had a seminal effect on film history for both technical and aesthetic reasons, such as *The Cabinet of Dr. Caligari* (1920), *Napoléon* (1927), *Citizen Kane* (1941), *Bicycle Thieves* (1948), and *Breathless* (1960). Others have been significant in less obvious ways like *His Girl Friday* (1940), *L'Avventura* (1960), *Easy Rider* (1969), *Taxi Driver* (1976), and *Annie Hall* (1977).

The list has been limited to one film per director, mainly because it would be only too simplistic to come up with 100 films that included only works by great directors, such as Alfred Hitchcock, Ingmar Bergman, Luis Buñuel, Federico Fellini, John Ford, Jean Renoir, Akira Kurosawa, and Billy Wilder.

Any of the films we have chosen to represent the directors above could be replaced by another: *North By Northwest* (1959), *Psycho* (1960), or *Rear Window* (1954) instead of *Vertigo* (1958); *Wild Strawberries* (1957) or *Persona* (1966) in place of *The Seventh Seal* (1957). John Ford, the maestro of the Western, is represented by *The Grapes of Wrath* (1940), a non-Western. Is *Rashomon* (1950) better than *The Seven Samurai* (1954)? Is *Some Like It Hot* (1959) better than *The Apartment* (1960)? One could make a strong case either way.

It was from this embarrassment of riches that we have made a final selection of our top 100 movies.

« **Ziyi Zhang** plays Jiao Long, an impetuous and physically skilled nobleman's daughter in *Crouching Tiger, Hidden Dragon*, Ang Lee's hit film of 2000.

Film poster, 1915

The Birth of a Nation

DIRECTOR D.W. Griffith

RELEASED 1915

The Birth of a Nation was a landmark in the development of motion pictures and remains one of the most controversial films ever made. The epic story follows two families on opposite sides during and immediately after the American Civil War.

At over three hours long, the scale of *The Birth of a Nation* was unprecedented in American cinema till then. All of the innovations of D.W. Griffith's earlier work – cross-cutting, close-ups, dissolves, and fades – reached maturity in this picture. One of its achievements was to integrate an intimate story within the progression of dramatically reconstructed historical events – for example, the assassination of President Lincoln and the swirling mass of soldiers on the battlefields. Apparently, Griffith wrote no script, carrying the film's complex structure in his head. However, much of the latter part of the film (in which slaves gain freedom; the hero forms the Ku Klux Klan; and a black man pursues a white virgin who kills herself rather than succumb to his attentions) was, even in 1915, considered by many to be racially offensive. As a result, the National Association for the Advancement of Colored People (NAACP) picketed and boycotted the film. Despite its racism, the film is acknowledged by many as a technical masterpiece.

CREDITS

Production	Epoch Producing Corporation
Producer	D.W. Griffith
Screenplay	D.W. Griffith, Frank E. Woods, Thomas Dixon Jr., based on Dixon's novels *The Clansman* and *The Leopard's Spots*
Cinematography	G.W. "Billy" Bitzer

In *The Birth of a Nation*, Lillian Gish plays Elsie Stoneman, the virginal heroine who is rescued from a "fate worse than death" by the newly formed Ku Klux Klan, led by her lover.

The deliberately distorted perspective of the sets have an almost hypnotic effect on the audience, reflecting Caligari's control over his servant Cesare.

The Cabinet of Dr. Caligari

DIRECTOR Robert Wiene

RELEASED 1920

Adapting its style from painting and the theatre, ***The Cabinet of Dr. Caligari*** (***Das Kabinett des Doktor Caligari***) was considered the first true example of expressionism in the cinema (see box). It had an important influence on German films in the decade after its release, and on horror movies in general.

Caligari (Werner Krauss), a fairground showman, hypnotizes his servant Cesare (Conrad Veidt) to commit murders in his sleep. The somnambulist carries off Jane (Lil Dagover), the girlfriend of the hero Francis (Friedrich Feher), though ultimately doesn't kill her because of her beauty. The film, meant as a metaphor for the Great War, has Caligari representing a government that controls the will of its people. However, the "twisty" ending shows him as the benign director of a lunatic asylum, with Francis a patient who has actually imagined the whole story. The distorted sets and grotesquely angled photography create a nightmarish atmosphere, a style that became known as "Caligarism". The film had a direct impact on James Whale's ***Frankenstein*** (1931) and ***The Bride of Frankenstein*** (1935), and influenced many later works, including those of Tim Burton, who modelled Johnny Depp's Edward Scissorhands on Veidt's character of the mesmerized slave.

CREDITS

Producer	Erich Pommer for Decla
Screenplay	Carl Mayer, Hans Janowitz
Set Design	Walter Röhrig, Hermann Warm, Walter Reiman
Cinematography	Willy Hameister

GERMAN EXPRESSIONISM

Expressionism was a movement in the graphic arts, literature, drama, and film that flourished in Germany between 1903–33. In film, the movement was characterized by the extreme stylization of sets, acting, lighting, and camera angles. Most of the major German directors of the silent period were influenced by ***The Cabinet of Dr. Caligari***.

The Cabinet of Dr. Caligari was the classic Expressionist film in Germany. The style inspired a series of horror fantasies known as "shadow films".

The film's feeling of terror is centred on the spectral, gaunt figure of Max Schreck's Vampire, who creeps through the film with menacing authority.

Nosferatu: A Symphony of Terror

DIRECTOR F.W. Murnau

RELEASED 1922

The film that marked the first appearance of the vampire Dracula on screen remains the eeriest and most magical of the multitude of movie versions of this supernatural tale.

F.W. Murnau made his debut as a film director in 1919, and a year later, ***The Cabinet of Dr. Caligari*** (see p.259) was released. He was clearly much influenced by that seminal work. However, unlike the stylized sets of the earlier film, much of ***Nosferatu*** was shot on location in Germany, with its Gothic atmosphere created by *chiaroscuro* lighting – a technique from the field of painting, in which the contrast between dark and light areas in an image is heightened (see box, p.99). Murnau also used special effects, speeding up the frames and using negative film to evoke a ghostly carriage ride. Murnau plundered Stoker's 1897 novel without permission and an action for breach of copyright was brought against him, but ***Nosferatu*** has become accepted as a classic of the horror genre.

CREDITS

Production	Prana Film
Producer	Albin Grau, Enrico Dieckmann
Screenplay	Hanrik Galeen, based on Bram Stoker's *Dracula* (uncredited)
Cinematography	Fritz Arno Wagner

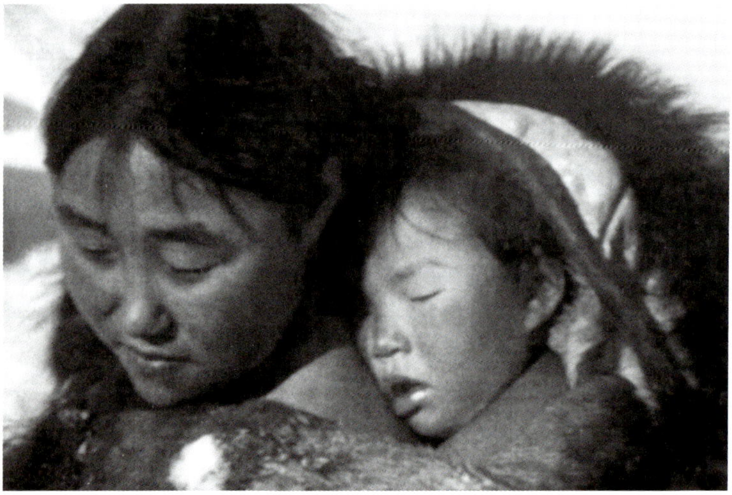

Nyla, Nanook's wife, carries her son through the bleak Arctic landscape. Nanook died of starvation two years after Flaherty filmed him.

Nanook of the North

DIRECTOR Robert J. Flaherty

RELEASED 1922

Robert J. Flaherty's ***Nanook of the North*** had a great effect on the evolution of the documentary film. The movie's strength lies in its basis in reality and in the unprecedented rapport between its Inuit subjects and the man behind the camera.

In order to make this extraordinary account of hardship and endurance, Flaherty spent 16 months living with the Inuit of Canada's Hudson Bay. He concentrated on a year in the everyday life of a family – Nanook, his wife Nyla, and their children – depicting activities such as trading, fishing, hunting, and the construction of an igloo. However, Flaherty directed them to re-enact their roles for the camera, including a scene in which a walrus is hunted. To be able to shoot inside an igloo, he had the dwelling built at twice the average size, with half of it cut away to permit sunlight to enter. Dubious as this sounds, such techniques allowed Flaherty to convey the drama and the struggle underlying the daily existence of the Inuit people, depicting a way of life threatened by encroaching civilization. It was a new approach to the presentation of reality on film, ennobling its subjects rather than exploiting them.

CREDITS

Production	Revillon Frères
Producer	Robert J. Flaherty
Screenplay	Robert J. Flaherty
Cinematography	Robert J. Flaherty

The Battleship Potemkin

DIRECTOR Sergei Eisenstein

RELEASED 1925

Soviet cinema and Sergei Eisenstein were brought to international attention by this magnificent film. Although full of dramatic scenes, it swirls around a central denouement that is universally known as the "Odessa Steps" sequence – one of the most memorable and exciting pieces ever produced.

Commemorating the 20th anniversary of the 1905 Revolution, *The Battleship Potemkin* focuses on an incident in which the crew of a battleship at Odessa mutinies rather than eat rotting food. The leader of the protest is fatally shot by an officer, prompting hundreds of civilians to pay homage to the dead man and lend their support to the mutiny. As many of them gather on the Odessa Steps to wave to the ship, they are mown down by the government troops. The soldiers march down a seemingly endless flight of steps, advancing on the fleeing citizens, the rhythm of their marching feet contrasting with the fall of injured and dying people, including a small boy trampled underfoot and an elderly woman shot in the face. With its rhythmic collision and contrast of images, the film was a splendid demonstration of Eisenstein's theory of montage (see p.201). What is sometimes forgotten, perhaps because of the film's revolutionary style, is that *The Battleship Potemkin* tells an exciting narrative through well-rounded characters.

A Russian poster for the film is a fine example of the particular graphic style of the Soviet period, which was known as structuralism.

CREDITS

Studio	Goskino
Producer	Jacob Bliokh
Screenplay	Sergei Eisenstein, Nina Agadzhanova
Cinematography	Vladimir Popov, Edouard Tissé

The "Odessa Steps" sequence shows the horrifying moment when a pram hurtles down the steps towards certain destruction.

The futuristic sets created for *Metropolis* are still impressive decades after the film was made. Mirrors were used to create illusions, including the flying machine that glided between the huge buildings.

A German poster shows the robot against the cityscape. *Metropolis* pioneered the use of science fiction to comment on contemporary society.

Metropolis

DIRECTOR Fritz Lang

RELEASED 1927

The visual legacy of Fritz Lang's *Metropolis* can be seen in a number of movies, from *The Bride of Frankenstein* (1935) to the *Batman* movies via *Modern Times* (1936), the *Star Wars* cycle, and *Blade Runner* (1982). The film's technical innovations influenced a number of Hollywood films of the 1930s and 1940s.

Set in a futuristic city, *Metropolis* tells the story of downtrodden factory workers (living underground), who are made to rebel against their masters by a malign robot created in the image of a saintly girl. Lang was given an unprecedented budget to create huge, realistic sets, inspired by the New York skyline, that anticipated the 21st century. To achieve futuristic effects, lighting cameraman Eugen Schüfftan introduced the Schüfftan process, which combined life-size action with models or artwork. Despite its ending – in which "Capital" and "Labour" are reconciled by the love of the factory owner's son (Gustav Fröhlich) for a working girl (Brigitte Helm) – *Metropolis* can be seen as an allegory of totalitarianism.

In 1984, composer Giorgio Moroder added a rock music score to the film, and tinted and optically enhanced several sequences, through which Lang's masterly control continues to astonish audiences.

CREDITS

Studio	UFA
Producer	Erich Pommer
Screenplay	Fritz Lang, Thea von Harbou
Cinematography	Karl Freund, Günther Rittau
Design	Otto Hunte, Erich Kettelhut, Karl Vollbrecht
Special Effects	Eugen Schüfftan

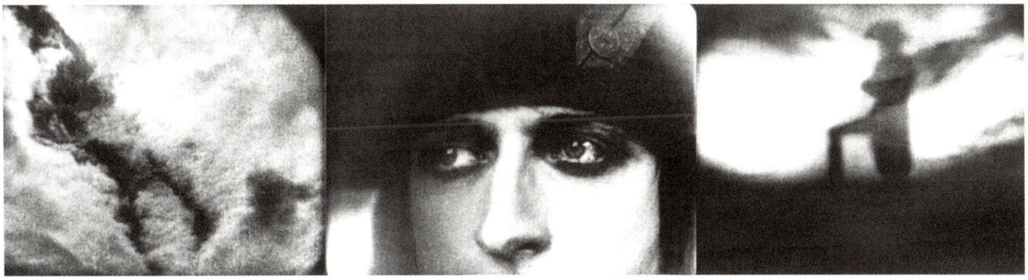

Polyvision was a revolutionary projection technique that used multiple frames to show a panorama of separate but thematically linked images.

Napoléon

DIRECTOR Abel Gance

RELEASED 1927

Abel Gance's most ambitious and personal film, ***Napoléon*** is a pyrotechnical display of almost every device of the silent screen and beyond. The use of a triple screen anticipates wide-screen techniques – such as Cinerama – which did not come into use for another 30 years.

Gance's historical and historic film presents, in six episodes, Napoléon Bonaparte as a Nietzschean Superman. It follows his life from childhood, through his military schooling, his meeting with Josephine (Gina Manès), and his rise to power. With a dazzling use of visual metaphors, Gance shows the boy Napoléon as a brilliant budding military strategist during a snowball fight shot to resemble a military campaign, the split screen filling with snowballs in flight. The most famous set piece is the symbolic sequence in which Napoléon sails back to France from Corsica through stormy, rough seas that threaten to enter the boat, cut with scenes of a political storm raging in Paris. In order to gain his effects, Gance used hand-held cameras, wide-angled lenses, superimposed images, and rapid cutting.

Napoléon was first shown at the Paris Opéra, in a version that lasted five hours. However, it was poorly received and was released in various truncated forms thereafter. In 1980, British film restorer Kevin Brownlow reconstructed the film, keeping as close to the original as possible, and ***Napoléon*** finally received the recognition it deserved, amazing audiences everywhere.

CREDITS

Production	West/Société-Générale de Films
Screenplay	Abel Gance
Cinematography	Jules Kruger
Music	Arthur Honegger

Albert Dieudonné plays Napoléon, here seen isolated after battle, surrounded by the dead and wounded. Such scenes typify Gance's desire to create a "richer and more elevated form of cinema".

The Passion of Joan of Arc

DIRECTOR Carl Dreyer

RELEASED 1928

This film is an intense depiction of individual suffering, a soul in torment transformed into cinematic images. It is the purest expression of Carl Dreyer's style, which he himself referred to as "realized mysticism".

Renée Falconetti, in her only film, wore no make-up and had to crop her hair to play the lead role.

Dreyer based his last silent film on transcripts of the 18-month trial of Joan of Arc before she was burned at the stake. By telescoping the entire trial into one day, the screenplay gives the film a formal intensity. Dreyer's constant and unforgettable use of long-held close-ups has led some to describe *The Passion of Joan of Arc* as a film consisting entirely of examples of this type of shot. In fact, the film also includes tilts, pans, medium shots, and cross-cutting. The faces of the heroine's judges, bare of make-up, are cruelly exposed to Rudolph Maté's camera; but it is the agonized face of Falconetti as Joan that burns itself into the mind. Dreyer's intention was to "move the audience so that they would themselves feel the suffering that Joan endured". Despite this, the film remains an uplifting experience.

CREDITS

Production	Société Générale des Films
Screenplay	Carl Dreyer, Joseph Delteil
Cinematography	Rudolph Maté
Costume Design	Valentine Hugo

An Andalusian Dog (Un Chien Andalou)

DIRECTOR Luis Buñuel

RELEASED 1929

A balcony at night. A man (Luis Buñuel) sharpens a razor blade. He observes a small cloud moving towards the full moon. Then the head of a girl comes into view, her eyes wide open. The cloud now moves across the moon. The razor blade slices open the girl's eye.

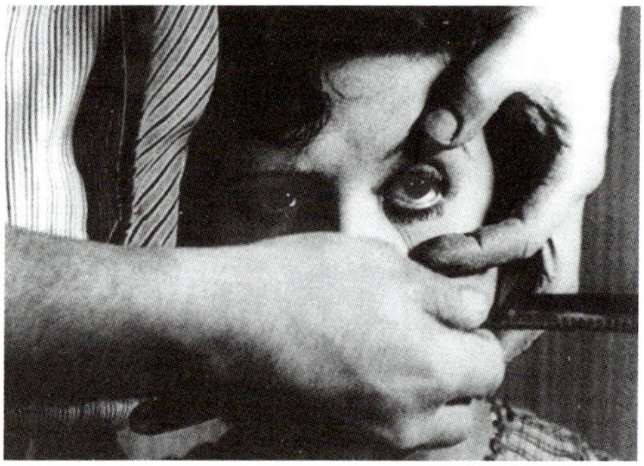

The opening sequence, in which a girl's eye appears to be slit by a razor, is the most memorable of the 17 surrealistic images in the film that are designed to shock or provoke the audience.

So began *An Andalusian Dog* (*Un Chien Andalou*) – the title is unrelated to anything in the film – and with it, Luis Buñuel's career. It has one of the most startling openings of any film, retaining the power to shock. According to French director Jean Vigo, "The prologue... tells us that in this film we must see with a different eye". Influenced by André Breton's "Surrealist Manifesto" (1924), and co-conceived with artist Salvador Dali, its series of unconnected incidents was intended to follow the logic of a dream: ants emerge from the palm of a disembodied hand (an archetypal Dali-esque image), priests are pulled along the ground, a woman's eye is slit open, and dead donkeys lie on two pianos. Although the film defies explanation, its rich supply of images from the unconscious can be read as a study of repressed sexual impulses.

CREDITS

Producer	Luis Buñuel
Screenplay	Luis Buñuel, Salvador Dali
Cinematography	Albert Duberverger

All Quiet on the Western Front

DIRECTOR Lewis Milestone

RELEASED 1930

Based on Erich M. Remarque's best-selling novel of the same name, this devastating film was a landmark in anti-war movies, particularly as the narrative is viewed from the German perspective. Its stark point – that war is hell for both sides – resulted in Germany and France banning the film for many years for fear that it would have a demoralizing effect on their armed forces.

The powerful pacifist message of Lewis Milestone's film, made at the dawn of the sound era, transcends cultures and generations. The film follows seven German boys who leave school in 1914, full of patriotic fervour, to fight for their country. Their enthusiasm is soon dampened when they are thrown into the horror of warfare and experience the brutality of life in the trenches. Particularly effective are the tracking shots, which show the attacks and counter-attacks of both sides, and the appalling deaths suffered. So realistic were these battle sequences that some of them have been incorporated into documentaries about World War I. The famous climax, in which Paul Bäumer (Lew Ayres) – the only one of the seven boys still alive – is killed as he stretches towards a butterfly, was shot some months after the film's completion. The director used his own hand for this shot, and later, to hold the Oscar for Best Director.

Film poster, 1930

CREDITS

Studio	Universal Pictures
Producer	Carl Laemmle, Universal Studios
Screenplay	Lewis Milestone, Maxwell Anderson, Del Andrews, George Abbott, Erich Maria Remarque
Cinematography	Arthur Edeson, Karl Freund
Awards	Academy Awards: Best Picture, Best Director

Paul Bäumer (Lew Ayres) takes cover in a church cemetery under heavy shell fire from French forces counter-attacking a German bombardment.

Dressed in a top hat, stiletto heels, and black stockings, Marlene Dietrich's Lola became one of cinema's most iconic images; the role was to launch her international career.

The Blue Angel

DIRECTOR Josef von Sternberg

RELEASED 1930

The first film with sound made in Germany, *The Blue Angel* (*Der Blaue Engel*) was notable for introducing Marlene Dietrich, one of cinema's greatest stars, to the world. The film also marked the start of one of the most remarkable collaborations between an actor (Dietrich) and a film-maker (Josef von Sternberg) that cinema has ever seen.

The film depicts the downfall of an ageing and puritanical teacher, Professor Immanuel Rath (Emil Jannings), who becomes infatuated with a sultry nightclub entertainer named Lola Frohlich (Dietrich). She marries the hapless man, but goes on to deceive and humiliate him. *The Blue Angel* is an impressive tale of a decent man lured to his doom by *un amour fou* – exemplified in a startling scene that shows the cuckolded Rath crowing like a cockerel, while dressed as a clown. However, despite a moving performance by Jannings, *The Blue Angel* is Dietrich's film. Von Sternberg saw sensuous, mysterious, and glamorous star potential in her, and she gives a splendid portrayal of an indolent *femme fatale*. Sitting astride a chair, scantily dressed, and huskily singing *Falling in Love Again*, Dietrich encapsulated an age and an impulse in German cinema. Shot concurrently in German and English, the film's seedy atmosphere is conveyed by director von Sternberg's masterful manipulation of lighting techniques.

CREDITS

Studio	UFA
Producer	Erich Pommerr
Screenplay	Josef von Sternberg, Robert Liebmann, Karl Vollmöller and Carl Zuckmayer, from the novel *Professor Unrath* by Heinrich Mann.
Cinematography	Gunther Rittau
Music	Frederick Hollander

City Lights

DIRECTOR Charlie Chaplin

RELEASED 1931

Four years after talkies had become *de rigeur*, Charlie Chaplin had the presumption to present a new silent film to the public. Only Chaplin – who not only acted in it, but also produced, directed, edited, wrote the scenario, and composed the music – could have got away with it. Audiences loved *City Lights* and critics called it his finest work.

Using his last cent, the Little Tramp (Chaplin) buys a flower from a blind girl (Virginia Cherill). Smitten, he is determined to restore her sight, and is able to do so with money obtained from a drunken millionaire he saves from drowning. Seeing the rather ridiculous looking tramp for the first time, and unaware that he is her benefactor, the girl puts money in his hands, only to recognize his touch. Chaplin's unique stamp is unmistakable in this film, which shows his ability to shift from satire to pathos. One of the funniest set pieces is a brilliantly choreographed boxing sequence in which Chaplin dances around the ring while keeping the referee between himself and his adversary. Although it had sound effects and music, *City Lights* was primarily a tribute to silent screen comedy.

Film poster, 1931

The Little Tramp, Charlie Chaplin's trademark character, seen here with a blind flower girl (Cherill), was inspired by his poverty-stricken childhood in Victorian London.

CREDITS

Studio	United Artists
Producer	Charlie Chaplin
Screenplay	Charlie Chaplin
Cinematography	Gordon Pollock, Roland Totheroh, and Mark Marklatt

Andy Lee (George E. Stone) rehearses a tap routine with the chorus line; Peggy (Ruby Keeler), the lucky understudy, is at the front.

42nd Street

DIRECTOR Lloyd Bacon

RELEASED 1933

Although an archetypal "backstage" musical of the early 1930s, *42nd Street* added a new dimension to the genre, with its potent references to the Great Depression contrasting with scenes of chorus girls slumming it in cheap apartments amidst Busby Berkeley's lavish kaleidoscopic production numbers. This was the first of three Warner Bros. musicals in 1933; followed by *Gold Diggers of 1933* and *Footlight Parade*. Economical, fast-paced, and down-to-earth, they revitalized the genre. While less escapist than its predecessors, *42nd Street* still contains all the essential elements of the genre, depicting the tribulations of putting on a Broadway show and ending with a successful opening night. Ingénue Peggy Sawyer (Ruby Keeler) takes over the lead role from Dorothy Brock (Bebe Daniels) at the last moment. The pep talk she gets from her director, Julian Marsh (Warner Baxter), before going on stage has entered showbiz lore, but most memorable are Berkeley's dance routines: *Shuffle Off To Buffalo*, *Young and Healthy*, and the title number, which, like the film, is "naughty, bawdy, gaudy, sporty".

CREDITS

Studio	Warner Bros.
Producer	Hal B. Wallis, Darryl F. Zanuck
Screenplay	Rian James, James Seymour
Cinematography	Sol Polito
Choreography	Busby Berkeley
Costume Design	Orry Kelly
Musical Numbers	Harry Warren, Al Dubin

Rufus T. Firefly (Groucho Marx), charms Gloria Teasdale (Margaret Dumont), the rich widow of the former President, at a party organized to welcome him as the new leader of Freedonia.

Duck Soup

DIRECTOR Leo McCarey

RELEASED 1933

In their fifth film, the Marx Brothers – Chico, Harpo, Groucho, and Zeppo – reached the height of their comic skills. This surreal satire lampooned war films (and war), authority and respectability, dictators, and the Ruritanian musical romances of the period.

The year 1933 was a time of immense social and economic upheaval: Hitler had seized power in Germany and the Great Depression was at its height in the US. So an outrageous comedy that begins with a political crisis and ends with a war would have seemed appropriate for its time. However, *Duck Soup* was both a critical and commercial failure when first released. Audiences were looking for reassurance, not the cynicism and anarchic humour of the Marx Brothers, hilarious as it is. In the film, Groucho plays the President of Freedonia, Rufus T. Firefly, who declares war on Sylvania, because he's "... already paid a month's advance rent on the battlefield". What follows is a series of lunatic set pieces, including the celebrated mirror routine in which Chico and Harpo are disguised as Groucho and all pretend to be each other's reflections. The film has the essence of the Marx Brothers' comic genius (without the piano and harp solos that interrupted many of their other films). After this film, straight man Zeppo became an agent, and the rest moved to MGM, where their lunacy continued.

CREDITS

Studio	Paramount
Producer	Herman J. Mankiewicz
Screenplay	Bert Kalmar, Harry Ruby
Cinematography	Henry Sharp
Music	Burt Kalmar, John Leipold, Harry Ruby

King Kong

DIRECTOR Merian C. Cooper/Ernest B. Schoedsack

RELEASED 1933

Despite two remakes – in 1976 and 2005 – and many imitations, the original black-and-white *King Kong* retains its ability to charm and astonish. It became the yardstick against which all later monster movies would be measured.

Kong, a gargantuan ape, inhabits the prehistoric Skull Island. When he sees Ann Darrow (Fay Wray), who is part of an expedition to the remote spot led by showman Carl Denham (Robert Armstrong), his primal instincts are aroused and he goes on a rampage. He is eventually captured and taken to New York, where he meets a spectacular death – the image of Kong on top of the Empire State Building (holding a scantily dressed Wray moments before he is shot down) is one of the most iconic in cinema history. The film was made one frame at a time, using a special effect technique known as stop-motion photography (see box). Although he appears huge, Kong was a model made out of metal, rubber, cotton, and rabbit fur, only 46cm (18in) tall. Part of the film's appeal is that the model seems to be a real actor, expressing human emotions.

STOP-MOTION PHOTOGRAPHY

One of the first special effects techniques used, stop-motion photography allows an otherwise inanimate object to move and change position by exposing a single frame of film at a time. The object is moved very slightly between exposures, so that when the film is projected, an illusion of motion is created. Because it takes 24 frames to create one second of film, several minutes of footage can take months to complete. Willis O'Brien was a pioneer of this technology, his crowning achievement being *King Kong*. Stop-motion sequences using real scenes of buildings and people was a variation on this technique and can be seen most effectively in *Jason and the Argonauts* (1963). The process is still used in animated films, such as Henry Selick's *The Nightmare Before Christmas* (1993) and Aardman Animations' productions (see pp.83–84).

CREDITS

Studio	RKO
Producer	Merian Cooper, Ernest B. Schoedsack, David O. Selznick
Screenplay	James Ashmore Creelman, Ruth Rose, Edgar Wallace
Cinematography	Edward Linden, J.O. Taylor, Vernon L. Walker, Kenneth Peach
Special Effects	Willis O'Brien

King Kong swats at the biplanes buzzing around him, while he balances on top of the Empire State Building in the movie's final sequence.

Juliette, a young city-dwelling bride, disappears after a quarrel but is reunited with her husband in a moving final scene.

L'Atalante

DIRECTOR Jean Vigo

RELEASED 1934

Any précis of this film's seemingly simple story cannot do justice to the richness of director Jean Vigo's only feature-length film. Much of it was shot along canals around Paris and in severe weather, contributing to Vigo's tragic death from tuberculosis just weeks after the film's premiere.

A young barge captain, Jean (Jean Dasté), takes his city-dwelling bride, Juliette (Dita Parlo), to live on his boat *L'Atalante*, which plies the waterways around Paris. Everyday life on the vessel is filled with magical moments, such as a waltz on a phonograph, the newlywed searching for his estranged sweetheart in water, and the joy of reconciliation. The film also contains rich characterization in the figure of Le père Jules (Michel Simon at his eccentric best), the master of the boat, who tells fantastic stories of his travels. Although it is ostensibly realist in setting and plot, the film has a surreal spirit, with a commitment to Freudian theories of dreams and the unconscious as well as the overthrow of bourgeois social and moral codes. Poorly received on its first showing, the film was badly edited and even the title was changed to that of a popular song. Fortunately, *L'Atalante* was restored to its original form in 1945 and has since gained the classic status it richly deserves.

CREDITS

Production	Gaumont-Franco Film-Aubert
Producer	Jacques-Louis Nounez
Screenplay	Jean Vigo, Albert Riéra, Jean Guinée
Cinematography	Boris Kaufman
Music	Maurice Jaubert

Jean and Juliette (Jean Dasté and Dita Parlo) stand at the prow of *L'Atalante*, the barge from which this haunting and beautifully visualized film gets its name.

« **Rotoscoped figures**, such as Snow White, the prince, and the wicked Queen, appeared in a Disney film for the first time. The most lovable characters were the dwarfs, whose names were chosen by a public poll.

Snow White and the Seven Dwarfs

DIRECTOR David Hand

RELEASED 1937

Walt Disney took an enormous artistic and financial risk by making the first feature-length animation film in three-strip Technicolor. However, ***Snow White and the Seven Dwarfs*** confirmed his position as the master of the cartoon movie.

Initially dubbed "Disney's Folly", the film was four years in the making and cost US$1.5 million, a huge sum for the times. Having produced only short cartoons till then, Disney had to make many changes for its first feature – the painted cells had to be enlarged to allow more detail in the images – and close to 750 artists worked on the two million drawings using drawing boards. The studio also devised a multi-plane camera, which enhanced the feeling of depth and was able to pan over each image without losing perspective. The result was possibly the most popular cartoon film ever, grossing over US$8 million on its initial US release. The songs, such as *Whistle While You Work* and *Someday My Prince Will Come*, became immediate hits. The film tells of how Snow White, the lovely stepdaughter of a jealous queen, flees the palace and takes refuge with seven dwarfs in their forest home. The queen changes into a wicked witch and poisons Snow White, who falls into a deep sleep until a prince finds her and awakens her with a kiss.

In 1938, Disney won a Special Academy Award for "a significant screen innovation which has charmed millions and pioneered a great new entertainment field for the motion picture cartoon". The success of ***Snow White and the Seven Dwarfs*** was followed by other Disney films including ***Fantasia*** (1940) and ***Pinocchio*** (1940).

CREDITS

Studio	Walt Disney Studios
Producer	Walt Disney
Screenplay	Ted Sears, Richard Creedon, adapted from the story by the Brothers Grimm
Cinematography	Maxwell Morgan
Supervising Director	David Hand
Awards	Academy Award: Special Award

The lighting of the Olympic flame is the culmination of the prologue, which links ideas of beauty in Greek antiquity to those in the Third Reich.

Olympia

DIRECTOR Leni Riefenstahl

RELEASED 1938

Riefenstahl's film on the 1936 Berlin Olympics is one of cinema's finest achievements. Nevertheless, admiration for its visual beauty is tempered by the fact that it was made under Hitler's orders as "a song of praise to the ideals of National Socialism".

Realizing the immense potential for propaganda through the Olympics, and for its dissemination by cinema, Hitler gave Riefenstahl all the time and resources she needed to make this four-hour documentary. She had planes, airships, and 30 cameramen at her disposal, and spent two years in the cutting room. It is easy to be seduced by the technical brilliance of the film's images, including the slow and reverse motion used in the diving sequence; the marathon forming "an epic hymn to endurance"; and the yacht racing under a darkening sky. However, the film is Nazi propaganda, and will always be associated with the atrocities against Jews.

CREDITS

Production	Tobis
Producer	Leni Riefenstahl
Screenplay	Leni Riefenstahl
Awards	Venice: Mussolini Cup (Best Film)

The Rules of the Game

DIRECTOR Jean Renoir

RELEASED 1939

Made on the eve of World War II, *The Rules of the Game* (*La Règle du Jeu*) is Jean Renoir's most complete film and his most complex in style. Inspired by the classic theatrical comedies of Pierre Marivaux, Pierre de Beaumarchais, and Alfred de Musset, the film shows French society of the time being disembowelled from within.

At a lavish shooting party of the Count and Countess la Chesnaye (Marcel Dalio and Nora Gregor), sexual tensions become apparent as relationships between aristocrats and servants are revealed. The structure, setting, and plot work to create a unique, dynamic juxtaposition of tragedy, melodrama, and farce.

Apart from memorable performances, particularly Renoir's own as the lovable buffoon Octave, there are some outstanding set pieces, such as the rabbit and bird shoots, and the after-dinner entertainment, which uses breathtaking tracking shots and deep focus. A commercial disaster on its release and banned because its exposure of class divisions in French society was "too demoralizing", the film gained recognition as a masterpiece only in 1956.

Julien Carette gives a sly, comic performance as the poacher Marceau (here displaying his quarry).

CREDITS

Production	Nouvelles Éditions de Films
Producer	Claude Renoir
Screenplay	Jean Renoir, Carl Koch
Cinematography	Jean Bachelet
Editor	Marguerite Renoir
Production Design	Eugène Lourié

Gone with the Wind

DIRECTOR Victor Fleming

RELEASED 1939

A film of superlatives, ***Gone with the Wind*** was, at the time, the most publicized and expensive film to date – and the most popular.

When David O. Selznick voiced his intention of filming Margaret Mitchell's bestselling novel on the US Civil War, for which he had bought the rights in 1936, Victor Fleming told him, "This picture is going to be the biggest white elephant of all time", while producer Irving Thalberg said, "...no Civil War picture ever made a nickel". Spectacular set pieces – such as the burning of Atlanta, the party at Twelve Oaks, and the sight of thousands of wounded Confederate soldiers – superbly evoked the Old South. The film's central relationship, between the roguish Rhett Butler and the wilful minx Scarlett O'Hara, is a monument of passion brilliantly played by Clark Gable and British stage actress Vivien Leigh.

CREDITS

Production	Selznick International Pictures
Producer	David O. Selznick
Screenplay	Sidney Howard, from Margaret Mitchell's novel
Cinematography	Ernest Haller
Production	William Cameron Menzies
Music	Max Steiner
Costume Design	Walter Plunkett
Awards	Academy Awards: Best Picture, Best Actress (Vivien Leigh), Best Supporting Actress (Hattie McDaniel), Best Director, Best Screenplay, Best Cinematography (Colour), Best Art Direction (Lyle R. Wheeler), Best Editing (Hal C. Kern, James E. Newcom), Technical Achievement Award (R.D. Musgrave)

Vivien Leigh plays tempestuous Scarlett O'Hara, who runs away from an afternoon house party in the first part of the film.

John Howard (George) and Cary Grant (Dexter) look on as a tipsy Katharine Hepburn (Tracy) languishes in the arms of James Stewart (Mike) after a midnight dip in the swimming pool on the eve of her wedding.

The Philadelphia Story

DIRECTOR George Cukor

RELEASED 1940

Although *The Philadelphia Story* has many of the elements typical of screwball comedy, the elegant, witty script and George Cukor's understated direction turned it into a sophisticated comedy of manners.

In a play of the same name, Katharine Hepburn scored a huge hit on Broadway as Tracy Lord, a role specially written for her by Philip Barry. She bought the film rights and chose her favourite director and co-stars. In a triumphant return to Hollywood, Hepburn plays Tracy, a domineering, spoiled socialite. All set for her wedding to the dull George Kittredge (John Howard), she finds she still has feelings for her ex-husband C.K. Dexter Haven (Cary Grant), and is attracted to cynical reporter Mike Connor (James Stewart), sent to cover her wedding. After a fight with George on the day of the wedding, she eventually succumbs to Dexter's dazzling charms and takes him back into her life. The film sparkles right from the celebrated wordless opening scene when Grant is tossed out of the front door by Hepburn, along with his bag of golf clubs.

Film poster, 1940

CREDITS

Studio	MGM
Producer	Joseph L. Mankiewicz
Screenplay	Donald Ogden Stewart, based on the play by Philip Barry
Cinematography	Joseph Ruttenberg
Costume Design	Adrian
Awards	Academy Awards: Best Actor (James Stewart), Best Screenplay

His Girl Friday

DIRECTOR Howard Hawks

RELEASED 1940

Howard Hawks' scintillating adaptation of the Ben Hecht and Charles MacArthur Broadway comedy *The Front Page* is a fine example of screwball comedy, with its breakneck pace, sexual innuendo, rapid-fire wisecracks, and absurd situations. However, it is also a pointed satire on political corruption and journalistic ethics, as well as a commentary on "a woman's place" in the professional world.

By changing the role of a main character – the star reporter – from a man (in the original play) to a woman, Hawks created sexual tension between the ruthless and wily newspaper editor Walter Burns (Cary Grant) and Hildy Johnson (Rosalind Russell), his employee and ex-wife. Hildy is about to leave the newspaper to marry meek insurance salesman Bruce Baldwin (Ralph Bellamy). The editor is determined to win her back, both to the newspaper and his bed, and hatches a plot, realizing that she will not be able to resist one final scoop. The twist works brilliantly in the film, especially as played by Grant and Russell, who give sharp and witty performances in this sparkling battle of the sexes. Most effective is the quick, intelligent repartee and the use of overlapping dialogue while the characters are constantly on the move. Despite being limited mostly to two sets – the newspaper office and the pressroom at the jail, where the journalists await the execution of an anarchist for killing a cop – the film never feels staged. It eclipses Lewis Milestone's excellent earlier version *The Front Page* (1931) and Billy Wilder's tired remake (1974).

CREDITS

Studio	Columbia
Producer	Howard Hawks
Screenplay	Charles Lederer, from the play *The Front Page* by Ben Hecht and Charles MacArthur
Cinematography	Joseph Walker

Film poster, 1940

Rosalind Russell, as Hildy, poses between co-stars Cary Grant and Ralph Bellamy in a promotional shot for the film.

Dorris Bowden, Jane Darwell, and Henry Fonda face trouble on their way to California in their old jalopy.

The Grapes of Wrath

DIRECTOR John Ford

RELEASED 1940

John Steinbeck's novel – a desolate vision of America during the Great Depression – provided John Ford with the material for one of the few Hollywood films, until then, with a genuine social conscience. With its unpatronizing treatment of ordinary people, it retains the themes of family and home – typical of many Ford films – while making a social statement.

Forced to leave their land (in the dustbowl of Oklahoma), the Joad family struggle to reach the "promised land" of California. Only exploitation, disappointment, and hardship await them at the end of their arduous journey, when they find that the wages paid to migrant workers are barely enough for survival. Although it focuses on the recent past, the film has a nostalgic poetry in its bleak visual images and beautifully lit studio exteriors. It was filmed in documentary-style black-and-white textures and low-key lighting, to recreate the look and feel of rural 1930s America. Henry Fonda gives one of his most sincere performances as Tom Joad, the grassroots American buffeted by fortune but willing to stand up for his rights. As he says to his mother: "I'll be all around... Wherever there's a fight so hungry people can eat... And when the people are eatin' the stuff they raise and livin' in the houses they build – I'll be there too." Unlike the novel's bleak conclusion, the film ends on an upbeat note, with the indomitable matriarch Ma Joad (Jane Darwell) proclaiming, "They can't wipe us out. They can't lick us. And we'll go on forever, Pa, because we're the people", thus affirming the strength and human dignity of the individual spirit.

The courage and strength of Ma Joad (Jane Darwell) keeps her suffering family together.

CREDITS

Studio	Twentieth Century Fox
Producer	Darryl F. Zanuck, Nunnally Johnson
Screenplay	Nunnally Johnson, based on the novel by John Steinbeck
Cinematography	Gregg Toland
Awards	Academy Awards: Best Director, Best Supporting Actress (Jane Darwell)

Citizen Kane

DIRECTOR Orson Welles

RELEASED 1941

In 1998, the American Film Institute (AFI) voted *Citizen Kane* the greatest Hollywood film ever. It has also topped *Sight & Sound*'s poll of best movies, conducted every 10 years since 1962, and despite being burdened with the label of "greatest-film-ever-made", *Citizen Kane* usually lives up to expectations.

As a newcomer to movie-making, the 25-year-old Welles is said to have broken rules he did not know existed. Working against chronological narrative conventions, his newspaper tycoon, Charles Foster Kane, is seen from many subjective viewpoints, providing a deeper understanding of the protagonist. The innovative use of wide-angle and deep-focus lenses, the creative use of sound, the great set pieces, the titanic performance of Welles as Kane, were all in pursuit of the meaning of "Rosebud", the single word Kane utters on his deathbed at the beginning of the film. To facilitate the low-angle shots, nearly every indoor set had a visible ceiling, a rare device at the time. Newspaper magnate William Randolph Hearst tried to have the film banned, believing that Kane was a veiled portrait of himself. It was screened only after Welles threatened RKO with a lawsuit.

CREDITS

Studio	RKO
Producer	Orson Welles
Screenplay	Orson Welles, Herman J. Mankiewicz
Cinematography	Gregg Toland
Editor	Robert Wise, Mark Robson
Music	Bernard Herrmann
Art Director	Van Nest Polglase
Awards	Academy Award: Best Original Screenplay

A high-angle shot shows Kane (Welles) and his best friend, Jedediah Leland (Joseph Cotten) taking over a small newspaper, a shot echoed in the film's final scenes of Kane's amassed goods.

Film poster, 1941

The Maltese Falcon

DIRECTOR John Huston

RELEASED 1941

Considered the first film noir, *The Maltese Falcon* is one of the most assured directorial debuts and perhaps the greatest ever remake, effacing two other versions (1931, 1936) of Dashiell Hammett's classic detective novel.

Among the many firsts of this seminal film was the screen debut, at 61, of stage actor Sydney Greenstreet. He plays one of three people – the others being Joel Cairo (Peter Lorre) and *femme fatale* Brigid (Mary Astor) – searching for a treasured *objet d'art* named the Maltese Falcon. The trio hire private eye Sam Spade (Humphrey Bogart) to find it. Bogart's portrayal of the laconic Spade pushed him into the top rank of stars, inaugurating a succession of thrillers featuring hard-boiled detectives. Huston created a brooding, shadowy world, often placing characters in the foreground, giving their mute reactions greater weight than was usual at the time.

CREDITS

Studio	Warner Bros.
Producer	Hal B. Wallis
Screenplay	John Huston, from the novel by Dashiell Hammett
Cinematography	Arthur Edeson
Music	Adolph Deutsch

In a hotel lobby, Sam Spade (Bogart) confronts the hired gunman, Wilmer Cook (Elisha Cook Jr.). Bogart is superb as the sentimental anti-hero who lives by his own code of ethics.

Humphrey Bogart cornered the market in cool, streetwise investigators after his performance in *The Maltese Falcon*.

The Little Foxes

DIRECTOR William Wyler

RELEASED 1941

William Wyler's classy adaptation of Lillian Hellman's lush, hothouse stage drama about an avaricious Southern family in the early 1900s featured Bette Davis at her bitchy best.

Wisely refraining from "opening up" Hellman's play, Wyler and his cinematographer exploited the claustrophobic atmosphere of the house where the Giddens family's power struggles take place. At the film's centre is Regina Giddens (Davis) – passionate, thwarted, tyrannical, and greedy. She conspires with her brothers to grab the family fortune, only to deceive and blackmail them. The use of deep-focus photography is particularly effective in a scene in which Regina refuses to give her husband (Herbert Marshall) his medicine when he is in the throes of a heart attack, choosing instead to watch him from the background as he struggles in the foreground. This was the last of three films Davis and Wyler made together, the others being *Jezebel* (1938) and *The Letter* (1940).

Regina (Bette Davis), in an Oscar-nominated performance, talks business with her brother Ben Hubbard (Charles Dingle, right) and industrialist William Marshall (Russell Hicks) over coffee.

CREDITS

Studio	RKO
Producer	Samuel Goldwyn
Screenplay	Lillian Hellman, from her play of the same name
Cinematography	Gregg Toland

To Be Or Not To Be

DIRECTOR Ernst Lubitsch

RELEASED 1942

During the dark times of World War II, Lubitsch directed one of Hollywood's greatest comedies. *To Be Or Not To Be* took the Nazi occupation of Poland as its theme and, as anti-Nazi propaganda, it was more effective than many "serious" attempts.

Carole Lombard and Jack Benny play Maria and Joseph Tura, who head a troupe of Shakespearean actors trapped in Warsaw when the Nazis march into Poland. When asked his opinion of Joseph, the comic Gestapo chief, "Concentration Camp" Ehrhardt (Sig Ruman), says, "What he did to Shakespeare, we're now doing to Poland". Although the jokes come thick and fast, the situation comes across as horrific. When the film was released, no one was in the mood to laugh: Pearl Harbor had been attacked by Japan, the Nazis were sweeping across Europe, and Lombard had been killed in a plane crash; but over the years, the film has become a classic.

CREDITS

Studio	United Artists
Producer	Alexander Korda, Ernst Lubitsch
Screenplay	Edwin Justus Mayer, Melchior Lengyel
Cinematography	Rudolph Maté

Professor Alexander Siletsky (Stanley Ridges) raises a glass to Maria (Carole Lombard). The Polish academic is actually a Nazi spy intent on destroying the Resistance.

» **Captain Edward V. Kinross** (Noël Coward) addresses his crew before their ship is sunk by enemy forces.

In Which We Serve

DIRECTOR Noël Coward, David Lean

RELEASED 1942

A tribute to those serving in the Royal Navy during World War II, *In Which We Serve* captured the prevailing mood of Britain at the time.

This "story of a ship" is told in flashback by the survivors of HMS *Torrin*, a bombed British destroyer, as they cling to a life raft in May 1941. The *Torrin* has been patrolling Europe's coastline as part of Britain's defence against German warships, but is sunk by enemy action off Crete. Led by Noël Coward as Captain Kinross, an archetypal British commander, the crew hope and pray for rescue. While waiting, some of them look back on the events of the war, including the evacuation of Dunkirk in 1940, and the loss of many of their comrades.

Permeating the film is a deep love for the ship, which symbolizes the unity of the nation without resorting to false heroics or flag-waving. The behaviour of the crew, all of whom "knew their places" on the social scale, was presented as the ideal model for the behaviour of a society at war. Coward also wrote and produced the film, and composed its music. The movie also features a 19-year-old Richard Attenborough, in his debut role of a callow stoker who deserts his post.

CREDITS

Production	Two Cities Films
Producer	Noël Coward
Screenplay	Noël Coward
Cinematography	Ronald Neame
Awards	Special Academy Award for "outstanding production achievement"

» **Ordinary Seaman Shorty Blake** (John Mills), one of the crew of HMS *Torrin*, begins a courtship with Freda Lewis (Kay Walsh) on a train.

The love between Ilsa (Ingrid Bergman) and Rick (Humphrey Bogart) is rekindled as she makes one last effort to get the transit papers for her resistance-fighter husband to be able to escape Casablanca.

Casablanca

DIRECTOR Michael Curtiz

RELEASED 1942

The strong plot, the exotic setting, the quotable piquant dialogue, the cherished performances from a magnificent cast, and the emotional score by Max Steiner – not forgetting Dooley Wilson as Sam playing *As Time Goes By* – have ensured that *Casablanca* remains the epitome of the 1940s Hollywood romance.

American forces liberated French North Africa in the same year that *Casablanca* was released, which gave the movie a topical title. Most of the film takes place in and around the Café Américain, which is run by Rick Blaine (Humphrey Bogart), a cynical isolationist and gun-runner. He gets involved in the Free French cause in order to help Victor Laszlo (Paul Henreid), a resistance leader who is married to Rick's former lover Ilsa Lund (Ingrid Bergman). The poignant and passionate team of Bogart and Bergman, with flashbacks to their love affair in pre-war Paris, is one of the most celebrated relationships in cinema history. Strangely, this most structured and beloved of films was made in a manner that left everyone on the set confused as to what was happening, except Michael Curtiz, who brought together all the subplots and huge supporting cast of this romantic war melodrama with his expert hand. As time goes by, *Casablanca* looks better and better.

CREDITS

Studio	Warner Bros.
Producer	Hal B. Wallis, Jack L. Warner
Screenplay	Julius J. Epstein, Philip G. Epstein, Howard Koch
Cinematography	Arthur Edeson
Music	Max Steiner
Awards	Academy Awards: Best Picture, Best Director, Best Screenplay

Film poster, 1942

Massimo Girotti (Gino) and Clara Calamai (Giovanna) play illicit lovers whose relationship is beginning to descend into guilt and mistrust.

Ossessione

DIRECTOR Luchino Visconti

RELEASED 1943

Ossessione was the first film to be referred to as Italian neorealist (see box, p.286), a label given by critic Antonio Pietrangeli, one of the film's screenwriters. It was also the first film to be directed by Luchino Visconti, whose use of natural settings and working-class characters served to inspire other Italian film-makers.

Gino (Massimo Girotti), a handsome drifter, and Giovanna (Clara Calamai), the beautiful and desperately unhappy wife of Bragana (Juan de Landa), an elderly and boorish innkeeper, embark on an affair. Their passion leads them to kill Bragana, after which their relationship drifts towards inevitable tragedy.

Visconti took James M. Cain's study of fatal lust in the rural US, *The Postman Always Rings Twice*, and brilliantly transplanted it to provincial Italy. Because it was wartime, Visconti was able to buy the rights of the novel, and therefore retained only the outline of the original. He even introduced a new character, whose presence further disrupts the already guilt-ridden central relationship. Although having professional actors, a well-defined plot, and visual formality make the film less neorealistic than its successors, its down-to-earth characters and evident sensuality contrasted vastly with the predominant bourgeois melodramas of the day. Initially cut and then withdrawn by Fascist censors, the film only reappeared after the war. Cain's novel had already been made into a film in France – *Le Dernier Tournant* (1939). It was to be remade in Hollywood in 1945 and 1981, and then in Hungary in 1998, under the title of *Passion*.

Film poster, 1943

CREDITS

Production	ICI Rome
Producer	Libero Solaroli
Screenplay	Luchino Visconti, Antonio Pietrangeli, Giuseppe De Santis, Mario Alicata, Gianni Puccini
Cinematography	Aldo Tonti, Domenico Scala

Children of Paradise

DIRECTOR Marcel Carné

RELEASED 1945

Marcel Carné described his film as a "homage to the theatre" and the script exudes the life and soul of France's theatrical tradition. The larger-than-life characters, the witty and profound dialogue, and the narrative skill and sweep of the production have placed this on many critics' lists as one of the greatest films ever made.

Children of Paradise is as complex and broad as a novel, although its action is confined to the world of Parisian theatre in the 1840s. *Paradis* (in its French title *Les Enfants du Paradis*) refers to the upper seats of the theatre where poorer viewers sat. Among the crowds that throng the boulevards in the film are classical actor Frédérick Lemaître (Pierre Brasseur), mime artist Debureau (Jean-Louis Barrault), and criminal Lacenaire (Marcel Herrand) – all based on real historical figures. All three are in love with the sensuous, free-spirited courtesan Garance (Arletty).

CREDITS

Production	S.N. Pathé Cinema
Screenplay	Jacques Prévert
Cinematography	Marc Fossard, Roger Hubert
Production Design	Léon Barsacq, Raymond Gabutti Alexandre Trauner
Music	Joseph Kosma
Costume Design	Antoine Mayo

The film came about because the Nazi occupation of Paris forced Carné and scriptwriter Jacques Prévert to make "escapist" movies, with no political content. Nevertheless, some commentators viewed Garance as a representation of Free France. Today, the film is seen as a richly entertaining and intensely romantic evocation of an epoch. Ironically, Arletty's career suffered due to a liaison with a Nazi officer. She was put under house arrest, forbidden to work for three years, and was not invited to the film's premiere.

The great mime artist Baptiste Debureau (Jean-Louis Barrault) performs with his father Anselme (Etienne Ducroux) and the alluring Garance (Arletty).

In the climactic sequence, a celestial judge and jury use the "stairway to heaven" to visit the unconscious Peter Carter and decide his fate.

A Matter of Life and Death

DIRECTOR Michael Powell, Emeric Pressburger

RELEASED 1946

In their fourth collaboration as producers, directors, and writers, Michael Powell and Emeric Pressburger delivered a richly comic film, which juxtaposed highly stylized fantasy with a morale-boosting depiction of Britain during World War II.

A British pilot, Peter Carter (David Niven), survives a plane crash only to discover that the powers above have made a mistake and that he was actually scheduled to die. As he fights for his life on the operating table under the loving eyes of American radio operator June (Kim Hunter), a debate takes place in heaven about whether or not to save him. Avoiding the obvious, the directors decided to shoot the scenes on Earth in Technicolor and the sequences "in heaven" in black-and-white. The link between the real world and the one in the mind of the pilot, is wittily represented by a mechanical staircase that uses modern technology to express a fantasy. One of the underlying aims of the plot was to celebrate the Anglo-American alliance that prevailed during World War II.

CREDITS

Production	The Archers
Producer	Michael Powell, Emeric Pressburger
Screenplay	Michael Powell, Emeric Pressburger
Cinematography	Jack Cardiff
Production Design	Alfred Junge

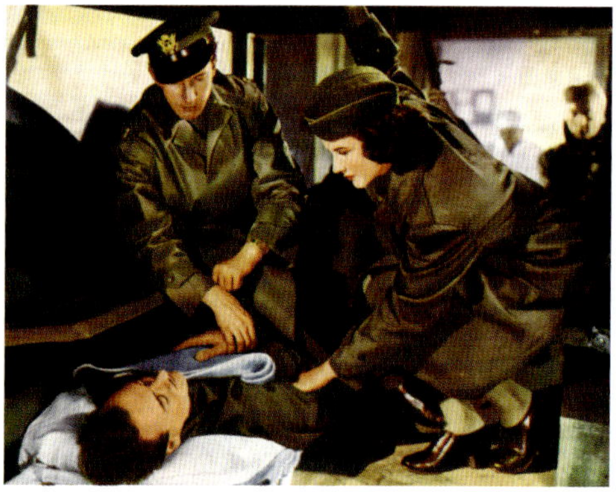

Back in the earthly realm, here represented by colour, June (Kim Hunter) comforts injured airman Peter Carter (David Niven) before he goes into the operating theatre.

It's a Wonderful Life

DIRECTOR Frank Capra

RELEASED 1946

Frank Capra called *It's a Wonderful Life* his favourite film and it is certainly loved by most audiences. It aims to impart the real meaning of the Christmas season, in a similar way to Charles Dickens' *A Christmas Carol*, and has certainly justified its perennial screening during the festive season.

The impetus and structure of *It's a Wonderful Life* recall Capra's pre-war successes, including *Mr. Deeds Goes to Town* (1936) and *Mr. Smith Goes to Washington* (1939), in which the heroes represent a civic ideal only to be opposed by the forces of corruption until they are redeemed by society as a whole. The character of George Bailey (James Stewart) embodies the quintessential Capra-esque "little man". He falls in love with Mary (Donna Reed), but financial troubles send him into a spiral of despair. Teetering on the verge of suicide, he is rescued by Clarence (Henry Travers), his guardian angel, who shows him how different the world would have been if he had never been born; Bedford Falls, the idealized small US town in which Bailey grew up, has become a cesspool of big-city ways in this alternate reality. Found too whimsical and sentimental for post-war audiences, the film failed on its initial release, but became popular with time.

CREDITS

Studio	RKO
Production	Liberty Films
Producer	Frank Capra
Screenplay	Frank Capra, Frances Goodrich, Albert Hackett, from the story *The Greatest Gift* by Philip Van Doren Stern
Cinematography	Joseph Walker, Joseph Biroc
Music	Dimitri Tiomkin

Film poster, 1946

In the celebrated final scene of the film, Bailey (James Stewart) realizes the value of the love of his family, having been rescued by his guardian angel.

Bicycle Thieves

DIRECTOR Vittorio De Sica

RELEASED 1948

Of all the movies dubbed "Italian neorealist" (see box), Vittorio De Sica's *Bicycle Thieves* (*Ladri di biciclette*) is the most beloved and moving. Despite improved social conditions in Italy, the film is still as poignant today as when it was made, because it contains one of the most believable portrayals of a father-son relationship on screen.

Bewildered and despairing, Bruno (Enzo Staiola) joins his father on the search for his stolen bicycle, showing his filial loyalty.

Filmed on location in the working-class districts of Rome, *Bicycle Thieves* tells the simple story of an unemployed man who is offered a job as a bill sticker, provided he has a bicycle. He borrows money from a pawnbroker to buy a bike, but it is stolen on his first day of work. He then spends the day with his young son, desperately searching for the bicycle and the thief. He discovers that the thief was just as needy as he is and considers stealing a bicycle himself, thus showing that anybody is capable of theft in certain circumstances. After De Sica's success in the US with *Shoeshine* (1946), American producer David O. Selznick offered to make *Bicycle Thieves* with Cary Grant, but De Sica refused, raised the money himself, and continued to work with non-professional actors in real locations. His insistence paid off – it was this un-Hollywood-like quality that gave the film its wide appeal.

CREDITS

Production	Produzioni De Sica
Producer	Giuseppe Amato, Vittorio De Sica
Screenplay	Cesare Zavattini, Oreste Biancoli, Suso D'Amico, Vittorio De Sica, Adolfo Franci, Gerardo Guerrieri
Cinematography	Carlo Montuori
Awards	Academy Award: Special Foreign Language Film Award

ITALIAN NEOREALISM

The origins of Italian neorealism can be traced to the "realist" or *verismo* style of Verga and others. It influenced Italian silent cinema, which portrayed human suffering in natural settings. The neorealists of the 1940s returned to these themes, reacting against frivolity. Films such as Vittorio De Sica's ***Shoeshine*** (1946), Roberto Rossellini's ***Paisà*** (1946), Luchino Visconti's ***La Terra Trema*** (1948), and Giuseppe De Santis' ***Bitter Rice*** (1949), dealt with the problems of working-class people and the social conditions that caused them.

Roma, Città Aperta (*Rome, Open City*, 1945) was an early neorealist film, shot in real locations, and using local people as well as professional actors.

Stefan (Louis Jourdan), a self-absorbed concert pianist, finally realizes the consequences of his actions as he reads a letter from a dying Lisa.

Letter from an Unknown Woman

DIRECTOR Max Ophüls

RELEASED 1948

The second of German émigré Max Ophüls' four Hollywood movies, *Letter from an Unknown Woman* is set in a lovingly evoked turn-of-the-century Vienna. It is the only one of his Hollywood films that came close to mirroring his sensuous and sumptuous European work, and is that rare thing – a Hollywood art movie.

In this bittersweet romance of unrequited love, Lisa Berndle (Joan Fontaine in a touching performance) hero-worships her handsome concert-pianist neighbour, Stefan Brand (Louis Jourdan), from a distance. After several years they meet and have a short-lived affair, but he disappears from her life again. The film, recounted in flashbacks, suggests that Lisa, blind to reality, lives in a romantic dream world in which her love can never be fulfilled. Seen from a female perspective, however, the movie also reveals the shallowness of a man's perception of a woman. Ophüls changed the original ending of Stefan Zweig's story by sending the hero to certain death in a duel. On its release in the US, it was dismissed as too sentimental, but it was later celebrated as one of the most evocative "European" films ever made in Hollywood.

CREDITS

Production	Rampart
Producer	John Houseman
Studio	Universal International
Screenplay	Howard Koch, from the story by Stefan Zweig
Cinematography	Franz Planer

> “By the time you finish reading this letter, **I'll be dead.**”

Opening lines of Lisa's letter to Stefan

In her modest apartment, Lisa (Joan Fontaine) reflects on her glamorous encounter with Stefan.

Fire wardens Shirley (Barbara Murray) and Arthur (Stanley Holloway) discover a centuries-old document that identifies Pimlico as French territory, not British.

Passport to Pimlico

DIRECTOR Henry Cornelius

RELEASED 1949

A tribute to the war effort and the stoical British character, *Passport to Pimlico* exudes good humour and social observation. It is also an expression of hope in the period following World War II.

EALING COMEDY

Although Ealing Studios made dramas and war films, they will always be associated with the particular brand of comedy they produced between 1947 and 1955. With rare exceptions, they used original scripts from the studio's own writers, principally T.E.B. Clarke, who wrote *Passport to Pimlico* (1949), *The Lavender Hill Mob* (1951), and *The Titfield Thunderbolt* (1953). The films generally dealt with a small group of people in a naturalistic social setting, making much of the indomitable, if somewhat idealized, British spirit.

The Ladykillers (1955), starring Alec Guinness and Peter Sellers, ended a short period of black comedy at Ealing Studios, which began with *Hue and Cry* (1947).

The film is set in the small district of Pimlico, in post-war London. A wartime bomb explodes, revealing treasures from Burgundy, France. Among these is a manuscript that claims, according to local historian Professor Hatton-Jones (Margaret Rutherford), that Pimlico is, by ancient law, a Burgundian possession. The inhabitants are no longer bound by wartime restrictions and austerity; instead they can operate outside British law by destroying their ration books and drinking at all hours. Border crossings are set up and customs officers patrol local trains.

An Ealing comedy (see box), this delightful film shows ordinary people in a small community making extraordinary things happen. It pokes fun at the new Labour government, but is too gentle to be classified as satire; when Pimlico is forced to rejoin Britain at the end, the spirit of compromise is celebrated.

CREDITS

Studio	Ealing
Producer	Michael Balcon
Screenplay	T.E.B. Clarke
Cinematography	Lionel Banes

The Third Man

DIRECTOR Carol Reed

RELEASED 1949

One of the most effective British thrillers, ***The Third Man*** derives its look from German expressionism (see box, p.259), Italian neorealism (see box, 286), and the work of Orson Welles. He appears for only about 20 minutes, but his presence is felt throughout.

Graham Greene's novella was meant to serve as the source material for the screenplay, but it was published after the film. This dark yet playful movie studies the effect of post-war economic and social corruption on war-torn Vienna. It was the first British film shot almost entirely on location. The sense of locale, making the shattered city an integral part of the action, and the black-and-white cinematography, add to the film's atmosphere. The moment when Welles – as the presumed-dead racketeer Harry Lime – reappears, is legendary. In the sequence, Holly Martins (Joseph Cotten) is searching for his friend through the night-time streets of Vienna. A cat miaows in a doorway. Martins turns and, as Anton Karas' zither music peaks, the cat is seen licking a pair of shoes. As the camera rises, Welles' face emerges.

The film begins and ends with the same scene: the funeral and burial of Harry Lime. The first funeral pronounces him the unfortunate victim of an accident, but the second identifies him as an unrepentant mass murderer.

CREDITS

Production	British Lion, London Film Productions
Producer	Carol Reed
Screenplay	Graham Greene
Cinematography	Robert Krasker
Art Director	Vincent Korda
Music	Anton Karas
Awards	Academy Award: Best Black-and-White Cinematography; Cannes: Best Film

Carol Reed told cinematographer Robert Krasker to keep the camera at an angle, heightening the drama of the moment when Harry Lime (Orson Welles) reappears.

Orpheus (Jean Marais) presses his face against a mirror before he enters the Underworld through the glass in search of his wife Eurydice (Maria Déa).

Orpheus

DIRECTOR Jean Cocteau

RELEASED 1950

This witty and haunting film can be considered the centrepiece of Jean Cocteau's entire *oeuvre*. It forms part of his Orphic trilogy, along with ***The Blood of a Poet*** (1930) and ***Testament of Orpheus*** (1960). Cocteau himself described ***Orpheus*** (***Orphée***) as "a detective story, bathed on one side in myth and, on the other, the supernatural".

CREDITS

Production	Films du Palais Royal
Producer	André Paulvé
Screenplay	Jean Cocteau, based on his play of the same name
Cinematography	Nicolas Hayer
Production Design	Jean d'Eaubonne

The poet Orpheus (Jean Marais) falls in love with the Princess of Death (Maria Casarés). In turn, her chauffeur (François Périer) – the angel Heurtebise – is in love with the poet's wife, Eurydice (Marie Déa). Heurtebise takes Eurydice to the Underworld through a looking glass, with Orpheus following in order to bring her back. "Mirrors are the doors through which Death comes and goes. Look at yourself in a mirror all your life and you'll see Death at work like bees in a hive of glass," says the angel.

Although Cocteau uses reverse slow-motion and negative images to evoke the Underworld, the domestic life of Mr. and Mrs. Orpheus is filmed "realistically". This helps to elaborate the theme of the poet caught between the real and the imaginary, in a perfect marriage between Greek legend and the director's own mythology.

Orpheus holds an open book showing a photograph of Eurydice. Her presence, both in person and in a photograph, reflects the subtle interplay of reality and illusion in the film.

Rashomon

DIRECTOR Akira Kurosawa

RELEASED 1950

Akira Kurosawa's ***Rashomon*** was the first Japanese film to be shown widely in the West. This makes it significant beyond its indubitable qualities because it set the stage for even greater works by Kurosawa.

In feudal Japan, a samurai named Takehiro (Masayuki Mori) travels through the woods with his wife Masako (Machiko Kyo). She is raped by a bandit (Toshiro Mifune), who also kills her husband. At the trial, the incident is described in four conflicting, yet equally credible versions – by the bandit, the wife, a priest (Minoru Chiaki), and a woodcutter (Takashi Shimura) – demonstrating the subjective nature of truth. The film's popularity was as much due to its intriguing story and forceful performances as for its unfamiliar background. By the time ***Rashomon*** (named after the ruined stone gate where the tale is told) awakened Western audiences to Japanese cinema, Kurosawa was already an established director in his own country. The film was remade in Hollywood as the Western ***The Outrage*** (1964), one of three Kurosawa samurai movies to be adapted in the Hollywood style.

POINT OF VIEW

Point of view (POV) is a shot filmed at such a camera angle that an object or an action appears to be seen through the eyes of a particular character. This is achieved by placing the camera beside the actor or at the spot he or she would occupy on set. The other actors look at the point where the character is supposed to be, rather than at the camera itself. One extreme example of POV was Robert Montgomery's ***Lady in the Lake*** (1947), in which a subjective camera was used to tell the whole story as seen by the film's protagonist Phillip Marlowe.

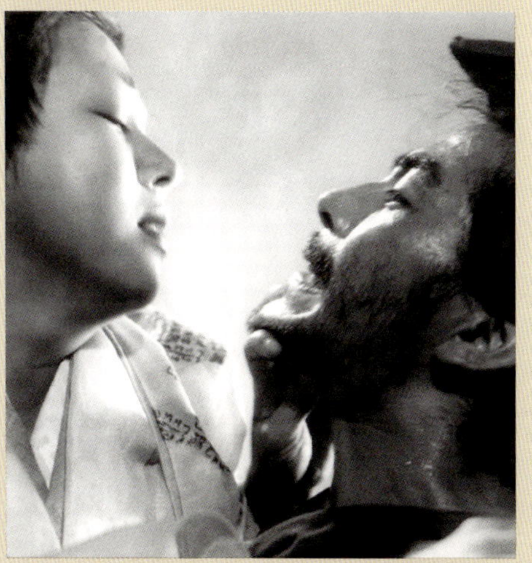

Masako cradles a dying Takehiro. Viewed through the multiple points of view of ***Rashomon***, the events leading to Takehiro's death reveal the relativity of truth.

This combat scene in the woods displays stunning light and shade effects.

CREDITS

Studio	Daiei
Producer	Minoru Jingo
Screenplay	Akira Kurosawa, Shinobu Hashimoto, from two short novels by Ryunosuke Akutagawa
Cinematography	Kazuo Miyagawa
Awards	Academy Award: Honorary Award for "most outstanding foreign language film released in the USA in 1951" Venice: Best Film

Film poster, 1952

Singin' in the Rain

DIRECTOR Gene Kelly, Stanley Donen

RELEASED 1952

CREDITS

Studio	MGM
Producer	Arthur Freed
Screenplay	Betty Comden, Adolph Green
Cinematography	Harold Rosson
Music	Arthur Freed, Nacio Herb Brown, Betty Comden, Johnny Green, Roger Edens

Considered the apogee of MGM musicals, *Singin' in the Rain* is a delightful mixture of nostalgia and affectionate satire on the turmoil and triumphs that beset the transition from silent films to the talkies. The era is splendidly conjured up by the period settings and costumes, and a series of wonderfully staged numbers.

Producer Arthur Freed, the supremo of the MGM movie musical, brought together an expert team. Many of the songs he had previously written, along with Nacio Herb Brown, for *The Hollywood Review of 1929* (1929) were integrated into the plotline – including the liberating title number. This famous song showed off the balletic and hoofing skills of Gene Kelly as Don Lockwood to memorable effect. Kelly's talents were also seen in the Broadway ballet sequence, while Donald O'Connor's electrifying comedy-dance routine, *Make 'Em Laugh*, was the peak of his career. In one part, Kathy Selden (ingénue Debbie Reynolds, sparkling in her first major role) has to dub the voice of Lina Lamont, a movie star from the silent era (played unforgettably by Jean Hagen), because Lina's voice is found too squeaky for movies with sound. Ironically, Debbie's singing voice was, in turn, dubbed by Betty Royce, who remained uncredited.

During the fantasy dance sequence, Don Lockwood (Gene Kelly) is bewitched by the seductive nightclub dancer and gangster's moll (Cyd Charisse).

Chishu Ryu (left), Setsuko Hara (middle), and Chieko Higashiyama share a moment in a domestic scene, shot at floor level.

Tokyo Story

DIRECTOR Yasujirô Ozu

RELEASED 1953

One of the finest films of Yasujirô Ozu's last decade, and one which continually appears in "best ever" lists of critics, ***Tokyo Story*** (***Tokyo Monogatari***) belatedly made the Japanese director's name in the West, mainly when it was released in the US in 1972, almost 20 years after it was made.

An elderly couple (Chishu Ryu and Chieko Higashiyama), who live by the sea in south Japan, pay a visit to their children and grandchildren in Tokyo. No one shows them much affection, except for Noriko (Setsuko Hara), their widowed daughter-in-law. "Be kind to your parents when they are alive. Filial piety cannot reach beyond the grave" – so says a simple Japanese proverb. Instead, the old couple are made to feel like a burden on their grown-up children. When they return home, the wife dies, leaving her husband to face an unknown future.

Tokyo Story was a prime example of *shomin-geki*, defined as a family melodrama. Yet this radiant, gentle, heartbreaking, and perceptive investigation of the tensions within a family, generation gap, old age, and pressures of city life, is far from the West's idea of melodrama. There are remarkable performances in the film and a creative use of sound – chugging boats, train noise – and ravishing exteriors punctuating the subtle interior sequences. Ozu shoots his story with as little camera movement as possible, in an attempt to make the balance of every scene perfect.

CREDITS

Production	Shochiku
Producer	Takeshi Yamamoto
Screenplay	Yasujirô Ozu, Kôgo Noda
Cinematography	Yuharu Atsuta
Music	Takanobu (or Kojun) Saitô

This poster was for the Academy Cinema, London, now defunct.

Edie (Saint) talks to Terry (Brando) on a tenement rooftop beside a pigeon coop. The coop belonged to Edie's brother, for whose death Terry is partly responsible.

On the Waterfront

DIRECTOR Elia Kazan

RELEASED 1954

A shatteringly powerful melodrama of social conscience, *On the Waterfront* was shot on location in New York. It reveals Elia Kazan's mastery in dealing with realistic settings and personal conflicts, highlighted by a naturalistic, improvisatory style of acting, which the director brought to cinema from the Actors Studio.

The plot follows a group of dock labourers in the clutches of an unscrupulous union boss (Lee J. Cobb). The labourers eventually confront their exploiter with the aid of a former union henchman and washed-up boxer Terry Malloy (Marlon Brando), a liberal priest (Karl Malden), and a courageous young woman (Eva Marie Saint). The film is seen as Kazan's reply to those who criticized him for naming Communists during the McCarthy investigations in 1952 (see p.31). Brando's deeply felt characterization dominates the movie. Especially memorable is the scene that takes place in a taxi between Terry and his brother Charley (Rod Steiger), in which he says poignantly, "I coulda had class. I coulda been somebody. I coulda been a contender instead of a bum, which is what I am". The photography and music score greatly enhance the mood of the film.

CREDITS

Studio	Columbia
Producer	Sam Spiegel
Screenplay	Budd Schulberg
Cinematography	Boris Kaufman
Music	Leonard Bernstein
Awards	Academy Awards: Best Picture, Best Director, Best Actor (Brando), Best Supporting Actress (Eva Marie Saint), Best Story and Screenplay, Best Art Direction (Richard Day), Best Editing (Gene Milford); Venice Silver Prize

All That Heaven Allows

DIRECTOR Douglas Sirk

RELEASED 1955

Although Douglas Sirk's *All That Heaven Allows* has the appearance of a lush soap opera and is enjoyable at that level, it is also a thinly disguised, scathing critique of American suburbia and a potent analysis of a middle-class woman's social oppression.

Cary Scott (Jane Wyman) is an attractive widow in a prominent social position in a New England town. However, when she becomes romantically involved with her gardener, Ron Kirby (Rock Hudson, Sirk's favourite actor), a much younger man, she is ostracized by her peers and condemned by her grown-up children. One of the most effective scenes is when her children, after trying to break up her relationship with Hudson, give her a television set as a Christmas present to occupy her time. The sequence ends with her reflection on the television's blank screen as she watches it in her empty house. The fluid camerawork, the inventive use of colour, and the intensity of the performances transcend the usual "woman's weepie" format. Rainer Werner Fassbinder used the movie as a model for his film *Fear Eats the Soul* (1973), and Todd Haynes' *Far From Heaven* (2002) paid direct homage to it.

CREDITS

Production	Universal International
Producer	Ross Hunter
Screenplay	Peg Fenwick
Cinematography	Russell Metty

Film poster, 1955

Widow Cary (Jane Wyman) defies convention and finds troubled happiness in the strong arms of her gardener Ron (Rock Hudson).

Rebel Without a Cause

DIRECTOR Nicholas Ray

RELEASED 1955

Rebel Without a Cause, a disenchanted cry of youth alienated from the adult world, will always be synonymous with its star, James Dean, in the role that did most to create his image and posthumous fame.

At the core of this inappropriately titled film (the rebels do have a "cause" – to be loved and understood as individuals) are the rebels' strained relationship with their parents. The movie focuses on three youngsters: "Plato" (Sal Mineo), whose divorced parents have abandoned him; Judy (Natalie Wood), who feels her father has withdrawn his love; and Jim (James Dean), who is being torn apart by his domineering mother and weak father. Unlike many of the teen rebel films that followed, this one places the blame on the parents rather than the teenagers. The main action takes place over one day and includes a knife fight, a "chicken run" (a high-speed race in hot rod cars up to the edge of a cliff), and a love affair between Jim and Judy. Nicholas Ray, making his first film in CinemaScope (a format in which he would become a master), caught the immediate and timeless qualities of frustrated adolescence. Strangely, all three of the film's young stars died violent and unnatural deaths: Dean was killed in a car crash, Mineo was murdered, and Wood drowned in mysterious circumstances.

CREDITS

Studio	Warner Bros.
Producer	David Weisbart
Screenplay	Stewart Stern
Cinematography	Ernest Haller

Jim (James Dean, far right) goes to the police station after teenage gang leader Buzz (Corey Allen) is killed in a "chicken run", and meets Buzz's fellow gang members coming out.

« **Durga** (Uma Das Gupta) offers a stolen guava to her great-aunt Indir Thakrun (Chunibala Devi).

Pather Panchali

DIRECTOR Satyajit Ray

RELEASED 1955

Out of an Indian film industry at the time almost entirely dominated by formulaic, escapist musical films, Satyajit Ray suddenly appeared on the international scene with this Bengali-language masterpiece. *Pather Panchali* completely altered Western notions of Indian cinema.

Shot in natural surroundings with non-professional actors, the film revolves around Apu, a young boy who lives in a small Bengal village with his parents, his sister Durga, and an aged great-aunt, on the borderline of poverty. The title means "song of the little road", and the film's leitmotif is travel – of vistas beyond the confines of the tiny rural community. There are the travelling players viewed with wonder by Apu, and the lyrical sequence when he runs with his sister through a field of tall grass towards the railway line to see a train taking people to a big city. Apu was to take this journey himself in *Aparajito* (*The Unvanquished*, 1956), the second part of the trilogy that concludes with *Apur Sansar* (*The World of Apu*, 1959). Ray had difficulty raising funds for his debut film and was about to abandon shooting after 18 months, when he was rescued by the West Bengal government.

CREDITS

Production	Government of West Bengal
Screenplay	Satyajit Ray, from the novel by Bibhutibhushan Bandyopadhyay
Cinematography	Subrata Mitra
Music	Ravi Shankar

« **Harihar Ray** (Kanu Bannerjee), Apu's father, is shattered by the news of his daughter's death.

The Night of the Hunter

DIRECTOR Charles Laughton

RELEASED 1955

Actor Charles Laughton's only directorial venture is an eerily beautiful parable of good and evil, its bold visual style derived from German expressionism (see box, p.259) and American primitive paintings. The presence of Lillian Gish as Rachel, representing the spirit of healing, echoes the rural dramas of D.W. Griffith.

The plot focuses on psychopathic preacher Harry Powell (Robert Mitchum), who obtains money for "the Lord's work" by marrying and murdering rich widows. Powell sets his sights on Willa Harper (Shelley Winters), whose husband has hidden a huge sum of stolen money and is on Death Row. Only the couple's children, John (Billy Chapin) and Pearl (Sally Jane Bruce), know where the money is. Harry marries and kills Willa, but the children flee down a river, finding refuge with an old woman, Rachel (Gish). Evil (Powell) is destroyed by the forces of good and innocence as represented by the old lady, the children, nature, and animals – all atmospherically photographed. The singular Mitchum pursuing the children through a nocturnal landscape, Gish guarding the orphans like a mother hen, and the murdered Winters' hair flowing underwater are some of cinema's most haunting images. Sadly, the film's failure at the box office dissuaded Laughton from directing another film.

CREDITS

Studio	United Artists
Producer	Paul Gregory
Screenplay	James Agee (rewritten by Laughton, uncredited), based on the novel by Davis Grubb
Cinematography	Stanley Cortez

With the words "love" and "hate" tattooed on his hands, Robert Mitchum gives an unforgettable performance as a psychopath posing as a pastor in the hunt for prey.

Death (Bengt Ekerot) plays chess with the knight (Max von Sydow), who hopes to extend his time on Earth by beating the Grim Reaper.

The Seventh Seal

DIRECTOR Ingmar Bergman

RELEASED 1957

Ingmar Bergman's 17th film placed him firmly in the pantheon of great directors. Shot in only 35 days, this powerful morality tale depicts, in luminous images derived from early church paintings, the cruelty of medieval life – including witch-burning and flagellations – as well as the joy and noble aspirations of humankind.

Antonius Block (Max von Sydow), a 14th-century knight, returns from the Crusades with his earthy and cynical squire (Gunnar Björnstrand) to find Sweden ravaged by the plague. In his search for God, Block meets a group of strolling players, suffering peasants, and Death (Bengt Ekerot), with whom he plays a deadly game of chess in an attempt to save his life.

The Seventh Seal (*Det Sjunde Inseglet*), which Bergman called "a film oratorio", is one of the first in his mature works. Shot in a highly individual style, the film is full of religious imagery, which, paradoxically, expresses a Godless universe. Bergman's figure of Death expresses his thoughts about existence and religion.

Tall, gaunt, and imposing, von Sydow made his mark in cinema with his portrayal of a man in spiritual turmoil. The cast also included Bibi Andersson, who worked in 13 films with Bergman.

CREDITS

Production	Svensk Filmindustri
Producer	Allan Ekelund
Screenplay	Bergman, from his play *Wood Painting*
Cinematography	Gunnar Fischer

Silhouetted against the sky, Death is seen holding his scythe and leading the knight and his followers in a macabre medieval dance.

In the opening scene, police officer John Ferguson (James Stewart) is frozen by fear as he clings precariously to a rooftop gutter.

Saul Bass, one of America's most renowned graphic designers, created this poster for *Vertigo*.

Vertigo

DIRECTOR Alfred Hitchcock

RELEASED 1958

Although *Vertigo* was a commercial and critical flop when it was first released, its reputation has grown gradually over time, and it is now widely considered to be Alfred Hitchcock's finest achievement. The reassessment has come about because of a deeper understanding of Hitchcock's films – of which *Vertigo* is a supreme example – both in theme and style.

Private detective John "Scottie" Ferguson (James Stewart) quits the San Francisco police force because he has developed a pathological fear of heights. He is hired by a friend, Gavin Elster (Tom Helmore) to follow his suicidal wife Madeleine (Kim Novak) around San Francisco. Scottie falls in love with Madeleine as he watches her day after day, but is unable to prevent her fatal leap from a bell tower because of his fear of heights. Following her death, the distraught Scottie meets Judy (also played by Novak), who reminds him of Madeleine. He tries to turn Judy, a brunette, into the exact image of the blonde he had loved.

Vertigo is an absorbing study of sexual obsession, which makes the twists in the plot almost irrelevant. With its central tragic love story, it is one of the few Hitchcock films to move audiences emotionally. It has also been acclaimed for its innovative use of camera techniques, such as forward zoom and reverse tracking shots, to intensify the atmosphere of suspense. Seldom has picturesque San Francisco looked so alluring as in the film's sharp-edged Technicolor photography; nor has Bernard Herrmann's yearning music ever been so effective. Kim Novak's cool, somnambulist manner accords perfectly with the dream-like atmosphere as she lures James Stewart to his doom.

CREDITS

Studio	Paramount
Producer	Alfred Hitchcock
Screenplay	Alec Coppel, Samuel Taylor
Cinematography	Robert Burks
Music	Bernard Herrmann
Title Design	Saul Bass

Ashes and Diamonds

DIRECTOR Andrzej Wajda

RELEASED 1958

Polish cinema burst onto the scene with Andrzej Wajda's lively war trilogy about the young people's resistance movement in Warsaw. The third part, ***Ashes and Diamonds*** (***Popiól i Diament***), which followed ***A Generation*** (1955) and ***Kanal*** (1957), is perhaps Wajda's finest work, its enigmatic twilight world communicating the "Polish experience" during World War II far beyond the country's frontiers.

On the last day of World War II in 1945, Maciek (Zbigniew Cybulski), the youngest member of a Nationalist underground movement in a provincial Polish town, is ordered to kill Szczuka (Waclaw Zastrzezynski), the new Communist District Secretary. As Maciek waits in a hotel during the night, he meets and falls in love with a barmaid Krystyna (Ewa Krzyzewska) and learns that there is something more to life than killing – the possibility of love and happines. He is soon torn between his conscience and loyalty to the cause he has lived for. The assassination scene, the climactic slow-motion dance to Polish music known as Polonaise, and Maciek's death scene are all stunningly realized. In a complex characterization, the brilliant Cybulski, his eyes hidden by dark glasses, embodies the sceptical new generation and establishes his reputation as "the Polish James Dean". The actor was killed while running for a train in 1967 at the age of 40.

» **The remarkable Zbigniew Cybulski** plays Maciek, who, having been shot during a chase, besmirches white sheets hanging on a line with his blood.

CREDITS

Production	Film Polski
Screenplay	Jerzy Andrzejewski, Andrzej Wajda, from the novel by Andrzejewski
Cinematography	Jerzy Wojcik
Music	Filip Novak, Jan Krenz

Some Like It Hot

DIRECTOR Billy Wilder

RELEASED 1959

A high-water mark in American post-war comedy, Billy Wilder's *Some Like It Hot* is an amalgam of parody, slapstick, farce, and sophistication. With its modern, liberal sexual approach, the film is nostalgic in its tribute to the screwball comedies and gangster movies of the 1930s.

Two jazz musicians (played by Tony Curtis and Jack Lemmon), on the run from gangsters, disguise themselves as "Josephine" and "Daphne" and join an all-girl band on the way to Florida. On the train, they befriend Sugar Kane (Marilyn Monroe), the band's singer. Complications occur when "Josephine" falls in love with Sugar, and "Daphne" is courted by millionaire Osgood Fielding III (Joe E. Brown). When "Daphne" finally admits he is a man, Osgood replies, in one of the most memorable punchlines in cinematic history, "Well, nobody's perfect". Curtis and Lemmon give two of Hollywood's best cross-dressing portrayals, with Curtis offering a triple treat – as his wise-guy self, as a woman with a dark wig and a high-pitched voice, and as an oil tycoon who sounds like Cary Grant. Lemmon, in high-heeled shoes, a flapper's frock, and a blond wig, is hilarious, while Monroe brings sensitivity to her role, and sings two zippy numbers from the 1920s.

CREDITS

Studio	United Artists
Production	Mirisch Company
Screenplay	Billy Wilder, I.A.L. Diamond
Cinematography	Charles Lang
Music	Adolph Deutsch
Awards	Academy Award: Costume Design

Sugar Kane (Marilyn Monroe), in rehearsal with her band on the train to Florida, belts out *Runnin' Wild*; while Tony Curtis and Jack Lemmon can be seen over her right shoulder.

Film poster, 1959

Jack Lemmon and Tony Curtis as Jerry/ Daphne and Joe/ Josephine, on the set of *Some Like It Hot*.

The 400 Blows

DIRECTOR François Truffaut

RELEASED 1959

Francois Truffaut's first feature film, made when he was 27 years old, was based on his own deprived childhood. It was an immediate success, winning the Best Director prize at Cannes. It also helped to launch the French New Wave (see pp.42–43) and started a series of films following the character Antoine Doinel (Jean-Pierre Léaud) through adolescence, marriage, fatherhood, and divorce.

NOUVELLE VAGUE

This term described the New Wave of directors who made their first feature films in France during the years following 1959. The main impetus for the French movement came from the critics-turned-directors of the influential magazine *Cahiers du Cinéma*, headed by François Truffaut and Jean-Luc Godard. The latter was perhaps the greatest and most radical of the French New Wave directors.

CREDITS

Production	Les Films du Carrosse
Producer	Georges Charlot
Screenplay	Marcel Moussy from an original story by Truffaut
Cinematography	Henri Decaë
Music	Jean Constantin
Awards	Cannes: Best Director

A harsh critic writing for *Cahiérs du Cinéma*, Truffaut was challenged by his movie-producer father-in-law to make a film himself. ***The 400 Blows*** was the triumphant result. The title comes from a colloquial expression *faire les quatre cents coups*, meaning "to get into a lot of trouble". A 12-year-old Parisian boy, Antoine, neglected by his mother and stepfather, plays truant and takes to petty crime. He is placed in a reform school, but escapes to the coast. The film has a wonderful freewheeling atmosphere as it follows Antoine through the streets of Paris. Much of the film's quality is due to Jean-Pierre Léaud's spontaneous performance. The freeze frame shot of his face as he runs towards the sea is one of cinema's most celebrated endings.

Breathless

DIRECTOR Jean-Luc Godard

RELEASED 1960

This greatly influential film made the anarchic Jean-Paul Belmondo a star, revitalized Jean Seberg's career, and established 29-year-old Jean-Luc Godard, in his first feature, as a leading member of the French New Wave (see pp.42–43).

The story of Michel Poiccard (Belmondo), a dashing young car thief, who kills a policeman and goes on the run with his American girlfriend Patricia Franchini (Seberg), was based on an idea by François Truffaut and dedicated to Monogram Pictures – Hollywood's all-B movie studio. ***Breathless*** (***A bout de souffle***) attempts to recapture the directness and economy of the American gangster movie by the superb use of location shooting, jump cuts (which eliminated the usual establishing shots), and a hand-held camera. Cinematographer Raoul Coutard, who has worked on many of the French New Wave films, was pushed around in a wheelchair, and used as a camera dollie, following the characters down the street and into buildings. In order to achieve an immediacy in the performances, Godard cued the actors, who were not allowed to learn their lines, during the takes. A former critic, he consciously broke conventions of film. At the same time, however, he paid homage to what he regarded as worth emulating in Hollywood cinema.

CREDITS

Studio	Impéria
Producer	Georges de Beauregard
Screenplay	Jean-Luc Godard
Cinematography	Raoul Coutard
Awards	Berlin: Best Director

La Dolce Vita

DIRECTOR Federico Fellini

RELEASED 1960

Causing a sensation when it was released, Federico Fellini's most (in)famous film is an impressive three-hour, widescreen panorama of decadent contemporary society in Rome. It introduced into the English language the expressions *la dolce vita* and *paparazzi* – the latter now synonymous with intrusive photographers who chase celebrities.

The film's story follows jaded gossip columnist and would-be serious writer Marcello Rubini (Marcello Mastroianni) through seven nights and seven days, as he rootlessly and amorally wanders around the hot spots of Rome in search of himself. At the metaphoric ending, he glimpses innocence in the form of a young girl on the beach at dawn, but a stretch of water separates them and he cannot hear what she is saying. There is imaginative brilliance in the notorious set pieces – a vast statue of Christ is flown over Rome; Marcello and a bored heiress pick up a prostitute for a *ménage à trois*; a high society orgy takes place, at which the hostess Nadia (Nadia Gray) performs a striptease; and Marcello sticks feathers on a woman and rides her like a horse. Especially memorable is Anita Ekberg as blonde starlet Sylvia, who calls out to Marcello in seductive tones at the striptease party.

Anita Ekberg, playing American starlet Sylvia, wanders tipsily into the Trevi Fountain in Rome.

CREDITS

Production	Pathé Consortium Cinema, Riama Film
Producer	Guiseppe Amato
Screenplay	Federico Fellini, Tullio Pinelli, Brunello Rondi, Ennio Flaiano
Cinematography	Otello Martelli
Music	Nino Rota
Costume Design	Piero Gherardi
Awards	Cannes: Best Film

Arthur Seaton (Albert Finney), an amoral, disenchanted, blue-collar worker, goes to bed with the married Brenda (Rachel Roberts) while her husband is working a night shift.

Saturday Night and Sunday Morning

DIRECTOR Karel Reisz

RELEASED 1960

One of British cinema's key works of the post-war period, and arguably the best and most honest of the British New Wave (see pp.41–42) movies that dealt with working-class life, Karel Reisz's first feature, *Saturday Night and Sunday Morning* turned Albert Finney, as the rebellious anti-hero, into a new kind of star.

"Don't let the bastards grind you down. That's one thing you learn. What I'm out for is a good time. All the rest is propaganda," says a defiant Arthur Seaton (Finney), who works at a lathe in the Raleigh factory in Nottingham, in the north of England. He has an affair with Brenda (Rachel Roberts), the wife of his colleague who later finds out. Brenda gets pregnant; in the meantime, Arthur has met Doreen (Shirley Anne Field) in a pub and marriage soon threatens. Albert Finney's "angry young man" gives the film its punch as he reacts against his surroundings with energy and humour. The film, with well-rounded, recognizable working-class characters rarely seen in British films until then, splendidly evokes the drab midland industrial setting – the factories, backstreets, canal banks, and pubs – and its effect on human relationships.

CREDITS

Production	Woodfall Film Productions
Producer	Tony Richardson, Harry Saltzman
Screenplay	Alan Sillitoe, from his novel
Cinematography	Freddie Francis
Music	John Dankworth

FREE CINEMA

In the mid-1950s, a group of British film-makers challenged orthodoxy in society and cinema. They stressed the social responsibility of the artist to make films free from commercial considerations, and to express the "significance of the everyday". Karel Reisz, Lindsay Anderson, and Tony Richardson were connected with the "Angry Young Men" of literature and the "kitchen sink" drama of theatre.

This poster for Tony Richardson's film adaptation of *Look Back in Anger* aptly reflects the impact of John Osborne's revolutionary play.

L'Avventura

DIRECTOR Michelangelo Antonioni

RELEASED 1960

After five features in ten years, Antonioni's style reached its maturity in *L'Avventura* (*The Adventure*). The minimal plot, long takes and slow tracking shots, limited dialogue, and strong relationship between the characters and their environment redefined views of time and space in cinema.

Anna (Lea Massari) and her fiancé Sandro (Gabriele Ferzetti) visit a Sicilian island with a group of wealthy people. After an argument with Sandro, Anna disappears. Her friend Claudia (Monica Vitti) joins Sandro to search for her, and they become lovers. The bitter ending is not a conventional resolution. Antonioni's refusal to explain Anna's disappearance outraged and disconcerted many when the movie was first released, although this did not stop the film from becoming a success. What matters is the effect the unsolved mystery has on the alienated characters, especially the ravishing Vitti in the first of many roles for Antonioni.

Best friends, Anna (Massari, left) and Claudia (Vitti) prepare to go off to spend a few days on a Sicilian island, from where Anna disappears.

CREDITS

Producer	Cino Del Duca, Amato Pennasilico, Luciano Perugia
Screenplay	Antonioni, Elio Bartolini, Tonino Guerra
Cinematography	Aldo Scarvarda
Music	Giovanni Fusco

Last Year at Marienbad

DIRECTOR Alain Resnais

RELEASED 1961

By rejecting a chronological structure and objective reality, and by mingling memory and imagination, desire and fulfilment, with past, present, and future, Alain Resnais created one of the most enigmatic, haunting, and erotic of ciné-poems.

In a vast, baroque mansion with geometrically designed gardens, X, an unnamed man (Giorgio Albertazzi) tries to convince A, a female guest (Delphine Seyrig) that they had had an affair the year before, and that she should leave M (Sacha Pitoëff), the man who might be her husband, for him. Although the style and structure puzzled many at the time, the interweaving of past and present, and the instant "flash-ins", instead of traditional slow flashbacks, have now become part of the vocabulary of contemporary film-making. On one level, *Last Year at Marienbad* (*L'Année Dernière à Marienbad*) is a variation on the eternal romantic triangle, expanded from the age-old "chat up" line, "Haven't we met somewhere before?" The stylized dresses, the organ music, the tracking shots down endless corridors, the dazzling décor, and the mysterious Seyrig are all unforgettable.

CREDITS

Producer	Pierre Courau, Raymond Froment
Screenplay	Alain Robbe-Grillet
Cinematography	Sacha Vierney
Music	Francis Seyrig
Awards	Venice: Jury Prize

Delphine Seyrig plays A, the nameless woman who does not remember whether she had an affair.

Lawrence of Arabia

DIRECTOR David Lean

RELEASED 1962

One of the most intelligent and spectacular blockbusters ever made, *Lawrence of Arabia* is a travelogue, a history lesson, and an adventure movie. Above all, it is a study of an enigmatic and controversial military figure. Peter O'Toole, in the title role, became a global star overnight.

The movie follows the adult life story of T.E. Lawrence, a British army officer who fought in Arabia. Based on Lawrence's memoirs, *The Seven Pillars of Wisdom*, the film's narrative begins with Lawrence's death in an accident in England. A flashback retraces the major stages of his military career: his friendship with Sherif Ali (Omar Sharif); his support of Prince Feisal (Alec Guinness); his capture and torture by the Turkish Bey (José Ferrer); and the central role he played in dismantling the Ottoman Empire.

CREDITS

Production	Horizon
Producer	Sam Spiegel
Screenplay	Robert Bolt, Michael Wilson, based on the memoirs of T.E. Lawrence
Cinematography	Frederick A. Young
Music	Maurice Jarre
Awards	Academy Awards: Best Picture, Best Director, Best Colour Cinematography, Best Colour Art Direction (John Box, John Stoll, Dario Simoni), Best Sound (John Cox), Best Film Editing (Anne Coates), Best Music Score

The story brought out the best in director David Lean, who responded, like his hero, to the beautiful scenery of the vast Sahara desert, splendidly caught in all its shifting moods by the camera of Freddie Young. The first sight of Sharif, initially a mere dot on the horizon, is perhaps the most striking sequence in this epic film.

Film poster, 1962

Peter O'Toole plays Colonel Lawrence, a legendary war hero who leads the Arabs into battle in the campaign against the Turks in World War I.

Dr. Strangelove

DIRECTOR Stanley Kubrick

RELEASED 1964

Stanley Kubrick's *Dr. Strangelove* elects to view nuclear annihilation as the ultimate absurdity. A satire on those who have stopped worrying about the bomb, this masterpiece of black comedy gets as close to a 20th-century catastrophe as possible, and is far more effective than more sombre efforts.

Kubrick had planned to make *Dr. Strangelove Or: How I Learned to Stop Worrying and Love the Bomb* as a serious drama about the inevitable heated ending of the Cold War. He changed the tone to a comic one during the early days of working on the script, when he found he had to suppress some of the more absurd elements to keep it from being funny. The plot centres on the frantic attempts by the US government to call back the B-52s sent by mad Air Force Brigadier-General Jack D. Ripper to launch a nuclear attack on the Soviet Union. Sterling Hayden as Ripper, who is convinced the "Commies" are tainting the drinking water to reduce sexual potency, and George C. Scott as the hawkish General "Buck" Turgidson, embody Kubrick's anti-militarism. Peter Sellers gives three brilliant caricature performances: as an RAF group captain; in the title role as a sinister, wheelchair-bound German scientist whose artificial arm involuntarily jerks into a Nazi salute; and as a liberal President of the US. The ominous circular War Room, brilliantly designed by Ken Adam, is central to Kubrick's nightmarish vision. Through comedy, the director sought to bring about an awareness of the very real possibility of nuclear destruction.

Peter Sellers (in dark glasses), playing the title role of the mad scientist, gives advice to the President (Sellers again, offscreen) in the War Room.

CREDITS

Production	Hawk Films
Producer	Stanley Kubrick, Victor Lyndon
Screenplay	Stanley Kubrick, Terry Southern, Peter George (based on his novel)
Cinematography	Gilbert Taylor
Production Design	Ken Adam

> "Please **gentlemen**, you can't fight here, this is **the War Room**!"

President Merkin Muffley

The Sound of Music

DIRECTOR Robert Wise

RELEASED 1965

Film poster, 1965

This heart-warming musical features seven children, their handsome, wealthy widower father, and a fresh-faced singing governess. With its catchy Rodgers and Hammerstein songs, the film, set in spectacular Tyrolean scenery and shot in Todd-AO and De Luxe Color, has become for many, one of their favourite things.

The plot centres around Maria (Julie Andrews), a young, postulant nun, who quits the convent to take up the position of governess to the children of Captain von Trapp (Christopher Plummer). She eventually marries her employer, and the family becomes the internationally celebrated von Trapp Family Singers, but have to flee Austria during the Nazi annexation of the country. The film is based on the true life story of the Trapp family as told in *The Story of the Trapp Family Singers*, written by Maria Augusta Trapp and published in 1949. Shot on location in Austria and featuring a perfectly cast Julie Andrews who radiates a youthful charm – as well as showcasing her melodious voice – the film had an immediate advantage over the 1959 Broadway musical. An unashamed escape from the harshness of contemporary life, *The Sound of Music* grossed almost US$200 million worldwide on its first release.

CREDITS

Production	Twentieth Century Fox
Producer	Robert Wise
Screenplay	Ernest Lehman
Cinematography	Ted McCord
Choreography	Marc Breaux, Dee Dee Wood
Music & Lyrics	Richard Rodgers (music) Oscar Hammerstein (lyrics)
Awards	Academy Awards: Best Picture, Best Director, Best Sound (Twentieth Century Fox sound department), Best Film Editing (William Reynolds), Best Adapted Music Score (Irwin Kostal)

In this narrow alley in the Casbah, the Muslim section of Algiers, patrolling French soldiers pass by veiled women in an atmosphere fraught with tension.

The Battle of Algiers

DIRECTOR Gillo Pontecorvo

RELEASED 1966

Without recourse to any newsreel footage, director Gillo Pontecorvo managed to achieve a naturalistic quality in this stunning film about the French-Algerian War. In true *cinéma vérité* (see box) style, *The Battle of Algiers* probably comes closer to the truth and the complexities of the situation than any documentary.

The guerilla war fought for Algerian independence from the French in 1954 is seen through the eyes of some of the participants, especially the central character Ali La Pointe (played by Brahim Haggiag), imprisoned for petty theft. He joins the cause after seeing a fellow Algerian's execution, and when recruited by the National Liberation Front, goes on to become a hero. The film was shot in the actual locations, from the dingy backstreets of the Casbah to the tree-lined avenues of the French quarter. Except for Jean Martin as Colonel Mathieu, the cast are all non-professional, and the film mixes

Maria (Julie Andrews) sings the title song in a grassy, flower-filled meadow encircled by the Austrian Alps in the opening sequence.

the grainy texture of a newsreel with hand-held camera movements, depth of field, and dramatic close-ups. The subject of political controversy, it was banned in France for some years. Its main strength lies in its scrupulous attention to the views and problems on both sides. The torture of Algerians by the French is shown, but so is a devastating scene in which an Algerian plants a bomb in a restaurant, knowing it will kill innocent people. In the late 1960s, ***The Battle of Algiers*** (***La Battaglia di Algeri***) was watched by Americans opposed to the Vietnam War, and the Pentagon reportedly held a screening during the Second Gulf War.

CREDITS

Production	Casbah/Igor
Producer	Antonio Musu, Yacef Saadi
Screenplay	Gillo Pontecorvo, Franco Solinas
Cinematography	Marcello Gatti
Music	Gillo Pontecorvo, Ennio Morricone
Awards	Venice: Best Film

CINÉMA VÉRITÉ

Dziga Vertov's *Kino-pravda* or "film-truth" was adopted in 1960s' France as *cinéma vérité* (see pp.94–95). Improvements in 16-mm equipment (including the reduction in the weight of the cameras) made it possible to reduce a film crew down to two people. The movement developed simultaneously in the US as "Direct Cinema".

Basic Training (1971), directed by Fred Wiseman, eavesdrops on life in a US Army training centre in Fort Knox, Kentucky.

Andrei Rublev

DIRECTOR Andrei Tarkovsky

RELEASED 1966

This three-hour epic was shelved for some years by Soviet authorities, who felt it was too "dark" for the October Revolution's 50th anniversary. However, four years after it was made, the film was released in the West to great acclaim.

Anatoli Solonitsyn plays the monk and artist Rublev. For director Tarkovsky, a horse was a "symbolic image", capturing the essence of life.

The film consists of several imaginary episodes in the life of the great 15th-century icon painter Andrei Rublev (Anatoli Solonitsyn), as he journeys through feudal Russia. Rublev leaves the peace and seclusion of a monastery, and because of the cruelty and misery he witnesses – rape, pillage, and famine – he gradually abandons speech, his art, and religious faith. Finally, inspired by a young peasant who assumes the responsibility for making a huge bell, he realizes that creativity is still possible in the worst of conditions and regains his faith in the world.

CREDITS

Production	Mosfilm
Producer	Tamara Ogorodnikova
Screenplay	Andrei Tarkovsky, Andrei Konchalovsky
Cinematography	Vadim Yusov
Production Design	Yevgeni Chernyayev

The Chelsea Girls

DIRECTOR Andy Warhol, Paul Morrissey

RELEASED 1966

A milestone of American Underground cinema, *The Chelsea Girls* marks the zenith of pop artist Andy Warhol's movie career and his breakthrough to national and international exposure. It features all the resident self-styled superstars of the "Factory" (his art space in New York's Manhattan), such as "Pope" Ondine.

Consisting of twelve 35-minute reels, each representing the activities in one room of New York's Chelsea Hotel at 222, West 23rd Street, *The Chelsea Girls* is projected two reels at a time, side by side, bringing its six hours of footage to a running time of three hours. Each of the 12 reels, eight in black-and-white and four in colour, consists of a single unedited shot in which personalities from Warhol's entourage (junkies, homosexuals, transvestites, and rock singers) act out their fantasies, some of which involve sex and "shooting up". *The Chelsea Girls* is a consistently fascinating document of the counter-culture of the time.

Andy Warhol prepares to film (from bottom to top) Mary Woronov, Nico, and International Velvet.

CREDITS

Producer	Andy Warhol
Screenplay	Andy Warhol, Ronald Tavel
Cinematography	Andy Warhol
Production Assistant	Paul Morrissey
Music	The Velvet Underground

Gangsters Buck Barrow (Gene Hackman), Clyde Barrow (Warren Beatty), and Bonnie Parker (Faye Dunaway) hold up a bank.

Bonnie and Clyde

DIRECTOR Arthur Penn

RELEASED 1967

One of the most influential American movies in its amoral attitude towards the outlaw, seen from a modern psychological and social viewpoint, *Bonnie and Clyde* also depicts scenes of graphic violence – rare in mainstream films of the time.

"They're young...they're in love...and they kill people..." was the effective publicity line of this most stylish and uncompromising of gangster pictures based on a true story. Faye Dunaway and Warren Beatty excel as Bonnie Parker and Clyde Barrow, infamous gun-toting criminals who roamed the American Midwest during the late 1920s and early 1930s. They are joined by a boy who works in a gas station, C.W. (Michael J. Pollard), Clyde's brother Buck Barrow (Gene Hackman), and his wife Blanche (Estelle Parsons), in a crime spree that includes murder. In this film, the bank robbers are portrayed as heroic and romantic – star-crossed lovers caught up in a whirl of violence and passion, meticulously evoked by posed photographs in sepia and carefully selected music and décor. The black comedy moves inevitably towards the much imitated ending in slow motion – the pair die in a hail of bullets. The film gave both Gene Hackman, who was Oscar-nominated for his role, and Gene Wilder (in his screen debut) their first chance to shine. The script was earlier offered to Jean-Luc Godard and François Truffaut, who turned it down, though the influence of the French New Wave is evident in Arthur Penn's bravura direction.

CREDITS

Production	Tatira-Hiller, Warner Bros.
Producer	Warren Beatty
Screenplay	David Newman, Robert Benton
Cinematography	Burnett Guffey
Art Director	Dean Tavoularis
Awards	Academy Awards: Best Supporting Actress (Estelle Parsons), Best Cinematography

Film poster, 1967

The Wild Bunch

DIRECTOR Sam Peckinpah

RELEASED 1969

On its release, *The Wild Bunch* caused a stir due to its graphic violence and amoral depiction of Texas outlaws as heroes. Today it is seen as an elegiac examination of "unchanged men in a changing land" and a landmark in the Western genre.

In 1913, Pike Bishop (William Holden) and his band of ageing outlaws, trying to live under the codes of the Old West, find themselves stalked by bounty hunters – one of whom is Pike's former friend Deke Thornton (Robert Ryan). The outlaws flee to Mexico where, in a gory, surrealistically choreographed, slow-motion climax, the gang is riddled by bullets. *The Wild Bunch* adopts a nostalgic view of the morals of the Old West and is a contemplation of the more romantic old Western. Beautifully photographed in widescreen by Lucien Ballard, with multiple angles and elaborate editing (six Panavision cameras were run together at different speeds), the film emanates a lyrical disenchantment.

Outlaws Ben Johnson, Warren Oates, William Holden, and Ernest Borgnine march across a Mexican town for a final shoot-out.

CREDITS

Production	Seven Arts
Studio	Warner Brothers
Producer	Phil Feldman
Screenplay	Walon Green, Sam Peckinpah, Roy N. Sickner
Cinematography	Lucien Ballard
Editor	Louis Lombardo
Music	Jerry Fielding

Easy Rider

DIRECTOR Dennis Hopper

RELEASED 1969

Made for less than US$400,000, *Easy Rider* was a "sleeper" hit. The film's combination of drugs, rock music, violence, motorcycles, and its counter-culture stance caught the imagination of the young and earned over US$50 million.

Two hippies, Wyatt (Peter Fonda) and Billy (Dennis Hopper), hit the road on motorcycles "in search of the real America" but instead find hostility from small-town bigots. The odyssey ends when the two are shot down by a truck driver who despises their lifestyle. Stupidity, corruption, and violence are set against the potential freedom of America in Hopper's first feature as director (and Fonda's as producer). Derived from the American "Direct Cinema" (see p.95) documentaries of the early 1960s, the movie relied on the expertise of cameraman László Kovács. The folk-rock music soundtrack featured Jimi Hendrix, Steppenwolf, The Byrds, Bob Dylan, and other counter-culture artists of the time.

Peter Fonda (left) as Wyatt and Dennis Hopper as Billy are hippy bikers from Los Angeles, riding to New Orleans – and destruction.

CREDITS

Production	Columbia
Producer	Peter Fonda
Screenplay	Dennis Hopper, Peter Fonda, Terry Southern
Cinematography	László Kovács

Jean-Louis Trintignant (Marcello) carries flowers to a loved one through the streets of Rome.

Film poster, 1970

The Conformist

DIRECTOR Bernardo Bertolucci

RELEASED 1970

An ironic and stylish study of a pre-war Italy, hauntingly evoked by Vittorio Storaro's camerawork, *The Conformist* (*Il Conformista*) penetrates the mores of ordinary fascism. Bernardo Bertolucci's first commercially popular film, it is the most successful blend of his Freudian and political preoccupations.

A professor in Italy in 1938, Marcello Clerici (Jean-Louis Trintignant) has suffered the childhood trauma of shooting a chauffeur who tried to seduce him. This experience, together with his own repressed homosexuality, contribute to his decision to enter into a bourgeois marriage with Giulia (Stefania Sandrelli) and offer his services to the Fascist party. He is asked to assassinate his former teacher, Professor Quadri (Enzo Tarascio), leader of an anti-Fascist group, but then has doubts about his mission. *The Conformist* sees the full flowering of Bertolucci's flamboyant style, with elaborate tracking shots, baroque camera angles, opulent colour effects, ornate décor, and the intricate play of light and shadow. Trintignant brings conviction to his role and there are also enticing performances from Sandrelli and Dominique Sanda (as Anna, Professor Quadri's young wife), who dance a memorable tango together.

CREDITS

Producer	Maurizio Lodi-Fé
Screenplay	Bernardo Bertolucci, from the novel by Alberto Moravia
Cinematography	Vittorio Storaro
Music	Georges Delerue
Costume Design	Gitt Magrini

In his shuttered room during his daughter's wedding, Don Corleone (Marlon Brando) listens to one of several supplicants who want him to "deal with" their enemies.

The Godfather

DIRECTOR Francis Ford Coppola

RELEASED 1972

With this film, Francis Ford Coppola made the public "an offer it could not refuse". The story, covering the rise of the Mafia and the Corleone crime family in the 1940s, builds up a rich pattern of relationships, meticulously detailing the rituals of an enclosed group. The film was one of the biggest commercial and critical successes of the 1970s, making sequels (*The Godfather: Part II*, 1974, and *The Godfather: Part III*, 1990) seem inevitable.

Mafia boss Don Vito Corleone (Marlon Brando) is part of a society where murder is "nothing personal, just business". For all the excessive violence, justified by the plot and never arbitrary, the movie effectively conveys the codes of loyalty, love, masculine honour, and women's submissiveness that bind the family together. Even more than the killings, audiences seemed to have been shocked by the scene in which a Hollywood tycoon wakes up to find the bloody head of his horse in his bed. Coppola masterfully controls the material with the help of extraordinary *chiaroscuro* photography of the interiors and an outstanding cast led by Brando, who creates an iconographic figure with his throaty voice and papal hand gestures as he switches from stern Godfather to kindly paterfamilias. At the Oscars, Brando famously sent a Native American woman to the stage in his place to protest against their treatment in the US.

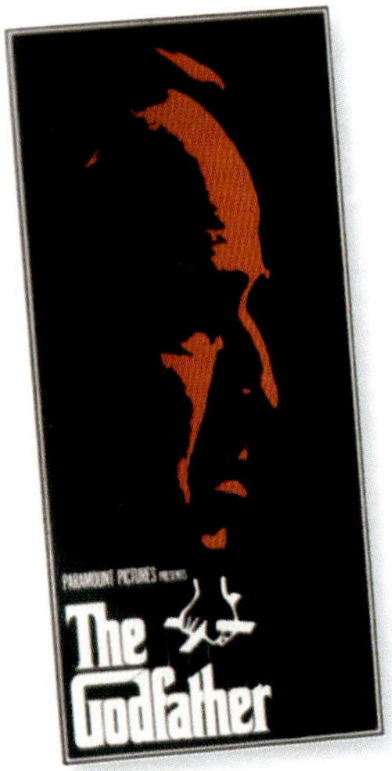

Film poster, 1972

CREDITS

Studio	Paramount
Producer	Albert S. Ruddy
Screenplay	Francis Ford Coppola, Mario Puzo, from the novel by Puzo
Cinematography	Gordon Willis
Production Design	Dean Tavoularis
Set Decoration	Philip Smith
Music	Nino Rota
Costume Design	Anna Hill Johnstone
Awards	Academy Awards: Best Picture, Best Actor (Marlon Brando), Best Screenplay

Aguirre, Wrath of God

DIRECTOR Werner Herzog

RELEASED 1972

This film, known in German as ***Aguirre, der Zorn Gottes***, features a megalomaniac hero and is a powerful, hypnotic, epic tale of the depravity of imperialism. The director, Werner Herzog, had to overcome difficult conditions while filming in the Andes but its success, due mainly to the striking images, was proof that the hardships paid off.

In the wilds of Peru, a 16th-century Spanish conquistador, Don Lope de Aguirre (Klaus Kinski), with the assistance of native slaves, leads a hazardous expedition over the mountains and down an uncharted river in search of the mythical kingdom of El Dorado. The fascination of this morality tale, presented in the guise of a true historical account, derives from the jungle atmosphere and pictorial flair, as well as Kinski's intense performance. (This was the first of five films he was to make with Herzog.) The opening long shot, of the expedition weaving its way down the mountain through the fog, is particularly effective, as is the final shot in which the camera circles rapidly around a raft littered with dead bodies and overrun with monkeys. The narrative is a steady stream of images, accompanied by brief pieces of dialogue, which not only set the pace of the film, but the mood as well. It is the topography of the landscape – the film was shot on location in the Peruvian rainforest near Puerto Maldonado – that dictates the action, rather than the actors. Indeed, the actors react strongly to their surroundings, which reflect and mirror the growing madness and the feverish hallucinations of the people on the doomed expedition.

CREDITS

Production	Hessischer Rundfunk, Werner Herzog
Producer	Werner Herzog, Hans Prescher
Screenplay	Werner Herzog
Cinematography	Thomas Mauch
Music	Popol Vuh

Klaus Kinski, as the film's protagonist, gives an enigmatic and frightening portrayal of human obsession and its consequences.

Nashville

DIRECTOR Robert Altman

RELEASED 1975

Karen Black plays Connie White, a country singer who uses Barbara Jean's (the reigning queen of Nashville) period out of the spotlight to bolster her own career.

This portrayal of a single weekend in the lives of people working in the music business in Nashville, US – the world's country music capital – is a *tour-de-force* in its manipulation of characters and sound.

To create this mosaic of characters, music, sights, and sounds, Robert Altman used 16 tracks for the sound-producing conversations, and a continuously moving camera, rhythmic cuts, and onscreen and offscreen commentaries. Particularly remarkable is the opening sequence at Nashville airport introducing all 24 characters. Conceived as a celebration of the US Bicentennial anniversary in 1976, ***Nashville*** ironically reveals the dark side of the US – racial prejudice, selfishness, and vulgarity.

CREDITS

Studio	Paramount Pictures
Producer	Robert Altman
Screenplay	Joan Tewkesbury
Cinematography	Paul Lohmann
Awards	Academy Awards: Best Song: *I'm Easy* (Keith Carradine)

In the Realm of the Senses

DIRECTOR Nagisa Ôshima

RELEASED 1976

Director Nagisa Ôshima's first big commercial success was, for many, in the realm of pornography. For others, it was a serious treatment of gender status and oppression, a link between eroticism and death, and an artistic breakthrough in the representation of explicit sex on screen.

After strangling her lover Kichizo (Tatsuya Fuji) while having sex, geisha Sada (Eiko Matsuda) prepares for her final, terrible act.

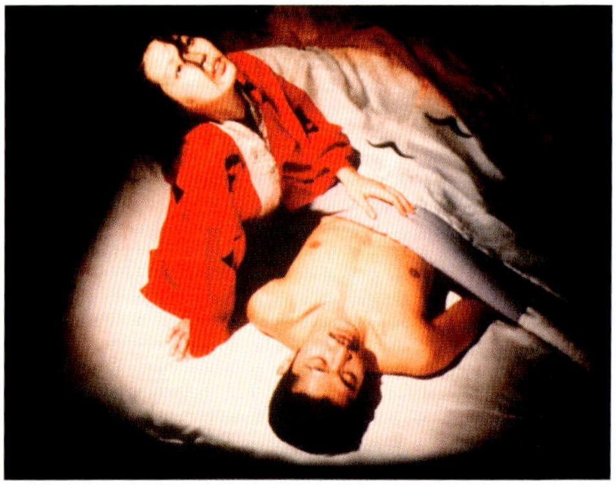

Kichizo (Tatsuya Fuji), a married man, and Sada (Eiko Matsuda), a geisha, retreat from militarist Japan of 1936 into a world of their own and act out their sexual fantasies obsessively. Finally, in a quest for the ultimate orgasm, Sada strangles and then castrates her lover. Based on a notorious murder case of the 1930s, Ôshima's voyeuristic masterpiece is a blend of tenderness and brutality, ritual and spontaneity. The original title, ***Ai No Corrida***, refers to a ritualized fight to death – *corrida* means "bullfight" in Spanish. In the 1970s, the film created controversy and faced censorship problems in many countries. However, when the original uncut version was re-released in 2000, it caused only a ripple.

CREDITS

Production	Argos Films, Ôshima Productions
Producer	Anatole Dauman
Screenplay	Nagisa Ôshima
Cinematography	Hideo Itoh
Awards	Cannes: Best Director

Taxi Driver

DIRECTOR Martin Scorsese

RELEASED 1976

This deeply disturbing drama, which examines alienation in urban society by combining elements of film noir, the Western, and horror movies, established Martin Scorsese as a major figure in world cinema and made Robert De Niro a star.

A Vietnam War veteran, paranoid loner, and taxi driver, Travis Bickle (De Niro) has no friends. He sees New York as "an open sewer" populated by "scum" and "animals". De Niro immerses himself in the complex character; his monologue to a mirror – "You talkin' to me?" – has become one of the most famous sequences from 1970s cinema. Bickle's diary entries – "Listen, you screwheads, here is someone who would not take it anymore" – force audiences into an ambivalent identification with him. Scorsese presents an apocalyptic view of the city, with steam hissing out of the streets, incessant traffic noise, and wailing sirens. This is contrasted with the haunting score by Bernard Herrmann (his last).

Robert De Niro's character, Travis Bickle, is perfectly described by the movie's tagline – "On every street in every city, there's a nobody who dreams of being a somebody..."

CREDITS

Studio	Columbia
Production	Bill/Phillips Productions, Italo/Judeo Productions
Screenplay	Paul Schrader
Cinematography	Michael Chapman
Music	Bernard Herrmann
Awards	Cannes: Best Film

Annie Hall

DIRECTOR Woody Allen

RELEASED 1977

Until *Annie Hall*, Woody Allen was considered one of America's brightest new funnymen whose films were little more than a series of revue sketches. He was catapulted into the big time with this "nervous romance", which won four Oscars, made a fortune, and gained a cult following.

The script, about the on-off relationship between Alvy Singer (Woody Allen), a television and nightclub comic, and budding vocalist Annie Hall (Diane Keaton), is semi-autobiographical, based loosely on the stars' real-life affair (Keaton's real name is Diane Hall and her nickname is Annie). In the film, their friendship begins during an indoor tennis match of mixed singles, which she wins, and continues through the Jewish Alvy's awkward and hilarious meeting with Annie's WASP family. The New York-loving Alvy then follows Annie to "mellow" California. The pair portray an intelligent, contemporary adult couple with wit, accuracy, and an undercurrent of anxiety. Highlights include media guru Marshall McLuhan, playing himself, who suddenly appears to refute what a phoney, standing in line to see a Bergman movie, is saying about him. Keaton's unisex costume of baggy trousers, white shirt, black waistcoat, knotted black tie, scarf, and felt hat oozed character and was a strong influence on what the well-dressed, liberated woman was to wear in the late 1970s.

CREDITS

Studio	United Artists
Producer	Jack Rollins, Charles H. Joffe
Screenplay	Woody Allen, Marshall Brickman
Cinematography	Gordon Willis
Awards	Academy Awards: Best Picture, Best Actress (Diane Keaton), Best Director, Best Screenplay

Film poster, 1977

Chewbacca (Peter Mayhew), Luke (Mark Hamill), Obi-Wan Kenobi (Alec Guinness), and Han Solo (Harrison Ford) set off to rescue Princess Leia from the evil clutches of Darth Vader and the Galactic Empire.

Star Wars

DIRECTOR George Lucas

RELEASED 1977

In *Star Wars*, a young man, Luke Skywalker (Mark Hamill), is chosen by destiny to lead the resistance against the Galactic Empire. George Lucas' fantasy film inspired generations of audiences – and forever changed the way movies are marketed.

Lucas modelled his universe – set "a long time ago in a galaxy far, far away" – on the Saturday action serials he enjoyed as a child, but he also studied Joseph Campbell's work on mythologies and borrowed significantly from Akira Kurosawa's samurai film *The Hidden Fortress* (1958). The structure of *Star Wars* was enough to fascinate adolescent boys – without complicating what is essentially a simple fable of good and evil. It was also able to hold two sequels and, 20 years later, three prequels. An unexpected hit (sci-fi didn't translate into box office returns then), it transformed the movie industry, and ushered in a new era of special effects-driven cinema aimed at a youth audience, released on as many screens as possible, and with a marketing budget offset by merchandising. Lucas became a billionaire and established Industrial Light & Magic, a leading special effects company.

CREDITS

Studio	Twentieth Century Fox
Production	Lucasfilm
Producer	Gary Kurtz
Screenplay	George Lucas
Cinematography	Gilbert Taylor
Awards	Academy Awards: Best Art Direction (John Barry, Norman Reynolds, Leslie Dilley, Roger Christian), Best Costume Design (John Mollo), Best Effects, Best Film Editing (Paul Hirsch, Marcia Lucas, Richard Chew), Best Music (John Williams), Best Sound

THE RISE OF THE BLOCKBUSTER

The word "blockbuster" refers either to a big-budget movie that catches the public's attention, or to a film that has broken box office records, such as *Jaws* (1975), the first film to earn US$100 million in domestic ticket sales. *Jaws* ushered in the "blockbuster era" during which *Star Wars* became the biggest blockbuster of the 1970s. The blockbusters of the late 1970s and early 1980s were mostly fantasy films, such as *E.T.* (1982) and *Back to the Future* (1985), while those of the 1990s, such as *Terminator 2* (1991) and *The Matrix* (1999), were darker and more violent.

The Deer Hunter

DIRECTOR Michael Cimino

RELEASED 1978

The first major American movie about the Vietnam War and its aftermath, *The Deer Hunter* won five Oscars. Because of its impact, Hollywood discovered that audiences were ready to accept the disastrous war as a subject – as testified by the number of films in the early 1980s that dealt with it.

Although there are several scenes set during the Vietnam conflict, the film's principal theme is friendship and the psychological and social effects of the war on a small community – here, a Pennsylvanian industrial town acting as the microcosm. Hunting and drinking buddies Michael (Robert De Niro), Nick (Christopher Walken), and Steven (John Savage) volunteer to go to Vietnam together and are thrown into the hell of war, which affects their lives forever. Steven ends up in a wheelchair, Nick shoots himself in the head, and Michael learns the dangers of the macho code he lived by. Director Cimino orchestrates the set pieces brilliantly – the wedding, the hunt, and the sequence when the American POWs are forced by their captors to play Russian roulette, which is a metaphor for the futility of war.

CREDITS

Production	EMI, Universal
Producer	Michael Cimino, Barry Spikings, Michael Deeley, John Peverall
Screenplay	Michael Cimino, Deric Washburn, Louis Garfinkle, Quinn K. Redeker
Cinematography	Vilmos Zsigmond
Music	Stanley Myers
Awards	Academy Awards: Best Picture, Best Director, Best Supporting Actor (Christopher Walken), Best Editing (Peter Zinner), Best Sound (C. Darin Knight, William L. McCoughey, Richard Portman, Aaron Rochin)

Mike (Robert De Niro) hunts for deer in the mountains for the final time before going to Vietnam.

Deckard (Harrison Ford) struggles to evade death, in a scene that brilliantly combines conventions of 21st-century sci-fi and 1940s detective film noir.

Film poster, 1982

Blade Runner

DIRECTOR Ridley Scott

RELEASED 1982

This movie is among the most discussed and influential science fiction films ever made. Ridley Scott's adaptation of Philip K. Dick's novel, *Do Androids Dream of Electric Sheep?*, filters the story through a retro noir sensibility appropriate to the Los Angeles setting.

Harrison Ford plays the role of Deckard, a "blade runner" hired to "retire" four rogue replicants – organic robots so lifelike that they don't even know they're not human. In the course of his pursuit, Deckard falls in love with another replicant (Sean Young), and comes to question his own – ambiguous – humanity. Although the plot is thin, the movie's visuals are astonishingly layered. Scott's imagination knows no bounds here. The movie's spectacular cityscapes are reminiscent of Fritz Lang's ***Metropolis*** (1927), while the street-level scenes give equally vivid impressions of a social fabric torn every which way. Although it was a failure at the box office, ***Blade Runner*** became a key cult movie, and was among the first titles to benefit from a restored "director's cut" when it was re-released in 1991. This version was actually shorter than the original; it dispensed with the lugubrious noir voice-over; and had a bleaker ending. Crucially, this version also carried clearer intimations that Deckard himself might be a replicant. Ironically, this makes him all the more human because he finally realizes his brotherhood with the android combatant (Rutger Hauer).

CREDITS

Production	The Ladd Company
Producer	Michael Deeley
Screenplay	Hampton Fancher, David Webb Peoples
Cinematography	Jordan Cronenweth

Paris, Texas

DIRECTOR Wim Wenders

RELEASED 1984

The film's title suggests a meeting between the old and the new world, and *Paris, Texas* expertly reworks elements of both classical Hollywood and European art cinema, in this successful collaboration between German director Wim Wenders and American writer Sam Shepard.

Wenders saw his chance to explore the vast American landscape – both urban and rural – in *Paris, Texas* and used the place of the same name as the setting for the story of Travis – his lost protagonist. Brilliantly portrayed by melancholy character actor Harry Dean Stanton, Travis does not speak for the opening 20 minutes, and is first seen walking alone in the Texan desert. Neither he nor the audience knows where he comes from or where he is going. Gradually, we learn that he wishes to see Hunter (Hunter Carson) – the son he left some years ago in the care of his brother Walt (Dean Stockwell) – and is trying to find his estranged French wife Jane (Nastassja Kinski), hoping, in vain, to put the pieces of his life back together again. He does find his wife and son, only to lose them once again. Wenders, with the help of Ry Cooder's haunting score and Robby Müller's stunning camerawork, evokes a poignant world in which communication between people has become complex but not impossible.

CREDITS

Production	Road Movies/Balin Argos
Producer	Don Guest, Anatole Dauman
Screenplay	Sam Shepard
Cinematography	Robby Müller
Music	Ry Cooder
Awards	Cannes: Best Film

Jane (Nastassja Kinski) listens to Travis (Harry Dean Stanton), separated by a one-way mirror, as he reminisces about their life together.

A gaunt and unshaven Travis (Harry Dean Stanton) wanders aimlessly across the bleak Texan desert.

Heimat

DIRECTOR Edgar Reitz

RELEASED 1984, 1992, 2004

Consisting of three series of 30 films, and running at 42 hours, Edgar Reitz's *Heimat* (*Homeland*) is an amusing, moving, and absorbing soap opera. Filmed in colour and monochrome, it mirrors Germany's history from 1919 onwards, through the eyes of ordinary people as the characters age and develop.

In Part III, *A Chronicle of Endings and Beginnings* (2004), Heiko Senst (centre) plays Tobi, a young construction labourer from East Germany.

Part I, *A German Chronicle*, depicts life in Hunsrück, a fictitious German village. The protagonist Maria (Marita Breuer) marries into the Simon family. Part II, *Chronicle of a Generation*, is set in 1960s Munich and focuses on a group of young people, including Maria's son Hermann (Henry Arnold), a struggling composer. Part III, *A Chronicle of Endings and Beginnings*, starts with the fall of the Berlin Wall in 1989, as Hermann, now an internationally respected conductor, returns to Hunsrück with his lover Clarissa (Salome Kammer). Particularly fascinating is the depiction of the Nazis and how their ideology filtered down to taint otherwise decent citizens.

CREDITS

Production	Edgar Reitz, WDR, SFB
Producer	Edgar Reitz
Screenplay	Edgar Reitz, Peter Steinbach
Cinematography	Gernot Roll, Gerard Vanderbergh, Christian Reisz
Music	Nikos Mamangakis

Come and See

DIRECTOR Elem Klimov

RELEASED 1985

This moving and powerful film, the last to be directed by Elem Klimov, depicts the war that took place in Belorussia in 1943, as experienced by a 16-year-old boy whose family and village have been destroyed by the Nazis.

Aleksei Kravchenko plays Florya, a teenage boy scarred by his nightmarish experiences during the war – he discovers his village destroyed and his family butchered by the Germans.

The viewer is invited to "come and see" Florya (Aleksei Kravchenko) as he wanders alone, witnessing a series of Nazi atrocities, until he joins a group of partisans as a hardened and active participant. Some unforgettable images include the agonizing struggle through a swamp to reach an encampment of lamenting women, and the journey to find food, accompanied by an effigy of Hitler. A sense of derangement is heightened by the film's soundtrack, most notably when the bombing of a village damages Florya's hearing. *Come and See* has no heroic catharsis or narrative symmetry. Instead, Klimov's apocalyptic vision focuses on the destruction of a young life and the horrors of war.

CREDITS

Production	Belarusfilm/Mosfilm
Screenplay	Ales Adamovich, Elem Klimov, based on the works of Adamovich
Music	Oleg Yanchenko
Cinematography	Aleksei Rodionov
Awards	Moscow International Film Festival: Golden Prize

▲ **Gangster Dennis Hopper** snorts gas through an insect-like mask and forces Isabella Rossellini – a nightclub singer known as The Blue Lady – to have sex with him.

Blue Velvet

DIRECTOR David Lynch

RELEASED 1986

David Lynch's radical fable is one of the seminal films of the 1980s, spawning a number of (inferior) imitations. Initially a satire on the complacency of small-town America, it turns into a parable of evil where corruption is found in the most unlikely places.

Blue Velvet opens with dream-like images of America: perfect houses with white picket fences and impeccably manicured lawns. A man collapses while watering his lawn, and the camera reveals a colony of swarming bugs in the grass. A little later, college student Jeffrey Beaumont (Kyle MacLachlan) finds a severed ear in a field; when he and Sandy (Laura Dern) try to solve the mystery, it leads them into film noir territory with a *femme fatale* (Isabella Rossellini) and a sadistic villain (Dennis Hopper). "Are you a detective or a pervert?" Sandy asks Jeffrey at one point. The answer, perhaps, is that he, the director, and the audience are being a bit of both.

CREDITS

Production	De Laurentiis Entertainment Group
Producer	Richard Roth
Music	Angelo Badalamenti, David Lynch
Screenplay	David Lynch
Cinematography	Frederick Elmes

"See that clock on the wall? In five minutes you are **not going to believe what I just told you.**"

Jeffrey Beaumont

Shoah

DIRECTOR Claude Lanzmann

RELEASED 1985

Lanzmann's monumental documentary, over nine hours long, on the calculated extermination of Europe's Jews by the Nazis is both a tribute to those who died and a warning. Although the film begins by saying, "This is an untellable story," it manages, as far as possible, to describe the indescribable.

An eyewitness arrives at Treblinka by train, one of many who recount the horror and tragedy of *shoah* (an Israeli word meaning "catastrophic upheaval").

In *Shoah*, survivors of the Nazi extermination camps (at Treblinka, Auschwitz, and elsewhere), Polish bystanders – who make no attempt to hide their past or anti-Semitism – and a handful of "former" Nazi officials, recall the Holocaust. Under Lanzmann's unwavering and detailed questioning, they reveal the barbarism of the atrocities and the minutiae of the planning that went into the Final Solution. The nightmarish conditions of the Warsaw ghetto are described, and harrowing stories told. Lanzmann spent 10 years travelling and visiting the scenes of the crimes to amass his towering document, edited from 350 hours of film. No archival footage is used in this terrible testimony, which is made all the more powerful for it.

CREDITS

Production	Les Films Aleph, Historia
Cinematography	Dominique Chapuis, Jimmy Glasberg, William Lubtchansky
Awards	Berlin: Caligari Film Award

A Room With a View

DIRECTOR James Ivory

RELEASED 1985

The first of three adaptations of E.M. Forster novels by director James Ivory, producer Ismail Merchant, and screenwriter Ruth Prawer Jhabvala (the others being *Maurice*, 1987 and *Howards End*, 1991) *A Room with a View* perfectly captures Forster's wit and idiom.

Lucy Honeychurch (Helena Bonham Carter) falls under the spell of Italy with free-spirited George Emerson (Julian Sands) in a lush field outside Florence.

The film deals with with the stultifying, hypocritical restrictions of Edwardian society. Sheltered Lucy (Helena Bonham Carter), holidaying in Florence with her chaperone Charlotte (Maggie Smith), shares a kiss with bohemian George (Julian Sands). Back in England, she seems to settle for stuffy Cecil Vyse (Daniel Day-Lewis) although her heart is with George. Ivory vividly contrasts Italy's untamed landscape, which triggers Lucy's sexual awakening, with the dampening effect of pastoral England.

CREDITS

Production	Merchant-Ivory, Goldcrest
Producer	Ismail Merchant
Screenplay	Ruth Prawer Jhabvala, from the novel by E.M. Forster
Cinematography	Tony Pierce-Roberts
Awards	Academy Awards: Best Adapted Screenplay, Best Art Direction (Gianni Quaranta, Brian Ackland-Snow, Brian Savegar, Elio Altramura), Best Costume Design (Jenny Beavan, John Bright)

Women on the Verge of a Nervous Breakdown

DIRECTOR Pedro Almodóvar

RELEASED 1988

Although Pedro Almodóvar had previously made seven features, it was this anarchic farce that sealed his career, becoming 1989's highest-grossing foreign film in North America and the most successful film ever in Spain, where it is called *Mujeres al borde de un ataque de nervios*.

Pepa (played by a smouldering Carmen Maura) is a volatile and attractive television actress who is pregnant by Iván (Fernando Guillén), her married philandering lover. Unaware of her condition, he blithely abandons her, leaving a message on her answering machine. As all her efforts to contact him fail, Pepa grows more and more hysterical, and is precipitated into a series of increasingly bizarre and surreal situations. As in the best of farces, the film's arrangement of irrational events is held together by an internal logic that is very funny. Like many a French bedroom farce, most of the action takes place in one setting – Pepa's smart Madrid penthouse apartment, which becomes overpopulated with eccentric, desperate women. Among them is Iván's deranged wife Lucía (Julieta Serrano), intent on taking revenge on her unfaithful husband, and Pepa's best friend Candela, who has fallen in love with a terrorist. Also making an appearance is a young, bespectacled Antonio Banderas as Carlos, Iván's 20-year-old son. There is a feminist message beneath the comic events, played out in true screwball comedy style, as all the women are frustrated by the childish egotism of the men with whom they get involved. Audiences were mainly attracted by Almodovar's campy brand of humour and distinctive visual style that was influenced by the Hollywood of the 1950s.

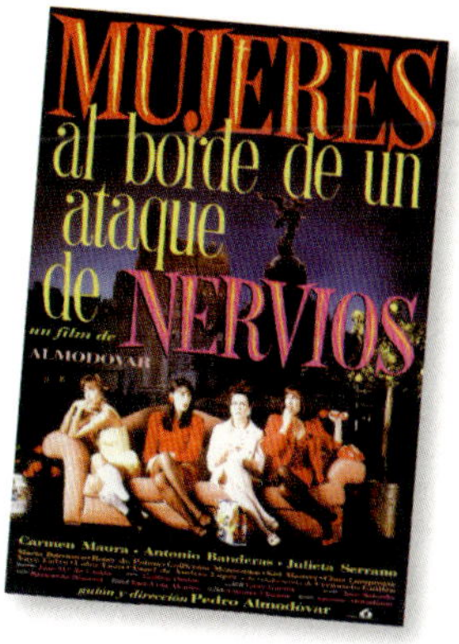

Spanish film poster, 1988

CREDITS

Production	Rank, El Deseo, Laurenfilm, Orion
Producer	Pedro Almodóvar
Screenplay	Pedro Almodóvar
Cinematography	José Luis Alcaine
Music	Bernardo Bonezzi

Lucía (Julieta Serrano), determined to kill her unfaithful husband, brandishes twin pistols in the "other woman's" apartment.

Salvatore (Salvatore Cascio as the young boy) is taught how to edit films and run the cinema projector by his mentor, Alfredo (Philippe Noiret).

Cinema Paradiso

DIRECTOR Giuseppe Tornatore

RELEASED 1988

This heartwarming film takes a nostalgic look at the lure of cinema and the death of the picture palace through the eyes of a child. Understandably, *Cinema Paradiso* has become one of the most popular Italian films of the last few decades, both in Italy and elsewhere.

The story, told in flashbacks, is about Salvatore (Salvatore Cascio), a little boy who lives with his harrassed, widowed mother in a small, grim, war-torn Sicilian village. He finds refuge from the daily misery of life by sneaking into Nuovo Cinema Paradiso, the local cinema hall. The projectionist, Alfredo (Philippe Noiret), soon becomes his friend and teacher. When Alfredo is blinded in a fire, he teaches the boy to take over his job, but ultimately encourages him to leave the stifling confines of the village. In his teens, Salvatore falls in love with a banker's daughter, Elena (Agnese Nano), and wins her over by taking Alfredo's advice to stand outside her window every night. Years later, when an older Salvatore (Jacques Perrin) has become a successful film-maker, he watches a montage bequeathed to him by Alfredo, of all the kissing scenes that had been deleted from the Paradiso's films over the years by the village priest (played by Leopoldo Trieste). A poignant reminder, helped by Ennio Morricone's haunting musical score, of how personal the cinema experience can be, *Cinema Paradiso* is a movie that stirs memories of childhood.

Father figure Alfredo cycles down a village pathway in Sicily with young Salvatore.

CREDITS

Production	Cristaldifilm, Ariane, RAI, TF1
Producer	Franco Cristaldi, Giovanna Romagnoli
Screenplay	Giuseppe Tornatore
Cinematography	Blasco Giurato
Music	Ennio Morricone
Awards	Cannes: Special Jury Prize; Academy Award: Best Foreign Film

Do the Right Thing

DIRECTOR Spike Lee

RELEASED 1989

A high watermark in US independent cinema and certainly the most important African-American film to date, Spike Lee's third feature is a stylized, provocative distillation of racial tensions in Brooklyn, New York, towards the end of the 20th century.

Set over the course of a swelteringly hot summer day, the film follows Mookie, a pizza delivery boy (played by Lee himself), as he goes about the neighbourhood. Along the way, we encounter various black and Hispanic youths, such as Radio Raheem (Bill Nunn) and Buggin' Out (Giancarlo Esposito); their elders (Ossie Davis and Ruby Dee); and Mookie's employers at the pizzeria, Sal (Danny Aiello) and his sons, the racist Pino (John Turturro) and colour-blind Vito (Richard Edson). Shot in bold, heavily saturated colours with a blaring rap soundtrack (*Fight the Power* by Public Enemy is prominent), the film bristles with energy and purpose. Tapping a rich vein of street comedy, Lee confronts racist attitudes before magnifying the tensions in a morally ambiguous climax that reflects contemporary controversies over police brutality. Although derided by some as inflammatory, the film is vibrant and searching.

CREDITS

Production	40 Acres and a Mule Filmworks
Producer	John Kilick, Spike Lee, Monty Ross
Screenplay	Spike Lee
Cinematography	Ernest R. Dickerson

Do The Right Thing featured varied and colourful characters such as Clifton (far left) and Buggin' Out (second from left).

Raise the Red Lantern

DIRECTOR Zhang Yimou

RELEASED 1991

One of the first Chinese films to be widely shown in the West, *Raise the Red Lantern* (*Da hong deng long gao gao gua*) was a great success. This can be ascribed to the gripping humanistic story it tells, its exoticism, stunning visual imagery, and the radiant, stately beauty of its star, Gong Li, the muse of its director, Zhang Yimou.

In the China of the 1920s, Songlian (Gong Li) becomes the fourth wife of Master Chen (Ma Jingwu), a rich and powerful landowner. It is the patriarch's tradition to light red lanterns outside the apartment of the wife he intends to join for the night. Most of the film takes place within one small compound where all four wives become rivals for their master's attentions. Intrigue and scheming mark the relationships between them and the young Songlian soon learns that she has to fight for her status in this convoluted domestic set-up. The house is seen through the seasons of a year; the interiors of the four apartments are in vibrant reds, oranges, and yellows in spaces marked out for passion. The Chinese government banned the film from the country, obviously seeing that, beneath the surface story, there is a parable of an authoritarian government, represented by the master, who allows no freedom of expression to the individual, represented by Songlian.

CREDITS

Production	Century Communications, ERA International, China Film Co-production Corporation, Salon Films
Producer	Chiu Fu-Sheng, Hou Hsiao-hsien, Zhang Wenze
Screenplay	Ni Zhen, based on *Wives and Concubines*, a story by Su Tong
Cinematography	Zhao Fei, Yang Lun

Gong Li plays Songlian, the beautiful new bride of a feudal patriarch. Here, she is bathed in the rich glow of the red lanterns in her bedroom as she awaits her husband.

Bill (Clint Eastwood), Ned (Morgan Freeman), and Schofield Kid (Jaimz Woolvett) team up to teach a ruthless sheriff a lesson.

Unforgiven

DIRECTOR Clint Eastwood

RELEASED 1992

The movie that finally gave Clint Eastwood Oscar recognition after 40 years in the business, *Unforgiven* is a gripping Western, a genre in which Eastwood made his name. Returning to the genre's roots, the veteran actor gave the Western a kiss of life.

Eastwood dedicated the film to "Sergio and Don" – the directors of low-budget Westerns, Sergio Leone and Don Siegel were his most important mentors. However, *Unforgiven* perhaps owes even more to John Ford than these two directors. When Little Bill Daggett (Gene Hackman), a dictatorial sheriff of a small frontier town, denies justice to a prostitute whose face has been viciously slashed by two clients, the brothel women hire Bill Munny (Eastwood), a once-ruthless gunfighter, now a hog farmer, to kill the culprits. He teams up with his old partner Ned Logan (Morgan Freeman) and the young Schofield Kid (Jaimz Woolvett), and embarks on the trail until the final showdown.

While exploring the darker side of the myths of the Old West, the movie is striking in its willingness to confront the effects of violence on both those who commit it and those who suffer it. For Eastwood, there are no heroes because even the good are capable of evil. He shatters illusions about heroism in the film, portraying the ugliness and pain that violence brings. According to Eastwood, *Unforgiven* "summarized everything I feel about the Western. The moral is the concern with gunplay".

CREDITS

Studio	Warner Bros.
Producer	Clint Eastwood
Screenplay	David Webb Peoples
Cinematography	Jack N. Green
Art Direction	Rick Roberts, Adrian Gorton
Awards	Academy awards: Best Picture, Best Director, Best Supporting Actor (Gene Hackman), Best Editing (Joel Cox)

Avenger Bill Munny (Clint Eastwood) is tormented by memories of his past crimes, but when the sheriff kills his friend Ned, he forgets his remorse and goes on a killing spree.

Film poster, 1992

Steve Buscemi (on the floor) plays Mr. Pink and Harvey Keitel plays Larry Dimmick alias Mr. White, seen here in the film's climactic shoot-out.

Reservoir Dogs

DIRECTOR Quentin Tarantino

RELEASED 1992

For many the most distinctive and exciting voice to emerge from US cinema in the 1990s, Quentin Tarantino announced himself with this bravura crime thriller. Smaller in scale than his subsequent output, *Reservoir Dogs* features all the elements that would soon become Tarantino staples.

The director begins the film in the middle of a failed diamond robbery, and carves the story into a series of chapters introducing each of the gangsters in turn. He borrows from the heist movie catalogue – Stanley Kubrick's *The Killing* (1956), Ringo Lam's *City on Fire* (1987), and the underworld milieu of Jean-Pierre Melville – all but omitting the robbery itself. The aftermath is a bloody trial of conflicting loyalties and festering suspicions as the crooks convene to figure out what (or who) went wrong. Tarantino's profane dialogue puts its own ironic spin on things – the heavies talk like movie-obsessed ordinary people, not like gangsters; scenes of blood-soaked gore are juxtaposed with well-known tunes from the 1970s. However, it is the disquieting ease with which post-modern cool shifts to violence – making it easy to overlook the pain beneath – that caused a stir at the time.

CREDITS

Production	Live Entertainment, Dog Eat Dog
Producer	Lawrence Bender
Screenplay	Quentin Tarantino
Cinematography	Andrzej Sekula

Three Colours: Blue, White, and Red

DIRECTOR Krzysztof Kieslowski

RELEASED 1993, 1994

The colours of the titles of Polish director Krzystof Kieslowski's trilogy, his final work, refer to the colours of the French flag, while the themes are allied to the country's Revolutionary slogan "Liberty, Equality, Fraternity". All three films offer sensual, emotional, and spiritual experiences rarely so well-depicted in contemporary cinema.

The trilogy is about people separated from those they love, but each film is different in tone, moving from meditative drama (*Blue*), through oblique social comedy (*White*), to a symbolic mystery-romance (*Red*). In *Blue*, after the deaths of her composer husband and young daughter in a car crash, Julie (Juliette Binoche) seeks to free herself from everyone and everything that reminds her of her past. In *White*, Polish hairdresser Karol (Zbigniew Zamachowski), returning to his homeland, makes a success of his life, aiming to take revenge on the wife who has spurned him. In *Red*, Valentine (Irène Jacob), a model, develops a relationship with an elderly, cynical judge Joseph Kern (Jean-Louis Trintignant). Kieslowski's stylish visuals and use of locations are a fitting epitaph to one of Europe's best directors.

In *Red* (1994), a film that explores the nuances of fraternity and platonic love, Valentine (Irène Jacob) models for a poster that visually illustrates the film's theme of loneliness.

CREDITS

Production	CED, Canal+, Fonds Eurimages, France 3 Cinéma, MK2, TOR, TSR
Producer	Marin Karmitz
Screenplay	Agnieszka Holland, Slawomir Idziak, Kieslowski, Krzysztof Piesiewicz, Edward Zebrowski, Edward Klosinski
Cinematography	Slawomir Idziak (*Blue*), Edward Klosinski (*White*), Piotr Sobocinski (*Red*)
Music	Zbigniew Preisner

In *Blue* (1993), Kieslowski's film about the imperfection of human liberty, Julie (Juliette Binoche) reflects on her vain search for freedom from the past.

Fifteen-year-old Tahereh Ladanian (as herself) stands on the balcony of her grandmother's house, listening to pledges of love from her co-star Hossein Rezai (out of shot).

Through the Olive Trees

DIRECTOR Abbas Kiarostami

RELEASED 1994

Although Abbas Kiarostami had been making feature films since 1974, it was only in the 1990s, with *Through the Olive Trees (Zire darakhatan zeyton)*, that he was recognized as the leading force behind the flood of high-quality Iranian movies that began to win prizes at international film festivals.

CREDITS

Studio	Abbas Kiarostami productions, CiBy 2000, Farabi Cinema Foundation, Miramax
Producer	Abbas Kiarostami
Screenwriter	Abbas Kiarostami
Cinematography	Hossein Djafarian, Farhad Saba

In 1992, Kiarostami directed ***And Life Goes On***, about a film being made on the survivors of an earthquake in Iran. ***Through the Olive Trees***, set in the same area, is a comedy about a director casting and making another picture. The most fascinating aspect of this film within a film is that the audience never knows what is real and what is fiction. The celebrated final sequence follows the two main actors, who are having a "real life" romance, in extreme long shot as the boy persuades the girl to marry him. The movie, at once simple and complex, intimate and distant, is full of insights into film-making, society, and human relationships.

Four Weddings and a Funeral

DIRECTOR Mike Newell

RELEASED 1994

After the highs and lows that British cinema went through during the 1970s and 1980s, it was this romantic comedy that hit the jackpot, making Hugh Grant an international star.

The habitually late Charles (Hugh Grant) and his flatmate Scarlett (Charlotte Coleman) race to the wedding of a friend, where Charles has been asked to be best man.

Fashioned around an ingenious structural conceit, Richard Curtis's deftly polished script is a love story filtered across several months and five ceremonies. At the first wedding, the chronically self-effacing Charles (Grant) is surprised to find himself flirting with Carrie, a forthright American (Andie MacDowell) engaged to another man. Subsequent encounters only prove that "the course of true love never did run smooth". Reminiscent of the screwball comedies of the 1930s in its depiction of wealthy socialites hindered by nothing but their own embarrassments, the film is an artful comedy of exquisite manners. Grant and Curtis reunited with production outfit Working Title for ***Notting Hill*** (1999), ***Bridget Jones's Diary*** (2001), and ***Love Actually*** (2003), all of them popular hits at home and abroad.

CREDITS

Production	Channel Four/Polygram/ Working Title
Producer	Tim Bevan, Richard Curtis, Eric Fellner, Duncan Kenworthy
Screenplay	Richard Curtis
Cinematography	Michael Coulter

Cowboy Woody (voiced by Tom Hanks) pretends to be friendly with Buzz Lightyear (voiced by Tim Allen), a fancy, high-tech action toy; the pretence is necessary because Woody feels threatened by Buzz.

Toy Story

DIRECTOR John Lasseter

RELEASED 1995

The idea that a studio brand might define the quality and characteristics of a film bearing its logo disappeared in the 1950s. However, starting with *Toy Story*, Pixar was an exception to this rule. It revitalized digital animated technology, becoming a hallmark for witty, sophisticated productions.

The first feature-length blockbuster by Pixar, a pioneer of computer-animated films in the 1980s, *Toy Story* was also its first feature to be released in cinemas. Based on an earlier short by John Lasseter, it is about a group of toys belonging to six-year-old Andy. Cowboy Woody is his favourite, but when Andy gets a new doll, Buzz Lightyear, Woody finds himself gathering dust with the rest of Andy's cast-offs. Consumed with jealousy, he tries to get rid of his rival.

Lasseter's CGI has a synthetic texture that suits the film, but also displays a fluidity and dynamism that the old animation style cannot match. However, Pixar's strengths go back to the drawing board: a rich story sense, fresh perspectives, and unforgettable characters created imaginatively, and with originality. Pixar developed a corporate culture that nourished creativity and was rewarded with one hit film after another: *Toy Story 2* (1999), *Finding Nemo* (2003), *Wall-E* (2008), and *Up* (2009).

CREDITS

Studio	Buena Vista/Walt Disney/Pixar
Producer	Bonnie Arnold, Ed Catmull, Ralph Guggenheim, Steve Jobs
Screenplay	Joss Whedon, Andrew Stanton, Joel Cohen and Alec Sokolow
Awards	Academy award: Special Achievement (John Lasseter)

Marge Gunderson (Frances McDormand), chief of police, bends down in the snow to examine the crime scene after a shoot-out in which a state trooper is killed.

Film poster, 1996

Fargo

DIRECTOR Joel Coen

RELEASED 1996

Brothers Joel and Ethan Coen hit the big time with their sixth film, *Fargo*, a cleverly plotted thriller set effectively in snowy Minnesota, "the abstract landscape of our childhood – a bleak, windswept tundra, resembling Siberia except for its Ford dealerships, and Hardee's restaurants".

A desperate Minneapolis car dealer, Jerry Lundegaard (William H. Macy), is in financial difficulties and hires two petty gangsters, Carl Showalter and Gaear Grimsrud (Steve Buscemi and Peter Stormare), to kidnap his wife so that his rich father-in-law Wade Gustafson (Harve Presnell) will pay a huge ransom. He plans to split the money with the kidnappers, but things go awfully wrong when they kill a state trooper – a murder that police chief Marge Gunderson (Oscar-winning Frances McDormand, Joel Coen's wife), seven months pregnant, investigates. Despite being overwhelmed by her pregnancy, Marge conducts the murder investigation with astute aplomb. The role, played brilliantly by McDormand, is probably the best (and warmest) female part written by the Coens. Superbly photographed against a snowy background, the film moves seamlessly between black humour, violent crime drama, and genial comedy, while weaving a good yarn. The semi-stylized dialogue, so important to the Coens' films, is given another dimension by the "yah-yah" rhythms of the local Minnesotan dialect.

CREDITS

Production	Polygram/Gramercy/ Working Title
Producer	Ethan Coen
Screenplay	Joel Coen, Ethan Coen
Cinematography	Roger Deakins
Music	Carter Burwell
Awards	Cannes: Best Director; Academy Awards: Best Actress (Frances McDormand), Best Screenplay

Crouching Tiger, Hidden Dragon

DIRECTOR Ang Lee

RELEASED 2000

The Chinese tradition of *wuxia* storytelling combines swordplay, martial arts, and Tao Buddhist philosophy. The movies' greatest exponent of the form was Hong Kong director King Hu, to whom Ang Lee pays tribute in this sweeping, romantic action film. The first Chinese-language movie to become a worldwide hit, ***Crouching Tiger, Hidden Dragon*** made more than US$100 million in North America alone.

It was produced by Sony (a Japanese company) through Columbia (its Hollywood division), with Chinese and European co-financing. Further, with a Taiwanese-born, US-based director, and both American and Chinese screenwriters, the film was global entertainment not centred on the American dream – perhaps a sign of things to come. Measured and flamboyant, the movie pits a reckless young couple, Jiao Long and Luo Xiao Hu (Ziyi Zhang and Chen Chang), against two older, wiser souls, Yu Shu Lien and Li Mu Bai (Michelle Yeoh and Yun-Fat Chow), to battle it out over love, duty, and the priceless jade sword "Green Destiny". For many Western audiences, this was their first exposure to Hong Kong cinema's gravity-defying wire-work, a craft enabling swordsmen not just to leap through the air but to bound over rooftops. The climax is a duel between Chow and Zhang, high up among the swaying bamboo trees – a scene at once perilous and mysteriously romantic. This was choreographed by Yuen Wo Ping, the kung fu director who helped realize Ang Lee's vision.

CREDITS

Production	Columbia Tristar
Producer	Li-Kong Hsu, William Kong, Ang Lee
Screenplay	Hui-Ling Wang, James Schamus, Kuo Jung Tsai
Cinematography	Peter Pau

Posing as a warrior, Ziyi Zhang as Jiao Long fights several men at once at a wayside station; her fiery passion shows that her fight is also for respect in a man's world.

In the Mood for Love

DIRECTOR Wong Kar Wai

RELEASED 2000

A touching, atmospheric romance of unconsummated love, Wong Kar Wai's *In the Mood for Love* (*Fa yeung nin wa*) is set in a dreamy, impressionistic evocation of Hong Kong in 1962, and stars Tony Leung and Maggie Cheung, two of Asia's biggest stars.

Maggie Cheung and Tony Leung play two reluctant lovers struggling to repress their passion for each other. Christopher Doyle, Wong's favourite cameraman, imbued the film with deep colours of red, yellow, and brown.

Chow Mo-wan (Leung) and Su Li-zhen (Cheung) have rented rooms next to each other. They fall in love while trying to deal with the infidelities of their respective spouses whom they discover are involved with each other. Adultery has desecrated their lives: "For us to do the same thing would mean we are no better than they are," Cheung says. What is unusual in a film about adultery is that we only see the wronged couple and not the adulterers. As the English title suggests, *In the Mood For Love* is a mood piece with nostalgic music in the background. Wong's skill in recreating the Hong Kong of the 1960s is so assured that it is surprising to discover that the film was actually shot in Bangkok.

CREDITS

Production	Block 2, Jet Tone, Paradis Films
Producer	Wong Kar Wai
Screenplay	Wong Kar Wai
Cinematography	Christopher Doyle, Mark Lee Ping-bin
Original Music	Michael Galasso, Shigeru Umebayashi
Production Design	William Chang

Traffic

DIRECTOR Steven Soderbergh

RELEASED 2000

At a time when American cinema seemed increasingly decadent and detached from the real world, director Steven Soderbergh took up the challenge of mapping out the drug trade in this panoramic, multi-strand drama.

In Washington, the US President's drug czar, Robert Wakefield (Michael Douglas), plans a renewed "war on drugs", not suspecting that his teenage daughter is addicted to heroin. In San Diego, Helena (Catherine Zeta-Jones) is shocked when her husband Carlos (Steven Bauer) is arrested for trafficking – but realizes that the only way to preserve her standard of living is for him to carry on where he left off. Meanwhile, Tijuana cop Javier (Benicio Del Toro) puts his life on the line to enforce the law even as his superiors profit from smuggling. Inspired by a British television series but reconceived in American terms by Steven Gaghan, *Traffic* was one of a number of millennial movies that adopted a multi-story structure to address a bewildering sense of individual powerlessness.

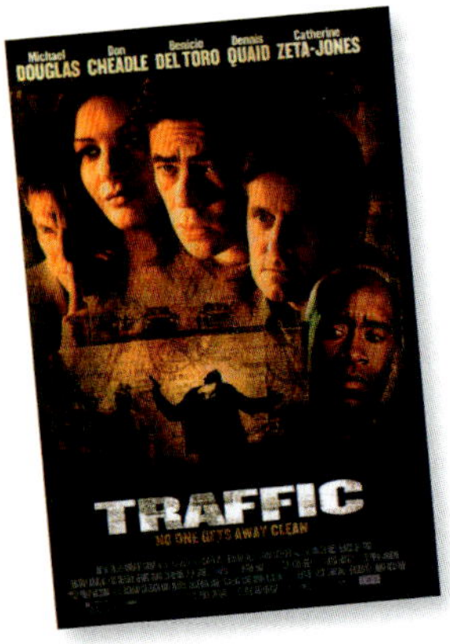

Film poster, 2000

CREDITS

Production	Entertainment/USA Films
Producer	Philip Messina
Screenplay	Steven Gaghan
Cinematography	Steven Soderbergh
Awards	Academy Awards: Best Actor in a supporting role (Benicio del Toro), Best Director (Steven Soderbergh), Best Editing (Stephen Mirrione), Best Screenplay based on previous material (Stephen Gaghan)

The Lord of the Rings

DIRECTOR Peter Jackson

RELEASED 2001, 2002, 2003

Released in three parts but filmed concurrently (with some additional shooting along the way), Peter Jackson's adaptation of J.R.R. Tolkien's saga of the land called Middle Earth was a massive undertaking, and a critical and commercial triumph. Using computerized special effects with great artistry, Jackson redefined the word "epic".

Immersing himself in Tolkien's richly imagined primordial world inhabited by hobbits, elves, and other strange creatures, director Jackson exploits the natural wonder of his native New Zealand to full advantage and gets the details just right. However, he never tarries for long – there are too many mountains, rivers, and valleys to traverse, armies to muster, and spells to cast. The narrative moves at a relentless pace as Frodo Baggins (Elijah Wood), a hobbit, is given a ring that gives its wearer great power. It is too dangerous to keep so Frodo has to travel with his friend Sam (Sean Astin) to Mordor, the only place where the ring can be destroyed. Understood as an anti-fascist allegory when Tolkien wrote it, the first part of the film trilogy took on an unwelcome militaristic zeal when it was released during US campaigns in Afghanistan and Iraq, yet at its roots, it remains a tribute to the resourcefulness and courage of common men confronted with the evil lure of absolute power. In the grotesque, schizophrenic swamp creature Gollum, Jackson and actor Andy Serkis created a compelling character, computer-generated yet imbued with humanity.

CREDITS

Production	Entertainment/New Line/ Wingnut (Barrie M. Osborne, Peter Jackson, Fran Walsh)
Producer	Grant Major
Screenplay	Peter Jackson and Fran Walsh
Cinematography	Andrew Lesnie
Awards	11 Academy Awards for *The Return of the King,* including Best Director (Peter Jackson), Best Picture (Barrie M. Osborne, Peter Jackson, Fran Walsh), Best Art Direction (Grant Major, Dan Hennah, Alan Lee), Best Costume Design (Ngila Dickson, Richard Taylor), Best Editing (Jamie Selkirk)

Frodo the hobbit (Elijah Wood), is mesmerized by the power of the ring in the first film, ***The Fellowship of the Ring***.

Ian McKellen plays Gandalf, the wizard who guides Frodo in his quest to destroy the evil ring; McKellen was nominated for an Academy Award for his performance.

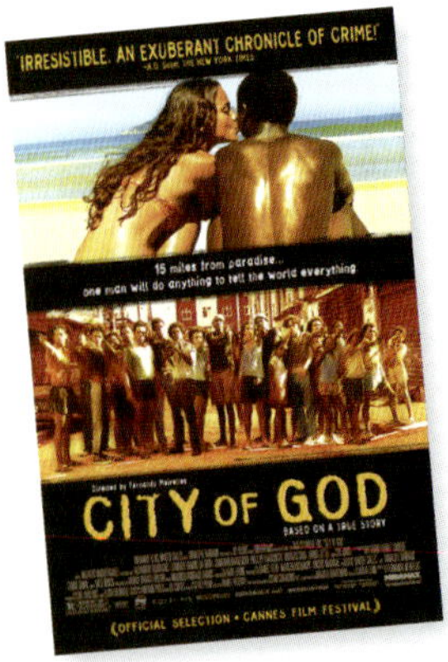

Film poster, 2002

City of God

DIRECTOR Fernando Meirelles

RELEASED 2002

This searing, anecdotal account of growing up in the slums of Rio de Janeiro, Brazil, has a startling immediacy and a punchdrunk, charged camera style that leaves the viewer reeling.

Working with a group of young non-professionals in front of the camera and creating episodes based on true stories, Meirelles and co-director Kátia Lund recreate 15 years in the downward spiral of crime (from the late 1960s to the 1980s) in Cidade de Deus, a Brazilian shantytown (*favela*). During this time, the cocaine trade had emerged in Brazil – and the *favelas* became the hideouts of drug gangs. Meirelles and Lund portray children growing up in these violence-ridden slums. They graduate from reckless but amusing high jinks to the ruthless terrorism of their neighbourhood, with a new generation of pre-teen sociopaths following hard on their heels. The narrator of the film's story, Rocket (Alexandre Rodrigues), escapes life in the gangs by virtue of his criminal ineptitude and his passion for photography. It is his one-time friend Li'l Zé (Leandro Firmino), known as Li'l Dice (Douglas Silva) in the 1960s, who becomes a vicious, cold-hearted drug lord – with Rocket as his reluctant court photographer.

This powerful and fast-paced epic speaks the brutal language of the streets – in this respect, it is reminiscent of Martin Scorsese's ***GoodFellas*** and the Wachowski brothers' ***The Matrix***. The film is a masterful depiction of urban violence and the chaotic combination of drugs, guns, and teenagers, and successfully portrays the horror of life in the *favelas*.

CREDITS

Studio	02/Video Filmes
Producer	Andrea Barata Ribeiro
Screenplay	Bráulio Mantovani
Cinematography	César Charlone

This scene captures the violence of life in a *favela*, as teenaged gangsters are chased by a rival gang down a street.

Clementine (Kate Winslet) is with Joel (Jim Carrey), who is reliving their first date on the frozen Charles river; her dyed orange hair indicates that the scene is a memory of a time gone by.

Eternal Sunshine of the Spotless Mind

DIRECTOR Michel Gondry

RELEASED 2004

This brainteaser of a love story proves there is something new under the sun. Written by Charlie Kaufman, ***Eternal Sunshine of the Spotless Mind*** drops viewers smack into an evaporating consciousness and demands that they make sense of what they are seeing.

Joel (played by Jim Carrey) gets on a train in the wrong direction and meets Clementine (Kate Winslet). He is reserved and conventional, while she is impulsive and extroverted. There is attraction, then there is heartache, resentment, and so much pain that they wonder if they ever really knew each other at all. If he could wipe all traces of her out of his mind Joel would do it – he can and he does, in this romantic comedy about erasing the memory.

Original thinkers are rare in the movie business but Charlie Kaufman really does project out of the box. The theme of amnesia is hardly unfamiliar territory, and the idea of a firm – Lacuna, Inc. – that specializes in memory erasing is reminiscent of Philip K. Dick's science fiction. However, the film's subjective stream of lucid and unconscious imagery is something else again – it is as if the movie is reinventing itself as it goes along.

CREDITS

Production	Focus Features/Anonymous Content/This is That
Producer	Anthony Bregman, Steve Golin
Screenplay	Charlie Kaufman
Cinematography	Ellen Kuras
Awards	Academy Awards: Best Writing, Screenplay written for the screen (Charlie Kaufman, Michel Gondry, Pierre Bismuth)

Glossary

Given below is a selected glossary of the technical and critical terminology used throughout this book.

Abstract film A type of non-narrative film that is organized around visual elements such as colour, shape, rhythm, and size. *Shots* are related to each other by repetition and variation.

Action The movement that takes place in front of the camera, or the series of events that occurs in the film's narrative.

American underground The world of films and film-makers that vary in production styles and exhibition venues from mainstream Hollywood film-making. Active in varying ways since the 1940s, the American underground has become noted for its inventive, usually low-cost methods of film-making and distributing, such as video film-making and online promotion.

Auteur The "author" of a film, usually referring to the director. The concept is the basis of the auteur theory, which originated with François Truffaut's theory of the *politique des auteurs* in *Cahiers du Cinéma* and was popularized in the US by critic Andrew Sarris.

Avant-garde An inclusive term for many varieties of experimental art forms. Avant-garde films flourished in France, Germany, and the Soviet Union during the 1920s and part of the 1930s, each taking various paths.

Cinema du Look A group of late 20th- and early 21st-century French directors who eschew mainstream film-making and are informed by the image-centred art of Music Television (MTV).

Cinéma vérité A type of film-making (its name means cinema truth) that aims to present the truth by recording real-life events in an objective, unadorned manner. It originated with the ideas of Russian theoretician Dziga Vertov and was practised in the documentary work of US film-maker Robert J. Flaherty.

CinemaScope A trademarked name for a wide-screen projection process developed in 1953 consisting of an anamorphic lens system drawn from an invention by Henri Chretien.

Computer-generated imagery (CGI) Images created on a computer, often animated and combined with live action.

Deep focus The effect of having objects close to and away from the camera in focus. This increase in the depth of field is brought about by the deep-focus lens.

Digital effects Special screen effects made by reconfiguring movie frames or art stored inside a computer. Their uses include creating scenes, enhancing them, or representing change (or morphing). The images used to make these effects exist in binary digital form.

Direct Cinema The term in the US since the late 1950s for *cinéma vérité*. Known through the work of Steven Leacock and Robert Drew as Living Cinema, it became Direct Cinema in the 1960s through the work of Albert Maysles and D.A. Pennebaker.

Direct film A film distribution system that bypasses traditional sales outlets such as television and periodicals to reach audiences via blogs and other online communications.

Direct sound Software that interacts with a computer sound card to allow applications to make *sound effects* and music.

Dolly (or dollie) A platform on wheels mounted with a movie camera, that makes *tracking shots* possible. Most move by hydraulics, sometimes on tracks. To dolly in means to move the camera towards the subject; to dolly out means to move it away.

Dynamic montage The arrangement of intrinsically uncontroversial film images to offer polemical expression. This film-editing practice is often used for propaganda works.

Iconography The elements of a film that allow its identification with a certain genre or type. These elements may encompass plot formulas, subject matter, locations, and style; together, these elements distinguish a Western from film noir or science fiction, and for most viewers, simplify movie decoding.

Intellectual montage A type of film editing that eschews now-traditional Hollywood spatial and time continuity and instead employs unexpected, quick images out of standard time to make a point or have a certain emotional effect. Practised by Russian director Sergei Eisenstein, these images often shock viewers.

Medium long shot A film *shot* that places the main object of interest in the centre of the composition, neither in the foreground or the background. Its angle is wider than a medium shot but not as wide as a long shot.

Mise-en-scène Literally the "setting in scene", this term refers to the existence and placement of actors and objects within the frame. Drawn from the French theatre, *mise-en-scène* may for some critics also refer to the tone and mood created by the film-maker.

Modernism An artistic movement of the late 19th and 20th centuries, marked by its concentration on the presentation of the story rather than standard story components. Often, the term is applied casually in recent films, which are are considered modern as they explore feelings rather than follow plots.

Montage The term referring to the juxtaposing of two opposing cinematic images to create a different meaning for the viewer. Deriving from the French word for assembling and mounting, montage was practised most famously by Russian film-maker Sergei Eisenstein. Particularly in the 1930s, montage of calendar dates and photo images was used in US films to indicate the passage of time.

Negative image A reverse light capture of an image in photography and film-making, or the unsympathetic presentation of a character or issue.

Painted cells (or cels) The individual components of traditional animation, each of which has been painted on paper and later on acetate (originally celluloid) by an animation artist. Each cell represents a discrete movement of the character or characters; thousands are used for an animated film.

Pan A compression of the words "panorama" and "panoramic", a pan is a movement of the camera on a fixed plane from one part of a scene to another.

Postmodernism An artistic movement arising in the late 20th century, concerned with the non-linear, non-traditional, and self-reflexive aspects of the arts. Postmodernist films often reflect an intimacy with non-cinematic forms, including computer art and literature.

Production Code The studio-generated self-governing system developed in 1930 to ensure acceptable levels of moral behaviour and good taste in films. The Code was revised in 1966 and a movie ratings system was begun in 1968.

Rapid cutting The editing together of many very short film *shots*, often to create a heightened sense of excitement or danger. An example is the series of short cuts used in Hitchcock's ***Psycho*** (1960), which present a murder.

Reverse slow motion A trick film effect in which a film is run backward in the camera at an accelerated rate. When projected, the *action* filmed appears to occur in reverse sequence and at a slow pace.

Reverse tracking shots A trick effect made by running the film backwards in a *dolly*-mounted camera, which is itself moving backwards, forwards, in, and out of a scene.

Sensurround The trademark for a special-effects process developed by Universal in 1974 to increase the feeling of tremors during watching a film.

Shock cuts A juxtaposition of widely varying images in a film to create a sensation of surprise or horror. Films employing the technique include ***An Andalusian Dog*** (1929) and ***2001: A Space Odyssey*** (1968).

Shot A single continuous *action* that is filmed or appears to be filmed in one *take*, from one camera setup. Many shots filmed are never seen by the audience: a single scene may be photographed from several different angles, with the director and editor selecting the ones that work best.

Slow motion A film effect of making an *action* appear to occur more slowly than it would in reality. The effect is created by putting the film through the camera at an accelerated rate. When the film is projected at a normal speed, events run more slowly than usual.

Special effects (SFX) Visual and mechanical effects used to create illusions on film.

Stop motion A technique in which inanimate objects appear to have lifelike action. The effect is created by repositioning the inanimate figures for each frame. The sequence of manipulated images is projected, with the effect of character movement.

Storyboard A progression of sketches or photographs that outline the sequencing of a film. They are used by directors for planning scenes.

Structuralism A theory of film analysis in which meaning is acquired through the study of dual opposing images. For example, desire may be portrayed by a seemingly unconnected image of a person followed by an image of another person or a costly item.

Superimposition The practice of photographing or placing an image or set of words over an existing image. The superimposed images are viewed as one. Superimposition is often used to supply subtitles; when several images are projected in rapid succession, they convey a colloquial Hollywood form of *montage*, usually for time passage or romantic dissolves.

Surrealism A 20th-century theory of art that pursues the expression of the irrational inner workings of the unconscious. Surrealist film-making draws upon fantasy and is often made of a series of seemingly unrelated images.

Take An uninterrupted *shot* taken by a camera. Directors may film many takes of the same *action*.

Technicolor A film colour process developed by Herbert Kalmus and Daniel Comstock during World War I and patented in 1922. Originally a two-colour process, it became a three-colour process in 1932; represented in movies including ***Gone With the Wind*** (1939).

Three-strip Technicolor Developed in 1932, this process is an advancement on the original two-colour *Technicolor* that uses a custom-built camera and three strips of film in red, blue, and green to render more realistic colour on screen.

Tracking shot A *shot* created by a camera mounted on a *dolly* or track that follows the movement of an actor or *action*. The shot may move in any direction to follow action.

Triple Screen A multiple-screen video display monitor for use in computer video editing.

VistaVision A wide-screen projection system developed by Paramount Pictures in the 1950s that creates its image through the technique of optical reduction from a large *negative image* to the standard release print image.

Visual formality The orderly arrangement of surroundings and players in the movie frame to convey a serious or settled tone to the film. Often the arrangement is meant to contrast with the world or characters in the film, as in the formality masking the disorder in ***Ran*** (1985).

Index

Page numbers in **bold** refer to main entries, *italic* numbers indicate illustrations.

Acknowledgments

The publisher would like to thank the following for their kind permission to reproduce their photographs:

(Key: a-above; b-below/bottom; c-centre; f-far; l-left; r-right; t-top)

Aquarius Library: Buena Vista / Walt Disney 337; Walt Disney 82bc; Warner Bros. 58bl. **Corbis:** Fabian Cevallos / Sygma 67; Keith Dannemiller 53tc; J. Emilio Flores 75; Douglas Kirkland 66; Jim Ruymen / Reuters 74bl; Sunset Boulevard 303. **Dorling Kindersley:** Museum of the Moving Image, London 65bl. **Getty Images:** J. R. Eyerman / Time Life Pictures 33cl, 33cr; RKO Pictures / Archive Photos 285b; Sotheby's / AFP 271.

The Kobal Collection: 20th Century Fox / Paramount / Wallace, Merie W. 57; 20th Century Fox 34cla, 40bl, 81tc, 97t, 112ca, 141t, 221tr, 251br, 276t, 276b, 310cla, 311t; 20th Century Fox / Paramount 180-181; 20th Century Fox / Seida, Takashi 93; A Band Apart / MiraMax 81br, 2, 17c, 18t, 21, 29tc, 31br, 51, 73tr, 89, 97br, 119b, 142, 167, 182tl, 267cl, 334tl; AFI / Libra 219cra; Akson Studio 248t; Alfa 247b; Allied Artists 92clb, 113tr; America 13tr, 40tr; Theo Angelopoulos 184b; Anglo Enterprise / Vineyard 244clb; Anhelo Prod / IFC Films 162bl; Anhelo Prod / IFC Films / Daza, Daniel 59bc; Anouchka / Orsay 43; Archer Street / Delux / Lion's Gate / Pathe / Buitendijk, Jaap 68b; Argos Films / Oshima Productions 226t, 318b; Arte / Bavaria / WDR / Spauke, Bernd 150b; Artistes Associes / PEA 228b; Assoc R&R Films / Paramount 121br; BAC Films 134t; Bandai Visual 173b; Lian Bang 169b; Basic Pictures / Media Asia Films Ltd 59tl; BBC Films / DreamWorks 182b; Bedford Falls / Initial Ent 340bl; Beijing New Picture / Elite Group 8b; Berit Films 236tr; Betzer-Panorama Film / Danish Film Inst. 147b; Biograf Jan Sverak / Portobello Pictures / Vavra, Zdenek 139c; BioSkop / Paramount-Orion / WDR 322br; Block 2 Pics / Jet Tone 340c; Bonne Pioche / Buena Vista / APC / Maison, Jerome 95tr; Bridgit Folman Film Gang 84t; British Lion 92t; Samuel Bronston 64; Bryna / Universal 214b; Bulbul Films / SFI / Aavatsmark, Erik 146b; Bunuel-Dali 264b; Cady / Discina 243t; Canal+ 161br; Carolco 113b; Casbah / Igor 310bc; CCC / CIPI / MGM 185; Chaplin / United Artists / Autrey, Max Munn 10-11; Chaumiane / Film Studio / Pierre, Georges 206b; China Film Group Corporation / Bai Xiao Yan 128-129; Devki Chitra 233t; CIBY 140; Cine Alliance / Pathe 191t, 191crb; Cinegraphic-Paris 85; Cino Del Duca / PCE / Lyre 307tr; CNC / Canal+ 95br; CNC / France 2 Cinema / Studio Canal+ / Jamet, Moune 234bl; Columbia 35b, 36-37, 37cb, 45, 117tr, 190cl, 190b, 192tl, 220tl, 231tr, 248bl, 275cr, 275b, 294, 308cl, 308bc, 314bl, 319tr; Columbia / Bass, Saul 231br; Columbia / Block 2 / Jet Tone Films / Shya, Wing 252t; Columbia / Bray,

Ken 216bl; Columbia / Caruso, Phillip 237tr; Columbia / Coburn, Bob 29b; Columbia / Danjaq / EON 116bl; Columbia / Lippman, Irving 25t, 32; Columbia / Sony / Appleby, David 103tc; Columbia / Sony / Chuen, Chan Kam 256-257, 339; Columbia / Tri-Star 187br; Concord / Warner Bros. 104br; Constellation-Cargo / Alive 53bc; Copacabana Films 165b; CristaldiFilm / Films Ariane 330t, 330bl; Crown Film Unit 27tr; Czech TV / Total Helpart / Spelda, Martin 138-139; Daiei 172bc, 291cr, 291bl; Danjac / EON 42tl; Danjaq / EON / UA 42bc, 116fbl; De Laurentiis 327; Dear Film 199t; Debra Hill Prods 44cb; Decla-Bioscop 259t, 259br; Dimension Films 99br; Dovzhenko Films 228t; Dreamworks / Aardman Animations 83b; Dreamworks LLC 84b; Duo Films / Arte France Cinema 132; Ealing 288t; Ealing / Rank 288bl; Edgar Reitz Film 326cla; Edison 122tl; Daiichi Eiga 171; El Desea-Lauren 329b; El Deseo / Renn / France 2 183t; El Deseo S.A. 329tr; El Deseo S.A. / CIBY 2000 183bc; Elias Querejeta Prods 159tc; Embassy 154bl; Embassy / Laurence Turman 41; EMI / Columbia / Warners 321; EPIC 258tl; Epoca / Talia / Selenia / Films Corona 158; Epoch 258b; ERA International 332; Europa Film 145; Excelsa / Mayer-Burstyn 286br; F.C. Rome / P.E.C.F.Paris 155tl; Factory Films 312b; Farabi Cinema / Kiarostami 336t; Figment / Noel Gay / Channel 4 157tr; Film Four / South Fork / Senator Film 131t, 166t; Film Polski 136br, 229br, 301, 302t; Films 59 / Alatriste / Uninci 189t; Films A2 / Cine Tamaris 245c; Films Aleph / Historia 328ca; Films Andre Paulve 195tr; Films Cisse / Govt Of Mali 131br; Films Du Losange 235br; Films Hakim / Paris Film 152t; Films Terre Africaine, Les 133tc, 238c; Filmsonor / Mirkine 194bc; First Light Productions / KingsgateFilms 121tr; First National 87ca; First National / Charles Chaplin 193br; Flaherty Prods 203br, 260clb; Focus Features 58tl, 125b; Focus Features / Lee, David 343; Focus Features / UIP 91; Fora Film / Hermitage Bridge Studio 144b; Fox 2000 / 20th Century Fox / Tenner, Suzanne 86c; Fox Films 15tr, 223crb; Fox Searchlight 86bl; Gamma / Florida / Oska 225; Gaumont 151, 209br; Geria / Bavaria / S.F.P. 202bl; Globo Films 342tl, 342b; Golden Harvest 104tl; Goldwyn / RKO 253tr; Goskino 201br, 261tc, 261b; Govt Of W. Bengal 297t, 297b; Guacamole Films / OK Films 166b; Guney Film / Cactus Film 141br; Hawk Films Prod / Columbia 309; Hepworth 156bl; Herald Ace / Nippon Herald / Greenwich 215b; Herzog / Filmverlag Der Autoren / ZDF 209t; HungaroFilm 137b; ICAIC 111tr, 163; Industria Cinematografica Italiana 282t, 282bl; Italia Film Torino 154ca; ITAMI 173t; ITV Global 30, 94bl, 105cra, 169t, 177, 230, 280b, 284br; ITV Global / Cannon, George 231bl; ITV Global / Gray, Eric 284t; ITV Global / Rosher, Max 280t; ITV Global / Weinstein, Michael 55t; Jet Tone Production 130b, 252b; Keystone Film Company 87br; Ladd Company / Warner Bros. 49, 324t, 324bl; Lasky Productions 14-15; Lazennec / Canal+ / La Sept 55cb; LenFilm 143br; Les Films Du Carrosse 245b; Les Films Du Losange / La Sept Cinema 235t; Lions Gate 59cr; Live Entertainment 334ca; London Films 289; LucasFilm 114tl; LucasFilm / 20th Century Fox 320; LucasFilm Ltd / Paramount 50, 68tr, 80tl, 116t; Lumen Films / Lama Prods 134bl; Lumiere 12c; Madragoa / Gemini / Light Night 160bc, 224; MaFilm / Hunnia Studio 212cl; MaFilm / Studio Objectiv 137tc; Makhmalbaf Films 135; Malabar / Cinema Center 208tr; Mars / Marianne / Maran 315t, 315cr; Mehboob Productions 174b; Melies 13c; Merchant Ivory / Goldcrest 328b; Metro-Goldwyn-Mayer / MGM 241b; Mezhrabpom Film, Moscow 232tl; MGM 6-7, 20b, 22tl, 24tc, 24bl, 26, 82tl, 90tl, 96, 107, 108t, 108bc, 112bl, 118ca, 188bl, 211tr, 222cla, 222b, 229c, 240bl, 274t, 274bl, 292tl, 292b; MGM / Longworth, Bert 19t; MGM / Samuel Goldwyn 220b; Mij Film Co / BAC Films 130t; Miraai / Jane Balfour 175b; MiraMax / Buena Vista 101br; MiraMax / Dimension Films / Tweedie, Penny 176b; MiraMax / James, David 109; Mirisch / United Artists 39t; Mirisch-7 Arts / United Artists 39cr; MK2 / Abbas Kiarostami Prod 213tr; MK2 / CED / CAB 213br, 335b; MK2 / CED / France 3 / CAB / TOR / Canal+ 335t; MosFilm 143tr, 144tc, 201t, 242b, 243b, 312ca, 326b; MoviWorld / MK2 / MiraMax 133b; Nero 20tl, 110c, 227; New Line 71tc, 71tr; New Line / Roger Birnbaum / Marshak, Bob 69; New Line / Saul Zaentz / Wing Nut / Vinet, Pierre 341t, 341b; Jacques-Louis Nounez / Gaumont 246b, 270t, 270b; Nouvelle Edition Francaise 272b; Nouvelles Editions / MK2 / Stella / NEF 219br; Olympia-Film 272t; Orion 125tc; P.E.A 124t; Palladium 200tl; Paramount 16, 52, 54, 89cr, 99tr, 120tl, 196t, 198, 240tl, 242c, 250br, 251t, 268bl, 300tc, 300cla, 316t, 316bl, 318t; Paramount / Bower, Holly 47; Paramount / Creamer, William 78-79; Paramount / Rafran 76-77; Paris Film / Five Film 189b; Paris Film Production / Panitalia / Pierre, Georges 192b; Pathe 62-63, 120b, 152bl, 205, 283; Andre Paulve / Films Du Palais Royal / Corbeau, Roger 290t, 290b; Polygram / Channel 4 / Working Title / Morley, Stephen 336b; Praesens-Film 111bl; Prana-Film 260tc; Priya 175t; Prods Artistes Associes / Da Ma 90bl; Prods Montaigne 221br; Produzione De Sica 199br, 286cl; RAI / Bibifilm 155br, 155fbr; Realisations D'art Cinematographique 233br; Recorded Picture Co. / Sahara Co. 187t; Republic 232b; Riama-Pathe / Pierluigi 305; Riama-Pathe-Gray / Astor-AIP 203cra; RKO 22cl, 28tc, 98, 102-103, 105br, 162c, 269, 277br, 285cr; RKO / Hurrell, George 31tl; RKO / Kahle, Alex 254-255, 277b; RKO / Samuel Goldwyn 279tr; Hal Roach / MGM 8tc; Hal Roach / UA 88br; Road / Argos / Channel 4 325t, 325b; Road Movies / Argos Films / WDR 150t; Road Movies / Films Du Losange / Filmverlag Der Autoren 249crb; Glauber Rocha / MAPA 164; Rome-Paris / De Laurentiis / Georges De Beauregard / Pierre, Georges 206ca; Saul Zaentz Company 204b; Sedif / Les Films Du Carosse / Janus 302cla; See-Saw Films 157b; Seitz / Bioskop / Hallelujah 149b; Selznick / MGM 273b; SGF / Gaumont 263t, 263b; Shochiku 223t, 293t, 293br; Shochiku Films Ltd 226b; Sippy Films 174tl; Societe Generale De Films 264c; Sony Classics 83tc; Sony Pictures Classics 56; Spectra / Gray / Alterdel / Centaure 153t; Svensk Filmindustri 146tl, 299t, 299br; Svensk Filmindustri / Gaumont / Tobis 186; Taehung Pictures 170; Tango 202tr; Terra / Tamara / Cormoran 234cla; Terra / Tamara / Cormoran / Pierre, Georges 307bc; Tevere / UGC 236b; Titanus / 20th Century Fox 247t; Tobis 194cl; Toho 172tl, 172tr; Toho / Albex 215t; Touchstone / Universal 195br; Touchstone Pictures 178-179; Trio / Albatros / WDR 322t; Trueba / LolaFilms / Animatografo 159b; Twentieth Century-Fox Film Corporation 114b; U.G.C. 153b; U.G.C. / Corbeau, Roger 188c; UA / Art Cinema 207br; UFA 148, 149t, 216tl, 218t, 218bl, 262t, 262bl; UFA / Ewald, Karl 266; United Artists 17tr, 19br, 35tc, 38, 48, 88tl, 122-123, 124bc, 156cra, 184tl, 193t, 246cl, 249tr, 267r, 279b, 298, 302bl, 302br, 319br; Universal 23cr, 44tl, 102tl, 103br, 115, 117b, 118bl, 210, 238bl, 241t, 250tc, 250bl, 265tr, 265b, 287t, 287b, 295cr, 295bl, 323t, 323b, 331; Universal / Amblin 239; Universal / Jones, Ray 99cl; Universal / Lee, David 217t; Universal / Wing Nut Films 72clb, 72br; Victorious Films 161tl; VideoFilmes / Mact Prod / Prandini, Paula 165t; Villealfa Productions 147t; VOG / Sigma / Voinquel, Raymond 23tc; VUFKU 94tl; Walt Disney Pictures 4-5, 110bl; Walt Disney Pictures / Walden Media 9; Wark Producing Company 207t; Warner 7 Arts 314c; Warner Bros. 34bl, 37tr, 46tl, 46bl, 60-61, 80b, 100tl, 101t, 106, 176ca, 197cr, 197b, 204tl, 208b, 211b, 212bl, 214t, 237br, 268t, 281br, 296, 313t, 313br, 333t, 333br; Warner Bros. / Alsbirk, Blid 70; Warner Bros. / DC Comics 5br; Warner Bros. / First National 20tr, 100bl, 278bl, 278b; Warner Bros. / First National / Julian, Mac 253b; Warner Bros. / Lee, David 217b; Warner Bros. / Wallace, Merie W. 200b; Warner Bros. / Woods, Jack 281t; Werner Herzog Filmproduktion 317; Frederick Wiseman 311bc; Woodfall / Associated British 306br; Woodfall / British Lion 306t; Working Title / Polygram 338cl; Working Title / Polygram / Tackett, Michael 338t; Xi'an Film Studio 168; Yash Raj Films 126-127; Zentropa Ent. / GER / Mikado Films 160ca; Zentropa Ents. / Konow, Rolf 244t; Zespol Filmowy Kadr 136cla; Zoetrope / United Artists 196bl. **Photo12.com:** ARJ 12cl. **Photoshot:** Picture Alliance 73bl. **Rex Features:** Jonathan Player 74t. **SuperStock:** 28bl.

All other images © Dorling Kindersley
For further information see:
www.dkimages.com